# The Cinem

## British Film Institute Cinema Series
### Edited by Ed Buscombe

The British Film Institute Cinema Series opens up a new area of cinema publishing with books that will appeal to people who are already interested in the cinema but want to know more, written in an accessible style by authors who have some authority in their field. The authors write about areas of the cinema where there is substantial popular interest, but as yet little serious writing, or they bring together for a wider audience some of the important ideas which have been developed in film studies in recent years.

Published:

Richard Dyer: **Heavenly Bodies: Film Stars and Society**
Thomas Elsaesser: **New German Cinema: A History**
Jane Feuer: **The Hollywood Musical**
Jill Forbes: **The Cinema in France**
Steve Neale: **Cinema and Technology**

**Series Standing Order**

If you would like to receive future titles in this series as they are published, you can make use of our standing order facility. To place a standing order please contact your bookseller or, in case of difficulty, write to us at the address below with your name and address and the name of the series. Please state with which title you wish to begin your standing order. (If you live outside the United Kingdom we may not have the rights for your area, in which case we will forward your order to the publisher concerned.)

Customer Services Department, Macmillan Distribution Ltd, Houndmills, Basingstoke, Hampshire, RG21 2XS, England

Jill Forbes

# THE CINEMA IN FRANCE
## AFTER THE NEW WAVE

First published 1992 by
THE MACMILLAN PRESS LTD
Houndmills, Basingstoke, Hampshire RG21 2XS
and London
Companies and representatives
throughout the world

ISBN 0–333–41429–2 hardback
ISBN 0–333–41430–6 paperback

A catalogue record for this book is available
from the British Library

Copy-edited and typeset by Povey–Edmondson
Okehampton and Rochdale, England

Printed in Hong Kong

For Alex

# Contents

## PART II  AUTEURS

# List of Illustrations

# Acknowledgments

This book is the fruit of many happy hours spent in the cinemas of Paris over the past twenty years and of many discussions with my filmgoing companions, foremost among whom must be mentioned Paul Joannides, Keith Reader and Jonathan Rosenbaum. I would like to thank the South Bank Polytechnic for its considerable financial support, the Archives du Cinéma Français, the Institut National de la Communication Audiovisuelle (especially Thierry Garrel and Louisette Neil), Unifrance Film, the British Film Institute Library whose resources, even for the study of French cinema, remain incomparable, as well as the BFI Stills, Posters and Designs Department and the Cinémathèque Française for illustrations. I have benefited from the advice, help and moral support of many individuals, but particular gratitude is due to Cathy Barlow, John Pym, my patient editor Ed Buscombe and Martin McKeand.

# A Note on the Text

Titles of films are given in French. Dates of films refer to the date of production, except where otherwise stated, and this may cause some discrepancies with the Filmography, where I have followed the convention and dated the films from their first French release. For ease of access I have translated all French material quoted into English, but scholars will find the reference to the French text in the notes.

# Introduction

This book has been written for both students and teachers of the cinema and for readers whose main focus of interest is France and French culture. Film lovers will not need convincing that French cinema is worth studying but they may not be familiar with many of the films discussed here. This is because I have deliberately attempted to look at a corpus of material which is not well known outside France. In doing so my aim has been to study works which are intrinsically interesting but also to change the conventional view of French cinema which prevails in English-speaking countries, a view which tends to concentrate narrowly on the survivors of the *nouvelle vague* and on the commercially successful works of directors such as Beineix, Besson and Carax, to the exclusion of much else that is worthwhile.

Students and teachers of French – or at least those who have been educated in the British tradition – may find the cultural significance of French cinema harder to take seriously. Yet we only need to recall the Surrealists' passionate interest in films, the eagerness with which Simone de Beauvoir and Sartre awaited and discussed new film releases or, more recently, the ease with which artists like Marguerite Duras and Alain Robbe-Grillet move between the media of film and print, to understand that film has long played a vital role in French intellectual and cultural life. I hope this book will demonstrate that this is a two-way process. Film makers in France, unlike some of their counterparts elsewhere, are not isolated in the ghetto of the film studio but are often themselves intellectuals who participate in the general artistic and cultural life of the country. Jacques Doillon, as will be seen, reads psychoanalytic literature, André Techiné was a friend and disciple of Roland Barthes, René Allio was influenced by the *Annales* school of history, and there are many more examples.

In the postwar period France has had a lively 'film culture'. Although the French industry does produce films for the mass audience, what is striking, characteristic and exceptional about it is that since the war it has provided an environment in which the art film can flourish. This is the secret of the survival and success of the French industry. Although it was damaged by the war, like the industries of Britain, Germany and Italy, and although it serves a relatively small domestic market and produces films in a language spoken by relatively few people, it has nevertheless managed to sustain production of wholly national films that have been both commercially viable and artistically interesting. Public policy towards the cinema has been marked by considerable lucidity about the role and impact of Hollywood and this has influenced the structure of subsidy, enabling the French industry to negotiate the postwar changes in film audiences more successfully than comparable western European industries. It has done this, essentially, by supporting the production of films that are intended not for the mass audience but for the smaller, educated, middle-class audience which has continued to frequent the cinema in the postwar period.[1] The continuing viability of film production has helped to sustain film making as a career along with the whole range of publishing and viewing activities associated with the cinema, and it is therefore no accident that many of the seminal modern writings on film were produced in France between 1950 and 1975. It is for all these reasons that the cinema has a central role in contemporary French culture.

Most of the film makers discussed here began their careers after 1968 in the period which might be defined as 'post-*nouvelle vague*'. This is why the reader will not find a detailed consideration of major film makers such as Bresson or Chabrol, Rivette, Resnais or Rohmer, since although all these directors continued to make films in the 1970s their period of innovative influence was over. This is clearly true of Chabrol who has devoted himself primarily to making commercial films, and of Rohmer, whose work is based on a deliberate and stylised continuity. Bresson's output was small after 1970 and the vagaries of distribution meant that much of Rivette's experimental work remained virtually unseen. Even Resnais, who retained his astonishing capacity for political prescience in films like **Stavisky** or **Mon Oncle d'Amérique**, made no film that could match the revolutionary impact of **Hiroshima mon amour**. Conversely, there were some film makers whose careers had begun in the 1950s or 1960s for whom the 1970s represented a new departure and who thus produced a body of work of new significance in the post 1968 period. This is the case with Agnès Varda, whose

2

films engage with the questions of feminism in a new and fascinating manner, with Truffaut, who embarked on a new career as actor–producer and fostered the talent of many younger film makers, and with Godard who in the 1970s began to work for television before returning, in the 1980s, to the more mainstream cinema.

Both inside and outside France the *nouvelle vague* is a powerful critical category. But whereas for critics who write in English its function is primarily nostalgic, serving both to define the art film and to deplore its demise, in France *nouvelle vague* signifies a specific kind of film practice, a complex of aesthetic, technical, political and social positions most usefully defined and thoroughly explored in Gilles Deleuze's magisterial essay on the cinema.[2] Thus in the films of Garrel and Eustache, but also those of Tavernier, Pialat and Blier, we can perceive a constant necessity for the film maker to position himself – or more rarely herself – positively or negatively in relation to the *nouvelle vague*. This necessity lends the post-1968 French cinema a productive coherence. Film makers did not waste much time in lamenting the passing of the *nouvelle vague*, but instead built on its achievements, whilst film makers such as Godard and Truffaut who had been central to the enterprise of the late 1950s and 1960s themselves continued to innovate.

The 'post-*nouvelle vague*' is also the period after May 1968 and it would be difficult to overstate the impact of this great social and cultural caesura on the cinema. May 1968 forced film makers to confront the influence of mass communications and to ask questions about the 'truth' and the 'reality' of the image. It presented film makers with the challenge of television and made them consider the politics of representation. It introduced new social actors to the screen and to film making, it called for the reinterpretation of history and, in exposing the problematical absence of the 'people' which in Marxist literature had long been unquestioningly assumed to exist, it forced all those working in the culture industries, but especially in the cinema, to reconsider the nature of this par excellence 'popular' art.

The structure of the book attempts to reflect the course of this process of upheaval and revaluation. After a brief account of the changes which have taken place in the French film industry, the first part of the book looks at the three main genres in which the *auteur* film flourished while the second part discusses the works of the most interesting and important film makers in the post-1968 period. Although the political and documentary cinema was the most immediate and tangible response to the Events of May, the different reaction to Hollywood and the American influence, and the growth and development of women's cinema are also expressions of the change which had occurred. Popular cinema was intimately associated in the minds of many French film makers and actors with the United States, and any redefinition of the popular meant a repositioning in relation to Hollywood. Similarly, women film makers did not owe their existence to May 1968 but the women's movement which grew out of the Events, and the concomitant investigation of subjectivity and of male and female identity, did have an enormous impact on the politics of representation which is reflected in women's films. The thematics of the post-1968 French cinema also mirrors these changes. It is perhaps most starkly apparent in the works of Godard, but history, the family, and the nature of the popular are all typical post-1968 themes, whilst the treatment of young people in the films of Garrel, Eustache, Pialat or Doillon bears the marks of the social revolution which occurred in 1968. The studies of film makers in the chapters which follow are therefore grouped in a way which is intended to bring out their common engagement with both the legacy of the *nouvelle vague* and the cultural issues arising from May 1968.

Finally, it might seem extraordinary or even provocative to study the *auteur* cinema in the period of post-structuralism for 'he' is surely dead and buried.[3] However, in film criticism, unlike literary criticism, the *auteur* has always been a fiction, a polemical device used to promote a certain kind of *reading* rather than a particular kind of writing.[4] The *auteur* is also an important intertextual reference, positive (for Tavernier), negative (for Pialat) or ironic (for Duras) and it would be perverse to ignore it. To talk of the *auteur* cinema is not to deny the essentially collaborative nature of film making or the social, political or ideological context in which it takes place. But for the post-1968 French film maker to be or not to be an *auteur* is to adopt a position in relation to the industry, to the *nouvelle vague*, to gender, and to the audience. It is, in short, an indication of the consciousness of status which is part of the reading of the film and, as such, essential to my purpose here.

# The French Film Industry since the War: A Very Brief History

Films were among the export commodities which figured in the general agreement of conditions surrounding the granting of Marshall Aid for postwar reconstruction.[1] These conditions imposed a volume of free trade which ran counter to the protectionist economic traditions of prewar France. Despite the pragmatic approach of French negotiators such as Jean Monnet, the view remained that, in areas where strategic considerations were felt to be paramount, support or protection continued to be necessary.[2] The cinema was seen as having both industrial and cultural significance and French politicians knew that if imports of American films were to be limited and the indigenous cinema was to have a significant cultural role then the film industry needed support. The First Plan (1947–50) therefore encompassed cinema in its brief and set out proposals to reduce taxes on the cinema, to build new studio capacity, to renovate and modernise existing cinemas and rebuild those destroyed in the war, and to set up a body to 'pursue a rational policy for the cinema'.[3] This led to the creation of the Centre National de la Cinématographie (CNC) in 1946 and the passing of the *loi d'aide* in 1948 which, although it did not introduce subsidies, as is sometimes suggested, set up a system which ensured, under the management of the CNC, that a proportion of the profits from production and exhibition were ploughed back into the industry. Financial assistance (*aide automatique*) was offered to producers as a proportion of the receipts of their previous film, provided a new French film was made, and in the 1950s this system of support provided some 17 per cent of total investment in film production. Clearly the percentage was high because the number of people going to the cinema remained high. Thus the success of these policies was due not so much to the quality of films produced, which was often described as mediocre,[4] as to the volume which was, in great measure, the result of the slow development of television.

Nevertheless, film audiences had begun to decline significantly and the critical reception of much French cinema was poor. By the time some permanent system of support was

5

required through the expiry of the 1948 law, parliament had come round to the view that the way to save the industry was to support quality as much as quantity. A *Fonds de développement* set up in 1953 added *aide sélective* to the *aide automatique* of the 1948 legislation by retaining a proportion of the fund specifically for projects which were 'French and of a kind to serve the cause of the cinema or to open new perspectives in the art of cinematography',[5] and the debates in the National Assembly manifested an acute awareness of the cultural significance of the cinema: 'We affirm our view that educational values have more weight and significance than exchange values'.[6]

Finally, in 1959 a *Fonds de soutien* was created which provided for *avances sur recettes*, or interest-free loans, granted on the basis of an outline or an idea and repayable if or when the film earned a profit. This, for the first time, allowed new film makers to benefit from support.

It can be seen that public policy towards the cinema concentrated on encouraging production. This was because until the end of the 1950s the problem seemed less to be how to get audiences into the cinema than what to put in front of them once they were there. The impact of the *aide sélective* is clear: in the mid-1950s it helped to support a group of makers of short films which included Marker, Resnais and Varda, all of whom went on to make feature films and, from 1959 onwards, it also assisted the production of low-budget independent feature films.[7] Its significance in the context of the French film industry is that it became available at a time when new technologies made possible the production of certain kinds of films much more cheaply, since lighter cameras and faster film reduced the size of film crews and encouraged the film makers to abandon the studios for locations. Thus the *aide sélective*, however modest, could be a determinant of whether or not a film was made.

The explanation as to why such films were successful lies elsewhere, in the changing composition of the audience and its changed expectations of cinema. The art film, as David Bordwell has rightly suggested, was a European phenomenon characterised by a narrative that is motivated by 'realism and authorial expressivity'[8] in some versions of which the author becomes a figure in the narrative.[9] It is therefore an 'auteur cinema' both in the sense that its realism is one of reflexion rather than action and because it is visibly the expression of the preoccupations of an individual (whether the protagonist,

**6**

the film maker or some conflation of the two). European art films, and particulary those made in France, successfully appealed to the audience that remained once cinema had ceased to be a mass entertainment, an audience that was relatively affluent, relatively middle class and highly educated. It was a cinema for the intelligentsia and the new middle classes which enabled the film industry to compete both against Hollywood's increasing investment in spectaculars and against television, which was spreading rapidly. In France a particular version of art cinema, the *nouvelle vague*, was popular at the beginning of the 1960s and offered an occasion for critics and policy makers to come together in support of the cinema.[10] Although the art film in general benefited from the structures of support, the *nouvelle vague* provided an instance of the combination of theory and practice that has remained exemplary.[11] An average of thirty to forty films a year benefited from the *avance*, which was some 25 per cent of total production, and the list of beneficiaries is impressive: Duras, Doillon, Tavernier, Truffaut, Godard, Resnais, Rivette, Bresson and so on.[12] During the 1960s, therefore, the French film industry achieved an uneasy equilibrium with attendances declining but the production of films of artistic interest remaining significant.

At the beginning of the 1970s it entered a period of recession. From just over 400 million in 1957 attendances dropped to 180 million in 1969 and then levelled off. What had been perceived as a crisis of production was now and henceforward seen as a crisis of exhibition – 'The economic crisis of the cinema increasingly placed the fate of the industry in the hands of the distributors' – and it resulted in a number of significant changes.[13]

First, public policy was changed so that from 1967 onwards exhibitors were able to benefit from the *Fonds de soutien* from which they had been excluded in 1959. This undeniably assisted the modernisation of cinemas, but it also led to rationalisation and greater concentration of exhibition. The large chains benefited more than independent exhibitors since support was based on box-office takings. At the same time the number of distributors declined, limiting the effective choice of filmgoers. Pathé and Gaumont merged their distribution divisions in 1969; the Parafrance company bought up a number of provincial circuits; and in 1971 the nationalised UGC group was sold off to the private sector. The dominant forms of exhibition changed too. The existence of financial support encouraged the creation of multi-cinema complexes, especially in large towns, so that, instead of a film playing 'exclusively' in a single cinema for a long period, followed by second showings in suburban halls, it became the practice to open a film in a large number of cinemas in order to maximise takings rapidly. Whereas in 1957 a film might hope to recover three-quarters of its costs in the first year of exhibition, by the 1970s it might recover half in the first three months, after which it would disappear from the screens. A film's profitability therefore increasingly depended on its capacity to succeed rapidly.

Second, the kinds of film produced changed. This was because the combined effort of subsidies to exhibitors and the relaxation of censorship after 1968 encouraged the production and exhibition of sex films to such an extent that they accounted for more than 25 per cent of all production. With titles such as **Emmanuelle, Histoire d'O** and **Exhibition** they were also made for an audience that was wider than the traditional 'X' category movie audience. By 1976, under considerable pressure from both the public and the industry, a law was enacted preventing sex films from benefiting from the *Fonds de soutien* and a tax was instituted on the production and exhibition of such films intended, in the words of Michel Guy, the Minister of Culture, to 'bring pornography back to the marginal situation that it always used to have, that is to 10 per cent of the market'.[14]

Third, television became the most important influence on French cinema. Throughout the 1960s and into the 1970s, French television was in continuous expansion which was all the more rapid for having begun comparatively late. Thus households with television rose from 2 million in 1960 to 11 million in 1970 and the coverage of black and white television was virtually total by the mid-1970s. During the same period second and third channels began broadcasting and colour was introduced. The cinema lost ground to television for two reasons. The first was that television offered an alternative leisure pursuit. In this, however, it was in France as elsewhere merely an indicator of affluence, for the cinema lost audiences as soon as disposable income rose and the French began to spend more on leisure in general.[15] The other reason was that television acted as an exhibitor of films and between 1965 and 1975 the number of films it screened doubled, as did the amounts the television networks spent on purchasing screening rights.

Why was there a sudden expansion of the number of films on television? Essentially because programme costs were rising steeply at a time when audiences had ceased to expand, so that films offered a relatively cheap means of filling the increased hours of viewing time and were also attractive to audiences. The reform of French broadcasting in 1974 further increased the number of films shown on television. The reform consisted in breaking up the ORTF – the French broadcasting corporation – into seven separate companies and requiring the television channels, TF1, Antenne 2 and FR3, to compete with each other. The reform was in part an attempt to control costs by making a proportion of each channel's income dependent on audience figures, so that feature films which were cheap and popular became even more frequently scheduled. However, although the number of films that were screened rose, especially at prime time, the number of art films which had received the *avance sur recettes* inevitably fell.[16]

The 1974 reform also established television as a significant producer of films. At first, only FR3, the Société Française de Production (SFP) and the Institut National de l'Audiovisuel (INA) were allowed to act as producers. This made it possible for both FR3 and INA to pursue a policy of financing difficult or experimental films, although such productions were not always screened, and during the latter half of the 1970s INA developed a significant catalogue of such films.[17] In 1979 TF1 and Antenne 2 also received their 'producer's ticket' together with a special budget allowance of 8 million francs for film production. Their *cahiers des charges* were also modified with respect to cinema films: the number they were permitted to programme was reduced, the quota for French or EEC films was raised, screening at prime time was limited and the obligatory period between theatrical release and television screening was raised to two years. Nevertheless, by 1980 over five hundred films were being shown every year on television compared with half that number in the 1960s and films represented some 40 per cent of viewing time.[18] The *Bredin Report* on the French cinema, published in 1982, concluded: 'Whether we like it or not, cinema–television co-productions and the advance purchasing of broadcasting rights now form an essential part of the economy of the film industry'.[19]

Between 1968 and 1986 film production in France increased in volume (even when the 'X' category is excluded from the figures) but the industry changed from being production-led to being exhibition-led. The proportion of total investment deriving from the *Fonds de soutien* declined significantly while the number of co-productions, especially those with minority French participation, increased.[20] This has meant that public policy can now exert an influence on film making only in an indirect way and that television has become the effective controller of the industry, with the result that the production of difficult films for minority audiences has declined while the number of international co-productions has increased. An extreme example might be the film version of Simone de Beauvoir's **Le Sang des autres** directed by Claude Chabrol but made in English with North American actors in two versions (for television and for the cinema) and co-produced by the cable network HBO. Despite its origins, this cannot be considered a French film.

The end of the 1980s may conveniently be seen as the end of an era. In 1986 the Socialist government which had attempted some measures of protection for the film industry lost power and its right-wing successor embarked on a programme of privatisation and deregulation in television with the sale of the major channel TF1 to the private sector; the kind of production hitherto sustained by the French industry will find it difficult if not impossible to survive these changes.

# PART 1

# GENRES

# 1:

# Political and Documentary Cinema

May 1968 is a watershed not only in modern French politics but in French political and documentary cinema. The French documentary film before May 1968 is best exemplified in the work of the so-called Left Bank Group which included Resnais, Marker and Varda. Works such as Resnais's **Guernica** (1950) and **Nuit et Brouillard** (1956), Varda's **Du Côté de la côte** (1958) or **O Saisons, ô châteaux** (1988), Marker's **Lettre de Sibérie** (1958) or **Cuba si** (1961) are inspired by a socialism of a broadly humanist kind. What characterises such films is their frequent choice of an issue of politics or human rights as subject matter. This is then presented as an appeal to the viewer's intelligence by means of a highly literary and sometimes poetic script usually delivered in voice-over, which enables the otherwise fragmentary montage of the film to be understood as the film maker's personal point of view. As Raymond Durgnat has pointed out, the Left Bank films owe their rigorous formal concentration and their elliptical continuity to the example of Bresson and their liking for the capricious, the whimsical and the 'stream of ruptures' to that of Queneau.[1] These techniques later spilled over into feature films. Resnais's work is celebrated for its ellipses, its dazzling montage and its oblique political statements, while Varda's combination of fiction and documentary, still photography and moving images, in works such as **L'Une chante, l'autre pas**, is strongly influenced by documentaries made earlier by herself and her colleagues.

Left Bank documentary and political films took the form of personal statements, for two significant reasons. The first had to do with the hierarchical structure of the French film industry and the financial assistance available to beginners. The film makers who were young in the 1950s found that it was necessary to serve a long apprenticeship as an assistant to an established film maker before gaining the opportunity to take charge of their own films. In addition, the only financial aid for non-established film makers, before the introduction of the *avance sur recettes* in 1959, was the *prime à la qualité* for shorts and documentaries available from 1954 onwards. They therefore took advantage of a subsidy which fostered *auteurism*, albeit in a narrow and marginalised genre.

The second reason was the effect of the political struggle in France in the 1950s and early 1960s. The postwar period was a time when French intellectuals, under the influence of the Cold War superpower confrontation but also as a result of the experience of defeat and occupation, were preoccupied with the dialectic of the domestic and the foreign.[2] The major political struggle was in some sense extra-territorial since it concerned primarily the decolonisation of Indo-China and North Africa. Domestic politics seemed strongly determined by the course of foreign wars, nowhere more so than in the fall of the Fourth Republic, and yet it was difficult for film makers to speak of such events. This was partly the result of a prevailing sense of bad faith which Resnais's protagonists in **Hiroshima mon amour**, **Muriel** and **La Guerre est finie** all exemplify with their guilty secrets and their petty betrayals. But it was also because censorship was extremely oppressive. One only has to recall that films as disparate as **La Bataille d'Alger** and **La Religieuse** were refused certification to appreciate how tightly the film industry was kept under government control, so that a film maker wishing to engage with a political question of domestic concern, as Resnais so frequently did, always did this obliquely and elliptically.[3]

The self-imposed exoticism and the expatriation of concern were beginning to give way even before the events of May 1968, while personal anguish was also coming to seem an inadequate political response. **Loin du Vietnam** (1967), a film made by members of the Left Bank Group and others, already illustrates the changes in politics and film making practice that had begun to occur before the events of 1968. It was produced and edited by the SLON (La Société pour la Création des Oeuvres Nouvelles) Cooperative, created by Chris Marker for the purpose and the first of several such collectives he inspired.[4] Episode films, such as **Paris vu par...** (1965), were a popular French and Italian formula in the 1960s, but producers were always careful to identify the director of each episode and to market such films as a collection of *auteur* statements. The sections filmed by each of the six contributors to **Loin du Vietnam** are not identified within the film

14

(although they are fairly easy to recognise). Instead the *auteur* is a collective entity which matches the political message of the film. **Loin du Vietnam** abandons character-istic Left Bank exoticism, and although it takes events in a distant country as its subject, it addresses the here and now and specifically relates present events to the lives of individuals in France and America. In other words it states clearly that Vietnam impinges not just on the emotions and sensibilities of individuals who are observers but that everyone in France and America has a collective responsibility for the war and the colonialist oppression of the Vietnamese. It also suggests that the cinema can help the Vietnamese in their struggle for independence.[5] In this way **Loin du Vietnam** prefigures the collective production groups, the assumption of collective responsibility ('we are all German Jews') and the attribution of an interventionist role to the cinema which was character-istic of political and documentary film making after 1968. It is a film which points the way forward from the increasingly political subject matter to be found in the films of directors such as Resnais and Godard from the mid-1960s onwards.

## The Events of May 1968

It is worth recalling, briefly, the principal actors in the May 1968 Events and the impact of the Events on the country at large, since these things are often reflected anecdotally in post-1968 cinema. There were two distinct groups with distinct motives and aspirations involved. On the one hand, there were the young people (students and others). Their social and economic importance had massively increased in France as it had in most other western countries as a result of postwar demographic changes and of affluence. The phenomenon of 'youth culture' had arisen in France as it had in Britain, Germany, the United States and elsewhere, but changes in social relations had not occurred at the same time.[6] On the other hand, there were the 'workers' who had not benefited as much as they felt they ought to have done from France's postwar economic success, particularly the expansion recorded in the ten years since De Gaulle had returned to power, either through an appropriate rise in their living standards or through new styles of management and labour relations.[7] The analysis of the May Events in the cinema and elsewhere frequently turned on the relationship between these two groups and on the *mise en scène* of what have been called the new social actors.

It is also worth recalling that the political conse-quence of May 1968 was the death of Gaullism and the rebirth of the left since, again, this is reflected in post 1968 films. Although the Gaullists won the general election of 1968, De Gaulle retired after his referendum defeat in 1969 and died in 1970. By 1974 his party had lost office to the more centrist Giscard d'Estaing and it was never to return in force. The Left underwent similar restructuring. In 1972, the parties of the Left signed the *Programme commun de gouvernement*, a common electoral platform which enabled them almost to win the general election of 1978 and to emerge victorious at the presidential and general elections of 1981. At the same time the oil crises of 1973 and 1979 ended the continuous expansion which had been characteristic of the years of Gaullist rule and helped to break up the populist alliance, based partly on expansion, which had underpinned Gaullism.

Above all, the Events of May 1968 led to a ques-tioning of the exercise of power in society. They revealed the possibility that power structures could change and that political activity could alter human relations, a theme that is amusingly illustrated in Jacques Doillon's idealistic film **L'An O1** (1972).[8] Such a possibility was glimpsed in the *Accords de Grenelle* which ended the strikes in 1968 and which provided not only for across-the-board pay increases but for greater recognition of trade union rights and participatory manage-ment. It was signalled in the *Loi Faure* which reformed the higher education system, ending the monolithic university dominated by the patronage of the *mandarinat*. Above all, the search for such change was expressed in the febrile political activity to be found in many sections of society in the years following 1968 and the politicisation of many areas of life which had remained immune from political influence up to that point.

## The Control of the Media: The Right to be Heard[9]

Film and television were inextricably bound up in the demands articulated by oppositional groups in May 1968. Because the communications media were heavily censored, through the Ministry of Information in the case of television, and through a system of certification administered by the CNC in the case of cinema, these demands first took the form of the right to be heard and seen and of a campaign against censorship. In television and radio, at the time run by a single organisation, the ORTF, news management became a major issue, particularly since the independent radio station Europe I reported the May Events very differently from the state broadcasting corporation. Journalists at the ORTF went on strike. Many were subsequently sacked and the credibility of the corporation was so damaged that it was disbanded in 1974. It took more than a decade for television to regain any kind of reputation for impartiality or comprehensiveness. Many film makers became involved in the rapid production of *cinétracts*, short films which recorded or commented on events in the streets, which were then shown in alternative venues to counter or contradict the 'official' point of view put out by television. Some of the film makers sacked from the ORTF later turned to documentary film making, often based on historical documents for which they ransacked the archives in an attempt to discover an 'alternative' truth. Their work, which was clearly influenced by their experiences in 1968, will be discussed further below.

In the cinema the question of state control or intervention was not at first so clear-cut. But in February 1968 an event occurred which appeared to confirm the view that France was governed in a paternalistic and authoritarian manner and which mobilised film makers to demand changes in the organisation and control of the industry. The Minister of Culture decided to remove Henri Langlois from his post as Secretary of the Cinémathèque. Langlois was particularly criticised for his failure to observe curatorial minima – a failing which even his most ardent defenders did not dispute.

However, many who took up Langlois's defence, including Pierre Mendès-France, suspected that the reasons for his removal were crudely political: 'The Government cannot accept the idea that the Cinémathèque might refuse to organise a festival of Argentinian or Iraqi films just because that would serve the Government's political ends'.[10] In support of Langlois were mobilised individuals in many countries and from all political persuasions because the educational function of his inspired programming was gratefully recognised. A defence committee was formed, which included Roland Barthes among its members, and the solution arrived at was the withdrawal of state funds from the

17

Cinémathèque, a move which enabled the reconstituted management committee immediately to reinstate Langlois.

The idea that the profession should mobilise was by no means new – it had done so very effectively in 1946–7 and had obtained protection for the French film industry. But many film makers and critics saw in these cinematic events a prelude to those in May. In particular, the Langlois Affair did pave the way for the criticisms of the organisation of the film industry which were made explicit by the May Events. *Cahiers du cinéma* published a questionnaire addressed to film makers which it entitled 'Towards a white paper for French cinema'. The questions posed concerned the role of the CNC, the working of the system of *avances sur recettes*, whether films on television discouraged people from going to the cinema, what film makers thought of television co-productions, whether they ought to form their own production companies and whether the state treated television more favourably than cinema.

A 'States General of the Cinema' began meeting in the middle of May 1968 and convened a series of commissions, or working groups, which made recommendations for the reform of the film industry which were then published as a single document. The work of the States General has been examined in considerable detail elsewhere,[11] but two major issues emerge from its agenda as well as from film makers' actual experience of recording events in the streets and in mass meetings. These concerned the structure of the film industry: who had the right to make films and how they were to be distributed. They also concerned the nature of realism, the authenticity and the truth of what films showed, the veracity of the single point of view. While it is true that government control of television was accentuated in the aftermath of the Events, May 1968 did lead to the birth of a new kind of political or documentary cinema as well as to the elaboration of theories of cinema which affected the way in which all films were viewed.

## How to make political films: 'Filming different things or filming differently'

*Cahiers du cinéma* published a 'collective text' on the occasion of the re-release of Jean Renoir's **La Vie est à nous** in 1970, in which it was suggested that Renoir's film exemplified what political cinema should do. The authors recall that **La Vie est à nous** was produced by the French Communist Party for the 1936 elections, financed by collections made at Party meetings (to the tune of 70 000FF which was a tenth of the average cost of such a film at the time) and that it was not commercially released but was shown at political meetings and rallies. They also point out that it was not a 'Renoir film' in the exclusive sense that many 'bourgeois' critics would have wished: 'critics enjoy noting the characteristic Renoir touches which, despite everything make him the authentic "father" of the work'.[12] They use it to define what they consider to be the essential problematic of a 'militant film', that is, 'not just what the film discusses and how, but whom it is addressed to',[13] and they conclude that **La Vie est à nous** is exemplary because although it 'precisely fulfils the conditions necessary for any militant film, using a single political signifier to carry a univocal message', it nevertheless avoids the flaw which generally vitiates such cinema namely 'being only the transparent statement of this single political signifier'. 'Instead of being just a statement of it, it reflects the conditions under which the statement is made'.[14] Thus both the audience, the question of authorship and the question of whether a reflection of its status was contained within the film itself were all issues which determined both the political and the aesthetic effectiveness of a political film. A further debate of some note was whether a political film should be documentary or fictional:

> The political film works with material that is contemporary to it such as social, economic and ideological data (...) and it has two methods for handling such material. Either it uses existing film documents or those filmed during events (news, current affairs, reports) which the editing and the commentary then place in some kind of order and render politically significant. Or it can reconstitute events in fictional form through mise en scène.[15]

The Events of May 1968 and parallel events in the United States and many other European countries meant that political cinema became fashionable. As *Cahiers* put it: 'There are very few films (...) today which do not show traces of the bitter class struggles which are currently taking place across the entire planet'.[16] But not all political films, could, in the eyes of the *Cahiers* critics, be considered authentically political. Alongside its reconsideration of **La Vie est à nous** the journal also published an analysis of Costa-Gavras's **L'Aveu** (1970) which Jean-Louis Comolli suggested provided a clear illustration of the way in which a film, despite the evident good faith of its director and actors, and despite its denunciation of events such as torture under Stalin, could end up establishing a complicity with, rather than a critique of, the events described.[17] For Comolli, **L'Aveu** contains no reflection on its own position in the relations of production and in the absence of such reflection reinforces the relations already existing. Furthermore, **L'Aveu** is pure spectacle. It is governed by a conception of cinema as a record of reality, as an illustration of the visible. The viewers must feel themselves 'really present' at the events depicted to the extent that they suffer torture with the tortured protagonist and, through their identification with the central character, are rendered incapable of criticising his position.

As the discussions of **La Vie est à nous** and **L'Aveu** show, it was held that a film needed to fulfil two conditions in order to be politically effective. On the one hand, it needed to operate some transformation of a personal, ideological or political kind, and therefore needed to distance itself in some way from the mainstream (Hollywood) cinema which functioned on the basis of identification and illusionism. On the other hand, it needed to demonstrate both a political and aesthetic self-consciousness – some form of reflection on and contribution to the art of film making, together with some reflection on its position in the relations of production – and only if it did these two things simultaneously could it make a significant political contribution. The intimate and necessary link between politics and aesthetics was what *Cahiers* called 'The struggle on two fronts'.[18]


## Political films in practice: *Coup pour coup* and *Tout va bien*

In order to explore what political film making meant, we shall look at two films which were released at more or less the same time (1972), and which apparently deal with the same subject matter, namely a strike and its consequences. The events depicted in both films were fairly typical of those that occurred in a number of industries at the time, and this apparent authenticity gave rise to an impassioned debate in the national press as well as to violent disagreements between partisans and opponents of the different approaches to political film making they exemplified that were published in the pages of the film journals. The two films in question are Marin Karmitz's **Coup pour coup** and J.-L. Godard and J.-P. Gorin's **Tout va bien**.

Karmitz trained at the IDHEC film school as a technician (he failed the director's examination) and **Coup pour coup** was his third film. Previously he had made **Sept Jours ailleurs** (1968) featuring a young composer and his brief affair with a dancer, and **Camarades** (1970) which reflected the political activity that had been a constant in Karmitz's life in the *Jeunesses Communistes* and which translated some of his political concerns to the screen. Although **Camarades** adumbrated some of the issues tackled in **Coup pour coup** it was vitiated, according to Karmitz, by 'the political heterogeneity of the team which brought together Maoists, Trotskyists and anarchists' and by the fact that 'instead of placing politics at the helm we placed (. . .) the cinema (. . .) [so that] the political discourse was not integrated into the description of real life'.[19] Hence the film was dismissed by Karmitz as petty bourgeois like its hero.

**Coup pour coup** therefore attempted a better and more useful political analysis and, in particular, strove to arrive at a unified political position and to let politics determine the development of the film. The film tells the story of a strike by the seamstresses in a textile factory in the north of France. The strike is provoked by the summary dismissal of two workers and the strikers, in line with the new, post-1968 tactics, do not simply withdraw their labour, they also lock up Boursac, the boss. The CGT (that is, trade union) representative arrives, negotiates a few concessions on wages and secures Boursac's release. But the seamstresses are not satisfied, the strike spreads to other parts of the factory and an occupation takes place. After three weeks, during which many of the women workers' domestic tasks such as childcare are taken over by their men, Boursac returns to his office and is again sequestered. Other workers in the town come out in sympathy. The Prefect advises Boursac to make concessions ('we'll make up for them later') and the women win their case.

The originality of **Coup pour coup** resides partly in the fact that it depicts a strike, partly in the methods the strikers adopt (this aspect caused considerable concern among

French management who feared a 'copycat' effect), and partly in the *mise en scène* of the strike. The strike as subject was not unknown in the French cinema but it was unusual (*Positif* called it 'insolite') in the *commercial* cinema for which **Coup pour coup** was intended.[20] Both the subject matter and the tactics adopted by the strikers are clearly the outcome of May 1968: sabotage, sequestration and occupation were all practices adopted in the immediate aftermath of May,[21] while the portrayal of the union representative as being objectively on the side of the bosses, although he belongs to the French Communist Party which is supposed to be on the side of the workers, reflects the disillusionment with the Party among certain sections of the Left, where it was felt that the settlement of the 1968 strikes amounted to a sell-out. In the same way the depiction of the Prefect as the Machiavellian arm of an authoritarian state reflects a point of view common at the time and often verifiable in practice.[22] Thus the topicality and immediacy of **Coup pour coup** meant that it derived a degree of authenticity from the pleasure of recognition as well as a notoriety which resulted from the presentation of hitherto unfashionable and therefore exotic subject matter.

Although it was intended for commercial release, the film was made in a way radically different from most commercial films. The script, for example, was not written by Karmitz or by a professional screenwriter but by a 'worker' and was developed with the assistance of real textile workers who commented on the speech, behaviour and attitudes of the characters.[23] It therefore has some claim to being a work of collective authorship. Furthermore, those who appeared in the film were workers as well as professional actors. Karmitz has recounted how his earlier film **Camarades**, for all its good intentions, remained the story of an 'act of individual awareness' and 'external to the working class' and how he had shown 'the Flins factory in the same way that TV reporters show a factory'.[24] Similarly, with the initial stages of **Coup pour coup**, 'we started off very much in the style of the progressive ORTF reporter' until the textile workers themselves became involved. The method of work, which consisted of discussions with female textile workers at Troyes and involvement with a strike at St Omer, with photos and video recordings which were discussed in order for the scenario to change and develop, enabled Karmitz and his team to understand that the first draft had shown a 'men's strike', not a women's strike, and that their conception of the conduct of the strike had been erroneous.

**Coup pour coup** can thus lay claim in a variety of ways to a superior authenticity and to political truth. Though the strike in the film is fictional, the unfolding of events is both plausible and historically accurate and the behaviour of the workers, their speech, their actions, their political views, are all apparently guaranteed by their non-fictionality.[25] In addition, **Coup pour coup** can lay claim to political significance as an agent of dialectical change and of a real *prise de conscience*. On the one hand, the team of film makers, petty bourgeois and intellectuals took instruction from the working class, who were thus instated, or reinstated, as the vanguard class. On the other hand, participation in the film caused the workers themselves to become more conscious both of their oppression and of the remedies available to them, In this way, the 'real' workers underwent an experience homologous to that of the fictional workers in the film. Finally, according to Karmitz, the presence of a film crew as participants in the strike at St Omer 'transformed their struggles. The local press was giving out inaccurate and even malicious information about events. So it helped them to fight back.'[26]

**Coup pour coup** was strongly criticised by the French employers' federation (CNPF) for inciting workers to revolution, but also by a variety of left-wing groups who did not accept the political stance taken by the film. Gérard Leblanc, for example, denounced 'the ideology of real life, of events "well filmed", of details which are guaranteed accurate: the ideology of the mirror which allows real women workers to look at themselves in a factory which is as authentic as the one in which they conducted their struggle at a given time'.[27] *Cahiers du cinéma* likewise criticised the 'serious philosophical error of an empirical kind' which underpinned the film, the notion that 'the truth is contained in reality, in life, and that it only has to be revealed, the agent of the revelation here being the sounds and the images'. This is characterised as 'outworn idealism inspired by religion'.[28] *Cahiers* also challenged the claim that the film effected the transformation that Karmitz suggested: 'The proletarian ideology is supposed to grow spontaneously out of the struggle as soon as it has been stripped of its bourgeois trappings. In this way we fall straight into a historicist conception of history (with the classes which embody a universal consciousness) invented by humanism'.[29]

A more measured criticism of the film might relate to the analysis of **La Vie est à nous** referred to above. Is **Coup pour coup** a film which might be described as vitiated by its 'single voice' or does it, by contrast, demonstrate a consciousness of its mechanisms and origins? Is any dialectic apparent in the film? First, there is the difference between the management and the workers, a difference which marks not simply the different fictional roles of 'them' and 'us' but also the fact that the workers are 'played' by workers whereas the management are 'played' by actors. Paradoxically, the decision to employ professional – albeit unemployed – actors for these roles was taken in an attempt to secure greater verisimilitude. It was, however, criticised as lacking credibility.[30] Jan Dawson described Boursac as a 'cartoon character' and remarked that 'as soon as the women start to articulate the oppression implicit in the factory's rhythms and routines (...) one becomes awkwardly conscious of a controlling presence behind the rough *cinéma-vérité* surfaces'.[31] There is clearly a discordance of discourses in the film which ought to derive from the differing objectives of the two classes portrayed in it but in fact occurs through a disjunction between reality and fiction that is avowedly unintentional. On the other hand, the alternation of rhythmical montage and long takes might be held to provide the politically and aesthetically necessary self-consciousness by breaking up the film's pictorial surface and interrupting the smooth flow of its narrative. Whatever its shortcomings, **Coup pour coup** is not a documentary film but a fiction film which looks as though it is a reconstitution. It might therefore be held to belong to a tradition exemplified by works such as Eisenstein's **Battleship Potemkin**. The title suggests a dialectical process, a refusal of resolution and closure, an insistence that the struggle goes on (it is not merely the workers but the bosses who think this is the case). The difficulty arises not so much in the experience of viewing the film as the comments made by the film makers who did, indeed, appear to subscribe to an ideology of authenticity and spontaneity.

There is no doubt that **Coup pour coup** had a great impact. As has been said, it was condemned as dangerous by management organisations and widely debated in the press for this reason. It also stimulated an examination of the question of realism and political cinema which led to some important theoretical advances. It was immensely significant in Karmitz's career since it gave him a reputation which prevented

Coup pour coup – the occupied factory

him from ever directing another feature film. Finally, and today this is perhaps its most interesting quality, it opened up new subjects to the French cinema. One of the tenets of the conclusions of the States General had been that workers should be given the means to make their own films and trained film makers should merely act as facilitators in this process. Karmitz took this policy literally, and his film was one of the first attempts to put it into practice within the commercial cinema framework. By the same token, **Coup pour coup** placed on screen a section of the population (female workers) that was virtually never seen, and allowed these workers a voice. The exploration of marginal or minority groups of all kinds was a feature of 1970s cinema, marrying the exoticism of earlier anthropological films with a new-found political commitment, and **Coup pour coup** was one of the first films to accomplish this.

By contrast, Godard and Gorin's **Tout va bien** takes a virtually opposite approach to what is almost the same story of a strike, which this time occurs in a sausage factory. During the strike the boss is locked up and the union negotiator, again a member of the CGT, is depicted as radically out of touch with the workers and as an objective ally of the bosses. His agenda of moderate pay increases and negotiation only wins him catcalls from those he is supposed to represent. But whereas **Coup pour coup** attempts to construct a fiction which resembles the enactment of unmediated experiences on screen, **Tout va bien** interposes a series of framing devices between the account of the strike and the viewer. The first fiction is framed by another which concerns two media workers (a radio journalist and a film maker, that is, a worker in sound and a worker in images) who go to report the strike and who are locked up along with the boss. This second fiction is itself framed by a third which purports to lay bare the financial mechanisms underpinning the making of a commercial film, showing the signing of a cheque to persuade the stars, Jane Fonda and Yves Montand, to act in the film which is then sold on the basis not of the roles they play in the fiction but of their 'real' personae as film stars.

Though **Tout va bien** is a political film it therefore emphatically rejects the unitary point of view in favour of a series of superposed perspectives which force the viewer constantly to revise and question what he or she thinks. In the same way, the visual style, in the manner characteristic of many Godard films, does not seek to create an impression of reality or authenticity, as **Coup pour coup** had done by, for example, using a disused factory as its set. Instead, through the use of sound, colour, camera movements and montage, it forces the viewer to be conscious that what is being watched is a construct, an artefact. Nowhere are these two procedures more clearly illustrated and combined than in the sequence where the image shifts rapidly from a scene within one of the rooms of the factory to the depiction of the factory in cross-section, as a series of boxes or frames, each containing its discrete activities. The multiple screen is familiar today in home video, but in 1972 it was not in use on television and virtually unheard of in cinema. Moreover its function is dissimilar. Generally, the multiple screen is used to show simultaneity in events separated in space or outside the camera's purview. In **Tout va bien** it is used to provide a conspectus of the struggles through the exploitation of precisely the rectangular framing devices that the visual media use. It is a *mise en abîme* of cinema, of its capacity to *donner à voir* and to create spectacle. It also has the effect of distancing the viewer from the struggle, as though he were examining a scientific drawing or sitting before an editing table choosing which frames to splice, demobilised by the spectacle rather than inspired by the struggle.

Julia Kristeva has rightly pointed out that Godard's films combine 'extravagant formalism and (...) extraordinarily poignant realism', that they mark a 'conjunction between the formal and the ideological' which is both 'very poetic and very militant'.[32] In **Tout va bien** the formal audacity is characteristically dazzling: the use of primary colours and the tricolour palette (blue, white and red) with its implicit reference to the state of France and the revolutionary tradition;[33] the brilliant parody of a television advertisement for *Dim* tights; the geometric counterpoint of the hypermarket raid sequence in which the long sideways camera movement, reminiscent of the traffic jam in **Weekend**, counters the vertical movements of the raiders as they dart up and down the aisles; the insertion of a black and white still photograph of an erect penis which comes as a shock because of what it shows and also because the image is contextually heterogeneous.

On the other hand, **Tout va bien** betrays an eclecticism which is also characteristic of Godard's work during the late 1960s and early 1970s,[34] an eclecticism which may derive from genuine political uncertainties or the desire, realised visually, to present a cross-section of political thinking, but which undoubtedly renders **Tout va bien** politically incoherent. A variety of post-1968 political positions are recognisable in the film, giving it the poignant realism referred to by Kristeva: the disaffected striking workers, the trade unionist,

Tout ba bien – Godard paradies the commercial for *Dim* tights

the feminist and the *gauchiste* (these latter 'liberate' the hypermarket shelves and subscribe to violent action). To these might perhaps be added the disaffected intellectual of Brechtian inspiration, in the person of Yves Montand, who has completely sold out and now makes commercials to pay the rent. The most sympathetic of these political types are undoubtedly the women: the factory workers who have a wit and self-assurance that makes light of their patently absurd and distasteful jobs, and the American journalist, played by Jane Fonda, whose outsider's attempts to understand what is happening at the factory are matched by her frequent failures at communication in her job – her voice is often censored, we frequently see her from the other side of a soundproof recording studio but cannot hear her – and her even less successful attempts to demonstrate the connection between the personal and the political to her husband. Thus **Tout va bien** may be said to have an aesthetic coherence in its commitment to visual experimentation, non-naturalistic images, and new forms of narrative, but its depiction of the strike is unconvincing and it is difficult to accept that Fonda in her role of feminist journalist embodies the beginnings of an attempt to 'struggle against the compartmentalisation of our lives'.[35] One of the reasons for this is the emphasis on visual compartmentalisation within the film, while the dynamically contrapuntal camera referred to above undercuts any sense of advance, resolution or synthesis. Thus despite the film's collective authorship it is not immediately obvious that it contributes

Tout va bien – Jane Fonda demonstrates the workings of patriarchy to Yves Montand

28

to the contemporary struggles depicted in it.[36] In this respect, the political intervention that might be ascribed to **Tout va bien** is far less significant than that of **Coup pour coup**.

It is essentially, however, as a film about the politics of the image that **Tout va bien** makes its statement. This, as we have seen, became one of the explicit concerns of film makers after May 1968, but it is also a concern which informed Godard's films virtually from the outset of his career. Where Karmitz tackled the issue of the right to be heard, and of extending to those traditionally excluded from it the possibility of speaking for themselves, Godard and Gorin explore the mechanism of such statements, the politics of representation, thereby accepting that someone is always speaking *for* someone else.[37] They do this first by posing the question of the relationship between sound and image. The two are frequently discordant in **Tout va bien**, either because the sound is silenced (when Fonda is cut off) or because it is incomprehensible (when Fonda speaks in English, when the trade unionist's rhetoric fails to match the circumstances of the strike), when the image says something different from the sound (the case of the apparently erotic image of the phallus denounced as oppressive by Fonda). The contention, throughout, is that both the temporal synchronisation and intellectual coherence between sound and image are not merely idealistic but also disguise the true politics of their production. Following from this, the structure of the communications industries is called in question, the freedom or otherwise to comment on events, to put an alternative point of view, and the responsibility of those working in the media industries to do so. The *Dim* advertisement sequence is critical both of the product's sales methods and even more critical of Montand, whose activities in advertising are presented as irresponsible. Finally, Godard and Gorin raise the issue of money in relation to the image. They stress the fact that film making is a commercial activity and without money films cannot be made, that certain kinds of film making, such as commercials, make more money than others, and that the actor's image is a marketable commodity like any other. This last point is also pursued in Godard and Gorin's film, **Letter to Jane**, which serves as a coda to **Tout va bien**. There the actress is criticised for using her image to sell a point of view about Vietnam, while in *Enquête sur une image* it is suggested that, because the actor's image is a commodity of exchange, he or she is incapable of portraying authentic emotion.[38]

The discussion in *Enquête sur une image* also helps to clarify a parallel strand in the critique of the politics of the image within **Tout va bien**. This is a more general attack on modern consumer societies of which advertising is seen as an epiphenomenon. In Godard's **Une Femme mariée** (1964), in his **Deux ou trois Choses que je sais d'elle** (1967) and incidentally throughout his work, consumerism is presented as perverse and immoral. In **Tout va bien**, the *gauchistes*' raid on the hypermarket, that temple of consumerism, is seen as having considerable virtuosity in the best Situationist tradition and is presented as justifiable and even admirable, though it may be politically naive. A persistent strand in Godard's work, exemplified here, is the nostalgia for the simplicity of an era in which fewer images circulated and where a direct and immediate relation existed between the image and its use value, a nostalgia perhaps for naive realism.[39]

Thus although the subject of **Tout va bien** is decentred from the strike to its representation, it shares with **Coup pour coup** a kind of utopianism. **Coup pour coup** has become increasingly poignant over the years as the class which it attempted to represent and to give a voice has continued to disappear, and it is a poignancy shared by Godard and Gorin's film.[40] This can be seen in the similarity in the points of detail such as the workers' refusal in both films to let the sequestered boss use the lavatory on the grounds that they themselves have been consistently harassed in this way. Such details are interesting because, whilst being clearly based on authentic cases, they form part of the repertoire of exoticism surrounding the real conditions of real workers in the wake of May 1968 that was most brilliantly exemplified in Robert Linhart's account of his own experiences working in a Renault factory.[41] They also belong to the much older tradition of criticising industrialisation as dehumanising which was renewed at this time,[42] but one which, if Jacques Rancière is to be believed, is always mediated through 'the extreme codification of characters and places in society' apparent in French cinema and which serves as a 'a bit of imagination added to the real'.[43] In **Coup pour coup** there is a mood of desperation which is almost tangible, a fervent desire to invest significance in a working class which was declining numerically and refusing to behave in an appropriately revolutionary fashion. The film reflects the concern with the absent or inadequate working class which is a theme that recurs in French political writing of the 1950s and 1960s, and is an attempt to give that class reality. **Tout va bien** evinces a comparable regret for a simpler world in which it was possible for an event to take place and for it to be represented without the accretion of the multiple connotations that the spread of the media industries has generated.[44] The Yves Montand character embodies the film's ambivalence. It sympathises, to a degree, with this weary and disaffected intellectual and former political activist, (a role already played by Montand in **La Guerre est finie**), whose professional life now consists in making a poor parody of a French film masterpiece. His commercial is a corrupt version of the French cancan which, when it was filmed by Jean Renoir, stood for Paris at the height of its opulence and artistic lustre, a corruption which is symbolised by the transformation of the stockings which once carried an extraordinary erotic charge into brightly coloured tights encasing the spindly legs of bored teenagers.

Thus **Coup pour coup** and **Tout va bien** both address, and to a degree answer, the question which after May 1968 became central to political cinema, namely whether different things should be filmed or whether things should be filmed differently. Both films portray the new social actors revealed by the Events: the workers, particularly the women workers, that the media industries had virtually never shown, the various marginal leftist groups, the feminists and the beginnings of the women's movement. **Tout va bien** explicitly tackles the subject of news reporting while **Coup pour coup** points the way, more generally, to the revival of interest in the documentary which was to be apparent throughout the 1970s and to the associated debates about the status (that is, the authenticity and the veracity) of the 'document'.

Both films also address the question of the control of the film industry which was central to the demands of the States General of the Cinema. This question is interestingly answered in the subsequent careers of both Karmitz and Godard who, each in his own way, used the experience of making what was to be his last commercial film for some considerable time to analyse what was wrong with the structure of the French film industry and to attempt to establish alternative practices outside it.

For Karmitz **Coup pour coup** marked the end of his career as a director: 'I'd had it as far as the *avance sur recettes* was concerned; they'd had enough of my projects'.[45] This, he believed, was because the production committees of the CNC, whose members were appointed by the Minister of Culture, had right wing majorities, and he was viewed as a man of dangerously influential left-wing opinions. However, the failure of the attempt to distribute the film commercially also showed Karmitz where a different intervention was possible and necessary. He established himself as an independent distributor (MK Diffusion) and opened a cinema in the Bastille area with the aim of 'getting out of the Latin Quarter ghetto and moving to a working class district where the cinemas showed karate and sex films'.[46] The intention was to create a countercultural centre with a cafe and a bookshop as well as a cinema. The '14 juillet' Cinema opened, symbolically, on 1 May 1974. Since that time Karmitz has become a wealthy and influential man with a production company and shareholdings in a French television channel, but his success is based on the promotion and more recently the production of independent films, an alternative and even marginal cinema for which there is a limited audience, which would find the conventional, commercial channels of finance unsympathetic.

Conversely, for Godard the experience of **Tout va bien** and, indeed, all the films of the Dziga Vertov group, implied an engagement with film production rather than distribution. This is quite explicitly stated in an interview he gave in 1970:

> *Whereas all political cinema is defined by an attempt to distribute films in a different way, we believed that this couldn't be done and that attempts to do so had always ended in failure. As Marxists we thought, instead, that production should determine distribution and consumption (...) only when we know how to produce films in the specific conditions of a capitalist country under the control of imperialism will we then know how to distribute them (...) so instead of considering distribution to be the main contradiction we considered the main contradiction was to be found in production: producing a film in a politically correct way should then show us the right way to distribute it, politically'.[47]*

**Tout va bien** might, arguably, be considered an attempt to exploit the commercial system to different ends. If so, it was not successful. But a more certain way of gaining greater control over production was to exploit the new technologies which could enable film makers to escape the managerial constraints of the industry and return to a craft-based approach to film making. This, in turn, implied an alternative distribution and exhibition circuit outside the Paris-based locations of the industry. In 1972 Godard established the Sonimage film company in the provincial city of Grenoble and, with his new partner Anne-Marie Miéville, devoted himself to the production of films which used video technology and the local distribution networks available in Grenoble. Because this equipment was both cheaper and easier to manipulate than film it offered a greater degree of autonomy to the producer/director, and Godard used it to make some of his most interesting and innovative works such as **Numéro deux** and **Sur et sous la communication**.

## The New Documentary

Alongside the traditional *cinéma militant* – the film records of the various political struggles being waged – there grew up a new kind of documentary film making directly influenced by the post-May 1968 processes of revaluation. These documentaries took as their premise that their product was a subjective fiction rather than an objective truth and they sought, for this reason, actively to implicate the viewer in the processes of interpretation.

The two seminal documentaries of the period were Marcel Ophüls's **Le Chagrin et la pitié** (1971) and André Harris and Alain de Sédouy's **Français si vous saviez** (1972). In their production history, the political position they adopt, their treatment of history, their explosion of the unitary point of view, and in the relationship they establish between sound and image, these two films, and others which were later influenced by their example, posed new questions as to the nature and purpose of documentary.

**Le Chagrin** and **Français si vous saviez** had common origins in pre-1968 French television. Harris and Sédouy were the producers of the current affairs programme, **Zoom**, on which Ophüls worked as a director between 1966 and June 1968. In 1967 all three had collaborated on a film entitled **Munich ou la paix pour cent ans** described by Ophüls as the first film 'in what should have become a whole series of programmes which attempted to demystify history (...) so as to counter the wave of complacent and jingoistic self-satisfaction which we thought dominated and determined the content of most of the history programmes on French TV'.[48] Clearly the team wished, even before 1968, to propose an alternative view

of history and an oppositional kind of television. The May
Events intervened to prevent the series being made and Ophüls,
Harris and Sédouy all left the ORTF. Subsequently **Le
Chagrin et la pitié** was produced by Harris and Sédouy with
a script by Ophüls and Harris, while **Français si vous saviez**
was scripted and produced by Harris and Sédouy. In both cases
European television stations other than the ORTF contributed a
major part of the production budget and acquired screening
rights to the films. The result was that although the films were
not shown on French television until much later in the decade –
though they did obtain theatrical release in Paris – they were
seen by wide audiences across Europe.

   **Le Chagrin** and **Français si vous saviez** adopt a
comparable political position. **Le Chagrin** is a portrait of a
French town – Clermont-Ferrand – during the Occupation,
while **Français si vous saviez** traces 'how we won one war
and lost two others' (First World War, Second World War,
Algerian War). But despite the fact that the first depends for
its coherence on unity of time and place, while the second,
which adopts a diachronic approach, depends on questioning
the relationship between power and legitimacy in the deeds of
the politicians, soldiers and statesmen who have led France in
the twentieth century, both have at their centre the historical
figure of De Gaulle (implicitly in Ophüls's film, explicitly in
Harris and Sédouy's) and both offer an examination of the
constitution of Gaullism and of its essential characteristics. In
addition, both films challenge to some degree the myth of
Gaullism, that of the unification of the people against a
common enemy, and of the creation of a national consensus
across the Left–Right political spectrum with, ultimately, its
political expression in the Fifth Republic. Indeed, Marc Ferro
has called **Français si vous saviez** 'a settling of scores with
De Gaulle',[49] for at the heart of Harris and Sédouy's film is
the suggestion that, if Gaullism, and by extension the Fifth
Republic, was not legitimately established, then the consensus
or acquiescence in its continuation was based on the falsehood
that Gaullism depended on agreement where none really
existed.

   **Le Chagrin et la pitié**, on the other hand, allows the
viewer to catch sight of an alternative tradition flowing from
the Popular Front through the movement of decolonisation
into the *Parti socialiste unifié* (PSU), a movement which is
embodied in the former Prime Minister and PSU leader Pierre
Mendès-France, so much so that Ophüls admitted, though he

claimed it was accidental, that Mendès-France becomes 'the narrator of the first part (...) almost the presenter'.[50] In the post-1968 context, after events which had shaken Gaullist power and, ultimately, forced the General's departure from the political scene, these films propose a different or a multiple interpretation of history, and they do so with astonishing prescience, since Pierre Mendès-France was an inspirational figure to the new left as it formed a parliamentary alliance under De Gaulle's arch opponent François Mitterrand in the early 1970s. The international success of **Le Chagrin et la pitié**, above all perhaps in Britain, which had cause to deplore De Gaulle's influence in Europe, can partly be explained by this oppositional stance.

Both **Le Chagrin et la pitié** and **Français si vous saviez** are historical documentaries in the sense that both consist of a montage of archive footage relating to the periods they depict. However, neither film adopts the traditional documentary procedure of a voice-over commentary offering the viewer an interpretation of the images. Instead the films intercalate newly shot interviews with survivors of and participants in the events portrayed in the archive material. These interviews have several functions: to place a present-day individual in relation to his own history, occasionally revealing that the individual has lied; to align individuals' memory of the past with what actually happened as revealed by the documentary footage; and to fill the gap left by the absence of commentary either with questions put by the film makers to the witnesses or with the original commentaries from newsreels of the period.[51] This procedure sets up new relations between sound and image and gives the film maker the status of innocent enquirer rather than omniscient reporter. In marked contrast to the documentary style prevalent in the 1950s which, with its interpretative voice-over, was often the film maker's *exercice de style*, this technique not only permits but requires conflicting interpretations.

In practice, it is quite difficult to attribute an ideological or political point of view to these film makers. It might be argued, for example, that in **Le Chagrin** the collaborators are better educated and more articulate than the members of the Resistance and therefore more persuasive or sympathetic. Conversely in **Français si vous saviez** the amount of time accorded one of the most right wing of the witnesses, Argoud, does not so much give him time to make his case as time to expound his extremist views on all kinds of matters not immediately related to the film. Opinions differ as

35

to the reasons why Clermont-Fcrrand and Lorraine were chosen as locations. By the same token, some might concur with Marc Ferro that, 'in order to be effective, the authors have sought out all the different strands of anti-Gaullism' while others might agree with Michel Foucault (followed in this by *Cahiers du cinéma*) who considered **Le Chagrin et la pitié** a reactionary film since what it shows is the *absence* of popular struggle.[52] The most significant feature of these films, therefore, is that after a decade of political certainties they promoted controversy, uncertainty and a multiplicity of views.

But these films, and especially **Le Chagrin et la pitié**, derive their force from a marriage of new ideological and new aesthetic forms. Ophüls consciously set out to update the documentary:

> *In montage films (. . .) documentary material is not used in a very modern way. The clip from the archives (. . .) is used over and over, and over again (. . .) It serves simply as a medium of transmission not even as an illustration, but as visual footage because something has to be shown while there is something on the sound track (. . .). Often archive material simply fills the gap in the commentary by the person making the film. And one of the really old-fashioned things in documentary montage films is the preponderance of spoken commentary so that you often feel the filming was added on afterwards.[53]*

Ophüls concurs here with the criticism of much militant cinema as expressed by Jean-Paul Fargier: 'Ninety-nine times out of a hundred political films are edited round the sound track (. . .) and the images – which are often grey and out of focus – are merely added on later'.[54] Ophüls restored the image to a position of supremacy and in so doing implicitly criticised television for being nothing but ameliorated radio. His approach also implied a degree of self-effacement on the part of the writer–director before the image. In fact, the director is merely removed a degree: he still makes choices but these are immanent in the film rather than dictated from outside. In **Le Chagrin et la pitié**, for example, Ophüls chose the locality, and then selected the various witnesses on the representative sample basis: 'we tried to have a – very large – cross section of different social groups, different political opinions, and different ways of reacting',[55] and at the editing stage (for although the film was long the quantity of footage shot was even longer) he claims that his choices were usually aesthetic and based on what made the greatest visual impression, what was most unfamiliar. Thus in **Le Chagrin et la pitié**, and perhaps even more clearly in **Français si vous saviez**, the documentary material and archive footage is used as a process of discovery, 'information becomes a voyage of discovery, a way of finding things out', rather than as a means of affirmation. It opened up the possibility of constant revision and reinterpretation, even or perhaps especially of well-known material (Ophüls remarked how certain items from the Coblenz archive were used and re-used), it showed what a truly innovative mass medium television could be, and it gave the image a role in meaning as great, if not greater, than that of the word.

**Le Chagrin et la pitié** and **Français si vous saviez** also called into question the nature of popular history and popular film making. Unlike the art documentaries of the 1950s or some of the militant films of the post-1968 period, they reached the mass audience of television by addressing themselves to a period – that of the Occupation and the origins of the Fifth Republic – widely acknowledged to be constitutive of modern France. In so doing, these films demonstrated the massive potential of the archive, which was held to be the repository of popular history. Although clearly not unknown until that time – indeed, in some respects this archive was too well known – it had nevertheless not previously been exploited on such a scale. Just as, after May 1968, certain film makers attempted to broaden the social scope of cinema to include the new actors who had emerged onto the political and social scene, so now the archive itself was revealed as having undreamt-of riches and as a potential weapon in the class struggle. For these films revealed, by their profusion of documents,the habitual processes of encoding at work in documentary (referred to by Ophüls as the conventions of documentary film making) as well as the ways in which the archive had been used to construct, repress or 'reprogramme' popular memory.

The discovery or rediscovery of the newsreel and television archive was linked to a movement in French historiography which can be traced back to the creation of the *Annales* school of history and, more immediately, to Michel Foucault's work on the 'archaeology' of knowledge in the 1950s and 1960s. For example, in an interview relating to René Allio's film version of Foucault's archive compilation **Moi, Pierre Rivière** the philosopher drew a distinction between 'official' and 'unofficial' history:

*These official histories are to all intents and purposes centred on Gaullism which, on the one hand, was the only way of writing history in terms of an honourable nationalism and, on the other hand, the only way of introducing the Great Man, the man of the Right, the man of the old nineteenth century nationalism as an historical figure. It boils down to the fact that France was exonerated by De Gaulle, while the Right (...) was purified and sanctified by him.*[56]

Foucault's thesis is that in the nineteenth century popular memory was kept alive as a tradition of struggles remembered and transmitted orally, while in the twentieth century a series of apparatuses was set up to impede the flow of the popular memory: 'It is vital to possess this memory, to control it, since what is at stake is popular struggle or the memory of that struggle.'[57] This is why he read **Le Chagrin et la pitié** as a reactionary film since it portrayed the absence of struggle, although he also saw in it a progressive function in demonstrating that the archive, in holding the key to memory, might also hold the key to popular struggle. As Stephen Heath put it in 1977: 'The problem is (...) that of a recovery and expression of history, a problem for the film maker [hence] the powerful appeal and currency of the conjunction 'cinema and history'.[58] Clearly, this activity could not proceed without challenge and recuperation. For the traditional Left 'the foundation of the archive and the creation of the nation state go hand in hand. Paper archives were created with the Revolution. The one and indivisible French Republic was based on the collective memory deposited in the *Archives Nationales.'*[59] On the other hand, for a revolutionary Marxist such as Jacques Rancière, this is 'intellectual nostalgia for the recovery of the "unity" of popular memory, (...) a Left anthology proceeding through village chronicles and memoirs of the people, to transform a voyeuristic relation to the people into one of inheritance'.[60]

## Nothing but the Image

The further exploration of the meaning and potential of the audio-visual archive became possible through a virtually fortuitous circumstance that led to the creation of INA — what is now called the Institut National de la Communication

Audiovisuelle.[61] The reform of the ORTF enacted under President Giscard d'Estaing late in 1974 (and in part provoked by the upheavals of 1968) unexpectedly brought together in one body the ORTF's television archives, which also contained the archives of the *Actualités Françaises* from the pre-television period, and the ORTF's former departments of research, experimentation and training. One of the functions of the newly created INA was to produce 'experimental' films and one of its unusual and original decisions was to view the archive as a source of new works: 'archives are most frequently used as documentary or pedagogic sources, to illustrate or provide examples. The conception we have adopted (...) is one that sees memory as a source of creativity (...). This is completely different from the kind of archive exploitation you find in America.'[62]

The creative possibilities of the archive were revealed in three compilation series produced for INA by Louisette Neil and Thierry Garrel: **Hiéroglyphes** (1975), **Rue des Archives** (four series 1978, 1979, 1980, 1981) and **Juste une Image** (1982). All three were 'magazine programmes devoted entirely to images' which progressively broke new ground.[63] In particular the structure of the series altered, with the first being highly didactic 'built up around various subjects under various headings, lasting between five and ten minutes each', while the later programmes, such as those in **Juste une Image**, were 'more complex because every episode was a work in its own right and we were much more interested in the combination of elements in each episode'.[64] Commentary was totally effaced and the images worked for themselves, creating out of the producers' individual and collective experiences what they called an 'imaginary cinémathèque'.[65]

These programmes all work through the confrontation, comparison and contrast of lengths of archive film documents which may have no other common denominator than that. In this sense, the newly formed relationships between images removed from one sequence and placed in another does indeed produce new meanings in the Eisensteinian sense. But there is more to these series than simply the virtuoso illustration of the aesthetic possibilities of montage or, at the other end of the scale, the postmodernist recycling of already existing material. This can best be seen by examining one of the contributions to the **Rue des Archives**, the **Petit Manuel d'histoire de France** (1979), a two-hour long montage created by the exiled Chilean film maker Raul Ruiz. The material Ruiz used is taken from television dramatisations of French history (beginning with the Gauls and ending with the Third Republic) such as Stellio Lorenzi's **La Caméra explore le temps,** Marcel Bluwal's **Les Enigmes de l'histoire,** Jean Chérasse's **Présence du passé** and Henri de Turenne's **Les grandes Batailles du passé.** There are, in addition, extracts from one or two feature films such as Gance's **Napoléon.** Ruiz organises this material in chronological sequence into periods under headings such as 'The Gauls', 'The Middle Ages', 'The Crusades', 'Joan of Arc', 'Modern Times', 'The Revolution' and so on. On the sound-track he retains what existed originally but he adds a commentary in the form of extracts from school textbooks such as those by C. Calvet (1903), A. Aymard (1929), David Ferré Poitevin (1956) and Audrin and Dechappe (1968).

As with **Le Chagrin et la pitié,** the film maker's contribution is implicit rather than explicit, though it is nevertheless very real, and is to be found in the overall conception of the series rather than any immediate message it conveys. However, the material Ruiz uses is complex and ideologically highly charged. The writing of French history is a well known site of ideological struggle and the advent of universal primary education in the 1880s had led to the production of history books designed to legitimate the newly restored Republic. This tradition is implicitly invoked in the extracts used, as is the conceit of having versions of history enunciated by youthful – and female – voices, the 'voices of innocence', who inform us, for example, that 'the Revolution was necessary'. Here, no doubt, Ruiz pays a belated compli-ment to Godard, whose **France/Tour/Détour** (1977), the title of which refers to perhaps the most celebrated of the Third Republic textbooks, *Le Tour de la France par deux enfants,* was also narrated by two children. Beyond that, of course, both film series refer to the pedagogic tradition of the early elementary schools, used in *Le Tour de la France,* of the *leçon de choses* or learning by a process of familiarisation.

But it is not just the commentary Ruiz uses which is already constructed. Virtually all the programmes from which he takes extracts were made in the early days of French television when the producers thought of themselves as having a 'mission' analogous to that of Jules Ferry's *instituteurs,* the so-called 'black Hussars of the Republic', so that their vision of History, and indeed of television, was very much a nineteenth century one, 'a period of humanism and faith in mankind'.[66] Ruiz's film, naturally, has many incidentally comic or sensitive moments, such as the comment, during the section devoted to the Crusades, 'How can one believe the word of an Arab?' or the expression of relief at the appearance of Joan of Arc in 'France saved by the French'. More generally, it uses the juxtaposition and confrontation of already existing texts to question the nature of all narratives of history so as to show their relativism and, indeed, to question the value attributed to documents by virtue of their entry into the archive.

It was probably no accident that a refugee from a Latin American dictatorship should have chosen to question, in this manner, the authority and official status conferred on fictionalised versions of history and on History itself by virtue of the process of conservation. The overthrow of democratic governments in Latin America and the exercise of various forms of cultural oppression meant that Paris in the 1970s contained a group of exiled film makers (Eduardo de Gregorio, Hugo Santiago and Edgardo Cozarinsky as well as Ruiz) whose films evince an explicable paranoia that no doubt derives both from political experience and the reading of the works of literary masters such as Borges. Certainly, the most consummate and brilliant example of the genre is Edgardo Cozarinsky's **La Guerre d'un seul homme** (1981), also produced by INA. This is a film whose images are entirely derived from archive sources and which, once again, looks at the period of German occupation, this time of Paris, but whose assumption is that the document is not merely a fiction but a lie.

**La Guerre d'un seul homme** sets up a relationship between three points of view or, perhaps, three dimensions. Firstly, there is the montage of archive footage, all of it taken from the *Actualités Françaises*, some of it extremely well-known.[67] Secondly, the spoken commentary consists of extracts from the *Paris Journal* of the German writer and poet Ernst Jünger, the 'one man' of the title, delivered in the powerfully suggestive voice of the actor, Niels Arestrup, and described by Cozarinsky as 'a voice that whispers in the viewer's ear'. Arestrup's presence is almost tangible, although he is never seen,[68] so that what he says comes to resemble the 'voice of conscience', the still small voice of the alternative point of view. This establishes a disjunction between voice and image, a disjunction which is exacerbated when it is recalled that Jünger, though an officer in the German occupying army, deliberately distanced himself, in his capacity as both a writer and a Prussian aristocrat, from the doings of the Nazis. He is not, of course, sympathetic to the French people, but he does have an intellectual respect for Paris as an artistic capital and he therefore welcomes his posting there. Finally, the film is orchestrated into 'movements' through the use of compellingly elegiac music, all of which turns out to be German: Pfitzner, Schreker, Schönberg and, above all, Strauss, in whose 'Last Songs' Cozarinsky detected something like 'the end of a culture'.[69]

For Cozarinsky, the notion that the truth may be grasped through documents is untenable: 'in most of what are called documentary films you have a presupposition which is foreign to me and which I am hostile to, that (...) sound and image cannot lie. I have always thought precisely the opposite.'[70] The result is an investigation of lies, an essay on lying: 'Instead of illustrating a truth which was defined in advance I wanted to study the play of lies because I knew there would be lies!'[71] The prejudice which Cozarinsky articulates in this matter-of-fact rather than embittered or disillusioned tone (whilst acknowledging the extent to which his personal history may have contributed to such a point of view) does not lead to any form of triumphalism. The tone of **La Guerre d'un seul homme** is far from suggesting that the truth is being revealed to the stupidly naive. Instead, Cozarinsky has woven together a series of brilliant variations on a theme, such that his film is one of the most poetic accounts in existence of the creation of modern France.

## Documentary and Truth

It was not until the 1960s that the communications industries expanded rapidly in France and not until the end of the decade, for example, that virtually all households owned a television. Nor did French sociologists begin to examine mass communications until that decade (the journal *Communications*, for example, was founded in 1961). May 1968 had the effect of bringing together into a debate on the politics of the image and the techniques of representation a curiosity and anxiety about the effects of mass communications, in particular television, and protests about government control and censorship of television which had first been revealed in the 1965 election.[72]

In order to follow the development of the debate, it is useful to look at Roland Barthes's essays on the media, since they give a good indication of the way perceptions and analyses changed. In 1968 Barthes noted, in an essay on Flaubert's realism, a trend in the modern age which was:

the (. . .) development of techniques, works and institutions based on the ceaseless need to authenticate reality: photography (the crude record of what was), news reports, exhibitions of old objects, tourists' visits to historical sites and monuments. All these things suggest that the real is reputed to be sufficient in itself, that it is powerful enough to deny any idea of 'function', that its statement has no need to be integrated into a structure, and that the fact that things have been there is (. . .) sufficient![73]

Barthes implies that the very profusion of opportunities for verification suggests anxiety about the truth. This proved to be the case with television, which had taken over the role that photography played for an earlier generation, that of furnishing access to the real. When it failed to do so, through censorship or omission, the question of its function was explicitly posed. In his analysis of images, Barthes started from the position that the photograph is 'a perfect analogon' a 'message without a code'.[74] But then he moved to consider images as a means of manipulating desire, and came to the conclusion that whereas the 'analogical plenitude' of photography has been seen as a 'factor of resistance against the investment of values' it was now clear that all images have a rhetoric, that they do not present the 'real' but the 'verisimilitudinous' which postulates something or attempts to persuade.[75] When applied to television and cinema the implications were enormous. As far as the institutional arrangements of television were concerned, it meant that the traditional search for objectivity was rendered pointless. More specifically it meant that what Bazin had called the 'ontology of the photographic image' could no longer be held to be its capacity to record reality.

In *Cahiers du cinéma*'s reassessment of Renoir's **La Vie est à nous** referred to above, it had been suggested that there were two ways of making a political film – either a *mise en scène* of a fictional political event or the montage of film events that had actually taken place. These two ways derive ultimately from the distinction between the Lumière and Meliès traditions conventional in French film criticism. But by the 1960s technological changes had eroded the distinction between the techniques of *mise en scène* and montage associated with fiction and documentary respectively. For example, lighter cameras, faster film and less cumbersome recording equipment all made montage and the methods of direct cinema possible in a fictional narrative, and the films of both the Italian neo-realists and the *nouvelle vague*, by their use of direct methods and montage, all blur the distinction between fiction and documentary.

But if documentary was penetrating fiction, fiction was even more interestingly perceived within documentary. In two fascinating articles Jean-Louis Comolli suggested that all films are based on *manipulation* (where to place the camera, when to start shooting) with the result that 'a certain coefficient of unreality, a sort of fictitious aura' is created round the events filmed.[76] According to Comolli, direct cinema is based on the paradox that 'it only begins to be valid as such when a fracture occurs in the reporting through which a film can enter, a fracture which betrays – or acknowledges – the basic falsehood underlying documentary, that at the heart of non-intervention is to be found manipulation'.[77] To illustrate the inevitability of manipulation Comolli cites one of the most famous of the May *cinétracts*, **La Rentrée des Usines Wonder**. Nothing in this film was set up for the camera and yet 'everything is so exemplary, more real than reality, that one cannot help thinking this the most Brechtian of screenplays in which the documentary appears to be the product of the most consummate act of fiction'.[78] It follows from this that all films are ultimately fictions and that there is no such thing as reality in the cinema but only representation.

When the re-examination of documentary techniques demonstrated, *contra* Bazin, that *mise en scène* was no 'closer' to reality than montage, the thoroughgoing rehabilitation of montage, and especially the work of Eisenstein, became possible.[79] *Cahiers du cinéma* published new and more complete translations of Eisenstein's writings, followed by two special issues on Russia in the 1920s,[80] and at the Aix-en-Provence festival in 1969 an event was devoted to montage, the proceedings of which were published in *Cahiers*.[81] The purpose of these exercises was in part to rescue Soviet cinema from the disrepute into which it had fallen as a result of Bazin's strictures, but it was also to explore an existing revolutionary cinema and the relationship between the political and the formal avant-garde.

Here advances in film theory and practice must be linked with – and were indeed to some extent dependent on – explorations in literary theory which occurred at the same time. The rediscovery was general in France and is exemplified in Todorov's edited volume, *Théorie de la littérature*, which was published in 1965.[82] The re-examination of the use of montage was associated with structural linguistics, the notion of film as a system in which meaning was produced by difference, 'the examination of ideas of linking, juxtaposition, combination and their corollaries'.[83] Montage, furthermore, need not be of single frames but could consist of the juxtaposition of whole sequences or the confrontation of texts and sub-texts such as Godard's deconstruction of an existing thriller in order to create another in **Made in USA**. In this way montage pointed to the cinema's inevitable intertextuality. Finally, it was stressed that montage was not be to confused with the editing that serves merely to make a narrative brisker, but was a dynamic and productive activity. Thus one finds in Eisenstein 'successive effects of transformation whose elements are linked by dynamic signs of correlation and integration (...) where the clash of two elements creates a decisive leap into a new concept'.[84] In the case of both montage and direct cinema, as in the case of literature, the viewer/reader is crucial to the production of the text: 'Fiction no longer pre-exists the shooting but is (...) its product, the spectator is the hero of the film and the film is his apprenticeship.'[85] This is where the formal and the political avant-garde come together. For direct cinema, the cinema of montage, and indeed, any film which displays its own processes of representation, serves as a challenge to the illusionism of the dominant Hollywood codes and to the bourgeois ideology which these embody.

Hence in the twenty years after May 1968, political and documentary cinema moved from the subjectivity of the 1950s, through a period of militancy in which the cinema was seen as a mobilising force and a means of concrete intervention in political struggles, towards a profound interrogation of the politics of representation and, in the case of a film maker like Cozarinsky, a reconciliation of the formal and political avant-garde. Indeed, as a result of the works of film makers discussed here, and others like them, all film making took on a political dimension deriving from the notion that the relationship between truth and fiction, reality and its representation is profoundly uncertain. This is reflected in the growth of women's cinema, in a different articulation of the relationship between French and American cinema, in a reinterpretation of the recent history of French cinema, as well as in the work of individual film makers such as Jean Eustache, Luc Moullet, Maurice Pialat or Agnès Varda, all of which are discussed in the chapters which follow.

# 2:

## Hollywood–France:
## America as Influence and Intertext

At the end of the Second World War the French rediscovered
the American cinema. American films had not been seen
during the Occupation, and after the Allied victory the
backlog of six years of Hollywood production flooded into
France, attracting large audiences.[1] Cinemas such as the Paris
Cinémathèque and the MacMahon embarked on programmes
exploring the American cinema and the film journals which
sprang up in the late 1940s and early 1950s all devoted
considerable space to the analysis of Hollywood. Indeed,
film critics today owe the definitive codification of certain
genres such as the western and the *film noir* to work that took
place at that time.[2]

But the American influence on postwar cinema and
postwar French culture in general was not universally welcomed. The immediate postwar period was a time when
France underwent rapid and sometimes brutal modernisation,
part of which was imposed by the United States as a condition
of aid for reconstruction,[3] so that the cinema and the culture
industries as a whole were only a minor part of a major
enterprise. The French cinema rapidly recovered most of the
audience it had temporarily lost to American films, re-
established its production capacity and, helped by the slow
growth of television, went through a period of relative
prosperity in the 1950s. This did not, however, prevent the
French industry experiencing considerable anxiety about
American competition, an anxiety which is reflected in the
combination of admiration and fear to be found among film
makers of the period. The ambivalent attitude towards the
American influence may be traced throughout the films of the
1950s and 1960s and is essential for understanding many
aspects of French film production after 1968.

# America in French films of the 1950s and 1960s

Although attitudes towards America varied across the political spectrum and fluctuated with the development of the Cold War,[4] film makers continued to see Hollywood both as an attractive model and as a potential instrument of destruction. In the 1950s, the French industry began, with great success, to imitate popular American cinema by producing thrillers, known as *polars* or *série noire* films, which were often adaptations of American detective stories transposed to the French context.[5] The *série noire* films have continued to flourish to this day and they form the principal means by which the French cinema's relationship to Hollywood has been articulated.

The first two such films, Bernard Borderie's **La Môme vert-de-gris** and Jacques Becker's **Touchez pas au Grisbi** (1954) manifested different responses to Hollywood and created two different points of reference for later film makers. However, both films inscribe in their text a version of the ambivalent relationship they maintain with the Hollywood model. Thus Jean Gabin, who plays the ageing gangster in **Grisbi**, wants nothing better than to retire to his good food and wine but is threatened by a younger gang leader who practises American methods and has adopted American habits. This, with minor variations, was a character that Gabin was to portray in films throughout the 1950s and, because of his peculiar position as the major international star of the French cinema, he incarnated the stark contrast between the old world and the new, both between prewar and postwar France but also between postwar France and postwar America influences on it. His roles thus became emblematic of the French cinema as a whole as it struggled to survive under the new dispensation created by the *pax americana*. Conversely, the American actor Eddie Constantine, who plays the FBI agent Lemmy Caution in **La Môme vert-de-gris**, testifies both to the attractiveness and the efficiency of the American approach by simultaneously recovering the loot and getting the (French) girl. However, his identity is as uncertain as Gabin's in **Grisbi**, since he is highly Gallicised, acting, in French, an American in a French film, and delivering lines in an impeccable *argot* which cannot be authentic since it is translated, while his performance, like that of the female lead Dominique Wilms, is played for laughs in a crude pastiche of the American genre. This immediately divorces the film from the social context which frequently gives American *film noir* its force, removes the existential dimension, but nevertheless leaves Constantine as a seductive performer whose qualities depend on his nationality – his energy, agility, charm and verbal delivery are all identifiably American.[6] As with Gabin's role as Max le Menteur, Constantine's Lemmy Caution returned in a series of films as well as exerting a strong influence on the style of actors such as Jean-Paul Belmondo in **A Bout de souffle**.

The relationship between the French and the American cinema in the 1950s and early 1960s might best be described, therefore, as one of tension perceptible in an elaborate intertextuality. When some of the critics of the 1950s became the *nouvelle vague* film makers of the 1960s they often exploited American genres such as the thriller, quoted or referred to American films and film makers in their own films and, when they did not write their own scenarios, frequently made adaptations of American thrillers.[7] These habits are often interpreted as evidence of either 'intellectualism' or the 'clannishness' of the *nouvelle vague*. They certainly testify to a highly developed film culture which is also presupposed in the audience, but references to Hollywood cinema have a serious point as well as being a set of winks, nods and in-jokes.

It is often suggested that the main outcome of extensive familiarity with Hollywood films was the creation of the *auteur* cinema, and it is true that the *politique des auteurs*, as originally developed in the pages of *Cahiers du cinéma*, stressed the importance of personal expression in the cinema and of *mise en scène* as a reflection of it. In France the *politique des auteurs* was also, at times, a voyage of discovery into unknown territories as well as an instrument of classification and exclusion. But an important aspect of the *politique des auteurs*, which is frequently ignored by Anglo-American critics, is its emphasis on the classicism of American directors. Thus Eric Rohmer, in a typical passage, wrote of the 'elegant sobriety', of 'the art of economy, the purity of line, the elegance of means'[8] that characterises American production. However, an admiration for the classicism of Hollywood cinema in turn indicated an ambivalence on the part of *nouvelle vague* critics and directors. For when Godard wrote, 'To quote Fénelon, I seek "a sublime so familiar that everybody will believe that he too could have achieved it effortlessly" ', and that 'the poise of transatlantic film makers echoes that which was to be found among the writers of our own delightful but unfortunate eighteenth century',[9] he was pointing to the cultural as well as the aesthetic significance of Hollywood.

American cinema was considered classical not merely because it was the aesthetic *summum* of the medium, like Greek sculpture or eighteenth-century French literature, but also, as with these forms, because of its globally pre-eminent role, confirmed and reinforced in America's international, political and economic influence. It was neither regional, marginal nor provincial, but the model to which all national variants sought to conform, to such an extent that little-known episodes of frontier history or a tale of cops and robbers in San Francisco could, despite the apparent triviality or parochialism of the subject matter, have universal significance. Naturally this meant that the cinema did not have to tackle grandiose subjects in order to achieve depth of meaning – a virtue which the *nouvelle vague* turned to great advantage[10] – but it also meant that French cinema could not hope to compete with the American on its own ground, that it had lost whatever national, cultural dominance it might once have had, and that it was condemned, in the postwar world, to the small-scale, the marginal and the regional.

Hollywood thus induced in the *nouvelle vague* directors a combination of pessimism and nostalgia of which Godard's **Alphaville** and Truffaut's **Tirez sur le Pianiste** are excellent but by no means unique examples. In **Alphaville** (1965) the themes of **La Môme vert-de-gris** are reprised in the story of how Eddie Constantine/Lemmy Caution, the FBI agent, in a slightly altered role, comes on a mission from America to a futurist city which is run by brainwashed automatons and a large computer. This city is, of course, the Paris which is in the process of radical modernisation (a theme Godard returned to in **Deux ou trois Choses que je sais d'elle**). Although the 'high tech' of the early 1960s looks dated now, the critique of a society dependent on machines, on dehumanising technology and the suppression of interpersonal relations remains forceful and apposite. However, this film is based on an unexpected reversal provided by the role and character of Caution and, as in **La Môme vert-de-gris**, the Americans are seen as having a beneficent influence.

In Borderie's film Caution is more attractive, more energetic, more resourceful and, above all, more competent than either the French gangsters or the Casablanca police. In **Alphaville**, Caution is now a journalist who poses a threat to the forces policing the city because he retains his autonomy and spontaneity. He awakens in the French automaton Natasha, played by Anna Karina, the feeling and reactions which had been programmed out of her, he restores her emotions and her conscience and, through him, she rediscovers her humanity by falling in love. In contrast to the conventional view, this film does not associate modernity with America, nor does it criticise American influences. Instead, through Caution, America is seen as the repository of the authentic and humane. **Alphaville** is a sombre and pessimistic film whose references to the *série noire* and the thriller genre are permeated with nostalgia for an era which has passed and a kind of film which is no longer made. In this sense the positive view of America which it offers is also an acknowledgment of the capacities of Hollywood and the limitations of the French cinema.

A similar nostalgia is apparent in **Tirez sur le Pianiste**. Adapted from the David Goodis novel, *Down There*, it recounts the downfall of a pianist: 'from the great concert halls of the world he descended the stairway to hell'.[11] This is 'a journey into the past, a return to the origins, towards Charlie's childhood, but this return is also that of the repressed, a return of violence to the childhood that the hero thought he had escaped by leaving his brothers for ever'. The film also recounts, in a highly misogynistic fashion, Charlie's inability to form relationships with women and shows him as the indirect cause of death of the two that he loves. Thus the artist escapes from his family, has a brief moment of glory and success, is struck with 'shyness' which is a form of egoism, discovers that he owes his success to the fact that his wife prostituted herself, and falls inexorably back into the misery from which he had come.

David Goodis had already served as a source or scriptwriter for a number of American *films noirs* but here the *noir* elements are associated with a French family which, through the casting of Charles Aznavour, is specifically coded as immigrant. It is also one from which escape is impossible. The references to the American cinema are affectionate and comic, from the naming of Charlie's brother 'Chico' to the two supremely unfrightening gangsters, wearing flat caps and smoking pipes, who talk more than they act. The film is hybrid in genre and extremely uneven in tone, but it is one in which inventiveness and creativity, whether verbal or physical, are left to the minor players who, as in the Lemmy Caution model,

51

often parody American characters, whilst the central figure, who is the ostensibly creative personality, is frustrated and ultimately sterile, ending his days tinkling futile tunes on a bar piano. If **Tirez sur le Pianiste** is, indeed, 'a respectful pastiche of the Hollywood B-films from which I learned so much',[12] as Truffaut claimed, it is equally a sombre account of the creative possibilities of the artist in France. In some of Truffaut's subsequent references to, or imitations of, *films noirs*, notably his last film, **Vivement dimanche**, the jocular does prevail, but in this, his second feature, but the film he had planned before any others, the emotion that predominates is anxiety and the tone again is elegiac.

Ultimately, the lesson both **Alphaville** and **Tirez sur le Pianiste** teach about American cinema is that it is incompatible with the realist themes of the *nouvelle vague* and the close observation of aspects of French society which the films of the 1960s proposed. The incompatibility is expressed in the narrative discontinuities of **Pianiste** and the representation of the American as outsider in **Alphaville**, as well as in the dialectic of the familiar and the strange to be found in both films. And in both cases what is referentially 'American' is attractive but fundamentally extraneous and unassimilable. Thus the *nouvelle vague* represents the end of one era as well as the beginning of another.

At the end of the 1960s the relationship between French and American cinema began to be articulated in a different way, reflecting essentially the changes which had occurred since the end of the war both in French society and in the film industry. France completed her process of rapid modernisation and, to the extent that Americanisation had been associated with it, the fears and anxieties aroused disappeared before the *fait accompli* that France had become one of the richest of western societies. Concurrently, the economic structure of the French film industry evolved in such a way that the American presence was inescapable, and this coincided with a period of crisis in French television in the 1970s, which resulted in a large increase in the number of American films and series screened. The relative independence enjoyed by the *nouvelle vague* was over and American producers became so dominant in the media industries that their presence ceased to be a topic of debate. Hence reflections on the malign nature of the American influence tend to disappear as a theme in the cinema at this point. Third, the Events of May 1968 and their aftermath transformed the social and political context in which film makers worked and gave much popular entertainment a new or changed political significance.

Despite its American origins the thriller became, at this point, more identifiably French, a genre used by producers to guarantee box office success, and one which, in its popular appeal, became a vehicle for the articulation of the social and political concerns of France as well as a reflection of them. In the post-1968 films the reference to American models is still present but it no longer takes the form of explicit imitation or nostalgia evident in the Lemmy Caution series or the *nouvelle vague*. In casting, theme, narrative style and *mise en scène* the *polar* was naturalised as French in a variety of interesting ways and it became a significant sector of French film production in terms of the number and success of the films produced as well as their capacity to articulate trends in French society and French film making. All *polars* have in common their reference to a genre which is ultimately American, but in other respects it is helpful to distinguish three categories which might be described as the fetishist, the political and the postmodern, in all of which this relationship is handled differently.

## The Fetishist *Polar*

This category of films includes the work of directors such as Henri Verneuil (**Le Clan des siciliens**, 1969, **Le Casse**, 1971, **Le Serpent**, 1972, **Peur sur la ville**, 1974, **I comme Icare**, 1979, **Les Morfalous**, 1984), José Giovanni (**La Scoumoune**, 1972, **Deux Hommes dans la ville**, 1973, **Une Robe noire pour un tueur**, 1980) and Jacques Deray (**Borsalino**, 1969, **Borsalino & Co**, 1974, **Flic Story**, 1975, **Trois Hommes à abattre**, 1980) all of which might be described as thrillers which refer to America in a way which is significant in the context of the development of the French cinema.

First, they represent an attempt to introduce aspects of the American star system into France by means of an intelligent exploitation of the acting tradition established by Jean Gabin and Eddie Constantine in the 1950s. These thrillers are to a great extent dependent on the performances of Alain Delon and Jean-Paul Belmondo: 'There are only two formats here: Delon and Belmondo', commented Jean-Pierre Melville, 'That's not a lot for a national cinema.'[13] The remark is not strictly accurate since alongside the thirteen thrillers Delon made in the 1960s and 1970s and the fifteen made by Belmondo, Jean Gabin (who did not die until 1976) appeared in nine and Lino Ventura in fourteen, while both Yves Montand and Jean-Louis Trintignant contributed to the genre. Nevertheless the careers of Delon and Belmondo are exemplary and they run in parallel, so that it is useful to trace their development with this in mind.

They belong to the same generation (Belmondo was born in 1933, Delon in 1935), and they both began their film careers towards the end of the 1950s (appearing together in Marc Allegret's *polar*, **Sois belle et tais-toi**, 1958). But they first made their names in the art cinema, Delon in Visconti's **Rocco and his Brothers** (1960) and Antonioni's **The Eclipse** (1962), Belmondo in Chabrol's **A double Tour** and Godard's **A Bout de souffle** (1959) in which his refreshingly relaxed and naturalistic acting, inspired by that of Eddie Constantine, amazed the critics. Delon also went briefly to Hollywood in the early 1960s.

However, both these avenues proved limiting to an ambitious actor who had the misfortune to be French – the art cinema because its budgets were small and it remained a director's rather than an actor's medium; Hollywood because, as the careers of Maurice Chevalier, Jean Gabin or Charles Boyer prove, it was virtually impossible to secure parts which were not nationally stereotyped. The *polar*, on the other hand, offered the opportunity to build a career through the popular cinema in which the film could serve as a vehicle for the actor to display himself and, indeed, for him to age.[14] Thus the Delon image was retooled in three films directed by Jean-Pierre Melville through which the development of the actor's screen persona can be traced. In **Le Samouraï** (1967) Delon plays an outsider with virtually no links to the ordinary world, a schizophrenic hired killer who, as the title suggests, ends by killing himself. This is thus a combination of a conventional thriller, which includes a superbly orchestrated chase sequence in the Paris métro, and a psychological study of some subtlety. Costello's emotional austerity, his repression, and his adherence to an anachronistic code of honour which has ceased to be a necessity rooted in a social context and has become almost entirely abstract and formal, are all matched by the austerity of the *mise en scène* and by locations, such as the

**Un Flic** – Alain Delon on the set with Jean-Pierre Melville

tunnels of the métro, which emphasise a geometric formalism. To play Costello, Delon draws on two traditions, the French tradition of restraint and suppressed violence established by Gabin in the 1950s, which itself draws upon the American example, and the American thriller tradition of underplaying most evident in some of Bogart's performances; his heightening of one or two physical characteristics, in the context of general suppression, appears to be entirely motivated psychologically. In the two subsequent films Delon made with Melville, **Le Cercle rouge** (1970) and **Un Flic** (1972) these characteristics gradually become part of an identifiable Delon screen persona. **Le Cercle rouge** does resemble **Le Samouraï** in its use of a code of honour, in this case of that of the American west, which imposes a particular physical and psychological comportment, but in **Un Flic**, as the title implies, the category has become more important than the individual example of it. Both these films, however, contribute towards the transformation of the actor's performance into a pure display of physical characteristics and metonymic objects such as the trench-coat and the hat.

Borsalino – Jean-Paul
Belmondo and Alain
Delon in thirties
costume

Although his range is much narrower than Delon's, Belmondo effected a similar concentration on either *truand* (villain) or police roles during this period, even if his performances became increasingly repetitious and sometimes parodic. And in addition to developing their particular styles Delon and Belmondo serve as a foil to each other, with Belmondo relying on muscular agility, pugnaciousness and a capacity to appear to fill the screen, while Delon depends on a glacial perfection in which the merest twitch of eyebrow or mouth is significant. Belmondo is aggressively virile while Delon can, at times, suggest sexual ambiguity.[15]

These contrasts are most thoroughly and successfully exploited in Jacques Deray's **Borsalino** (1969) and **Borsalino & Co** (1974). It is clear from the fact that Delon produced both films that they were designed as actors' vehicles. However, the pair appeared together only in **Borsalino** and by **Borsalino & Co** Belmondo is cleverly represented as the icon which he has, in fact, become in the film industry, since the film opens with the funeral of the character he played in the earlier film and with a close-up of his cameo portrait lying on his tombstone. Delon's iconic role is similarly emphasised in **Borsalino & Co** both by the brief sequence where he is revealed as an ordinary and humble citizen in an asylum, stripped bare of all the fetish objects which compose his image, and by the sequence where, after exile in Italy, he returns to France to take his revenge at the head of what is disguised, precisely, as a theatre troupe. This is a world in which acting, appearance and image are pre-eminent and in which a character's image and indeed the recognition he can command may consist exclusively of one or two items such as the double-breasted suit or the enormous Borsalino hat which Delon constantly fingers as though to draw attention to its special significance in lending him identity.

The second point of American reference for Deray's films is the American cinema of the 1930s and the 1970s, the former explicitly, the latter implicitly, to be found in an elaborate play of quotations and pastiches. The gangster film of the 1930s, for example is one source of **Borsalino & Co** and it is apparent in such elements as the opening funeral scene, in the way the shoot-outs are staged, in the positioning of the hoods in triangular formation as they walk through the streets, and so on. An equivalence is also drawn between the Italians from Italy, led by Volpone, who attempt to take over Marseilles, and the Italians in the USA, who have imported gang warfare to Chicago. Thus when Delon escapes from the asylum he takes refuge in Italy and, having learnt the Italian methods and style returns in an excessively loud pinstripe suit and proceeds to liquidate Volpone and his gang in an extremely violent manner. However, these references are also mediated through the American cinema of the late 1960s and early 1970s, which had rediscovered Mafia films. Beginning with Roger Corman's **St Valentine's Day Massacre** (1966), the trend reached its apotheosis with Coppola's **The Godfather** (1972) while Friedkin's **The French Connexion** (1971) adumbrates much of the plot of **Borsalino & Co** but from the point of view of an American lawgiver.

It would, however, be wrong to consider Deray's films as derivative since they not only draw on the French cinema tradition as much as the American but they sustain a relationship of creative tension with America. The political context of the films is particularly interesting in this respect.

They are set in the 1930s, which was a period undergoing revaluation in France at the time, but they do not have the moral dimension of the *film noir* where chiaroscuro serves to point to moral ambiguities.[16] Much of **Borsalino & Co**, for example, is shot in 'day for night', so much so that it is often hard to make out what is going on, but the play of light and shade serves to spotlight, to reify and to fetishise the eyes, the hat, the car or any feature, object or item of clothing which then becomes disembodied or decontextualised.

Nor do they adopt the political stance of films such as **The Godfather** or **The French Connexion**, which contrast the corruption of Europe and European mores with the virtues of America. There is a moral and political dimension to these films, but one that is provided by the French film industry. Delon as producer clearly set out to establish a series which, had it continued, might have stood comparison with serials of the silent period such as **Judex** or **Fantomas** or, indeed, the spontaneous and accidental serial created by Eddie Constantine's films.[17] The character Delon creates has much in common with the criminals and detectives of such serials because he is more recognisable in his accoutrements than in his person and because he is endowed with superhuman powers of either detection or escape. The recourse to fetish objects, which is one source of the Surrealists' liking for the silent serials, is used to good effect in these films of the 1970s to signify a period, a profession and a genre. The plot of **Borsalino & Co** also bears some resemblance to those of the early serials, not least in its perfunctory improbability, since it concerns a fiendish Nazi who conspires to render the entire population of Marseilles incapable of action through the distribution of narcotics.

In the same way, the role Delon plays in the film may be interpreted as a commentary on his career and on the French film industry, for the Frenchman is imprisoned in his own country and, indeed, considered to be mad. He is then exiled to Italy, where his eyes are, seemingly, opened; he returns to France only long enough to take his revenge before setting sail to America, the land of freedom and opportunity. Interestingly, although in these films Belmondo's career is not subjected to any comparable analysis, it is implicitly criticised in Alain Resnais's contemporary work **Stavisky** (1974). For here Resnais addresses (as he had done in **La Guerre est finie**) the legacy of the 1930s by locating corruption firmly in France and the French ruling class and he casts Belmondo in the role of beneficiary and exploiter of this state of affairs by making use of the qualities of charm, virility and so on which were the source of his success as a popular actor, in his portrait of the decade's most notorious con-man.

Like the *série noire* films of the 1950s and the *nouvelle vague* films of the 1960s, the French thrillers of the 1970s often expose and reflect a relationship with the United States in which cinema and the film industry serve to figure a broader economic and political relationship. It is interesting that whatever the film maker's political views (whether of the Left, like Resnais or the Right, like Delon) the 1970s manifest a general acceptance of Europe's role in American corruption. These films undoubtedly reflect both a new attitude towards America in Europe following the ending of the Vietnam war, and a new direction in American foreign policy and the beginnings of a disengagement from Europe. On the European side, there is a concomitant realisation that America cannot serve as a symbol of uncomplicated modernism and that much of what happens in Europe has its sources in Europe and not America. These films, it might be argued, therefore mark a certain disengagement from the Hollywood model, along with a disengagement from the naturalism for which Hollywood was renowned.

## The Political Thriller

The second version of the *polar* to become popular in France after May 1968 was the political thriller. Its genesis can be related to the political events of that year in France and around the world and it became a particularly appropriate vehicle for political discussion because of the nature of the political questions raised in 1968. In France itself, the May Events called into question the nature of the Gaullist regime, especially in its repressive aspects such as censorship and the use of the army and the police to enforce state power. They also demonstrated that the forces that were supposed to provide leadership for the people, the Communist Party and, to a lesser extent, the trade unions, practised a politics that was out of touch with the grass roots and complicit with the state and the government. Hence the interest in *gauchisme* – extra-parliamentary left-wing organisations – whether Trotskyist, Maoist or of any other persuasion, as well as a renewal of interest in the traditions of late nineteenth-century anarchism.

Outside France, in addition to the longstanding opposition shown by French film makers to the American presence in Vietnam, the Colonels' regime in Greece and the Russian invasion of Czechoslovakia in the summer of 1968 placed the issue of human rights at the centre of preoccupations. Once again, this was an opportunity to question the nature of supposedly left-wing regimes and, in particular, the practice of Communism. Thus the conventional content of the thriller, the portrayal of hunter and hunted, the interrogation of the nature of crime and corruption, the depiction of the work of the police, all acquired a strongly political resonance in the climate of iconoclasm subsequent to May 1968. This was not the first time that the French cinema had served to reflect such a climate and such an atmosphere. The Occupation and its aftermath had earlier provided the backdrop for an exploration of espionage and corruption and of the relationship between criminals and police in Clouzot's two masterpieces, **Le Corbeau** (1943) and **Quai des orfèvres** (1947), but these two precursors only serve to emphasise that at times of national ferment or crisis the thriller often becomes a vehicle for political discussion. In addition, in the early 1970s, the *série noire* novel series, which often provided the inspiration for thrillers on film, itself became highly politicised, as can be seen in the works of Jean-Patrick Manchette and of ADG.[18]

The Costa-Gavras trilogy **Z** (1969), **L'Aveu** (1970) and **Etat de siège** (1973), which discussed respectively the Greek Colonels' regime, the repression of the Prague Spring and an unidentified Latin American dictatorship, all illustrated that the denunciation of totalitarianism, whether of the Left or the Right, in the name of human rights, was capable of achieving box office success. An interesting feature of these films, however, is that they star Yves Montand in the central role; just as Melville had provided Alain Delon with the means to modify his image, so now Costa-Gavras, who had worked with Montand on his earlier thriller, **Compartiment tueurs** (1965), made use of Montand's extra-cinematic reputation as a man of the Left and helped to reinforce it through these films. And just as he later did with Belmondo, so Alain Resnais had provided the ironic commentary for what was to become the Yves Montand persona, the isolated agent or the lonely lawgiver placed not in an American city but in an exotic situation where events of world importance were taking place. For Resnais had given Montand the starring role in **La Guerre est finie** (1966) a film which was premonitory in its portrayal

60

of a tired revolutionary, disillusioned with the activities of the European Communist parties, weary of working for the overthrow of Franco's government from his exile in France. Here the use of a film star who had both an international reputation and a political record serves to underline what Costa-Gavras's films illustrate, namely that under the pressure of world political events the thriller has ceased to be the parochial concern of a small-town detective, has become a matter of human justice and has turned into what Jeancolas has called the 'cinéma civique'.[19]

However, in metropolitan France the figure of the lawgiver, or 'justicier', however heroic in the American west, whether urban or rural, remained extremely ambiguous. Whether he is a member of the official forces of law and order or a lone operator, the virtual interchangeability of *flic* and *truand* is a theme which runs through the films of this period. The idea is, of course, an old one, but its novelty here resides in the absence of the heroism from which the lawgivers, inspired by the American tradition, derived their charm, as well as the lack of the moral ending that was so common in the 1950s. The work of Yves Boisset is an interesting illustration of the general mistrust and disillusionment felt with the institutions of the state. In **Un Condé** (1970) the distinction between the police and the criminal community is hard to find: 'Thieves or policemen, they're all the same', as Vidocq put it, but by the time of **Le Juge Fayard** (1977) the sense of ambiguity has disappeared and the film is a straight denunciation of illegitimate political pressures on virtuous officers of the law, the simplicity of this moral configuration, as well as its cinematic antecedents, being underlined by the judge's sobriquet 'le shérif'. By the same token, anarchism in its various forms was not necessarily, or no longer, the province of the Left, all parties being attracted by the possibility of action outside the confines of conventional society. Whether in Melville's **Le Samouraï** or in Mocky's **Solo**, solitude and isolation, the pitting of the individual against society, the desperation of the small man in his inability to arrest the big machine, are all implicitly a critique of collective solutions, while the group of anarchists portrayed in Chabrol's **Nada** (1973) are as ineffectual as are those in Fourastié's **La Bande à Bonnot** (1968).

The interesting exception to this rule might be **Etat de siège**, in which Montand plays an American embassy official kidnapped by the Tupamaros in Montevideo and mercilessly interrogated by them until he agrees that his activities have contributed to the persistence of the totalitarian regime, after which he is killed. Costa-Gavras's view of collective action is therefore much more positive than that of many of his contemporaries and he equally finds no difficulty in justifying extra-parliamentary or criminal action when the opponent is both as powerful and as hypocritical as the United States. This was, however, a point of view which rapidly became unfashionable as the denunciation of American imperialism gave way by the mid-1970s in France to the denunciation of Soviet totalitarianism.

## The Postmodern Thriller

The third category of thrillers may usefully be considered 'postmodern' since the term helps to define both their form and content and to suggest new ways in which the films relate to contemporary discussions of art and culture and of the new to the old, in which the reference to America is explicit but is articulated differently.

What is meant if a *polar* is described as postmodern? In France, at least, the 'postmodern' was developed as a critical term to describe aspects of the art and culture of postwar societies. The postmodern was held to follow modernism by analogy with the post-industrial society which followed industrial society – a process of development in which America played a locomotive role and which was first analysed by American sociologists such as Daniel Bell. The identification of the postmodern is closely linked with the growth of cybernetics and its impact on our daily lives as well as with the critique of authenticity launched by Walter Benjamin in his seminal essay, 'The Work of Art in the Age of Mechanical Reproduction', and in the Frankfurt School's studies of what are called the 'culture industries'. In France this question has been explored by Guy Debord in *La Société du spectacle*, by Jean Baudrillard in *Le Système des objets* and other works and most notably by Jean-François Lyotard in *La Condition postmoderne*, subtitled 'a report on knowledge', published in 1979. To a degree, postmodernism, its exegetes and its critics, all attempt to come to terms with the impact of technology on art, and this is why cinema offers a privileged field of study. The question of the relationship between technology and culture as well as what this implied for the work of art, for social organisation and for the human mind were thus in the forefront of critical discussion in France throughout the 1970s.

'Postmodernism', however, has become a portmanteau term which means different things in different contexts and, more important, when applied to different art forms. For instance, most of the examples in Fredric Jameson's influential essay 'Postmodernism, or the Cultural Logic of Late Capitalism', published in Britain in 1984,[20] are drawn from architecture and this enables postmodernism to be identified with a worrying eclecticism and a habit of reference and quotation not motivated by reference to 'nature'. Postmodernism is frequently defined by what it is not: it disturbs the conventional relationship between nature and art or nature and culture and posits no organic link between the two, with the result that it breaks not merely with classic realism but with the realism we have come to discern in high modernism. To pursue the formulations offered by Jameson in another essay, postmodernism is the 'reaction against high modernism', 'the effacement of key boundaries or separations most notably in the erosion of the older distinctions between high culture and so called mass or popular culture' and the correlation of 'the emergence of new formal features in culture with the emergence of a new type of social life and a new economic order'.[21]

Furthermore, postmodernism also has a preferred form which is pastiche, the indiscriminate re-use of formal features from previous generations or periods without the observation of the hierarchical or canonical rules, either for different ends or for no apparent end at all, neither quoting nor referring with an object in mind but simply in order to recycle. Thus postmodernism amounts to abandoning definitively the orders of culture, whether these are architectural, dramatic or indeed social, handed down to us from the Greeks and reconstituted at the Renaissance. The artistic and cultural idioms remain but they are not used to speak the same language.

In one sense it is clear that film is a postmodern form par excellence. It is the product of a technology which permits endless repetition and reproduction, it is constructed (through editing and montage) by literally assembling bits and pieces which may have come from anywhere and whose unity is provided only by a temporal continuum and by contiguity rather than thematic coherence or a common origin. And it is, as early film critics often pointed out, a 'bastard form', since it is heavily dependent both on adaptation, imitation and, indeed, pastiche. However, the *polar* in France might be considered characteristically postmodern since, as we have seen, it is voluntarily imitative of an American genre which is referred to, quoted and recycled. Jameson would, however, emphasise the distinction between parody and pastiche to suggest that the norms (linguistic or otherwise) on which parody depends for its effects have fragmented into a series of private languages or idiolects, so that the creative possibilities of parody are no longer available and the only possibility that remains is pastiche. The very tension with which America and the American are referred to in French *noir* films of the 1950s and 1960s suggests that parody was still possible and that reference had a meaning, and it is evinced in the Lemmy Caution series. By the 1970s America had become a formal figure in the *polar*, at the same time as the questions raised by postmodernism as well as its practices came to figure in the films themselves. This trend can be illustrated by looking at two films, J.-J. Beineix's **Diva** (1981) and Alain Corneau's **Série noire** (1979).

**Diva** takes the form of a thriller with two chases becoming accidentally interconnected and confused, to non-naturalistic and sometimes comic effect. One chase concerns the search for a recording in which it is revealed that Police Inspector Saporta has been involved in a prostitution ring. We do not take this chase seriously: the protagonists are either absurd or comic, the alleged trade in prostitutes is a theme so hackneyed that it is scarcely credible and the deaths that arise are not played realistically. The murder of Nadia, as Tom Milne has pointed out, is filmed like a classic *noir* sequence so that it not only stands out from the remainder of the film but is read as nothing more than an interpolation, a diversion from the real business of narration.[22] The other chase, which is in a sense the mirror image of the first, we do take seriously, although not for the usual reasons. It is not that we wish to prevent a murder taking place and to see justice done, which is the normal reaction of a thriller audience, but that we experience deep sympathy towards the melomaniac messenger boy who has made a pirate recording of his favourite 'Diva' and wishes to recover the tape he has lost. The plot, naturally, is motivated by the fact that the two tapes are transposed.

Both the non-linear construction of the narrative and the sets and design of the film (buildings faced with reflective glass, apartments made out of rehabilitated warehouses) might earn **Diva** the epithet 'postmodern' in some quarters. Yet it is above all the plot which carries this distinction, for it depends on the existence of the technologies of cultural reproduction and circulation which are, paradoxically, employed by the messenger boy – this 'facteur de la vérité' as Derrida might have called him – because of his desire for the authentic. The Diva herself refuses to make recordings, believing that music is a living (that is, organic) thing which will be destroyed by endless reproduction. An irony naturally dictates, therefore, that a recording of her voice, because of the uniqueness which such a recording in normal circumstances cannot have, becomes a priceless object, more prized in fact than the Diva herself. The film thus pivots on the dialectic of the natural and the artificial or beauty and truth (one of the tapes is true, the other is beautiful) which is a Romantic theme par excellence. Through the confusion of the tapes it also posits a homology between the moral corruption of the police and the artistic corruption of recording techniques. But it is characteristically postmodern because, in making the messenger boy the central actor in this drama, it demonstrates that it is the circulation of information rather than its production which motivates both the narrative and social organisation.

Diva – messenger boy Jules (Frédéric Andrei) talks to Alba (Thuy An Luu)

**Diva** nevertheless acquires a moral dimension which tends to be obscured by the dazzling virtuosity of its photography. The character of the messenger boy, named Jules to suggest, perhaps, his exemplarity,[23] has neo-naturalist antecedents in Claude Faraldo's **Bof** or in the Antoine Doinel of Truffaut's **Baisers volés**, both of which, like **Diva**, portray young men who, because of economic circumstances and the cruelty of modern societies, are forced to subsist on *petits boulots* when their tastes and aspirations lead them to wish for something more rewarding. It is so clearly Jules's social position, his poverty and the discrepancy between his humble means and his elevated desires that renders him sympathetic and exonerates him whilst suggesting that for such people art should be democratised and mechanical reproduction permitted.

**Diva** articulates a number of traditions – American *film noir*, the naturalism of the *nouvelle vague* (especially in the scene where Alba goes shoplifting), the early French cinema (Gorodin closely resembles Feuillade's Avenger) and, as has been seen, the postmodern. The relationship between **Diva** and the American tradition is therefore complicated. On the one hand, the *noir* sequences (such as Nadia's death) are pastiche as Jameson defines it, purely formal exercises with no further moral or artistic dimension. On the other hand, modern America is represented by the beautiful black opera singer who, by her colour, profession and ultimate kindness towards Jules, offers a total contrast to the conventional *femme fatale*. By the kiss she bestows on Jules (reminiscent of Eddie Constantine kissing Anna Karina in **Alphaville**) she transmits a little of the beauty he is seeking. This is not the spiderwoman's kiss but the kiss of life momentarily transfiguring the puny, underprivileged Jules and allowing him to enjoy, briefly, the lush beauty of America.

Alain Corneau's **Série noire** (1979) betrays a similar ambivalent relationship with America. This was the fourth film made by a director whose works offer an excellent illustration of the way the thriller developed in France in the 1970s. Corneau's own education and experience testify to a deep interest in America which is undoubtedly characteristic of the generation of French film makers born in the 1940s. He was brought up in Orléans (where his second film, **Police python 357**, is set), a city which, at the time, contained an American base where the young Corneau was able to listen to all the American musicians who passed through.[24] He in fact hesitated between music and film making as a career before choosing the latter, and traces of his interest in American music can be found in his films, not least in **Série noire**. He was formally trained at the IDHEC film school and worked as assistant director for numerous film makers, acquiring an extensive film culture which is apparent from the range of references in his films. He has also lived in the United States, where he went to work with the thriller-writer Jim Thompson on an adaptation of *Pop 1280* (the book was later filmed by Tavernier as **Coup de torchon**), and his deeply held interest in the American thriller came to fruition in **Série noire**, which is an adaptation of Thompson's *A Hell of a Woman*. Corneau is thus typical of his generation in his enthusiasm for certain aspects of American popular culture and in his breadth of knowledge of the cinema, and his films are designed to appeal to an audience with comparable interests.

Corneau's first film, **France S.A.**, is, as the title (France Ltd.) suggests, a virulent critique of the prevailing economic order which is cast in the form of science fiction. Michel Bouquet is the leader of a drugs ring (as we have seen, a theme much in evidence in the early 1970s), who has been preserved in a plastic bubble until the year 2000, from which vantage point he looks back at the 1970s. What he sees is conspiracy on the part of the French leadership, to whom he once sold drugs until he himself became an addict and a member of the Front Révolutionnaire des Toxicomanes, to sell out the interests of the country to the United States in order to preserve their own power. Corneau himself described the theme of the film as 'how America will finally eat France alive'.[25] This film is typical, in some ways, of the political climate of the early 1970s when the traditional political parties (of the Left as well as the Right) were often felt to be demonstrably ineffective or corrupt and when, as has been seen, anarchist groups briefly flourished.[26] It also adumbrates the debate over France's realignment within the Atlantic Alliance and the end of Gaullism that was marked by Giscard D'Estaing's election in 1974. The originality of **France S.A.**, however, resides in the Bouquet character, who has no name other than a generic one ('Le Trafiquant' – The Dealer) and who is presented not merely as a victim of manipulation by unseen forces but of himself and his own impulses. Corneau contrasts very clearly the two 'zones' in which his anti-hero moves: 'a zone where the roads glisten with rain, with dim

67

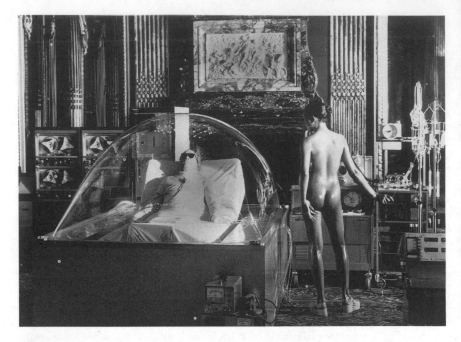

street lights and empty houses' in contrast with 'a world of
meeting rooms, modern buildings, computers'.[27] The first
recalls Fritz Lang, the second **Alphaville** or Kubrick's urban
decors. So that, although Bouquet represents the little man
oppressed by an unknown force condemned to haunt the grim
periphery of the big city, what happens to him is also his own
fault. **France S.A.** is a sombre portrait of despair, futility and
self-destruction.

   Corneau's second film, **Police python 357** is based
on a similar socio-political analysis although the genre has
changed from science fiction to thriller (the title, in fact refers
to the 357 calibre gun rendered famous in American films
such as **Magnum Force**). This film marries the traditions of
the French and the American thriller in the character of Marc
Ferrot, who is as solitary and self-sufficient as any transatlantic lawgiver, but who is characteristically French in the
Simenon or Clouzot manner in such details as his passion for
crosswords, his bachelor life, the disposition of his office and
the conduct of his love affair.[28] The film depicts the upper
classes of Orléans – 'which I believe is a town typical of the
big bourgeoisie in France'[29] against whom Ferrot can do
nothing. The plot hinges on the murder of a young woman
whom Ferrot/Montand loves but who turns out also to be his

boss's mistress. So Ferrot discovers, in investigating the murder, that 'like Oedipus'[30] all clues lead to himself. The investigation is therefore his own death sentence. This is both a political comment and a portrait of total social and psychological alienation, of a man who may well be a victim of society but who is, even more, a victim of himself. This role is resumed in Corneau's third film, **La Menace**, in which Montand, this time playing the director of a haulage company, appears to assume responsibility for the murder of his mistress when she had in fact committed suicide, and disappears by faking his own death in Canada, only to encounter his real death at the hands of the teamsters who believe, wrongly, that he has killed one of their number.

Corneau's fourth film, **Série noire** (1979), demonstrates the capacity of the *polar* to articulate contemporary trends and preoccupations, and is remarkable for the way in which it exploits the postmodern narrative whilst being firmly rooted in an identifiable social context. The title **Série noire** refers back to the celebrated series of thrillers created by Marcel Duhamel in 1945 for Gallimard, which initially published translations of British and American writers and only later took on French authors. The series was thus a vehicle for the dissemination not so much of American popular culture in France but of a certain French view of American popular culture. This is particularly evident in the use of language in *série noire* books since, in an attempt to render the so-called 'hard-boiled' style, the translations evolved a literary argot reminiscent of Céline or Queneau that attempted to be both exotic and relatively comprehensible. The first-person narrative of many such works lent added credibility to the conversational register, the colloquialisms or grammatical solecisms characteristic of such translations.[31]

From the 1950s onwards many films were adapted from the *série noire* books (for example, **La Môme vert-de-gris**, **Touchez pas au Grisbi**) and, indeed, a film with the title **Série noire** was made in 1955. Corneau's **Série noire** is therefore an explicit generic reference. But what is original and interesting about this film is that, from the opening sequence onwards, it becomes apparent that the reference exists less in order for the audience to take its bearings and look out for *noir* sequences than as a means for the central character Frank Poupart to situate himself. The beginning of the film shows Poupart in long shot standing by a beaten up car in the middle of a patch of waste ground with high-rise

buildings in the background, miming the actions of a sax-
ophone player while on the soundtrack we hear strains of
'Moonlight Fiesta'.[32] This enables us to understand that the
reference to the **Série noire** exists as much for Poupart to
conduct his affairs as for us, the audience. It is what enables
this unsuccessful door-to-door salesman to envisage murder-
ing an elderly woman who lives with her niece Mona in an
isolated house, and to steal her money in order to reimburse
the petty sums he has stolen from his employer. As a drama of
poor white America, Jim Thompson's *A Hell of a Woman*,
from which **Série noire** is adapted, commanded a degree of
realism and possessed a literary ancestry which can be traced
back to Faulkner. Transposed to the Paris suburbs, the plot
becomes entirely fantastic, the requirements of realism are
suspended, and the audience accepts the narrative as the poetic
equivalent of Poupart's frame of mind. He is a schizophrenic
who believes he is an actor in an American thriller, the logical
culmination of a line of Corneau characters.

In **Diva** the technologies of reproduction served, as
we have seen, to motivate the narrative. In **Série noire** it is
language that fulfils the same function. As a door-to-door
salesman, Frank Poupart (played by Patrick Dewaere) lives by
language, by his 'patter'.[33] In the novel, recounted in the first

Série noire – Frank
(Patrick Dewaere) talks to
Mona (Marie Trintignant)

person, much of what is written passes for a transcription of Poupart's thoughts. In **Série noire**, instead of using the voice-over, which is the conventional approach to adapting first - person narrative thrillers, Poupart speaks his thoughts out loud so that they serve to characterise him, presenting him as a histrionic who is incapable of being silent, constantly trying out new registers and new commonplaces, to ward off disintegration in an attempt to fix his personality in and through language.[34] It is an attempt which fails.

The extraordinarily brilliant dialogues of the film were written by the novelist Georges Perec. Corneau explained his choice thus:

> *I really related to his book* Je me souviens. *It's written in the form of aphorisms and is a source not of commonplaces but of remarks on a period which appeal to me because I belong to it too, the period of Dario Moreno, Dalida... The language is simple but it isn't naturalistic. I needed someone who could 'place' the characters, and provide a whole stock of expressions and mythological clichés.*[35]

Perec's interest in American detective fiction, in jazz, and in the cinema, together with a capacity to identify the obsessions and clichés of a period, his strong sense of place, his predilection for intertextual games all made him an appropriate choice for **Série noire**.[36]

In Perec's view Poupart is 'a character who has completely lost his way, who is off his trolley, who makes up stories and who keeps ending up with his back against the wall because he operates according to stereotypes'.[37] For him the protagonist is 'someone who in a way has no language. He has to look for his language and his reactions in other people. He is totally conditioned by the world around him (...) He reminds me of Monsieur Ripois. In fact Queneau's dialogue inspired me considerably.'[38] Unlike characters in many films adapted from the *série noire*, therefore, Frank Poupart does not speak *argot* or the *langue verte*. Whereas *argot* is always defined by relation to standard speech, Frank, it is suggested, speaks a parallel language: 'He is delirious in the psychiatric sense of the word.'[39] Like the viewers of **Série noire**, Frank is familiar with the language of the genre, but this is simply one point of reference against which the dialogue of the film is judged, and it is never wholeheartedly or consistently embraced.

Frank is also familiar with the *verlan* of *La Zone* – *verlan* being the thieves' slang, based on the inverting of syllables in words, which became popular among young people in the late 1970s,[40] and *La Zone* being the run-down areas of public housing and waste land on the outskirts of Paris. But because of his personality disorder he cannot consistently embrace any one form of language and instead switches register and dialect according to the identity of the interlocutor or the identity he himself is attempting to assume. Thus he refers to the death of Tikides in a style reminiscent of Céline: 'Dommage que ça n'arrive pas plus souvent. S'ils pouvaient tous crever (...) la gueule ouverte à la queue-leu-leu.' (Pity it doesn't happen more often. Why don't they all just snuff it, one after the other.)[41] He refers to himself as a crusader 'bloodied by my travails, but never bowed'.[42] And in a brilliant, but failed, attempt to use *verlan*, he betrays his disorder with the superb metathesis 'foin pinal' (for 'point final' – full stop).[43]

But Perec and Corneau's screenplay combines social observation with a psychological dimension and, indeed, posits a relationship between Frank's language and his social alienation. The original novel was set in Kentucky, but in **Série noire** this is replaced by *La Zone*. This is the world of violence, alienation and racism produced by the rapid modernisation of the 1960s, which attracted considerable attention from sociologists in the 1970s. 'What interests me about the outskirts of Paris,' Corneau has said, 'is that these places are a complete wasteland where anything can happen (...) It's the urban area of the greatest alienation.'[44] In **Série noire** the sense of place is defined by its absence. The streets of the city have become strange, the familiar contours have disappeared because in such suburban areas the decor is simultaneously formless and uniform, with the alternation of high-rise blocks and patches of waste ground and isolated houses, such as the one Mona inhabits, stranded or left over from an earlier period. The sense of community and belonging, itemised by Perec in *Espèces d'espaces*, is exploded. This is an international phenomenon and it is reflected, therefore, not merely in other French films of the period such as Blier's **Les Valseuses** (1974) in which Dewaere also starred, and Pialat's **Loulou** (1980) but in Kurosawa's **Dodes' Kaden** and Coppola's **Rumble Fish**. This is *La Zone* of ill repute, so that Frank's difficulties with language, his failure to achieve, so to say, the authentic inauthenticity of the conventional *série noire*, becomes the sign of his real alienation from both himself and his milieu. He is dispossessed in every sense.

## The Meaning of the French Thriller

The French thriller or *polar* is, as we have seen, a genre which developed in the postwar period. It drew inspiration from the American literary and film genre and became a crucial means through which the relationship between the French cinema and the American was articulated. This relationship evolved over the decades so that both the kind of films made and the references to America within them change from period to period. The thriller also played a crucial role in cultural politics. One of the legacies of the 1950s was the creation of a film culture to which American cinema was central. This is the sense of the *politique des auteurs* developed in *Cahiers du cinéma* and of the promotion of directors such as Ford, Hawks and Hitchcock. The force of the American example has not diminished. When asked why he chose to adapt American authors to the screen, J.-J. Beineix replied: 'Because they embody a myth, a mystery and an exoticism. Our generation is really fascinated by America. It is part of our film heritage and therefore of our iconography.'[45] But if American cinema was exemplary and central, this left European national cinemas with a little more than a provincial role. The anxiety that this occasioned is frequently perceptible in French thrillers themselves which, through the inclusion of American characters or references to America, convey, metonymically, the unequal relationship between Hollywood and the French film industry.

French thrillers also serve to portray a relationship between France and the United States in its political and economic as well as its cultural dimension. The modernisation of France began with the postwar settlement and Marshall Aid. The debate about this process was conducted in terms of France's alignment with either one of the power blocs or with neither. From this process it became evident that the integration of the French economy into the zone of dollar influence and the integration of French defence into the Atlantic Alliance meant abandoning autarky and also, perhaps, national integrity and identity. The cinema was relevant to this process because the Americans and the French concurred in the belief that economics, politics and culture were a continuum and that the American cinema was a vehicle for the promotion of the 'American way of life' in all its forms. This point was very effectively made by the CGT-affiliated technicians' union at the time of the signing of the Blum–Byrnes agreement and it has remained a constant in all French

73

thinking about cultural policy.[46] The issue, in France, was whether it would be possible to retain cultural independence and a specific cultural identity or whether this too would disappear in the process of modernisation.

This process had two aspects which are characteristic of and perhaps peculiar to France. The first was that the rural exodus did not occur on any scale until after the Second World War, so that it was not until the 1960s that urban culture was sufficiently widespread to be the common experience of an entire generation. Even today politicians, for example, take care to refer to their roots in rural France. The second was that, because it occurred after the war, modernisation was inextricably linked with an increase in American influence, and ambivalent feelings about the loss of an old way of life were often translated into ambivalent feelings towards the United States.

This is why the thriller is such an interesting and important genre in France, for it provides an excellent vehicle for describing, criticising and coming to terms with modernisation. As is well known, the emergence of the detective story as a genre is linked with industrialisation, the growth of cities, the crimes associated with urbanisation and the mechanisms of policing developed to cope with them. However, the presentation of the urban environment in French cinema changed dramatically from the prewar to the postwar period. Before the war, the film makers saw the city as a serendipitous playground (one thinks of films such as René Clair's **Paris qui dort**) in which there are some evil-doers such as Fantomas. After the war, the city ceased to be the ludic environment of Surrealist fantasy, or the mysterious space created by Trauner's sets, and became part of ordinary, everyday life.

*Nouvelle vague* films reflect and question these changes. Not simply are they frequently shot on location but the locations are often clearly identified: Nantes, Clermont, Geneva as well as the inevitable Paris. *Nouvelle vague* films also address the problems of urbanisation. **Alphaville**, as has been seen, shows the modern city as both dehumanising and menacing; **Deux ou trois Choses que je sais d'elle** (1967) examines how modernisation and urban renewal have expelled the poor from the centre of Paris to the outlying suburbs and forced them to adopt stratagems like prostitution to make ends meet. A decade later **Des Enfants gâtés** (1977) criticises property speculation as the origin of difficulties in personal relationships.

Through its handling of action, particularly violent action, the American cinema in general taught French film makers after the war that the physical can have a moral dimension. This was an important lesson for a national cinema that was allegedly interested in 'filmed theatre' rather than the depiction of the individual in his environment. The virtue of the American *film noir*, at least in the eyes of French critics, was that it posited an organic relationship between the individual and an urban rather than rural setting, suggesting how the city affected the behaviour and emotions of those who lived in it. This is a theme common to **Diva** and **Série noire**, as we have seen, but which can be found in innumerable recent films from **Les Valseuses,** to **Subway,** to **Police**.

Thus, to sum up, the French thriller serves to articulate France's relationship with the United States, it offers French cinema a means to reconcile psychology and action and, finally it serves as a vehicle for the discussion of the processes of modernisation.

# 3:

# Women Film Makers in France

The tradition of women making films in France stretches back to the silent period. The country produced one of the pioneers of the silent cinema in Alice Guy and one of the most talented of Surrealist film makers in Germaine Dulac. However, our interpretation of women's films, our attitude towards women film makers and our appreciation of the prospects for the growth and development of women's film making have all been profoundly affected by the women's movement, so that the very category 'women film makers' has a quite different connotation from that of the 'femmes cinéastes' of Charles Ford's study of Arzen, Riefenstahl, Chytilova, Zetterling and others.[1] This is as true of France as of Britain, the United States or Germany, but where France differs from comparable western countries is that French women film makers tend to work within a tradition which, both in its thematics and its formal expression, is less explicitly linked to the political agenda of the women's movement.

It should be said at the outset that the mere fact of being a woman film maker in a profession so predominantly male is itself noteworthy, so that some comment on the opportunities for women film makers is required.[2] Furthermore, it is possible to read any film 'as a woman' and there is now a considerable body of writing devoted to doing just that.[3] Indeed within the Anglo-American tradition there have emerged three main ways in which gender has had a significant impact on film making and film analysis.

The first is the production of films where women's issues (abortion, for example) or the women's movement are investigated from a feminist perspective. In the American independent sector, with films like **Rosie the Riveter** or **Born in Flames**, and more particularly in Britain with its strong documentary and realist traditions, the last fifteen years have seen the production of a large number of such films as well as the development of production and distribution systems to support women's cinema.

Second, there is the question of the 'image of women', the material for which is supplied by the mainstream cinema and the associated media industries (television, advertising and so on). Critics have noted an evolution in the way women are represented: in the 1950s they were invariably housebound; in the 1980s they tended to have jobs (albeit a limited range of jobs). In other words the mainstream cinema reflects the documented changes in the socio-economic status of women in the postwar period. But despite the apparent gulf between 1950s melodrama and 1980s melodrama, it has been pointed out that the narrative resolution of many apparently progressive texts such as **Klute** or **Looking for Mr Goodbar** (to cite two frequently analysed examples) invariably amounts to the reassertion of male hegemony, so that any change in the representation of women must probably be considered superficial.

Hence the investigation of the third area in which gender has had an impact on film analysis and film making: the mainstream cinema's failure to come to terms with the women's movement is related, or so the argument runs, to the cinematic apparatus itself which is not gender-neutral. Thus considerable effort has been devoted to the exploration of the construction of the subject through representation with a view to answering the question so succinctly posed by Ann Kaplan, 'Is the gaze male?'[4] If, as many feminists believe, the cinema constructs the viewer in a gendered way, then the feminist viewer/film maker must explore the use of various narrative and visual strategies which attempt to disrupt or in some way fissure these ways of seeing. Once again, there now exist a considerable number of films and critical texts which make this attempt.

In France things have taken a rather different course. The three approaches outlined above are all to be found within a feminist intellectual tradition which differs from that of Britain and the United States. The Events of May 1968 are usually considered to have provided the impetus for the development of the women's movement in France and, in particular, to have stimulated the creation of women's organisations and an upsurge of women's publishing.[5] But the emphasis of the French women's movement – at least in the eyes of many British and American feminists – has been on theory at the expense of practical politics.[6] In fact it would be more accurate to say that the theoretical orientation of the two traditions is dissimilar. Their divergence can perhaps best be apprehended – especially with respect to the cinema – in relation to what has been called the 'problem of the body'. Anglo-American feminists, as has been suggested, are typically concerned with the question of representation, whether this consists of the way women are portrayed in films or the way the cinematic apparatus constructs sexual identity. They descend from an influential current in postwar film criticism which believed, as Merleau-Ponty put it in the late 1940s, that

> *the cinema does not give us man's thoughts, as the novel did for so long, it gives us his conduct or behaviour, it provides us directly with this particular way of being in the world (...) The cinema is particularly well suited to bringing out the union of mind and body, of mind and world and how the one is expressed in the other.*[7]

This existential approach to the cinema was adopted and popularised by the *Cahiers* critics in the 1950s, who were thus able to claim a moral significance for *mise-en-scène*, and it thence became generalised.[8] This is why the canonical issues of postwar feminism – sexual difference, biological determinism, the exploration of the body as origin, and of 'anatomy as destiny' – have been related to the cinema in Anglo-American writing through the question of representation, whether the approach is Marxist, psychoanalytical or semiotic. Claire Johnston, for example, states: 'What the camera in fact grasps is the "natural" world of the dominant ideology.'[9] For Jacqueline Rose, on the other hand: 'One of the chief drives of an art which today addresses the presence of the sexual in representation [is] to expose the fixed nature of sexual identity as a fantasy and, in the same gesture, to trouble, break up, or rupture the visual field before our eyes';[10] while for Teresa de Lauretis: 'In cinema the stakes for women are especially high. The representation of women as spectacle – body to be looked at, place of sexuality, and object of desire – so pervasive in our culture, finds in narrative cinema its most complex expression and widest circulation.'[11]

The body is of no less significance in French feminist thinking but is mediated through – or perhaps physically attached to – a preoccupation with language, with the phallus as signifier, and indeed many of the major French feminist thinkers are heavily indebted to Lacan and Derrida. This is immediately apparent if one looks at the texts produced in the 1970s, an astonishing number of which translate the need and desire to recover speech (*prendre la parole*): Marguerite Duras and Xavière Gautier's *Les Parleuses* (1974), Annie Leclerc's *Parole de femme* (1974), Claudine Herrmann's *Les Voleuses de langue* (1976) and others.[12] One of the most interesting, perhaps, is Hélène Cixous's essay 'Le Sexe ou la tête' in which she analyses a Chinese fable in order to show that in our cultures a woman can only 'keep her head' (that is, not be decapitated as in the fable) 'on condition that she loses it' (that is, remains silent).[13] The intellect in general, but particularly the power of speech, is criticised as conventionally opposed to the body and the repression of the body is frequently seen as the condition of all discourse. Discussion in the French women's movement has therefore tended to concentrate on the relationship between the body and the text, while writing – feminine writing – is seen as a way of circumventing or transcending the patriarchal dualism of mind and body: 'Political reflection cannot do without a reflection on language or work on the language.'[14] The body, it is held, cannot have a referential status independently of language[15] and 'more body hence more writing' ('plus corps donc plus écriture').[16]

> *She must write herself because this is the invention of a new, rebellious writing which at the moment of her liberation will allow her to make the breaks and changes needed in her history (...) by writing herself the woman will return to the body which has been confiscated from her many times over (...) By censoring the body one also censors breath and speech* [17]

By the same token silence also has a significance: 'Their silence is aphonic, it is a loss of speech, the silence of women who have not entered language.'[18]

Women's cinema in France has therefore differed from Anglo-American or German women's cinema in two important ways. On the one hand, the political activities of the women's movement have not tended, except in the early 1970s, to take the form of struggles for material equality, so that the realist portrayal of women's lives has been less significant to women film makers than it has elsewhere. However, the women's movement has, on occasions, provided the inspiration for feature films. On the other hand, a theoretical preoccupation with language rather than visual representation does not *a priori* lend itself to work on the cinema, which is usually considered to be a quintessentially visual medium.

Nevertheless, this theoretical stance has in fact stimulated some fascinating films which attempt to engage with the theorisation of the relationship between the body and the text.

## Cinema and the Women's Movement

As might be expected, the cinema reflected both directly and indirectly the raising of women's consciousness that was implied by the constitution of the women's movement (MLF) in 1972. This was frequently, though not always, associated by male directors with a political realignment in relation to the trade union movement and the working class. The post-May 1968 world was peopled by new social actors, hitherto marginal groups such as 'women', 'the workers' and 'the peasants'. Thus in Godard and Gorin's **Tout va bien**, as we have seen, the female protagonist explains 'phallocracy' to her partner, in the context of the reporting of an industrial struggle. Similarly, the difficulties of working women are reflected in Marin Karmitz's **Coup pour coup** or again in some episodes of Godard's television series, **Sur et sous la Communication** (1976). At this time Godard also made, in collaboration with a woman, Anne-Marie Miéville, an extraordinarily violent denunciation of male power within the family in **Numéro deux** (1976).

However, the distance between the approach of male and female directors can also be measured in their respective treatment of women's work and of the domestic arena in general. For Godard or Karmitz women are exploited to the extent that they are industrial workers like any others.[19] However, within the women's movement at the period there was considerable discussion of the question of domestic labour, which many considered constituted an additional source of oppression (hence the 'wages for housework' campaigns) and this formed the subject of several documentaries.[20] Yet it is in fiction that the difference is most clearly revealed. For Godard, in the **Nanas** episode of **Sur et sous la communication**, the housewife is a pathological figure, her desire for order and cleanliness to be explained, it is implied, by other absences in her life. She is, in fact, an object of ridicule. By contrast, for Marguerite Duras, in **Nathalie Granger** (1972), the house itself is a female domain in which men are intruders, and within that sphere laundry is a specific

Jeanne Dielman –
Delphine Seyrig at her
household tasks

preoccupation. Hence the washing machine salesman (Gérard Depardieu) is made to feel extremely uncomfortable; his patter, whose futility is emphasised by the silence of the women, turns him into a buffoon. Chantal Akerman, in the short film **Saute ma Ville** (1968) and at much greater length in **Jeanne Dielman 23 Quai du commerce** (1976), reverses the male order of things more throughly. Though housework is a symptom of the pathological state to which the heroines are reduced and, in **Jeanne Dielman** is shown as boring, time-consuming and repetitive, the women escape through acts of violence inflicted on themselves or others. The protagonist of **Saute ma Ville** kills herself. Jeanne, on the other hand, confronted with a situation where the housework which structures her existence is ultimately the most redundant of tasks, only interrupted by the male clients whose regular arrival inhibits narrative closure, finally takes her destiny into her own hands and kills one of them, bringing the film to a satisfactory end.

Other interesting ways in which the impact of the women's movement is reflected in the cinema might be the attempt to explore personal history and to locate women's experiences in a historical context and the change in the role of men. Thus, although Jeanne Moreau's **L'Adolescente**

(1978) is highly sentimental, as is Diane Kurys's portrait of adolescence in the 1950s, **Diabolo menthe** (1977) – though the latter is extremely funny – many of Chantal Akerman's films have an autobiographical sub-text, with the film maker herself acting in **Je tu il elle**, while **Rouges Baisers** attempts to draw a comparison between a girl's adolescence and the evolution of the French Communist Party. Claire Clouzot's **L'Homme fragile** looks at a divorced man's relationship with his daughter, while Coline Serreau, again in comic mode, explores a similar theme in **Trois Hommes et un couffin**. Finally, the issue that was central to the politics of the beginning of the women's movement in France, namely freedom of abortion and contraception, was also the subject matter of one of the most celebrated of militant films, **Histoires d'A** (1973), banned for over a year but nevertheless shown outside the normal distribution circuits as a campaign document, and a significant contribution to the successful campaign for the legalisation of abortion and for women to have the right to control their bodies.

## Women's Voices

It was not until Coline Serreau made **Mais qu'est-ce qu'elles veulent?** (1975) (the title of which echoes Freud's famous question) that a woman produced an overview of the change in women's perceptions of themselves and the public perception of them in this crucial decade. This film consists of a montage of interviews with eight different women of differing ages and from very different walks of life (a minister of the Swiss church, the star of sex films, an anorexic girl, a worker in a garment factory, a concierge, a peasant woman, a widow and an upper middle class woman) together with the sex film director and the factory boss, both of whom are men: Intercalated with the montage of interviews are shots of the sea, no doubt to connote an eternal feminine, the 'great, sweet mother'. As Françoise Audé has perceptively written, the richness of this film lies initially in the surprise caused by these women's speech, the variety of their accents and turns of phrase, akin, in her view, to the experience offered on first seeing some films from Quebec.[21]

    A comparable richness is apparent in parts of **Sur et sous la communication**, although it is perhaps not confined to women, and, more significantly, in Akerman's **Les Rendez-vous d'Anna** (1978) where the film maker heroine meets a variety of different people talking varieties of regional French as she travels south from Germany through Belgium to Paris.[22] It is perhaps of some note that Akerman is Belgian and Godard Swiss and that both, for this reason, are no doubt more sensitive to the peripheral, regional or marginal aspects of French culture, as expressed and signified through accent and dialect. It is also significant that, in a film which allowed women to be heard, they should come across not simply as various, but also as regional, marginal, and in some way non-standard, in their speech.


## The Power to Communicate – The Right to Speak

The notion that the control of the audio-visual media is a necessary part of any political struggle was acutely brought home by the Events of May 1968 in France. The ability to do so was assisted, thereafter, by the availability and rapid propagation of cheaper film formats, such as Super 8, and by video. Nevertheless, in France as elsewhere, far fewer women than men produce or direct films. Thus in the survey conducted by Claire Clouzot in 1973 only thirty out of some 160 film producers in Paris were women and only two of these, Véra Belmont and Nicole Stéphane, admitted to any particular interest in producing films written or directed by women.[23]

To a degree this reflects the structure of careers in the French film industry as well as the characteristics of the French education system. The training of film makers was, until very recently, carried out by the national film school, IDHEC, which recruited its students on the basis of a competitive entrance examination of an academic kind, and then distributed them into its various sections – editor, director and so on. This, in itself, was not favourable to women as Annie Tresgot explained: 'All the women who passed the entrance examination knew that they wouldn't be allowed into the film directing course.'[24] This partly accounts for the preponderance of women film editors and the absence of women directors. However, by the mid-1950s, IDHEC was no longer training primarily for the cinema but for television and, once again, those who benefited from the 'pioneer atmosphere' of the early days of French television were men: 'As far as I am concerned television is a very hard environment, a very negative place to work, a jungle,' observed Jeanne Labrune of her difficulties in making a career as a director.[25] From the 1960s onwards the *nouvelle vague* provided an alternative structure of production but, as Suzanne Schiffman movingly shows, this did not benefit women either, even though the opportunity to circumvent the normal constraints of production might have been expected to do so.[26] Where an *auteur* cinema flourishes women generally do better than they do in a highly commercial cinema, but their success is relative. Thus it has been a leitmotif in every interview given by Agnès Varda for more than a decade that the fact she is an established film maker has not helped her raise the capital to make films.[27]

The career of Yannick Bellon is a dramatic illustration of the disproportionate difficulties encountered by women wishing to direct films. Though born in 1924, and therefore of the same generation as Varda and Resnais, and though she began by directing short films, many of which were extremely well received in the 1940s, Bellon did not have the opportunity to direct her first feature film, **Quelque part, quelqu'un** until 1972. Perhaps because of her early setbacks, many of Bellon's subsequent films tackled the theme of women in society. Thus **La Femme de Jean** (1974) tells the story of a woman who was completely overshadowed by her husband until the day he left her for someone younger and she was forced to find a new identity; **L'Amour violé** (1978) tells the story of a woman who has been raped; and **L'Amour nu** (1981) that of a woman who has breast cancer. Because of her willingness to engage with social issues Bellon is sometimes compared to André Cayatte. But the comparison is unfair since Bellon's films palpably arise from a commitment to improving the lot of women, and as her career has progressed she has taken a less sociological approach to her subject matter and become more interested in psychoanalysis, so that her most recent film, **Les Enfants du désordre** (1989) is a study of the treatment of psychologically disturbed adolescents.

Since financing a film is essentially a question of confidence, women in France, like women in other countries, have not found the backers as ready to trust them as they are to trust male directors. It was in October 1973 that the Musidora group was created to improve this situation. Its published objectives, as described by Françoise Flamant, were to encourage the production, direction and distribution of women's films and videos, to pursue research on the role of women in the cinema and on women film makers, and to organise meetings and events to improve the reception of women's films.[28]

The organisation was not uncontroversial. Though Musidora denied any separatist intentions it was often accused of 'racism' and denounced as irrelevant to the real concerns of the day which were 'action to promote jobs for women in careers related to the cinema (...) the salaries paid to women editors (...) the number of women's films financed through the *avance sur recettes* (...) the proportion of women at IDHEC and (...) their future'.[29]

However, Musidora had two significant achievements. One was the publication in 1976 of a series of texts about the cinema written by women film makers, critics, and viewers, significantly entitled *Paroles...elles tournent*.[30] In addition to essays on films such as **Jeanne Dielman** or **India Song** which were felt to be exemplary *mises en scène* of women's experience, it is clear how much the question of language preoccupies many of the contributors: 'We are waging a struggle over language: collectively and individually we are seeking the feminine language which we have all been discovering on our own. We all knew intuitively that it was important to seek a qualitative change in narrative and thought so as to bring a really revolutionary content into our writings and our films' (p. 7); 'absent speech' (p. 17); 'words, speech and language belong to Men' (p. 21), and so on. The Musidora texts therefore contributed towards placing women's cinema squarely in the realm of language rather than in the conventionally conceived categories of political and militant cinema.

Musidora's second and perhaps more immediately obvious achievement was the creation of a festival of women's films, the first two of which (1974 and 1975) were clearly feminist in inspiration (the themes for programming and discussion were training and women's careers, women film crews, pioneers of women's cinema and the representation of women's sexuality).[31] However, the festival subsequently moved to Sceaux and thence to Créteil, was taken over by different groups of women and rapidly demarcated itself from the feminist inspiration of the first two events: 'The way we differ from the first festivals is that on the one hand the sessions will be open to men and also that our selection will be made on the basis of filmic quality.'[32] Nevertheless the festival became an excellent instrument for the promotion of women's cinema.


## Two Examples of Women's Cinema: Varda and Duras

Contemporary French women's cinema is extremely rich and various. It includes talented film makers like Aline Issermann, whose brilliant first feature **Le Destin de Juliette** (1982) is an original portrait of a young woman from a rural environment forced by the absence of social and professional opportunities into an impossible marriage, as well as commercially successful directors such as Coline Serreau, whose film **Trois Hommes et un couffin** was granted the somewhat dubious accolade of a Hollywood remake. However, the remainder of our discussion will concentrate on the films of Agnès Varda and Marguerite Duras since their work is a particularly good illustration of the characteristic problematic of French women's cinema, namely the relationship between body and text.


### Agnès Varda

Agnes Varda is a film maker whose career exemplifies the impact of the women's movement and, to a degree, the consciousness of a need to make films 'as a woman'. Her early films were well received but retrospectively criticised, often violently so, by women viewers. Thus **Cléo de 5 à 7**, a film which remains the *locus classicus* of the use of 'real time', portrays a singer waiting for two hours (the duration of the film) for the result of a test that will confirm she has cancer. It is dismissed by Françoise Audé in this way: 'She moves a short way from the status of desirable object to that of subject, but it is a movement which is hardly perceptible.'[33] Even at the time, the perceptive Françoise Giroud wrote: '...is she beautiful? Rather she is intellectually dormant, not awake to the world, an object. For some she represents Woman. For others nothing, and she'd better keep quiet'.[34] Yet the film was also premonitory. The theme of the voice, evoked by Giroud, is omnipresent: Cléo, after all, is a singer – like Pomme in the much later **L'Une chante, l'autre pas** – whose voice is about to be extinguished. The fear of illness and death obliges or enables the heroine to speak to people, such as a soldier in the street,

86

whom she would not otherwise have encountered and she does so unadorned in her usual costume and wig. The theme of time is dazzlingly mobilised, looking forward to Akerman's **Jeanne Dielman**, but it might be argued that it is specifically a woman's time since it consists in waiting for something to happen rather than controlling events. On the other hand, Varda's **Le Bonheur** remains for many viewers, not simply many women, an unforgivable film. Not only does it offend by its uncritical portrayal of a man who, though blissfully happy with his wife and children, embarks on a simultaneous relationship with another woman, causing his wife to kill herself, but it is filmed in 'an idiom that sets one's teeth on edge',[35] a visual repertoire that is reminiscent of soap powder advertisements. This film gave Varda a reputation for idealism, conventionality and an inability to be socially critical.

This approach is not evinced, however, elsewhere in her work. She has a long, though not widely acknowledged, career as a maker of documentary films which often serve as an oblique commentary on her fiction. Moreover, from the time she first went to the United States in 1967, her feature films have all had documentary elements in them, making her an excellent weathervane of the movement of ideas, and showing her attentive to changes in the way people live and the detail of their lives: 'Reality is very lyrical and very unexpected.'[36] It has been rightly said that Varda is a poet of the everyday, a characteristic which she shares with contemporary writers such as George Perec. But she is equally preoccupied with the subjective nature of reality, as in **Cléo** where the urban environment begins to bristle with signs of death. The best non-fiction example of the subjective interpretation of the everyday is perhaps Varda's television series **Une Minute pour une image** (1983) in which she would show a randomly chosen person a photograph for a minute and ask him or her to interpret it for another minute.

It might be argued, nevertheless, that Varda is specifically feminine in the aspects of the everyday she chooses to focus on, in her sympathy for the marginal and in her *mise en scène* of women. Thus **Uncle Yanco** (1967) is a portrait of her hippie painter uncle whom she discovered living in California, **Black Panthers** (1968) is a portrait of the eponymous revolutionary group, **Nausicaa** (1970) an essay on the Greek immigrant community in France, **Mur murs** (1980) a documentary on the murals painted by the Chicano community in Los Angeles, and so on. Other documentaries specifically link women with the marginal. The early **Opéra Mouffe** (1958) portrays the encounters between a pregnant woman and the tramps in the Mouffetard market, while the much more recent **Documenteur** (1981) shows a woman, this time with a young child, as an exile in Los Angeles desperately searching for a new identity. Finally, **Daguerréotypes** (1975) is a film not so much of feminist criticism – even though the small shopkeepers in the rue Daguerre who are its main protagonists all work in couples with a highly traditional division of labour – as a film made under the typically female constraints of domesticity. Varda had just had a baby at the time: 'I was stuck at home. So I told myself I was a good example of women's creativity which is always boxed in and stifled. And I wondered what could possibly come out of such constraints.'[37]

Alongside the search for what might be called a specific social space for women there clearly runs the search for an authentically feminine voice. The titles of the films **Réponse de femmes** (1975) (reply), **Mur murs**, the 'menteur' (liar) in **Documenteur**, **Les Dites cariatides** (1984) (sayings) a film showing the sculptures of women on Paris facades, indicate the uncertainty or perhaps the untrustworthiness of these voices, and this is reflected in the fiction films. **Cléo**, as we have seen, is a singer whose voice is about to die. In **Sans Toit ni loi** (1985) the protagonist Mona rarely says anything, her portrait is constituted precisely of what others say about her. It is only in **L'Une chante, l'autre pas** that women unequivocally and positively express themselves, with Varda herself in voice-off adding a narrative commentary for good measure, while in her most recent film, **Jane B. par Agnès V.** (1988), though the portrait is not entirely positive, the film maker herself is again heard in commentary on this portrait of herself and of Jane Birkin.

Some of the central preoccupations of women, such as housework, pregnancy and childcare, and of the women's movement, such as the search for a women's voice, are therefore to be found in Varda's documentaries, not always as a central subject or theme but with what appears to be greater and greater insistency. Her feature films, on the other hand, more clearly demonstrate her awakening to women's issues so that **L'Une chante, l'autre pas** and **Sans Toit ni loi** require to be read 'as a woman'. Varda's career is thus a fascinating illustration of the inevitability of the feminist perspective.

An accident of history took Agnès Varda away from France during the late 1960s. But when asked why May 1968 did not figure in the historical panorama of **L'Une chante** she replied: 'If there is a struggle recounted in this film it is the struggle for contraception, for sexual freedom and for women to control their bodies. Bobigny [that is, the abortion trial in 1972] is more important in this struggle than '68.'[38] In this Varda departs from the position of directors like Godard or Karmitz, who subsume the women's struggle into the general workers' struggle, and aligns her film, whose first version, entitled **Mon Corps est à moi** (My body is my own) dates from 1971, with **Histoires d'A**, of which it is to a degree a fictionalised version.[39]

**L'Une chante, l'autre pas** recounts the story of a friendship between two women, Pauline/Pomme and Suzanne. They first meet in 1962 when Suzanne is the impoverished mother of two children and expecting a third. Pauline helps her to secure an abortion (illegal at the time) and Jérôme, Suzanne's partner, commits suicide. Suzanne then goes to live with her parents and gradually becomes involved in the family planning movement (MLAC). By 1972, when they meet again during the Bobigny trial demonstrations, Pauline has become the singer Pomme, who lives with an Iranian, Darius. She goes to Iran, becomes pregnant, returns to France to have the child and then decides to allow Darius to take the child with him to Iran so that she can pursue her career in singing. After this meeting, Suzanne and Pomme stay in regular contact, leading parallel lives and deepening their friendship. The film ends with a vision of the women, their children and their friends in an ideal community.

This is not an entirely successful film. The mixing of genres, part pseudo-documentary with voice over narrative, part fictional narrative which is voluntarily novelettish (Jérôme's suicide, Suzanne's second husband's instant divorce), does not seem completely motivated. The central characters are difficult to admire and occasionally unsympathetic in their very exemplarity. They are too conventionally radical, too programmatic, in the manner of Pomme's songs which are women's movement jingles: 'Ni cocotte, ni popote, ni falote/Je suis femme, je suis moi.' (Neither tart, nor cook, nor bore/I'm a woman, I'm me.) Unlike the community portrayed in **Lion's Love**, which was of interest because of the people in it, the way in which 'underground' actors such as Viva presented themselves to the camera and their witty

commentary on their own and others' way of life, the
community in **L'Une chante** seems factitious. The visual
codes of the film, finally, have proved unpleasing because
they are too unrealistic or perhaps hyper-real 'acidic colours
like the girls in the *Dim* commercial', while Pomme and
Suzanne appear too resplendently beautiful by the end of the
film. As in **Le Bonheur** Varda has been accused, with some
justice, of prettifying the world in **L'Une chante**.

But it is perhaps in its shortcomings that this film is
interesting. It does represent, first, an attempt to show that the
personal is political, not simply in the impact of political events
on personal lives, in this case the campaign for abortion and
contraception, but also because we know that at the time the
first version of the film was completed Varda herself was
pregnant.[40] The slippage from fiction to documentary in **L'Une
chante**, in the use of Gisèle Halimi to play herself, for example,
is illustrative of this attempt at social comprehension, even if it
is not successful. But it is in its recourse to the thematics of the
voice that the film requires to be taken seriously. The title is a
reference to the utopian slogan 'les lendemains qui chantent' (a
brighter tomorrow), invariably articulated in the context of the
working class struggle but here reappropriated by women.
Furthermore, the contrast between Cléo and Pomme, both

90

singers, is startling: Cléo is ill and dying; Pomme (the name
of the fruit implying fullness and mellowness) is bursting with
good health and vitality and her voice is not silenced, she takes
charge of her own life. **L'Une chante** does chronicle a political
and personal victory, even if its optimism appears exaggerated.

By **Sans Toit ni loi** the tone had changed and this is
perhaps the only Varda film to date to achieve tragic dimensions. It is certainly more emotionally complex than her others.
Mona, the central character, sets off one day in winter with a
pack on her back and roams the Midi, sleeping rough, eating
little except bread and sardines, begging the odd franc here and
there. As she goes she encounters various inhabitants of the
region and finally she freezes to death in a ditch. **Sans Toit** has
two primary cinematic references – the road movie and the *film
noir*. Traditionally, the road movie is associated with an
existential quest, resembling in this the literature that inspired
it (Kerouac's *On the Road*, for example). It is strongly
associated with a search for male identity and frequently
visually coded as such: in **Easy Rider**, for example, the
roadsters travel on exaggeratedly phallic motorbikes. However, the notion of a road movie in which the central character
is female is not original, since in **Messidor** (1979) Alain
Tanner had already portrayed two women hitting the road.

**Sans Toit**, however, is a pessimistic response to Tanner's film. The revolutionary month of 'Messidor' runs from late June to late July, so called because, in France at least, this is the month of the harvest (traditionally finished by 14 July). The two girls in **Messidor**, probably of comparable age to Mona, depart in summer on what turns out to be a circular adventure, the reaping of some psychological crop. There is a harvest to be had in the film, however bitter; there is some community to be created through adversity and adventure and, as in many road movies, there is a political lesson to be learned for protagonist and viewer alike.

Mona sets off in winter (historically, one of the hardest winters since 1946–7). This is the south of France but emphatically not the Riviera. It is the part of France which, as Varda reminds us, was historically Protestant: 'The landscape of the Hérault and the Gard in winter is not full of pretty villages: it's a harsh, Protestant area.'[41] Nor is it simply midwinter. Nature is dying, the plane trees are afflicted with some fatal disease and their disappearance will radically alter the landscape. Whereas the classical road movie might be considered the expression of the optimism of the 1960s, **Sans Toit ni loi** is, by contrast, highly critical of the political consequences of that decade.

Thus Mona refuses to adopt a life similar to that of the philosophy graduates turned goat-rearers she meets at one point in her travels. These proponents of the ecological life offer her a piece of land, but she prefers staying in bed to working it. Only then does Mona come anywhere near to offering an explanation of why she is on the road, and it has more to do with sexual harassment 'I was fed up with petty bosses', with patriarchy in other words, than with any concern for the environment or for the dignity of manual labour. This reflects both the feminist sympathies of the film maker and the educational gap between Mona and the *soixante-huitards* – for, while they have benefited from the privileges of higher education, Mona has been an office employee. The film equally presents the remnants of the drug culture in an unfavourable light. A group of drug users are terrorising passers-by at the Nîmes railway station but they do not know what to make of Mona, who evinces a complete serenity and an almost total indifference to money.

The second cinematic reference is to the thriller and since the central character is a woman of mystery, specifically to the *film noir*. The narrative device used in **Sans Toit** is a flashback, although the viewer rather loses sight of this fact. The film opens with the police noting the details of Mona's death, measuring the position of the corpse. Thereafter, the film develops as an enquiry into a death, through a series of 'eye witness accounts' relating to the deceased woman, statements by people Mona has encountered by chance along the way, each of whom, however admirable or reprehensible they may have found her, describe her as an enigma, beyond rationality, inexplicable. They do not know what she wanted or what she was seeking. Despite the very different filmic code, therefore, the flat washed colours of the Midi in winter, the absence of the urban decor and the emotive chiaroscuro of *noir* films, Mona is nevertheless comparable to the mysterious unknowable women of *noir* films such as **Woman in the Window** or **Laura**.[42] Finally, she is both immensely sympathetic and immensely repulsive. She is the opposite of the female cinematic icon: she is dirty, unkempt, overweight, repulsive in her personal habits and her moral practices (she is undiscriminating in her sexual partners) – she is a female Boudu and all the more remarkable for being female, moving in ungainly fashion (followed by long travelling shots) weighed down by her backpack.

This is perhaps the first Varda film to have an insistent moral dimension and to address, directly, the question of social values. **Sans Toit ni loi** is quite without the jokiness and knowingness of **L'Une chante**, it does not manifest the uncertainties of genre apparent in the earlier film and, as a result, is a much more unified structure, much more homogeneous in tone. It contains both a critique of the way people live and of Varda's own earlier films. Occasionally, the social critique is too emphatic. Mona's encounter with a young couple who are waiting for an old aunt's inheritance and the way their obsession with money is destroying their relationship strikes a false note because it is slightly farcical and out of keeping with the elegiac pessimism of the remainder of the film. By contrast, Mona's refusal to allow sex to be used as a value of exchange, her sympathetic interaction with immigrant workers, the commitment of the botanist (Macha Méril) to her work, all these things are positives and presented as unusual in French society. Even the unaccustomed view of the South of France (reminiscent of Varda's early film **Du Côté de la côte**, whose first title was **Eden toc** (that is, artifical Eden) is itself an implicit criticism of the moral values which derive from affluence.

But above all it is as a woman that Mona moves us. She is both single, solitary (the name Mona no doubt recalls both the Greek for name, *onoma*, and for single, *monas*, as well as the eternally mysterious woman, Mona Lisa) and the eternal feminine. The first shot of her in the film is as Venus rising from the sea. But although she is all these things, she is also virtually silent, manifestly oppressed and she dies, her death resulting from elemental forces after a primitive bacchanal in which she is symbolically raped. The colour purple, here, in the dregs of wine which are daubed all over her, evokes the blood of a sacrificial violation. It is thus impossible not to read **Sans Toit ni loi** as a highly pessimistic vision of women in society and in the cinema.

## Marguerite Duras: The Discovery of Pleonasm

The films of Marguerite Duras are unlike those of Agnès Varda: they are more cheaply made, more marginal, more voluntarily experimental. But Duras shares with Varda a preoccupation with women's cinema and its possibilities. It might be argued that Varda disrupts our conventional notions of cinema by the production of mixed genre films – half

**Jane B. par Agnès V.** – Jane Birkin parodies Goya

94

fiction, half documentary; that she distances conventional narrative by her refusal of realism, as in the frequently melodramatic plots of her films, and that she calls attention to the issues of women's cinema both by appearing in her own films (**Jane B. par Agnès V.**) and by the use of voice-over in **L'Une chante**, for example. Although voice-over is generally considered to arise from 'a space absolutely other than that of the image' and in this way to confer an authoritative reading on the images, a woman's voice-over and moreover one known to be that of the film maker cannot have the same effect. Varda's voice over the images in **L'Une chante** implies identification with the images, because she is a woman and because she has herself created them, and in this respect it is pleonastic: it confirms and repeats what the images already say. In exactly the same way, the film maker's voice, in **Jane B. par Agnès V.** confirms and repeats the images of the *tableaux*, reprises of Goya's *Maya* or the Urbino Venus, and is therefore pleonastic.

Duras's films are not narrative in the conventional sense although they are intense and moving. But her experimentation has concentrated particularly on the use of sound or its absence, and it is thus by recourse to the thematics of the voice and to pleonasm, the figure inevitably associated with the voice in the cinema, that Duras's cinema is characteristically that of a woman.

During the silent period cinema was viewed as a plastic art, a succession of visual compositions, and most discussion of its artistic resources concerned the effects of visual montage. But after the advent of sound such a position was no longer tenable. As has already been suggested, there developed an existential account of cinema which considered films as a way of presenting man's, and pre-eminently woman's, being in the world, and present-day discussions of questions of representation almost all derive directly or indirectly from this account. Merleau-Ponty was not alone in suggesting that cinema shows us the individual's relation to the world. Also in the immediate postwar period, the critic and film maker Alexandre Astruc published a famous series of articles in which he reflected on the impact of the talkies. On the one hand, he welcomed sound as an addition to the cinema, because it gave greater scope for drama and psychological depth: 'The miracle is that because of speech and thanks to the talkies (...) there is now a need for a dramatic style which can recount stories of life and death.' But these images are not purely illustrative, for it is in its capacity to envisage the relations between things that the cinema achieves depth:

*All thought and all feeling is a relationship between one human being and another human being or certain objects which form part of his world. It is by making these relationships explicit and by describing the visible indication of them that the cinema can make itself into the real means of expressing thought.*[43]

Although these views were set out over forty years ago, at a time when sound cinema was still a relative novelty, they continue to inform mainstream film making practices, as Mary Ann Doane points out in her fascinating essay entitled 'The Voice in the Cinema'.[44] Even today, as Doane rightly emphasises, cinema continues to be a *mise en scène* of bodies', a kind of 'somatography'. Indeed, in a general way our culture attaches more significance to the visible than to the audible and the result, for sound recording in the cinema, is, on the one hand, the establishment of a hierarchy of sounds which subordinate everything to the dialogue, although this is not naturalistic and, on the other hand, the creation of the impression that sound derives from a unitary source which is the human body. Hence, the immense significance attached to synchronisation, the rejection of dubbing as inauthentic, and the 'grammar' of shot/reverse shot to figure the interchanges implicit in dialogue.

Cinema as somatography is unacceptable for the avant-garde cinema, and from the late 1960s onwards the political and artistic avant-gardes began to experiment with sound in the same way as they began to show the filmic apparatus in an attempt to render the viewer conscious of how and where the film is produced and of the materiality of the image. The films of Godard and Resnais are good examples, although in different ways, of the new consciousness both of the resources of sound and the need to use it differently. Godard frequently broke the conventions of shot/reverse shot – for example by rapid panning in **Vivre sa vie** – and refused sound mixing which respected the conventional hierarchy that allowed speech to be heard above ambient sound, preferring a more 'natural' mix. Indeed, he once wrote how much he admired Scorsese for his use of sound, and that his own ambition was to make a film with a single recording track. In later films, such as **Luttes en Italie, Sur et sous la communication** and, above all, **Passion**, Godard abandons the canonical synchronisation of speech and image, while in some of his video films he disrupts sound in a different way by offering an alternative written text which is printed out on the screen in accompaniment to speech or dialogue.

In political terms it was always maintained that experiments such as Godard's were instances of dialectic, that they served to 'foreground the materiality' of the film so that the viewer would be aware that what was being viewed presented an ideological position. In psychological terms, however, the effect is, as Doane points out, to fracture the imaginary cohesion of the body, which is dispersed and fragmented by avant-garde practices. An interesting instance of this is Godard's **Passion** (1982) which contains the most radical dislocation of synchronisation he has achieved to date. The body is reconstituted in **Passion**, but factitiously, by the recomposition of pastiches as *tableaux vivants* of famous paintings which are held together, in a manner imitated from Resnais, by a beautiful and romantic continuous music track. Thus the unity of composition is at once artifical and excessive in this film.

The approach of Alain Resnais has been somewhat different from Godard's and is of considerable significance here since Marguerite Duras collaborated with Resnais on **Hiroshima mon amour** (1959). Resnais always accorded as much significance to sound as to image: 'The cinema is a combination between a visual rhythm and a sound rhythm, but it is a combination, it is not an image alone.'[45] From **Nuit et brouillard** onwards, music became a structuring element in Resnais's films, entering into a dynamic relationship with the images. And, from the time that Resnais began to make feature films, music became a narrative element, underlining his characters' quest for themselves and the themes of memory and forgetfulness, history and the abolition of history, by its capacity for recall and repetition within a unified structure, its symphonic and contrapuntal richness which the human mind, in Resnais's films, seeks but cannot find. The sound track in Resnais serves to underscore the profound anti-naturalism of his narratives in for example, Emmanuelle Riva's artifical diction in **Hiroshima mon amour** or in the non-naturalistic rhythms and bodily movements in **L'Année dernière à Marienbad** (1961).

Marguerite Duras's first film text, **Hiroshima mon amour**, as filmed by Resnais, was premonitory in its establishment of a new relation not simply between sound and image

97

but between voice and image.[46] The opening sequence is a montage of shots of Hiroshima and its inhabitants whose bodies have been wounded and fragmented by the atomic blast, intercut with shots of fragments of two other bodies (arm, hand, leg) which appear to be those of a couple making love. A woman's voice, which we gradually assume to be that of one of the lovers, although we do not know, apostrophises both Hiroshima and her lover in a language which is complex, stilted and theatrical. Without the voice, the relation between the lovers, love and Hiroshima would not be comprehensible, so that the voice is a source of intelligibility and composition or recomposition: it is constitutive of the film in that it allows the fragments to be pieced together (an important political point of course is that those shattered by the bomb can never be put together). In this way **Hiroshima mon amour** figures the somatic function of speech in the cinema and prefigures Duras's own films, having done which it returns to a more conventional narrative structure. It is thus an interesting pointer to the way Duras uses the voice and the body in her films.

But it is in Duras's own film, **India Song** (1975) and its companion piece, **Son Nom de Venise dans Calcutta désert** (1976) that all the elements of Duras's cinema would appear to be assembled. The themes of time past and ruin, the slow deliberate movements of the actors, the use of stilted language and rhetorical devices such as periphrasis, repetition and hyperbole in the speech of the characters producing entirely non-naturalistic sentences which cannot be called dialogue but which more resemble the antiphonic structure of some classical poetry, together with an insistent, beautiful and repetitive musical score which consists in variations on a theme, all these things are a pursuit, in greater depth, of the experiments of **Hiroshima mon amour**, with the important exception that Duras disposed of a budget which was far smaller than that of Resnais.[47] However, the most striking feature of **India Song**, confirmed a year later by **Son Nom de Venise**, is the pre-eminence given to the sound track. None of the characters in the film speaks, their movements vaguely correspond to what they are described as doing, but not precisely. Instead, two female voices-off narrate the story of Anne-Marie Stretter and her lovers. Once again a woman's voice composes the film, but in a quite compelling and moving way, and as if this were not entirely obvious the companion piece uses the same soundtrack but over images of deserted landscapes from which all corporeal representation has been expelled.

**India Song** and **Son Nom de Venise** thus represent a new kind of cinema, one in which sound is as important as, if not more important than, image, and one which is composed of a montage of sound and image.[48] In order to appreciate how radical this is one has to imagine both what the film would mean without the soundtrack – unlike most fiction films it would be unwatchable and virtually unintelligible without it – and the way in which the soundtrack, by juxtaposition with and counterpoint to the images, changes our perception of those images. Hence the meaning of images depends as much on the audio as the visual context and this is what Duras's diptych demonstrates. The sound cinema has always been concerned to avoid what it considers redundancy: you do not say what you can show. But because in Duras's films the soundtrack has a fully-fledged and autonomous existence, the pleonasm so feared by conventional film makers can become a positive quality. Thus Duras has talked of 'the vulgarity which is inherent in the realism of direct cinema'[49] and gone on to say that, whether rehearsal or repetition arises visually with 'the reflection of the protagonists in the mirrors [which] represent the state in which one listens to oneself' or whether it is voices-off describing the physical and emotional movements of the actors, in both these cases 'pleonasm is totally positive (...) it gave me fantastic pleasure to discover its joys'.[50]

Nevertheless, **India Song** and **Son Nom de Venise**, though they are films by a woman, are not women's films in the sense that the viewer is not aware that the film maker has particularly engaged with the politics of women's cinema. The reverse is the case, however, with **Nathalie Granger** (1972) and above all with **Le Camion** (1977). In **Nathalie Granger**, it has been rightly said, a sharp contrast is established between the inside and the outside, the women's domain and that of the world – a contrast which is already familiar from anthropological literature and rendered all the more abrupt by the irruption of a man (Depardieu) into the inside for a brief period.[51] The women's world is thus in some sense autistic, and it is also one of silence. It has been argued that the silence of these women represents a form of resistance, and it is certainly true that this idea had some currency in the women's movement at the time. Hélène Cixous, for example, was asked 'Don't you think that silence can be a response?'.[52] In addition, silence in a sound film is extremely disturbing: the viewer expects some noise, background noise if not speech, so that as well as showing ways in which women continue to resist, **Nathalie Granger** points towards the more radical disjunctions of sound and image to be found in **India Song** and **Son Nom de Venise** and, above all, **Le Camion**.

     **Le Camion** is a film which does not exist or which, rather, exists as the product of a woman's voice. Marguerite Duras herself and the actor Gérard Depardieu sit in a room with the curtains drawn and the lamp lit, reading the script of a film.[53] This is intercut with shots of a large articulated lorry driving through the ugly landscape on the outskirts of Paris (between Plaisir and Trappes). It is, Duras emphasises, a game of 'let's pretend'. The mood used is the conditional, traditional for children when they imagine a scenario ('you be the mummy and I'll be the daddy') and used also, in French, for what is supposed, imagined or alleged to be the case. And just as **India Song** managed to rupture the eternal present of the cinema and introduce a past so **Le Camion** has managed to introduce a future in the past – a future anterior.[54]

     The film is related to episodes in Duras's novels, *Le Marin de Gibraltar* and *Détruire dit-elle*, where the narrators imagine they are writing novels, but it is the first text in which a

Le Camion – Gérard Depardieu and Marguerite Duras reading Duras's text

woman is the creator.[55] **Le Camion** takes up the same dialectic of inside/outside as **Nathalie Granger**, with Depardieu as the same representative of the male 'outside'. This time, however, he is entirely dependent on the woman's creativity, her voice and her writing, and speaks only what she has already written. Visually, too, the film is structured in a series of ironic reversals. A lorry is a traditional male symbol, often frightening, as in Spielberg's **Duel**, and always coded as masculine. By extension, lorry drivers combine both an excessive masculinity and an excessive proletarianisation. The dialogue in **Le Camion** makes it clear, indeed, that the lorry driver is an almost caricatural member of the CGT/PCF. The choice of Depardieu, himself as it were a *poids lourd* (heavyweight), to play the driver of a *poids lourd* (heavy goods vehicle) is the kind of pleonasm which Duras enjoys, but equally, as in Chantal Akerman's **Je tu il elle** (a film whose title indicates a similar work on the verb), a lorry driver is the source of frightening and uncontrolled sexuality – at least in fantasy – capable of raping women on sight. However, in **Le Camion** the physical contrast between Depardieu, who is young and large, and Duras, who is elderly and small, reinforces the astonishing and ironic reversal operated in this film: the film maker has represented herself not as an object of desire – that is the *poids lourd* – but as an anti-heroine. The woman's body, and by extension woman's writing ('plus corps donc plus écriture') is 'maigre' as Madeleine Borgomano interestingly puts it,[56] it has corporeal austerity, a paucity of signifiers which makes it characteristically female although not characteristically cinematic, and thus, paradoxically, well-suited to signify both women's condition and women's cinema. But above all **Le Camion** is a woman's film in its appeal to the thematics of the voice. Referring to her use of voices-off Duras has said: 'For a long time I thought that they were voices from outside, but now I don't think so, now I think they are me if I didn't write (...) it's a sort of multiplicity inside oneself',[57] but in **Le Camion** the voice-off is also present in the film, a diminutive figure shown reading the text that she has written, the ultimate cinematic pleonasm.

In both Agnès Varda's and Marguerite Duras's films there are silent characters – Nathalie Granger and Mona – moments of indirect speech in the unincorporated or unattributable voice-off and moments when, for the space of a sequence or a film, as in **Jane B. par Angès V.** and **Le Camion**, the film maker speaks. By contrast, neither Varda nor Duras has been able to 'write the body', according to Hélène Cixous's injunction, with anything like the same success. If Anne-Marie Stretter was Duras's fantasy alter ego, the colonial queen that Duras dreamed of being during her impoverished childhood, Stretter is nevertheless not shown as capable both of physical presence and speech but always suffering cinematic disjunction or dislocation, unable to be the subject of perfect synchronisation, perhaps because her image is so erotically charged. Similarly, although Varda is occasionally able to celebrate plenitude in lyrical fashion, in the round and pregnant forms of **Opéra Mouffe** and **L'Une chante**, these figures are always distanced by a documentary framework and the consciousness of the film maker's gaze.

Both Duras and Varda deliberately refuse to offer women's bodies as erotic spectacles for the male gaze. Anne-Marie Stretter, as we have seen, is physically absent from **Son Nom de Venise**; Marguerite Duras herself is present in **Le Camion** but 'thin' and diminutive in relation to Gérard Depardieu. Mona, in **Sans Toit ni loi**, is an anerotic figure, as are Varda's portraits of the androgynous icons of the 1960s, Viva in **Lion's Love** and Jane Birkin in **Jane B. par Agnès V.**, while **Réponse de femmes** represents naked women almost clinically and **Les Dites cariatides** sees them as beautiful but unfeeling and physically fragmented by the camera. It might be said, therefore, that although Varda and Duras have extended the repertoire of the cinema and have altered the relationship between sound and image in a way which has stimulated many radical film makers, both have also made films whose message is one of pessimism for the possibilities of women's cinema.

# PART II

# AUTEURS

# 4:

# Truffaut and Godard in the 1970s

## Truffaut: the film maker as producer

In the 1950s Truffaut had been a mordant film critic with a mission to transform film making in France. In the 1960s he got his chance to do so with a series of brilliantly original films such as **Tirez sur le pianiste**, **Jules et Jim**, and **Farenheit 451**. By the 1970s, it is sometimes felt, his career as a pathbreaker was over and it is true that he often repeated himself notably, if deliberately, in the Antoine Doinel cycle.[1] His films cease to be as visually exciting and he often appears concerned with commercial success rather than with continuing his radical break with mainstream practices. It is also true that, despite an appearance at the States General of the cinema in 1968, Truffaut seemed virtually untouched by the Events of May 1968 and continued to affirm in interviews a complete lack of interest in politics or the public sphere and to promote himself as an intimist film maker whose concerns were interpersonal relations and domestic interests The viewer of a film such as **Le dernier Métro** (1980), which was a huge commercial success, experiences a certain malaise at the depiction of the momentous events of the war and the Occupation from a point of view which is entirely personal and from which history has apparently been evacuated. Conversely, **Le dernier Métro** in its use of history as a source of spectacle is useful in indicating how Truffaut's post-1968 films can be read, as well as the nature of his influence on contemporary French cinema. Though he turned into a film maker whose visual conventionality was a sad contrast with the inventiveness of his early years, the thematic development of Truffaut's cinema is fascinating to explore.

First, Truffaut completed and dispensed with the semi-autobiographical Antoine Doinel cycle by destroying it from within. In **L'Amour en fuite** (1978) Doinel has become the author of a novel, *Les Salades de l'amour*, the title of which implies both that he a mediocre actor and that the tales told by the book are inventions or lies. And while Colette (Marie-France Pisier) is glancing through this opus in a bookshop the audience is shown extracts from **Les 400 coups**, the film in which the Doinel character had first appeared. Furthermore, Doinel's divorce is filmed on television because he and his wife Christine are the first couple to separate by mutual consent, and this event is accompanied by retrospective extracts from the other films in which he has figured. All the events of Doinel's life therefore seem destined to be fictionalised and this has two consequences. On the one hand, **L'Amour en fuite** retrospectively lends a coherence to a series of fictions which are in reality somewhat disparate in tone and in style and provides them with a narrative closure. Rather as the fictional Doinel recounts his life and perhaps lies about it in *Les Salades de l'amour*, so his inventor, by creating intertextual references where none previously existed, provides his own retrospective on what has become his *œuvre*. On the other hand, the writing of a novel, the appearance on television and, in general, the treatment of Doinel's 'adventures' as though they were source material for fiction or documentary, reinforces the impression that Doinel

L'Enfant sauvage –
Truffaut (left) as Dr Itard

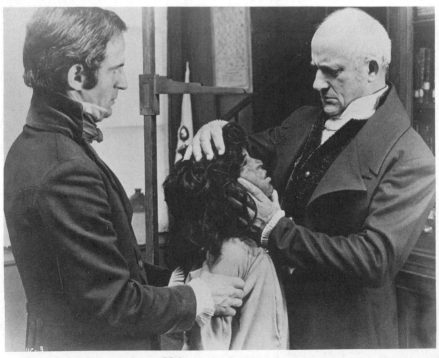

is 'real', opening up the possibility for the 'real' Truffaut to be fictionalised.

Such intertextual composition – what used to be referred to as 'quotation' – was habitual with Truffaut in his earliest films, from **Tirez sur le Pianiste** onwards. But what happens after the 1970s is that the film maker is himself seen as a producer in a way that is new. As the character Antoine Doinel becomes progressively more 'fictional', that is to say as he loses whatever earlier autobiographical relationship he bore to Truffaut himself, he begins to behave like the real Truffaut by creating himself as a character in a fiction (in *Les Salades de l'amour*, for example). Concurrently Truffaut appeared as an actor in three of his own films, as Dr Itard in **L'Enfant sauvage** (1970), as the film director Ferrand in **La Nuit américaine** (1973) and as the journalist Julien Davenne in **La Chambre verte** (1978)

The link between the three characters played by Truffaut is that they are all, themselves, producers of other characters. **L'Enfant sauvage**, which is set in the eighteenth century, is a film about the dialectic of nature and culture in which Dr Itard sets out to educate Victor, a wild boy he found roaming in the woods, so that by playing the role of Itard who

**La Nuit américaine –** Truffaut as Ferrand directing Jacqueline Bisset and Jean-Pierre Léaud

La Chambre verte –
Truffaut as Julien
Davenne with Nathalie
Baye in Julien's
mausoleum

moulds, forms, and ultimately invents Victor's personality Truffaut is acting out in proxy form his own role as film maker and inventor of fictions. Similarly, in **La Nuit américaine** the director of the film is seen as the source of the fiction. He holds together the team of actors and technicians, deals with their bouts of hysteria and relates their behaviour to what he knows of their circumstances, but also disposes these adults in a configuration of his own invention, moulding them to his own view of what their behaviour should be. Finally, in **La Chambre verte** Julien, who is responsible for the obituaries column in the local newspaper and who has miraculously survived the First World War while many of his contemporaries died, sustains a necrophiliac obsession with his wife Julie who died fifteen years earlier. The green room of the title is her shrine, full of objects that were hers as well as her life-size model. Through his worship of her, expressed finally in his own death, Julien hopes not merely to preserve her memory but to create the woman she was. The film is an adaptation of three short stories by Henry James, with an obvious *fin de siècle* resonance, and it may well be that Truffaut was also recalling in this film the celebrated Bazin dictum that the photographic image was invented to resurrect the dead.

However, Julien's activities are also comparable to those of Itard and Ferrand, since his job is to produce versions of other people's lives in the obituaries he composes. With this in mind it is tempting to see the three film roles that Truffaut played as symbolising the life-cycle of a producer, moving the creative process through three ages of man from childhood to maturity and to death.

Truffaut simultaneously pursued a practice of encouraging projects by other, usually younger, filmmakers where these correspond to his own preoccupations, so much so that several filmmakers might almost be said to have been 'invented' by Truffaut. This is the case, for example, with Jean Eustache whose pre-1968 films share many Truffaldian themes but whose masterpiece **La Maman et la putain** is clearly an attempt to come to terms with this paternal heritage by rejecting it. But it is also true of Maurice Pialat who, although he was nearly a decade older than Truffaut, had a much later start to his film making career and was encouraged by Truffaut in his making of **L'Enfance nue**.[2] And it is of course the case with Jacques Doillon, whose film **Les Doigts dans la tête** was so strongly admired by Truffaut that he helped to set up the financing of Doillon's subsequent film, **Un Sac de billes**.[3]

However, Truffaut's best known disciple is Claude Miller, who was 'directeur de production' on several of Truffaut's films before making his own first full-length feature, **La meilleure Façon de marcher** (1976).[4] This film is thematically interesting because it adapts some of Truffaut's preoccupations in the 1960s to the changed conditions of the 1970s in a way that Truffaut himself seemed unwilling to do. It is set in a *colonie de vacances*, an institutional environment which might be compared with the borstal in **Les 400 coups**, since although the *colonie* is a holiday village it is extremely regimented and Spartan and the children are supervised almost as closely as in the borstal. This merely forms the background of the film, however; the foreground concerns the persecution of one of the *moniteurs* or supervisors, the intellectual Philippe, son of the director of the *colonie*, by his colleagues. Philippe is, in particular, accused of always having his head in a book and of preferring to direct a play with his charges instead of playing football with them. One evening during a power cut Marc, a fellow *moniteur*, surprises Philippe in his room dressed in women's clothing and wearing full make-up, possibly trying out a role for a play. Thereafter, the film traces the vicissitudes

**109**

of the relationship between the two men and the mutual attraction which is not explicitly acknowledged by either, and it ends during the *colonie*'s farewell fancy dress party when Philippe, now publicly dressed, or disguised, as a woman, dances with Marc, kisses him on the mouth and then, in the ensuing brawl, knifes him in the leg.

Here Miller makes fascinating use of material which, in Truffaut, is often disguised as an exercise in genre. The theatrical, for example, is central to both **La Nuit américaine** and **Le dernier Métro**, where it is treated as a means of revealing truth and as a way of handling the emotions to such a degree that spectacle replaces time and history. This is emphatically not the case with Miller, whose film is given a specific historical or 'period' dimension since it is set before the 1968 'revolution'. In the same way in Truffaut's **Tirez sur le Pianiste**, **La Mariée était en noir**, and **La Sirène du Mississippi**, all of which refer in some way to the *noir* tradition, disguise and mistaken identity are all means of dealing with dangerous and sometimes fatal sexuality; they are all films in which women are not magic, as Antoine Doinel suggests, but murderous and dangerous, while in *Jules et Jim* Catherine's cross-dressing is used to indicate her ambivalence towards both her lovers.

It is not merely that Miller looks back at the period when Truffaut first began his career with, as it were, a more lucid and more penetrating gaze. In fact, **La meilleure Façon de marcher** reads as critique of those aspects of Truffaut's films which had caused them to become profoundly unsatisfactory, in particular their repressed misogyny, their unwillingness to engage with the world of the 1970s (most of his post-1968 films are in some way historical) and their use of spectacle as a means of eliding emotional difficulties. By setting the film in the period Truffaut drew on for his own material, Miller and his co-writer Luc Béraud wish to promote an alternative history to the familiar Truffaut version. In Miller's film it is a man who becomes sexually dangerous by cross-dressing, the spectacle is not real but actually an amateur theatrical which cannot substitute for the real emotional drama, and the children in the film are not presented as the privileged conscience of the time.

After a series of excellent films including the thrillers **Dites-lui que je l'aime** (1977) and **Garde à vue** (1981) Miller returned to the Truffaut heritage with **La petite Voleuse** (1988), an adaptation by himself and Béraud of an idea by Truffaut. The film is again set in the past ('1950, a small town in the centre of France' as the credits state) and it turns on the classic Truffaut themes of emotional deprivation and compensating criminality. The novelty here is that the central protagonist is the girl, Janine, where Truffaut's films invariably cast boys in the central role. During the course of the film, she is compared by the choirmaster whom she seduces to Victor Hugo's street urchin, Esmeralda, yet she is not the conscience of the people, she has none of Esmeralda's innate goodness, and she is not presented with the sentimentality with which the nineteenth-century writers surround their child characters and which Truffaut himself frequently adopted. Throughout the film Janine continues to steal and to betray those who love her. Her intellectual and emotional horizons are provided by the cinema, which offers a technicolour world that contrasts strongly with the drab existence of the aunt and uncle to whom her mother abandoned her as a baby. She runs away to become a maid in the house of a rich family. She meets a married man, older than herself, and a church choirmaster, who becomes her lover. He tries to educate her but fails. She then betrays him for Raoul, an unemployed youth (played by an actor bearing a strong resemblance to Jean-Pierre Léaud) and becomes pregnant. She steals her

**111**

employer's silver and runs off to the seaside with her
boyfriend, is arrested and placed in a girls' borstal which is
run by sadistic nuns. There she is placed in solitary confine-
ment for attacking another girl and is finally rescued, in a
Bonnie-and-Clyde-style escape, by a fellow inmate's boyfriend who has a car. She sets off to look for Raoul, who
has disappeared, and finally thinks she sees him in a newsreel
showing troops embarking for the war in Indochina.

The treatment of Truffaut's habitual themes is
fundamentally altered by placing at the centre of this film a
girl who has no moral sense, no sense of sexual or material
property, and who therefore does not play by society's rules.

112

The shift from male to female consciousness is reinforced by Miller's recourse to the conventional thematics of the women's movement, namely that the defeat of oppression comes through women's control of their own fertility and through economic independence. Here the heroine is uneducated, becomes a live-in maid and discovers that her only route to professional advancement is through secretarial evening classes. Unlike her employer who chooses to become pregnant, Janine gets pregnant by the ne'er-do-well Raoul, who abandons her, as her father had her mother, leaving Janine to consult a back-street abortionist and, finally, to go through with the pregnancy nevertheless. Miller's film does not promote the view that progress has taken place but rather the idea that by accepting her situation Janine channels her rebelliousness into taking charge of her own destiny.

Miller also takes a sceptical view of the influence of the mass media. One of Janine's few distractions in her home village is going to the cinema. There she learns of the relationship between romantic love and consumer objects and she is inspired to steal silk underwear to make herself an object of desire. Indeed, the cinema has a consistently negative influence on her life since it serves as an ironic counterpoint to her own experience. After an unsatisfactory and inconclusive conversation with the Choirmaster in which she asks her lover what he would do if she were pregnant, she views a newsreel depicting the wedding of Rita Hayworth and the Aga Khan, to which the commentary offered is: 'And so, even today, princes still marry shepherdesses.' Again, after she is apprehended at the seaside while on the run with Raoul, a newsreel shows a group of young women in swimming costumes lining up for the 'Miss Eiffel Tower' contest, with the title 'Horizons du monde' (world horizons). Finally, when she is contemplating the necessity for an abortion back in her home village, the tragic element of the drama takes place in the cinema into which she wanders only to see Raoul in uniform walking up the gangplank and turning to wave at the camera as if to emphasise her desolation and abandonment. By contrast when sent to a girls' reform school, she strikes up a friendship with a fellow inmate whose hobby is photography and who initiates her into the art. Janine and her friend are given a degree of autonomy in the institution because of their photographic skills and this allows them to plan their escape. Once outside the borstal, the camera becomes a valuable object for Janine: she uses it to pay for her abortion and when she decides against an abortion after all the camera is the only object she steals back. Thus a powerful subtext of this film is the need for women to control not merely their lives and their bodies but also their images.

Some of Truffaut's demonology is retained, principally in the depiction of a series of cold and sadistic women. Janine's aunt is both cruel and cold and is neither a mother herself nor a good mother substitute. She mistreats Janine when her niece lives with her and when Janine returns from the reform school refuses to let her sleep in the house and pretends that Janine's natural mother's most recent letter contained no word about her daughter. The back-street abortionist is presented as a mercenary and exploitative; the nuns who run the borstal take pleasure in torturing their charges emotionally and physically. Like Truffaut, Miller presents all institutional environments as repressive, whether it be the school Janine first attends, the church she steals from, the secretarial college she briefly attends, or the reform school. A life on the run is seen as infinitely preferable to life as a maid (though she is well treated) with a bookish and diffident lover.

Whilst remaining in some way very close to Truffaut's idea, **La petite Voleuse** places the drama recounted in a historical perspective and so relativises it. It also shows a different kind of female consciousness from the stereotypical phalanx of inadequate mothers and *femmes fatales* which normally people Truffaut's films. By choosing to treat a plot which originally had many elements of melodrama as a means to expose the gender assumptions of an earlier period, Miller continues the thematic critique of Truffaut already to be found in Eustache, Pialat and Doillon. The paradox of Truffaut's career after 1968, therefore, is that his own films became widely criticised but that he acted to foster new talents where he thought he detected kindred spirits, so that a whole strand of film making developed which can be traced in the films of the 1970s in which women and young people are depicted in a way that is a specific challenge to Truffaut's own ideas.

## Godard: Television and Sexual Politics

Whilst Truffaut became an actor in his own films and a producer of those of others, Godard, as we have seen, responded to May 1968 and its aftermath by distancing

114

himself from Paris and, after **Tout va bien**, from conventional film making. Because of this, perhaps, the decade proved to be one of Godard's most innovative and productive periods, and one in which he experimented with the different medium of video and with different forms of distribution, including television. He was as attentive as ever to the social and political concerns of the time. The influence of the women's movement, for example, is particularly apparent in **Numéro deux** (1975), while the challenge to power in all its forms, that was so characteristic of the decade, is interpreted by Godard as a questioning of himself as author, so that, although he is almost always present in the films he made in the 1970s, he deliberately fragments his authority by showing it as incomplete, either as sound or as image, either as voice-off or as bodily presence. Similarly, he attempts to get beyond the binomial and sometimes Manichean oppositions that had been so characteristic of his films, to a structure which includes communication and interaction, in particular suggesting not only the considerable social and aesthetic significance of television, but ultimately how two warring media and their respective industries, once described as 'Cain and Abel', could be reconciled in such a way that the creative possibilities of television could feed back into the cinema.

     **Ici et ailleurs** (1974) is a seminal film: it marked the beginning of Godard's collaboration with Anne-Marie Miéville at the Sonimage studio in Grenoble and it shifted the discussion of politics of the image from the denunciation of censorship and the exposure of bias, to be found in **Tout va bien** and **Letter to Jane**, to a consideration of the significance of the various technologies of image production. In **Ici et ailleurs** footage of the Palestinian struggle shot in 1970 is intercut with images of a French family watching television in 1974, while Godard and Miéville discuss what Godard and Gorin had intended to do in **Jusqu'à la victoire** and what meaning the images have in 1974. The film turns on the juxtaposition of several moments in time and several periods of technological development. The political situation has changed for the Palestinians, for the French family looking at TV, for Godard and Miéville, just as the film embodies not merely film and video footage but a celebrated scene recalling the early history of the cinema when five people each wearing a still photograph (re-used in **Photos et cie**) file past the video camera in a dramatic demonstration of the principles on which cinema works. Since Miéville and Godard are commenting on

**115**

a film made with Godard's previous collaborator, this might imply that the previous stance has to some degree seem naive or wrong, but as Godard was later to say in **Sur et sous la communication** it is the conjunction that counts, the 'and' linking the 'here' and 'elsewhere' which, thanks to technology, can be a continuum, a series of juxtapositions, a simultaneity. The invention of each visual medium – photography, film, video – belongs historically to a different period and is coded to signify different genres and different forms of distribution. With **Ici et ailleurs** Godard experimented for the first time with a montage of technologies of production and delivery, rather than of images or of sequences, and his subsequent films were to demonstrate how rich this discovery could be.

The reflection on his previous work and manner is also a feature of **Numéro deux** (1975), so called because Godard stated it was a remake of his first feature film **A Bout de souffle**. If so, this is not in the sense that it reworks the same plot but perhaps because it signals a new departure in Godard's career. **Numéro deux** engages with domestic politics in the same way as **Tout va bien**. It is a film in which the struggle is explicitly and specifically brought back home not merely to France but within the family. Where previously Godard had engaged with the liberation struggles of oppressed peoples the world over, now in **Numéro deux** it. is domestic politics which retains his attention. The film opens with a framing sequence in which Godard himself presents the film to come from inside what he calls his 'factory', a dimly lit studio with a film projector and video monitors playing images that include a television report on the annual May Day parade, a Kung Fu movie and episodes from two contemporary films, Bergman's **Scenes from a Marriage** and Sautet's **Vincent, François, Paul et les autres**. This long sequence serves both to establish the subject of the film as 'sex and politics',[5] work and relations between the sexes, and to establish the origin of the film and, perhaps, films in general. Rather as **Tout va bien** opened with the propaedeutic sequence in which the financing of the film and the presence of the stars are accounted for, so Godard explains that Georges de Beauregard offered to finance **Numéro deux** and the film will be about 'playing on words', 'short circuits' and 'interferences'. The viewer is then, as it were, handed over to the diegetic space as the voice of Sandrine, one of the central characters, takes over from that of Godard, and the

monitors begin to show scenes from her marriage. Thereafter
**Numéro deux** depicts the home life of an extended family
consisting of the central couple, Sandrine and Pierre, their
children Vanessa and Nicolas, and two of the children's
grandparents. This is a working class family living in a block
of flats that is not well built (there are constant complaints
about the plumbing). Sandrine has no job but we see her
ironing, doing the washing, cooking and generally accom-
plishing the domestic chores. Pierre, on the other hand, leaves
every day for a factory job where he claims he feels exploited.

  **Numéro deux** is the first of Godard's films in which
the family and children play any significant role – hitherto his
protagonists have been childless although thise in **Tout va
bien** did examine the relation within the couple – and it is also
the first to place sexuality as the centre of politics. In doing so
it reflects the mood of the times. Sandrine is the key sensibility
in the film and it is her voice which first takes over from that
of the film maker, followed only later by those of Pierre and
. the grandparents. Sandrine is a double object of desire and
oppression, both as the wife of a worker and the product of a
film maker's imagination. The dialectic of production/con-

**117**

sumption, outside/inside, male/female which structures **Numéro deux** pivots round Sandrine. Other contemporaneous films such as Chantal Akerman's **Jeanne Dielman** draw links between housework and exploitation, but in **Numéro deux** Godard's originality is to have linked sexual politics with the politics of representation. The film engages with the sexuality of old people, young people and with homosexuality; the children are shown asking about menstruation and sexual intercourse; the grandmother discourses at considerable length on the subject of men's sexual oppression of women; and in common with the men in **Vincent, François, Paul et les autres** Pierre experiences anxiety about his masculinity and describes the uncertainty about his own sexual identity that he sometimes experiences when making love with Sandrine.[6] However, the scene of crucial symbolic significance is, as described by Pierre, a moment when he learned that Sandrine had been to bed with another man, felt that he wanted to rape her, and forces her to accept anal intercourse, only to discover that this 'primal scene' had been witnessed by Vanessa their daughter.

We see clips of the rape recurring throughout the film, edited in a variety of different ways – in more or less long shot, in different colours, and with different superimpositions. The scene clearly figures male domination of women but also the importance of how this is represented and in what medium. In **Numéro deux** the narrative of family life is always represented on one or more monitors inside the larger film frame, giving the impression that we are watching a series of television programmes. The content, similarly, reinforces this impression since it consists, essentially, of the banal, domestic concerns that are the staple of soap opera. However, repetitiousness and the refusal of narrative closure (obliquely referred to in the recurrent problems of Sandrine's constipation) are characteristic not just of soap opera but also of pornography, in particular the sex films which Godard clearly parodies in his insistent return to the scene of the rape.[7] Just as **Ici et ailleurs** depended for its effect on a montage of genres, so the visual presentation of **Numéro deux** invites the comparison between a variety of themes rendered similar and perhaps indistinguishable by their common representation on television: the soap opera, the rape, the May Day parade, the Kung Fu movie. And just as Vanessa is forced to witness a perverted form of the primal scene so, it is implied, we are forced to look at a perverted form of the image. Vanessa is shown the origins of life, we are shown the origins of the cinema, but both produce violent, perverted or debased forms.

Like **Ici et ailleurs**, but in a more thoroughgoing fashion, **Numéro deux** mixes and juxtaposes images of technologically different status and apparently different genres. It will not settle down either to one medium (film or television) or to one genre (documentary, fiction, sex film, soap opera) but constantly shifts, sometimes lending itself to illusionism and sometimes destroying it. Though **Tout va bien** overtly questioned the politics of the image it also dazzled the viewer with its aesthetic virtuosity. By contrast, **Numéro deux** adopts the greyness of the most banal of television programmes to depict a rather grim reality. Here the viewer is not so much dazzled as daunted by the sheer quantity of visual information within the frame and the pessimism of the film's message. Its originality lies, in a sense, outside the images which compose the film in the identification of television as the site of struggle, the medium which must be changed if the critique of the family that arose after 1968 was to be pursued through a new politics of the image.

Godard was to spend the remainder of the decade exploring the creative possibilities of television in two series, **Six Fois deux/Sur et sous la communication** (1976) and **France/Tour/Détour/Deux enfants** (1978). He remains the only major French film maker to have worked so extensively and creatively with television and he was able to do so largely. thanks to the experimental programme production policy developed by the L'Institut National de l'Audiovisuel (INA) between 1975 and 1979.[8] **Sur et sous la communication** consists of twelve 50-minute programmes scheduled for broadcasting in groups of two.[9] The penultimate programme, **Avant et après**, insists that the series should be understood as a whole, which would itself be unusual in television, and suggests that each block of two programmes can be read across the horizontal axis with the first programme in each block examining a question or a problem of general interest while the second consists of an interview of some kind. Thus the third block, **Photos et cie** shows a photograph of a massacre which took place during the war in Bangladesh and discusses with the photographer Don McCullin some of the technical problems of photo journalism, moving then to a clip from the footage covering the Communist Party conference in which the General Secretary, Georges Marchais, attacks television. **Marcel**, the second programme in the same block, consists of an interview with a watch maker who is also an amateur film maker, in which he explains his notion of beauty and how he sets about selecting landscapes to film, and it includes some of Marcel's material.

The comparison between the professional and the amateur, the public and the private is implicitly a contrast between the corrupt and the authentic. But, of course, these two films also establish a series of intertexts. Some of the stills shown in **Photos et cie** already figured in **Ici et ailleurs**, having already figured in a magazine report on the Palestinian struggle. The clip of Marchais addressing his comrades is reminiscent of the footage of the Communist Party in **Numéro deux**, while it is tempting to suggest that Marcel, the real-life watchmaker with clear-cut aesthetic views, is intended to mock Tavernier's fictional character in **L'Horloger de Saint-Paul**, released the preceding year. **Avant et après** also suggests that **Sur et sous la communication** could be read down the vertical axis which might allow all the 'personal' interview programmes, including an interview with Godard himself, to be juxtaposed. Indeed, the intersection of the axes is a figure which is frequently inscribed on the screen throughout the series to explain or reinforce points.

The richness of **Sur et sous la communication**, however, lies not just in its structure but also in what Godard has managed to put on screen. His own presence is more modest than that of the inevitably oppressive film maker in **Numéro deux** and the use of his forenames in **Jean-Luc** suggests diffidence, if not anonymity. Though he is often the interviewer, his presence is rarely visible in the interviews he conducts. As Gilles Deleuze has pointed out, Godard has great talents as an interviewer and contrives to ask the apparently simple or naive questions that others do not dare to pose.[10] He is completely even-handed in his treatment of people, showing the same respect and open-mindedness towards the peasant farmer Louison as he does towards the famous mathematician René Thom, and he exaggerates his Swiss accent perhaps to reassure his interviewees that he is not a prying representative of metropolitan culture. In **Y a personne** he manages to persuade a job applicant to act out the part of a cleaning lady (another reference to Chantal Akerman), in **Jacqueline et Ludovic** he talks to the inmates of a psychiatric hospital, in **Nanas** he gets a group of women pensioners to reminisce (rather like the grandparents in **Numéro deux**), in **Marcel** and **Louison** he explores the world of work rarely presented on television. Whether in its deconstruction of official images in **Photos et cie** or its programming of unofficial images in **Marcel**, its steadfast refusal to interview the professionals, politicians and experts who usually appear on television, in its sympathetic treatment of people who lack confidence and, above all, in Godard's attitude as an interviewer, **Sur et sous la communication** breaks the habitual codes of television.

It also proposes a relatively coherent theory of communication which represents a continuation of and an advance on **Numéro deux**, where Sandrine, meditating on her constipation and her oppression, intones 'numéro un, numéro deux, enfin numéro trois, moi enfin'[11] as though to propose a way forward which would allow her signifying plenitude, signifying in her own right rather than as what Mulvey calls an 'empty sign' for male desire. Through a variety of formal means, such as the structuring of the series and the generation of text on the screen, Godard arrives at a notion of interaction. **Avant et après**, as has been seen, suggests a mode of reading which might be considered a witty exploitation of the syntagmatic and paradigmatic axes fashionable in structuralist analysis of narrative at the time, but tempers this formalism with the constant intersection of axes.[12] Again in **Avant et après** thoughts on the nature of television are communicated from an unseen transmitter, who may be Godard, through the headphones worn by a young man on screen who receives the prompt and transmits the messages. In this way it is asserted that television is a mystification, that there are actually 'three of us' (*nous trois*) in television: the transmitter (speaker), the receiver (citizen) and the set (screen),[13] so that, in a way that recalls **Numéro deux**, television becomes a 'family affair' intervening 'between you and me'.

Just as in **Tout va bien** Godard evinces a nostalgic yearning for a prelapsarian regime of image production, so here he plays with the idea of a pre-revolutionary or utopian world of communication which would be 'direct'. In his view television transmission, which necessitates a passage through Paris, is the equivalent of the communications network in pre-revolutionary France which imposed the passage through numerous internal customs barriers. Thus, in attempting to place itself at the interface where two becomes three in an effort at interactivity, **Sur et sous la communication** also offers a poignant demonstration of the communicative power of television when in **Nous trois** a pair of lovers communicate not through speech (there is no sound track) but 'through' television as their changing relationship is expressed in the decomposed and recomposed forms generated by vision mixing and the reversal of light and dark shapes. Similarly, in the interviews he conducts, Godard not only casts himself as an outsider but often chooses to talk to men and women who are pursuing solitary occupations, like Louison and Marcel, often in a world they have created themselves, or who are self-sufficient to the point of solipsism, as in **Jacqueline et Ludovic**. The contrast with the highly conventional and coded format of television and newspaper journalism is thrown into stark relief, leaving Godard's strange cast of characters with a kind of innocence.

**France/Tour/Détour/Deux enfants** was Godard's second television series, which was also commissioned by INA, in 1977–8, but not screened until 1980. It takes its name from the celebrated nineteenth century school textbook by G. Bruno, **Le Tour de la France par deux enfants**, itself inspired by the tour that journeymen traditionally made round France to complete their education as apprentices before being admitted to their guild as master craftsmen. The book was designed to provide a series of object lessons for the pupils in the newly created elementary school system and it imagines two children travelling around France observing details of its natural landscape and economic activity and presenting these observations as answers to naive questions. Godard, in turn, uses the consciousness of two children, Camille and Arnaud, whom he questions directly or obliquely on the state of the nation in the *faux naïf* manner of the nineteenth-century pedagogue. Like a television magazine programme, **France/ Tour/Détour** is framed by two presenters, Betty Berr and Albert Dray, who appear at the beginning and end of each episode and attempt to place in context the things that the children have said or noticed. But throughout the series Godard complicates and confuses the issue of authority, who is 'in' the fiction, who is 'in' television, and who is outside. Like Godard in **Numéro deux**, the children are shown handling the film making equipment at the start of the first sequence, yet Betty Berr and Albert Dray are allowed to be privileged commentators on the action, sometimes with ironic force reminiscent of Michel Lonsdale's commentary in **British Sounds**. The children who are seen in their ordinary domestic and scholastic context are asked questions of great philosophical complexity, some of which they answer in an interesting fashion and some of which pass over their heads.

The series is therefore less successful than **Sur et sous la communication** in subverting the social function of television, particularly since the children are so obviously conditioned by their environment that they do not succeed in recapturing the innocent or untutored attitudes that Godard clearly sought.

Though **France/Tour/Détour** is less politically and ideologically innovative than **Sur et sous la communication** it nevertheless enabled Godard to recapture a kind of aesthetic innocence. Where previously Godard had insisted on the materiality of sound and image in order to denounce a system of production or to demonstrate how cinema works, **France/Tour/Détour** points to the more sensuous use of images and music that characterises Godard's films in the 1980s. Each episode of **France/Tour/Détour** is opened and closed by a haunting musical sequence which sets up a profound contrast with the matter-of-fact attitude of the commentators and the ordinariness of the children's daily lives, while Godard attends to the composition of the children's gestures by slowing down the video image in such a way that it decomposes the shot entirely, distracting the viewer's attention from what action is being accomplished and focusing on beauty of the movement.

Beginning with **Sauve qui peut (la vie)** (1979), which he described as his 'second first film', Godard returned to mainstream film making in a series of works in which music, movement and painting all function as autonomous aesthetic elements, beautiful and sensuous in their own right, compositions of sound and colour pegged onto narrative structures of decreasing importance. It is significant, perhaps, that in the 1980s Godard's films often rework culturally familiar material: from the Annunciation in **Je vous salue, Marie** (1983), from well-known plays or operas in **Prénom Carmen** (1982) and **King Lear** (1987) and from well-known paintings in **Passion** (1981). It is as though Godard deliberately wished to reintegrate his films into the mainstream of western culture and to abandon his long-held position of marginality in order finally to allow the expression, as **Passion** suggests, of feelings and of the emotion that in **Pierrot le fou** Fuller had said was the essence of cinema. The roots of this return to the western cultural tradition are to be traced back to **Numéro deux**, where the children discuss the distinction between a a factory and a landscape. In **Sauve qui peut (la vie)** Godard inaugurated a new pastoralism, rediscovered the natural world and chose the landscape rather than the factory, as the journalist Denise Rimbaud, like her illustrious nineteenth century namesake, quits the metropolis for the countryside. She is shown cycling along a country road while the image is slowed down and decomposed into a thousand points of colour. This is Godard at his most painterly, attempting to recapture the innocent image.

The broadcasting history of Godard's television series has been unfortunate. **Sur et sous la communication** was shown in the holiday months of July and August to small audiences, while **France/Tour/Détour** waited three years after completion before it reached the television screens. In part the failure of these series to reach the wide audiences for which they were intended can be attributed to the increasing financial pressure on French television at the end of the 1970s and the resulting conservatism in the design of its schedules. But it also had to do with the fact that Godard's films are extremely subversive of television practice, both in the way they ask questions about the medium and most of all, in their de-professionalisation of it. Godard's work for television showed that the medium could be genuinely popular on condition that it regained its lost innocence by using social actors such as children or peasant farmers who are far removed from and uncontaminated by metropolitan life, and by technical simplification. It is hardly surprising therefore that a message which questioned their working practices and their social function should not have found favour with television professionals.

# 5:

# The Heritage of the *Nouvelle Vague*

## Philippe Garrel

Philippe Garrel has been called the Rimbaud of the French cinema, a sobriquet which derives both from the youthfulness of his début, his apparent iconoclasm and his total commitment to art. It does not (as yet) refer to the course of his career. His willingness to stand in a marginal relation to the mainstream of the French cinema has been a considerable source of strength. He began his career working as a technician in French television, where he made a 60-minute film, **Anémone** (1967) produced by the ORTF. He later called this work 'very bad, completely Godardian'.[1] Nevertheless admiration for Godard has been a constant of Garrel's career: 'I saw all Godard's films, I was crazy about them (...) In fact, those were the only films I saw,' he remarked in 1968.[2] The compliment is reciprocated. A further premonitory feature of **Anémone** was Garrel's casting of his father Maurice in the role of father, a role to be played by Maurice Garrel in many of his son's subsequent films.

Garrel first attracted significant critical attention with two short films also made in 1967, **Droit de visite** and **Les Enfants désaccordés**, both of which well exemplify one thematic strand of his work. **Droit de visite** portrays an adolescent boy whose parents live apart, on a Sunday outing with his father (played by Maurice Garrel) and his father's girlfriend, while **Les Enfants désaccordés** describes the adventures of an adolescent couple who, finding life with their parents intolerable, decide to run away. The subject matter of these films is very much of its period: the problems of young people, and particularly questions of their sexuality, figure in many of the early *nouvelle vague* films; they were also a subject of sociological research and journalistic preoccupation at the time. Young people's difficulties are earnestly discussed in the face-to-camera 'interviews' with a

125

schoolteacher and with the father of the boy in **Les Enfants désaccordés** and are reflected in the fact that Françoise, the girlfriend in **Droit de visite** has, at the age of twenty-five, more in common with the son than with her lover the father. Thus these two films embody the conflict between the generations and elements of the youth culture that the term 'nouvelle vague' originally referred to. To some degree Garrel adopts a realist style that is consonant with these themes, particularly in **Les Enfants désaccordés**, where street shots of the youngsters discussing their next move could have come from a Rozier, Godard or Chabrol of the early 1960s and where the 'interviews' are filmed in television style.

However, these two shorts also offer hints of Garrel's later style and preoccupations. One of these is his use of landscape. **Droit de visite** features a superb long tracking shot from the back of the sports car in which the father, girlfriend and son leave Paris for the country, and a sequence in the forest (probably Fontainebleau) where the pattern of trees has a clarity and depth that renders it almost abstract. Similarly, although the street scenes in **Les Enfants désaccordés** are neo-realist, the destination of the adolescents' escapade turns out to be a château set in a clearing in a forest, which is emphatically not realist. Seen from a distance and distanced by the way the shots are framed, the château becomes mysterious, poetic and menacing by turns, so that the viewer never believes that this is an authentic place of refuge but assumes, instead, that the film has shifted onto a plane of fantasy. This is a magic castle and, not unlike the one in Resnais's **La Vie est un roman**, it is indeed entirely romantic. Of this film Garrel has said: 'it is (. . .) about a guy who leaves home (. . .) and because I didn't really know where he was going, I filmed something abstract, a sort of château with people hanging out of the windows and people in the woods who didn't move.' He added: 'When I look at the film today [1968] I think that it shows exactly what is happening to our generation, the way in which we are completely at odds with the cycle of consumption.'[3] The second premonitory feature of these films is the length of the shots that compose them. Though Garrel eschews, like most of the *nouvelle vague*, classic narrative techniques, he does not use montage to anything like the extent it is used by Godard, for example, preferring instead the lengthy shots which in later films turn into virtuoso exercises. Garrel has claimed this both as a challenge – 'it's a sort of little game organising the length of the shots' – and as an aesthetic element – 'composing a shot which lasts a long time is much more musical'.[4]

We find in these films, therefore, both the concern for certain aspects of modern life and, more important, a challenge to the way modern life is represented, particularly by television. The concern is evident in Garrel's remarks about the consumer society and the statement he made to *Cahiers du cinéma* in 1968, agreeing that he was 'completely against culture', that innovative film making required a certain cultural innocence.[5] To illustrate how widespread such concerns were, an interesting comparison might be made between these Garrel films and Godard's **Weekend**, also made in 1967, a film which combined trenchant and at times violent denunciations of social trends (consumerism, second homes) and virtuoso camera exercises in the long sideways tracking shot of a traffic jam and the 360-degree rotation of the camera while Jean-Pierre Léaud declaims from the works of St Just. Indeed, the last part of **Weekend** is comparable to the château sequence of **Les Enfants désaccordés**, though it is more violent and more comic, since it too takes place in a landscape peopled by extraordinary characters.

In 1968 Garrel made a *cinétract*, **Actualités révolutionnaires**, which again gave him an opportunity to define his position in relation to the dominant culture and politics. Here, too, the political issue is couched in aesthetic terms, that of the representation of the barricades on film and television.

> *I wanted to show that it was crucial not to continue with spectacle, not to go on filming the barricades because doing so was a way of playing the government's game by making films so that people could get off on the images. I simply wanted to show, in an abstract way, an analysis of what is going on (...) and to completely avoid showing the barricades just as one would avoid showing a naked girl.*

This statement challenges the position of the film maker: 'it is completely contradictory to film the barricades because (...) doing so means that you are away from the barricades and that you are reporting the event in the present by saying, "look, this is what happened while I was carrying on with my life", which is a way of not thinking.' It also challenges the pleasure that the cinema procures: 'the cinema must never be a place where the viewer finds pleasure (...) The film must always be something that disturbs (...) it must be completely intolerable for the viewer'.[6] Within these two statements are to be found the belief that the dominant narrative and visual codes, those established by the Hollywood cinema, have an ideological role in constructing our lives, a belief that was commonplace in film circles in 1968, though the role of such cinema was rarely as systematically attacked in practice as it was subsequently by Garrel.

Garrel defines the film maker as an artist in much the same way that a painter might be defined. This has both negative and positive aspects. On the one hand, it entails a rejection of modern forms of mass consumption and mass communications, particularly advertising and television, as we have seen. On the other hand, it leads the film maker to attempt to exploit the technical possibilities of the apparatus whilst simultaneously refusing to be constrained by narrative and photographic conventions. These two imperatives can be traced through virtually all of Garrel's subsequent films.

The break with the realist practices of **Droit de visite** and **Les Enfants désaccordés** can be found in two short films made also in 1968. **Le Révélateur**, with Laurent Terzieff and Bernadette Lafont, was shot in Germany, 'using what we come across along the roads', that is to say without any of the usual preparatory work (finding locations, planning shots, rehearsals) and is a completely silent film, without either words or music.[7] Its companion piece, **La Concentration**, was continuously shot on a single set over a 72-hour period and edited in a week. Both films show Garrel attempting to explore and practise some of his film making precepts, especially his notion that film making should be an entirely craft activity, without technicians, purely the product of the film maker's personal needs: 'I dreamed of having a Cameflex so that I could make a film like a diary the whole day long, by which I mean shooting a shot here and there, then putting it away for a week and then taking it out for another shot',[8] and his belief that making a film is the reflection of and product of a process of mental or internal struggle: 'Jean-Luc says: "The cinema for me is an image and a sound." For me it is an image. It is completely silent for me. The dialogue is all interior dialogue as in a dream. It is spoken but cannot be heard.'[9] The experimental nature of this activity, as has already been noted, leads Garrel to explore many technical processes, such as the use of light or the length of shots, further than is conventional, so that occasionally his shots seem to explode into light; and it is mirrored in the spatial disposition of his characters in later films, their spiritual or aesthetic quest being expressed in movement through often barren or featureless landscapes (notably in **La Cicatrice intérieure**).

But the film which best illustrates Garrel's transition from realism is **Marie pour mémoire** (1967) which opens with a parody of oppositional film making but moves on to the themes and images which were to be characteristic of Garrel's mode in the 1970s. In the beginning it appears that **Marie pour mémoire**, like the contemporaneous **Le gai Savoir**, will explore the intellectual trends of the 1960s, with its discussion of Lacan, Situationism, Bosch and Stroheim. The opening sequence is filmed like a tribute to the *nouvelle vague*, with the camera panning from side to side following the speakers' interventions, much as in **Le gai Savoir** Godard exploits the shot/reverse shot convention by his use of a panning camera. It moves then to a portrayal of the father, played by Maurice Garrel, who is characterised as an instance of the repressive exercise of power, of authoritarianism and of the 'ordinary fascism' that Michel Foucault discussed in his writings and that May 1968 was to challenge. When the father behaves in a militaristic fashion the portrait verges on caricature. However, in the study of the girl, Marie, the emotional charge is too great for what occurs to her to be read as anything other than entirely serious. For Marie desires a child and, like the Virgin Mary after whom she is named, she believes herself to be pregnant. However, her desire and belief are treated as a phantom pregnancy, she is seized by two ambulance drivers who turn out to be doctors, hospitalised and infantilised – we see her in bed with a teddy bear, cutting pictures out of a magazine. She is later placed in a straitjacket, interrogated and obliged to undergo psychiatric treatment. The treatment of Marie is brutal and frightening since she is virtually tortured for her desires.

**Marie pour mémoire** prefigures Garrel's later films in its recourse to Christian imagery, its association of the experience of gestation and childbirth with the life of the artist and in its depiction of the violent exercise of power. However, it is a difficult film to follow since it mixes realist styles of acting and a modern setting with a narrative which is, at least in part, mystical. Aspects of it have dated rather badly, in particular the portrait of the father as an exploitative crook which, today, looks like a simplistic parody of many of the political slogans of the 1960s, and it does not have the visual richness of his two subsequent films. On the other hand, **Marie pour mémoire** is a film made by a very young man whose constant return to these themes in later films testifies to the seriousness of his concerns.

There followed a triptych composed of **Le Lit de la vierge**, **Athanor** and **La Cicatrice intérieure** (1972) (in practice **Athanor**, which went through several versions, is an offcut of **La Cicactrice intérieure**). The first was made in Morocco and the second two in Egypt, locations chosen for the simultaneous poverty and splendour of their landscapes, which for viewers brought up in the Judaeo-Christian tradition are associated with the founding events of Western civilisation. Indeed, the search for and interpretation of the origins of life and of man recur throughout Garrel's films and are reflected in their titles – 'lit' (bed), 'berceau' (cradle), 'origines' (origins) and so on. These works were produced by Zanzibar Films, the company financed by Silvina Boissonas,[10] and their visual richness, together with the unhurried unfolding of their shots, particularly in **La Cicatrice intérieure**, clearly have to do with the comparatively generous resources Garrel had available.

**Le Lit de la vierge** returns to the imagery of the Christian nativity but with some departures from the received version of the story. The film opens with shots of the sea and then positions the camera above the head of a woman who is apparently lying on a rock jutting out to sea. For some considerable time the camera looks through her knees, which are drawn up in the classic posture of parturition, before it draws back and a young adult male figure appears from below and to the side of the woman. We assume this is Christ. Thus Garrel marries an image of the virgin birth with a witty reversal of the genesis myth (here man is born from a woman's rib and not vice versa) and a gesture towards theories of evolution and our universal origin in the sea. Pierre Clémenti is cast in the Christ role, his thin, frail-looking body, dark beard and sombre eyes perfectly incarnating the attitude of slightly epicene suffering characteristic of portraits of Christ by the Mannerist School that Garrel has said he admires.[11] However, the life of Christ is updated and its sequence scrambled. His baptism, teaching in the temple, encounter with Mary Magdalen, Calvary, and descent into hell are all referred to but in a way that suggests they are cultural reference points rather than episodes in the exemplary biblical tale. Thus the Calvary sequence occurs early in the

film. The Roman soldiers are dressed like members of the Klu
Klux Klan and they pursue Clémenti, who is on horseback,
through the streets of mud houses in much the same way as an
enemy might be run out of town in a Hollywood western. It is
a frightening and violent sequence filmed in a continuous
tracking shot, which adds to its relentlessness, and it perfectly
succeeds in universalising the Christian myth by associating
biblical and contemporary forms of persecution. However,
Christ's baptism to the accompaniment of rock music and in
the company of a group of hippies is less convincing, and
when he descends into a hell which consists of a series of
underground tunnels, poorly lit by braziers and torches, we
have little sense of fear. For Garrel it is clear that terror is
primarily psychological and he has said of this film 'It is post-
1968. Everyone is unhappy.' Thus **Le Lit de la vierge**
embodies the quest for spiritual values and different ways of
living which is typical of one aspect of post-1960s politics, the
feeling that western civilisation, and in particular the consumer society, is pointless and corrupt. It is an attitude which
is parodied in a work such as Georges Perec's novel, *Les
Choses*, in which the protagonists leave the 'developed' world
of Paris for North Africa in the belief that they will find a
simpler but somehow more authentic life there. Such attitudes
were no less real for being naive and Garrel was clearly
influenced by and to some extent subscribed to such ideas
even though he attempts to place them in a broader cultural
context and, above all, to draw on a wider visual tradition
which embraces both western painting and the Hollywood
cinema.

131

**Le Lit de la vierge** might be considered a modern pastoral. **Athanor/La Cicatrice intérieure** (1972) which followed it is more sophisticated and visually extremely beautiful but it is also more mannered and difficult to follow than its predecessor. Garrel has explained that he took the title of **Athanor** from the crucible in which alchemists brew their concoctions in their search for the philosopher's stone (alchemy also figured in one of the scenes of hell in **Le Lit de la vierge**).[12] He has similarly remarked of **La Cicatrice intérieure**: 'you must not look at this film and ask yourself questions, you must look at it in the same way as you might enjoy walking in the desert. The film consists of traces and of what goes through my head at the time I'm filming. It can only be traces or milestones'.[13] In these films (treated as one for the purposes of discussion) landscape comes into its own both as pure visual experience, with the barren expanses of the Egyptian desert providing the freedom for Garrel to develop his long pans and tracking shots, and as a laboratory for observing the play of light, with the shimmering brilliance of these hot lands generating naturally some of the lighting effects Garrel had sought elsewhere. The desert landscape also serves as a canvas or *tabula rasa* on which to inscribe the past and the future and on which to pose human figures, perhaps as 'milestones', a neutral backdrop against which to explore spatial and temporal relationships or to throw the human face into strong relief.[14] Finally, at a metaphorical level, the emptiness and barrenness of the desert perfectly figure the film maker's need to search for traces and indications on which to hang interpretation.

This quest is reflected elsewhere in the film's iconography which, like that of **Le Lit de la vierge**, is used to refer to a mythical or cultural tradition. It is apparent in references to both Oedipus and Theseus when the naked Pierre Clémenti wanders with bow and arrow or when the sails of his boat change from black to white. These are two heroes of Greek myths defeated in their quest for knowledge. However, whereas **Le Lit de la vierge** convincingly modernised traditional Christian imagery, **La Cicatrice intérieure** relies heavily on that of Ingres and the Symbolist tradition, both in its reference to Greek mythology and in its numerous other references to the Arthurian legends and the Grail quest. Because Garrel chooses to see such myths in terms of the nineteenth century the film appears at times extremely mannered and even precious.

132

Garrel has referred to **La Cicatrice intérieure** as a new departure: 'my films begin with **La Cicatrice intérieure**; the others are all in the past', adding that it constitutes 'a film based on the couple'. It therefore adumbrates the theme that was to be explored in depth in **L'Enfant secret**. With **Athanor**, **La Cicatrice** was the first film he made with his partner Nico and he also casts himself in the role of her partner. Both the dialogue, which is in English, and the acting have moments that are painfully stilted, as the pair play out the dialectic of dependency and rejection that the film explores. When Garrel described it as being 'anti-fascist' he was presumably referring as much to interpersonal relations as to national politics. Moreover, because the Garrel–Nico relationship is the centrepiece of these two films the director violates his own rules about pleasure in the cinema. Thus in **Athanor** Nico and Zouzou are seen sitting with their backs to the camera looking out through the embrasure of a castle. Both actresses are naked and their pose is stylised, resembling that of Ingres's women, yet it also introduces an almost tangible sensuality which is rare in Garrel's films. The result is that both in **Athanor** and in **La Cicatrice intérieure** the use of autobiographical material is uncomfortable, intrusive and not entirely convincing.

In the mid and late 1970s, Garrel made a series of films, **Les hautes Solitudes** (1974), **Un Ange passe** (1975), **Le Berceau de cristal** (1976), **Voyage au jardin des morts** (1977) and **Le Bleu des origines** (1978), which have been described by Alain Philippon as having 'a pronounced taste for the hermetic and the rarefied' and in which the film maker deliberately and perhaps almost stubbornly adopts the attitude of the artist in exile, so much so that towards the end of the decade he appeared to have run himself into an impasse.[15] With hindsight it is clear that Garrel also suffered some kind of breakdown at this time. However, the period of depression in which references to exile and suicide are frequent (in, for example, **Le Berceau de cristal** and **Le Voyage au jardin des morts**) came to an end when Garrel began making **L'Enfant secret**, a project which continued over three years, between 1979 and 1982.

The film is clearly autobiographical. But instead of proceeding as he had previously done in an effort 'always to transgress the laws of the modern cinema and to look for something even more modern', instead of attempting to treat his life as a pretext for poetic abstraction which had, to some dcgrcc, been the case with **La Cicatrice intérieure**, Garrel adopted a more realist approach. He wrote down a series of things that had happened to him and gave the list to the well-established scriptwriter Annette Wademant, whom he describes as 'a doctor for my soul, someone who cured me of being hermetic and who made it possible for me not to be afraid of having something to say'.[16] As a result Garrel dropped his 'puritanism' and his 'artist's pose' but acquired the freedom both to create a structured narrative and to engage with contemporary society.

     **L'Enfant secret** is divided into four parts, each of which might be said to correspond to aspects of Garrel's biography or to the preoccupations which run through his films, and which are titled 'The Caesarian section', 'The last of the warriors', 'The ophidian circle', and 'The disenchanted forests'. The central characters in the film, the actress Elie and the film maker Jean-Baptiste, bear names which perhaps refer back to Garrel's earlier religious preoccupations, but the film traces the relationship between the couple and with Elie's child, situating them squarely in contemporary society.

     A child is central to the film but the 'secret' child in question is also absent – from the thoughts of his father who ·refused to recognise him and from the life of his mother who declares herself, at one point, incapable of looking after him. The child's birth, it is implied in the title of the first section, is difficult and painful and his existence requires those responsible for him to sacrifice other concerns. Art and the family are seen here as virtually irreconcilable so that when her mother dies Elie tells Jean-Baptiste, 'I would have gone to see her more often if I hadn't made your film.' Similarly, when Jean-Baptiste is accosted by a prostitute who says she lives with her daughter, the film maker retorts 'I have no children, I prefer the revolution!'

     But despite the central characters' ambivalence about parenthood it is nevertheless seen not just as desirable but as correlative to artistic creation and difficult and painful for that reason too. The life of the artist is certainly seen as one in which personal relationships become entangled and ultimately intolerable, but nevertheless remain a positive force. In **L'Enfant secret** the confident revolutionary that Jean-Baptiste appears to be in 'The last of the warriors' becomes the depressive of 'The ophidian circle', in which he is admitted to psychiatric care and, with the consent of his mother, given electric shock treatment. These sequences, which are analogous to the hospital scenes of **Marie pour mémoire**, are disturbingly realistic, and it is clear that an artist is being tortured for his inability to come to terms with the world. On the other hand, Jean-Baptiste secures the love and assistance of Elie and another woman friend, and emerges from hospital. He then finds, however, that his relationship with Elie deteriorates; she becomes distant from him and depressed at her mother's death. Jean-Baptiste finally realises that Elie is a heroin addict and that her momentary absences, which had previously puzzled him, had been at times when she was buying or taking drugs. Elie is withdrawing from emotional involvements and her distance from Jean-Baptiste is demonstrated in one extraordinary sequence which begins with the couple sitting in a cafe conversing. She then tells Jean-Baptiste she no longer visits her son and he remonstrates. At this point she says she has to leave the cafe for a while, but Jean-Baptiste is able, from her image reflected on the window pane of the cafe, to witness her encounter with a drug dealer that is taking place behind his back and on the other side of the glass. This is a wonderful metaphor both for their distant relationship and of the cinema's capacity to show and to look, but at one remove, as it were, from reality.

**L'Enfant secret** places identifiable characters with human concerns and a capacity to suffer emotion and loss in a realistic social setting. It is, after a period of withdrawal, Garrel's acknowledgement that society exists and his expression of the pleasures and difficulties of showing it. On the other hand, it is not a naturalistic film. The firm structure permits thematic organisation rather than linear narrative development, enabling Garrel to concentrate on heightened or significant moments and sequences. Despite the apparently naturalistic material, therefore, **L'Enfant secret** does not differ in its approach to visual composition and narrative from **La Cicatrice intérieure**, except that its iconography is contemporary. Similarly, although the film concerns a couple with relatively ordinary preoccupations such as work and children this is less, in Garrel's eyes, an opportunity for sociological investigation or comment than a form of artistic purity or austerity. He has said that his politics centre on the couple: 'after all, a man and a woman are all that there is', but this is not the unit of consumption that Lelouch portrays but a form of restraint, a return to the elemental that is also perceptible in Garrel's use of landscape, what he calls 'completely refined elements'.[17] Garrel's achievement in this

135

film is to have portrayed a couple whose predicament is so exemplary as to be virtually abstract, at the same as rendering their pain so convincing it is almost tangible.

L'Enfant secret might be seen as the adult version of Droit de visite and, in the context of Garrel's career, it seems to have marked both a summing up and a new departure, since his two following films, Liberté la nuit and Elle a passé tant d'heures sous les sunlights reflect on the successes and failures of his earlier work. Elle a passé tant d'heures is a film about a film which is not made: 'the film is conjugated in the perfect conditional. It has not existed', recalling Duras's Le Camion in the process. It casts Garrel as Garrel and as film maker, together with other film makers such as Chantal Akerman and Jacques Doillon, and it consists of attempts at sequences, outlines or sketches which ultimately lead nowhere. But as with all Garrel films it has its moments of exquisite beauty, particularly in the filming of the human face.

Liberté la nuit, on the other hand, engages squarely with personal and political history. It is set at the time of the Algerian war and its central characters, played by Maurice Garrel and Emmanuelle Riva, are actors whose presence refers to that past (Garrel to his son's earlier films, Riva to her performance in Resnais's Hiroshima mon amour). The father is to some extent rehabilitated and forgiven in this film. Though he abandons his wife, his passion for a younger woman is seen as redemptive and he dies, if not heroically, then at least for a respectable cause, namely the Front de libération nationale (FLN).

The film is not merely set in the historically identifiable period of the 1950s, a period in which political loyalties were notoriously complicated and when even some of the most admirable individuals were compromised. The climate of uncertainty and betrayal is well depicted in Resnais's earlier films, Hiroshima mon amour and Muriel, so that the casting of Riva may be seen as a gesture towards Resnais. But the climate of the Algerian war, in which secrecy and conspiracy were so much the norm that a husband and wife could be ignorant of the fact that each was working for the same side, provides the perfect vehicle for Garrel to express his constant anxiety about the relationship between the personal and the political and between the personal and the cinema. The subject also provides an artistic answer to the question of history and of time through the use of black and white photography, which convincingly lends the images a period look, thereby obviating the need to be more explicit about location or even public events.

Throughout his career Garrel has succeded in making his films an expression of his personal concerns, whether or not these are fashionable, to the point where his *œuvre* as a whole can be read as an account of his life. He does this by casting himself, family and friends in his films, and by making intimate human relations the very centre of his preoccupations. He is thus an extreme example of the *auteur* if, by that, is meant the personal in cinema. However, such preoccupations have a political and artistic significance which are the source of his reputation. On the one hand, he explores the political concerns of the post-1968 generation, often impatient with existing political parties of the Left, concerned with issues such as fascism, torture and the environment but also with the relationship between the personal and the political. On the other hand, his constant variations on a theme, worrying at the same subject matter, only serve to foreground his vigorous experimenting with the resources of the camera. Ultimately it is the beauty of Garrel's films which have created his reputation, while his critique of TV and of mainstream cinema as mere offshoots of consumerism have led to an anti-naturalism which distinguishes him as a film maker.


## Jean Eustache

It is a decade since Jean Eustache died and his films are seen less and less frequently. Yet in the eyes of his contemporaries he was the major French film maker of the 1970s. His reputation is based on a combination of technical originality and the capacity to identify the concerns of a generation, which he did so magnificently in his three-and-a-half hour-long portrait of a group of young people, **La Maman et la putain** (1973). In his films he deliberately reworked many of the themes of the *nouvelle vague*, but in a manner appropriate to the new decade, by exploring his own biography in both documentary and fictional form so that he appeared, in the words of Philippe Garrel, to have 'said virtually everything about the problems of the generation born during and just after the war'.[18] Although, as we shall see, he disclaimed *auteurism*, his approach to film making was always innovative, and the powerful conjunction of life and art, rendered clearer and more poignant by his suicide in 1981, meant that Eustache came to be considered the *auteur* par excellence. His *œuvre* is, in the words of Philippe Garrel, 'difficult to rival',[19] and is therefore central to the post 1968 French cinema.

## The Film Maker as Ethnographer

Eustache made seven documentary films and edited several more.[20] His most interesting documentaries are those which explore aspects of life in the area where he was born (he was a native of Pessac in the Gironde) since, from his account of the making of these films, it becomes clear that the exploration of his own roots went hand-in-hand with an exploration of the sources of the cinema. The two versions of **La Rosière de Pessac** (1968, 1979), **Numéro zéro** (1971) and **Odette Robert** (1980), have much to teach about the methods and preoccupations of his fiction films and about his approach to the cinema in general.

The 'Rosière' is a young girl elected every year for her virtue and crowned in a ceremony presided over by the Mayor of Pessac. Eustache described how, in filming the event for the first time, he tried to intervene as little as possible. He used three cameras and three sound recordists and attempted to 'let the participants speak for themselves' without a voice-over commentary and without the need for obtrusive montage. The result is a film composed of long sequences which gives the impression of having been shot in real time.[21] The film was commissioned by the ORTF and one counter-model present in Eustache's mind was the conventional television documentary and its approach to sound and image. He vehemently rejected what he called the 'canalisation' imposed by voice-over commentary: 'as soon as a working class man is given five minutes on television, his particular way of speaking is immediately framed by that of other speakers who repeat what he says but in a way that is specifically re-coded to conform to television in France today'.[22] Like Garrel, Godard, and many other contemporaries, Eustache dreamed of an unmediated realism 'in which I did not speak myself but in which [I tried] to present the viewer directly with the events',[23] with the added desire to avoid a class-inspired patronisation. He sought a form of realism based partly on allowing formerly excluded groups to have their say and partly on a return to earlier techniques of film making in which the film maker's role, modelled on that of Louis Lumière, was merely one of recorder and facilitator:

*I would have liked the camera not to move (...) when it moves a great deal (...) it may be to make the viewer believe that something is happening or that cinema is being created (...) what I wanted was for the cinema to be simply the recording of reality without any subjective intervention or interference.*[24]

Eustache claimed a similar attempt had been made with **Le Cochon**, another documentary of country habits which he shot with Jean-Pierre Barjol in 1970: 'I challenged the notion of the director's eye (...) Since **Le Cochon** was filmed by two people who collaborated totally I really do not see how it is possible to talk of an *auteur* or of *co-auteurs*'.[25]

The anti-auteurist stance that Eustache seemed to adopt towards his documentaries, which was a direct contrast to the theories of the *nouvelle vague* if not their practice, has two distinctive elements within it. The first is a belief, consonant with the May 1968 movement, that the mass media corrupt reality for the viewer. In this context it is interesting that the first version of **La Rosière de Pessac** records the ceremony that took place in June 1968, while the Events were in full swing in Paris, and that the film crew, who agreed to continue with the film despite the turmoil in the industry, worked as a result 'without any passionate involvement which went very well with the tone I wanted to give my film'.[26] The second, which is linked to the attempt to be dispassionate, is that the film maker is an outsider looking in without preconceptions. Eustache's documentaries have an ethnographic dimension strongly influenced, as was the *nouvelle vague* in its realism, by Jean Rouch and the school of ethnographic film making, for they treat France, especially rural and provincial France, both as a subject worthy of study and as territory unknown to metropolitan television film crews and audiences. This was a stance which Eustache claimed to have sought since his first film and which he continued with **La Rosière**, which he called 'sort of a civilised version of **Les Maîtres fous**'.[27]

**Odette Robert** evinces a similar approach to film making. This work, which was again commissioned by television and broadcast in 1980, was in fact an edited version of the unshown **Numéro zéro**, shot in 1971. As the title of the earlier film suggests, it was intended as a prototype for a new departure when Eustache emerged from a depression into his greatest creativity in the first half of the 1970s. **Odette Robert** is a portrait of Eustache's grandmother, a frail, old peasant women in her eighties at the time of filming. Many of the elements of **La Rosière de Pessac** are to be found here: the anti-auteurist style which, apart from a short introductory sequence where Odette is shown walking down the road with her great-grandson, consists of simply placing the camera in front of the old woman and inviting her to talk; the record of an aspect of French life which has different values and virtues from those of the metropolis; above all, perhaps, the rejection of spectacle through the depiction of an old woman whose age, blindness, and consequent lack of narcissism, block any possible complicity with camera or audience. Thus **Odette Robert** is a cruel as well as a tender portrait, matching **Le Cochon** in its brutal realism and pointing to another assumption in Eustache's approach to film making, that lack of sentimentality is in some sense a guarantee of authenticity.

As with all ethnography, however, the dialectic of purity and danger is ever-present in Eustache's documentaries. First, whatever his claim to be dispassionate, he is massively implicated in these films. In the case of both **La Rosière** and **Odette Robert** the return to the film maker's origins, to his native village and his ancestors, is associated with a return to the origins of the cinema (with **La Rosière**) and to personal creativity (with **Odette Robert**). The old-fashioned virtue that the Rosière ceremony celebrates is posited as analogous to the aesthetic innocence of the primitive cinema: sexual innocence and aesthetic purity go hand-in-hand. However, by the paradox of documentary, Eustache is also aware that such innocence is a fiction, for in the second **Rosière**, times having changed, the woman elected is virtuous but married, while in **Odette Robert**, aesthetic honesty, based on refusal of both authorial intervention and of spectacle, amounts to emotional brutality.[28]

Thus Eustache's documentaries in fact imply approval of certain moral values among which are female virtue and peasant life (which is lent a moral dimension). The documentaries embody a fascinating dialectic of truth and fiction both with respect to the individuals they portray and in their approach to film making. On the one hand, reality is virtuous, but rarely found and rapidly disappearing; on the other hand, what makes reality objectively filmable is the existence of a spontaneous *mise en scène*, a fictionalisation which through filming gives the real its reality. Hence Eustache stated his desire in **La Rosière** to 'get back to a Louis Lumière approach in which as soon as something is filmed it goes directly in front of the viewer. There was no question of me making my mark on the film. I made **La Rosière** against the notion of the word art'.[29] But at the same time he remarked that

> *any ceremony [such as that of the 'Rosière'] 'is a model of* mise en scène *in the way it unfolds. It is a function of reality which constantly refers back to the* mise en scène *of the hierarchies in life (tradition, protocol, authority) (...) But none of these exist except as a function of the ceremony and of the film which confirms their existence. So thanks to the film they have enacted their own reality.*[30]

This perception is extremely significant in relation to Eustache's fiction films. These make no pretence at objectivity in their subject matter. Unlike the documentaries, whose titles adopt the objectivity of proper names or generic nouns, the titles of the fictions – **Les mauvaises Fréquentations, La Maman et la putain, Une sale Histoire** – often imply moral judgments. However, the power of Eustache's fiction films derives from the fact that these provocatively immoral stories create the illusion that they are a *mise en scène* of reality and that they are, in this way, self-authenticating, like the documentaries.

## Explorations of class, sexuality and gender

The ethnographic style is also a marked characteristic of Eustache's feature films, which are all impressive, not just for their apparently realistic portrayal of contemporary society but also for their capacity for the close observation, almost monitoring, of the detail of individual lives. To some extent, of course, Eustache does no more that follow a trend apparent in virtually all French cinema from the 1960s onwards of taking up themes of contemporary social concern, particularly in relation to young people.[31] Eustache's subject matter and *dramatis personae* are often shared with his *nouvelle vague* predecessors, especially Truffaut, and when **Du Côté de Robinson** and **Le Père Noël a les yeux bleus** first opened they were both discussed as contributions to the public debate about 'youth'.

However, what is perhaps exceptional about the young male characters which dominate Eustache's films is their highly developed anxiety about class and social origins, an anxiety which invites the assumption that the Daniel of **Mes petites Amoureuses** and **Le Père Noël** and the Alexandre of **La Maman** are partly autobiographical portraits. Indeed the films sometimes incorporate episodes known to have occurred in Eustache's life, such as the childhood spent with a loving grandmother, evoked in **Mes petites Amoureuses** as in **Odette Robert**. Eustache consistently and movingly relates class to poverty and social inferiority. Because they are poor his characters are often rootless or obliged to uproot themselves. The unfortunate woman in **Du Côté de Robinson** has left her violent husband and is wandering around a strange town; in **Le Père Noël** the young Daniel has to make ends meet in a strange town by disguising himself; in **Mes petites Amoureuses** Daniel had experienced life in the country, in that 'douce France' celebrated in the Charles Trenet song played over the title sequence, but is brutally removed from this existence and taken away from his grandmother to live with his mother and her lover in town, there to discover that he is poor. Above all, perhaps, whereas in **La Maman et la putain** all the women have professional or gainful occupations (Gilberte is a teacher, Veronika a nurse and Marie owns a dress shop), Alexandre has no visible means of support and no home and, indeed, describes himself, with only a touch of self-deprecation, as 'a young man who is poor and not very clever'.[32] Alexandre accuses Gilberte of rejecting him on the grounds of class: 'You were careful who you fell in love with, weren't you? You didn't choose a Portuguese worker, an Algerian immigrant or even a French worker.' He believes his rival has 'a prestigious job and a cultural inheritance' and accuses Gilberte of marrying him for money.[33] But this is also a political statement: Alexandre is as he is because of the political situation. **La Maman et la putain** is shot through with a sense of post-revolutionary sadness: '... we had the cultural Revolution, the Rolling Stones, May 1968, the Black Panthers, the Palestinians, the Underground and then nothing for the last two or three years'.[34] The list, in its comprehensive cosmopolitanism, draws attention to the constraint of Alexandre's life in St-Germain-des-Prés. It deliberately mixes personal and political liberation movements in a way typical of the period post-1968 but which also implies that Alexandre's personal failings are as much those of a society.

Eustache's realism is based on the authenticity of his locations, his refusal of spectacle (especially in **La Maman et la putain**, where the characters do not appear to be dressed or made up for the camera), naturalistic dialogue enhanced by sound recording, the refusal to 'prettify' (**La Maman et la putain** is shot in black and white since this is the dominant tone of the Paris streets) and an extreme austerity of *mise en scène*. Yet his films also depend on the emotional verisimilitude which is expressed in the social anxieties of the characters. Nowhere is this more true than in the field of sexuality. The problematical and changing nature of the relations between the sexes is a constant theme of Eustache's fiction films which, like those of the early *nouvelle vague*, take 'la drague' as their subject matter.[35] But whereas seduction is a narrative or comic device for the *nouvelle vague auteurs*, for Eustache it is an emotionally charged activity, and it is this approach to sexual encounters that gives his films much of their force and conviction.

In Eustache's investigations of the psychological and social dimensions of sexuality it has been suggested that he consistently adopts a male point of view, that he is a sexist and even, on occasions, a misogynist. To a degree, this would appear to be borne out by his documentaries which, as has been seen, are far from being dispassionate but imply approval of old-fashioned female virtues and values and link these with authenticity. In all Eustache's fiction films except for **La Maman et la putain** the central characters are indeed male while the women are given thankless roles and are treated either as insignificant, passive, to be exploited, or all of these things. In **La Maman et la putain**, however, this is not the case. Both Gilberte and Veronika are independent-minded women who, far from being used by Alexandre, oblige him to conform to their needs. Marie is a slightly different case. When the film opens Alexandre is living with her and is clearly supported by her (for example, he asks her to bring him back some clothes from her business trip to London). Alexandre then introduces Veronika into the ménage making it clear to Marie that he has a sexual relationship with her. Marie is jealous but she does not throw Alexandre out. It might be argued, therefore, that he fulfils her emotional needs just as much as she fulfils his material needs, or that in her capacity as 'mother', she takes a benevolent view of Alexandre's relationship with Veronika.

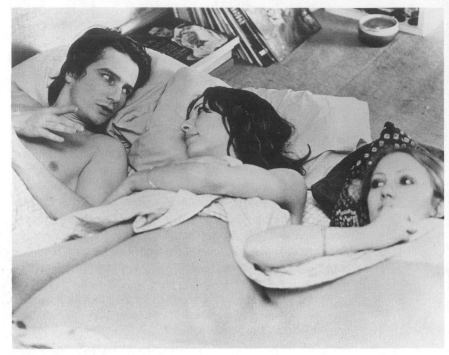

Veronika is a striking contrast to Marie. She is younger and, though employed, claims that she works purely to pay for her pleasures. Veronika is, apparently, a typical, liberated young women influenced by the ideas of the MLF (which is referred to anecdotally in the film) and who has symbolically given up wearing a bra.[36] And yet her long, drunken soliloquy at the end of the film is both an impassioned statement of liberty and an impassioned plea for love: 'Just because a girl is screwed by a lot of men in all kinds of different ways it doesn't mean she's a prostitute. I don't believe prostitutes exist, that's all.'[37] 'I only lost my virginity quite recently, when I was twenty (...) Since then I've had as many lovers as possible.'[38] And yet her sexual freedom proves to be unsatisfactory: 'the only really wonderful thing is to make love because you love each other so much that you'd like to have a child that looks like you, otherwise it's just sordid fucking'.[39] Coming from Veronika, whose freedom of language and conduct and whose apparent contempt not just for Alexandre but for all her lovers seems to designate her as the quintessential exponent of sex without attachment, this may seem a surprising statement and it is one which certainly runs counter to the tenets of sexual liberation and of feminism

La Maman et la putain – design for living with Jean-Pierre Léaud, Bernadette Lafont and Françoise Lebrun

144

predominant in the early 1970s, which rejected motherhood and the nuclear family as primary sites of female oppression. But in Veronika's moving address to camera what comes across is not her need for Alexandre, although that is present, so much as her need for the haven of the Alexandre–Marie couple: 'I love both of you.'[40] Any claim that Eustache is a 'sexist' or a 'misogynist' must therefore take account of the forceful character of Veronika, even to the extent that her final admission that she loves Alexandre and wishes to marry him is qualified by the violent attack of vomiting which immediately follows it.

Nevertheless, Eustache's male characters lend more weight to this claim. They follow an interesting evolution as his *œuvre* progresses, moving from sometimes aggressive physical relationships, to the mainly verbal interactions of **La Maman et la putain** (both Alexandre and Veronika existing primarily in and through words) to a virtual absence of male–female interactions in **Une sale Histoire**, where the women have been reduced to bit players, voices off or, indeed, an implied audience. A key figure in this process is that of the prostitute, even though it is only in **Le Père Noël** that Daniel actually visits a brothel. In **Du Côté de Robinson** the two young men rob the young woman out of revenge for having failed to seduce her. It is an exercise of male prerogative, a symbolic violation but also an inversion of the conventional venal relations between men and female prostitutes. Similarly, in **La Maman et la putain**, the financial traffic is from the women to the man, from Marie to Alexandre, although this time it is voluntary, while the designated 'whore' flouts the conventions by pursuing sex for pleasure not money.[41] Money and sex can therefore be interchangeable, always provided that the women in some way pay the men: because the young woman does not give the young men what they want she has to pay them; because Alexandre gives Marie what she wants, she has to pay him. The advantage of prostitution is that it avoids the dialectic of dependency and rejection that Veronika movingly and indeed violently expresses. Perhaps, therefore, Eustache might more accurately be described as misanthropic rather than misogynist since it is the individual's sexual desires, whether that individual is male or female, that make him or her vulnerable to others and this is seen as a weakness: 'People's sex lives are totally unimportant' as Veronika puts it.[42]

Any statement about Eustache's attitudes must be qualified by the knowledge that he is consciously working in

145

both a cinematic and a literary tradition. In his depiction of the lives of young men he both imitates and criticises the *nouvelle vague* in general and Truffaut in particular. Like Truffaut in the Antoine Doinel series, Eustache traces the life of a young man, Daniel/Alexandre, from childhood through adolescence to the age of thirty; as Truffaut had done, he casts the same actor, Jean-Pierre Léaud, in two out of three of the films;[43] and in **La Maman et la putain** he has Alexandre refer to the petty crime and delinquency which had characterised Doinel in Truffaut's **Les 400 coups**: 'When I was a child I used to steal books. I claimed that poverty was no reason for not getting an education.'[44] Like those of Truffaut, Eustache's films contain a series of inadequate mothers and maternal prostitutes;[45] **Mes petites Amoureuses** is a virtual remake of **Les Mistons** and it tempting to see the *ménage à trois* in **Jules et Jim** reworked to Eustache's taste in **La Maman et la putain**.[46]

Where Eustache differs from the *nouvelle vague* is in tone. At least after his initial films, Truffaut had none of Eustache's seriousness and commitment to innovation: 'Today, dare one say that Truffaut and Chabrol are almost making the kind of films they attacked when they were critics? That's how I see it,' was how Eustache put his reservations in 1978.[47] By the same token, casting Jean-Pierre Léaud in a role which exaggerates some of the characteristics of Doinel to the point where they become mannered and even caricatural is surely strongly critical not merely of Truffaut's films but, given the relationship between Doinel and Truffaut, of Truffaut himself.

In addition to the *nouvelle vague*, the film makers to whom Eustache owes his greatest debt are Lubitsch and Renoir. In Lubitsch he appreciated the dialectic of appearance and reality and the use of play-acting which are to be found in **To be or not to be** and he imitated the *ménage à trois* of **Design for Living** in **La Maman et la putain**. It is interesting, however, that Eustache's design for living is pessimistic and disillusioned where Lubitsch's (adapted from the Noel Coward play) is light and comic. The Lubitsch characters are real artists living in the Bohemian Paris of the 1920s, whereas Eustache's Alexandre merely hangs out in a former artists' cafe in St-Germain-des-Prés but has no creative activity whatsoever. Lubitsch's female protagonist tries bourgeois marriage but finds it excruciatingly dull and is delighted to be rescued from it by her Bohemian lovers, whereas Eustache ends with a proposal of matrimony. Finally, where Lubitsch has two men and one woman, Eustache inverts this situation to the advantage of the man, however inadequate he may be. ('You're lucky Alexandre, having two girls who love you,' says Veronika.)

The presentation of disillusionment and the reliance on actors was undoubtedly what Eustache primarily admired in Renoir. The stylised sexual interactions and the elaborate *mise en scène* of life depicted in the codes and conventions of **La Règle du jeu** were a clear inspiration to him, while **Une partie de campagne** (adapted by Renoir from the Maupassant short story) sums up much of what Eustache's characters elsewhere appear to believe about sexual or erotic encounters: that they are followed by hostility between the actors and that they have value only when recalled as past.[48]

Through Renoir Eustache's debt to the French nineteenth century becomes apparent, to the mores depicted not just in Maupassant but also in Flaubert and in Rimbaud. Indeed, his works might be seen as extended *éducation sentimentale*. For example, Eustache himself referred to Flaubert's novel in the context of **Le Père Noël**, recalling particularly a moment in the novel when Frédéric and his friends remember an evening spent in a brothel as 'the best moment of our lives' as a point of comparison with his film,[49] but also using the novel to illustrate how the film is a

Mes petites Amoureuses – Jean Eustache on the set with Maurice Pialat

```
MON
TON
SON    IMAGE
```

NUMERO DEUX

```
- c'est pas de la politique,
  c'est du cul.

- non, c'est pas du cul,
  c'est de la politique.
```

technique for distancing himself from his involvements. Thus **Le Père Noël** is viewed both as a 'sentimental education' in the obvious sense and as a portrait of 'a character who recounts what he has done in order to distance himself from it: look how young and stupid I was'.[50] A similar, if more vehemently expressed, sentiment is to be found in the Rimbaud poem from which **Mes petites Amoureuses** borrows its title.[51] The poem is sardonic, contemptuous and misogynist, with the speaker transposing his self-disgust on to the earlier objects of his affections:

> O mes petites amoureuses
> Que je vous hais
> (...)
> Et c'est pourtant pour ces éclanches
> Que j'ai rimé
> Je voudrais vous casser les hanches
> D'avoir aimé

('Oh, my little mistresses,/How I hate you (...) And yet after all it's for these shoulders of mutton/That I've made rhymes/ I'd like to break your hips/For having loved') (translation by Oliver Bernard).

This poem clearly embodies many of the attitudes explored in Eustache's films: the wish for revenge felt by the two young men in **Du Côté de Robinson**, the aggressive reaction towards the dependency induced by love experienced by Veronika, the tendency to blame women, a self-disgust which, like Veronika's, is Célinian in its violence. But above all the tense of the poem is important: 'having loved'. Alexandre and Daniel *recall* their lives, they do not live them. Gilberte, who is surely named after the object of Marcel's affections in Proust's novel, can play the role of lost love for Alexandre precisely because the relationship is finished. Where love ends art begins and, more important, love must end for art to begin. Alexandre can rehearse his speech and perform his act; physical passion is transmuted into discourse and even his present relationships are informed by role-playing: the 'mother' and the 'whore'. Eustache's male characters, and especially Alexandre, all watch themselves playing a variety of roles and reproduce in fictional form what has happened to them in the past. To adopt the expression used by Michel Foucault, they illustrate the *mise en discours* of sex characteristic of contemporary society, but they also treat human relations as *mise en scène*.[52]

Eustache's explorations of sexuality therefore have three main components. First, their general misanthropy and the particular difficulties experienced by characters such as Veronika challenge the contemporary view of sex as liberation. Second, they present male–female relations as existing essentially in the realm of fantasy, again challenging the innocence of liberationist beliefs by exploring expressions of desire or pleasure that are always already constructed and *mises en scène* because they are literary or perverse. There is no room for the conventional heterosexual couple in Eustache's depiction of prostitution, the *ménage à trois* or scopophilia. Third, if these films are the *mise en discours* of sex, this is a process which is surprising in the cinema, which is often held to be an essentially visual medium, but they are all the more remarkable because, as Réné Prédal has pointed out, the early 1970s was a period in France when 'explicit' and 'hard core' sex films became widely screened, so that Eustache practises a deliberate restraint which must be understood as another critique of the habits of the commercial cinema.

## Narrative Strategies

**La Maman et la putain** is a tour de force. Its examination of the futile lives of its three central characters is rendered pitiless by the film's exceptional length (it runs for over three and a half hours), its visual austerity, its discursive realism and its refusal of spectacle. It stands alone in contemporary French cinema as a monument to a style of film making and to a generation. Despite this, it is perhaps Eustache's last fiction film, **Une sale Histoire**, which draws together most effectively and most comprehensively the various strands of his work and best illuminates his narrative strategies. Since Eustache described **Une sale Histoire** as an episode 'left over' from **La Maman et la putain** it can be legitimately viewed as a coda to his masterpiece containing, as such addenda often do, the structure of the work as a whole in miniature or in *mise en abîme*.

**Une sale Histoire** consists of two films of more or less the same length (28 and 22 minutes), the first shot on 35mm in conventional Hollywood manner with clear framing and a recognisable set; the second on 16mm in documentary or direct cinema style with a naturalistic soundtrack and less clear cut framing. The first casts Michel Lonsdale, Jean Douchet and four women; the second Jean-Noël Picq and four women. The two male protagonists are in fact narrators. They speak the same text in which each recounts how he used to enjoy going downstairs to the ladies' toilets in a particular cafe, lying virtually flat on the floor in one of the cubicles and gazing up through the gap beneath the partition wall at women as they used the toilet. As a result of this each discovered the beauty of the female pudenda, that 'looking' is as exciting as 'having' and, following Sade, that eroticism depends on the anonymity of the object of desire but disappears as soon as a relationship based on knowledge or familiarity is established.

This film sums up Eustache's cinema in a number of ways. First, in its use of both a structure and an aesthetic style to question cinema's relation to reality. In the first, 'Michel Lonsdale', version there is apparently no doubt that the film is a fiction, albeit a surprising one. Both the style of filming and the discussion with the female audience are represented in such a way that we know a creative hand has been at work and that Lonsdale is an actor discussing a part with a producer. However, the addition of a second part, billed as 'adapted

Une sale Histoire – Jean Eustache talks to Michel Lonsdale

150

from a story by Jean-Noël Picq', which is a repetition of the first, calls into question the certainty of the fiction. The Picq version is shot as though it were a documentary. Must it therefore be true? Is part two the source of part one? Which is the reality and which the rehearsal of it? Is Picq describing what he used to do, or what Eustache used to do? Throughout Eustache's work, as we have seen, he juxtaposes documentary and fiction to question the assumptions on which both are based. He goes further than before in **Une sale Histoire** since the story told, whether true or fictional, is scandalous and perverse. If it is a fiction, then it is an extraordinary choice of subject; if it is true, then it is astonishing that the narrators should be so open about their sexual perversions.

Looking back over Eustache's *œuvre* it is possible to establish a whole series of doublets, remakes or stories within stories of this kind. There are two versions of **La Rosière de Pessac**, two of **Odette Robert**, **Les mauvaises Fréquent-ations** consists of a double bill of **Du Côté de Robinson** and **Le Père Noël**, alleged by René Prédal to be 'nostalgie cinéphilique du double programme';[53] **Mes petites Amoure-uses**, as Deleuze has pointed out, is structured like a diptych and there are two women in **La Maman et la putain**. This kind of formalism is probably typical of the literature and the cinema of the period. In the 1950s Godard had already expressed admiration for William Faulkner's *Wild Palms* and the hope that he would one day make a film structured in the same way. In the 1970s this was often the case, with Robbe-Grillet, Marguerite Duras and Raul Ruiz providing examples. Nevertheless in **Une sale Histoire** Eustache goes further than any of his contemporaries, in adopting almost exact repetition, and this leads to a very significant closure.

The second level on which **Une sale Histoire** typifies Eustache's *œuvre* is in its attitude to women and what it requires of them as spectators, a question which Picq informs us exercised Eustache's attentions considerably.[54] The activity described in the film is scopophilia – pleasure in looking – which Freud describes as the concomitant of exhibitionism.[55] As if to prove the point, one of the women listening offers to undress at one point during the tale. The scopophilia described here is at first autoerotic and it is dependent on the anonymity and objectification of the women looked at. In fact, however, the narrator follows the trajectory outlined by Freud from voyeur to exhibitionist himself, although he does not do so physically but verbally. In offering a narrativisation of scopophilia and providing an audience, Eustache imagines a perfect psychological economy of the perversion which is also an aesthetic economy since the film contains not merely the story but the audience for it. As Chantal Labre has suggested, this film blocks or closes off any discussion on the part of the 'real' audience by providing both the genesis of the work and the reception of it, and it is this that renders it misogynist.[56] **Une sale Histoire** may be read as a model of the structure of the cinema which consists of male voyeurs inspecting anonymous but female objects, divorced from context or 'framed' as one might say, so that their most private parts are aestheticised, and it obliges a female audience to watch a male creator fantasising this cinema.

Finally, **Une sale Histoire** completes Eustache's progress from relationships based on physical contact to those entirely based on words because they are progressively recalled, fictionalised and *mises en scène*. Eustache shares with Marguerite Duras the belief that the cinema is as much created by words as by images. In Duras's **Le Camion** the transgressive element is provided by the contrast between the lorry which is coded as male and the diminutive female creator. In Eustache, it is provided by narrating rather than showing perversion. But in the end, Eustache's masters are the novelists of the nineteenth century because their art consisted in the aestheticisation of sexual encounters, and he is one of the few film makers to have found an equivalent to the narrative modes of the nineteenth century rather than simply to have adapted nineteenth century fiction to the screen.

# 6:

# In Search of the Popular Cinema: Bertrand Tavernier and the Return to the 'Tradition de Qualité'

The opposition between the 'tradition de qualité' and the 'cinéma d'auteurs', so mordantly defined by François Truffaut in the 1950s,[1] did not die with the demise of the *nouvelle vague*, although it was often recast as an opposition between mainstream and avant-garde film making. As Jean Eustache remarked as late as 1978: 'What a large section of the public is interested in today is intelligence, sensitivity, how serious the subject is and how well it is tackled; but that has nothing to do with creativity, pleasure or the enrichment of cinema'.[2] Bertrand Tavernier's films closely match Eustache's definition of what is popular. They are accessible and easy to watch, their locations are often beautiful, their actors give polished and convincing performances and they discuss intelligent subjects seriously. But while Tavernier assumes the popular heritage of the 1950s, what is interesting is that he simultaneously pursues an *auteur* cinema, hence the inscription of the conflict of generations as a trope within so many of his films and most notably his first, **L'Horloger de Saint Paul**.[3] For Tavernier's is a highly conscious attempt to create a popular cinema through a rejection of the *nouvelle vague* and through a particular approach to history and to the influence of American cinema and culture.

## A New Traditionalist

Tavernier's first feature film, **L'Horloger de Saint Paul** (1973), clearly signalled his rejection of the *nouvelle vague*, since it was scripted by Jean Aurenche and Pierre Bost, authors, according to Truffaut, of all that was reprehensible in the cinema of the 1950s.[4] The collaboration was in fact so

153

successful that Tavernier himself wrote a further three films with Jean Aurenche: **Que la Fête commence** (1975), **Le Juge et l'assassin** (1976) and **Coup de torchon** (1981).[5] Taking this group of films as a whole we can attempt to define what Tavernier rejected in the *nouvelle vague* and what were the positive aspects of a return to the 1950s both in narrative and visual terms. Tavernier, it is clear, subscribes to a form of psychological realism which the *nouvelle vague* rejected. He has a highly developed sense of society, social processes and of the influence of history on the individual. Sometimes, as in **Des Enfants gâtés**, this can lead to crude attempts to equate social, sexual and emotional exploitation, but elsewhere the influence of society is more subtly treated. We are invariably told at the opening of Tavernier films where and when the action takes place and because history is seen as an important actor he often chooses to situate his films at moments which represent well-known and easily identifiable ruptures or turning points such as May 1968 in **L'Horloger de Saint Paul.**

By contrast, the typical *nouvelle vague* film has little sense of history or psychology and tends to show human interactions either in the form of dialogue rather than action, or if in the form of action then in caricatural or pastiche mode (such as Godard's imitations of American gangster films or musicals) usually divorced from cause and effect. Tavernier's films also tend to have a strong sense of cultural history, which is used to render them popular, and this undoubtedly explains his affinity with Aurenche and Bost. Literary adaptation was a major genre in French film making in the 1950s (and indeed in French television in the 1960s). The exploitation of well-known works of literature, particularly the classics of the nineteenth century, was a form of moral reconstruction specifically intended for the popular audience. What was said of television in the 1960s might equally be applied to cinema in the 1950s: 'If one looks closely at television drama at the beginning of the 1960s it can be seen that it is great nineteenth century television, designed to exploit the international cultural heritage'.[6] 'France is a country with a heritage and a country which is nostalgic for its period of power'.[7] What the television producer Marcel Bluwal called 'the *nouvelle vague* terrorism'[8] temporarily expelled popular moral didacticism from the cinema during the 1960s, and this was something that Tavernier, in films such as **Que la Fête commence** and even more in **Le Juge et l'assassin**, set out to recapture.

154

Tavernier's emphasis on history and psychology and on the influence of the social and historical environment on the individual has its visual counterpart. His actors are always filmed in relation to a landscape which provides their measure and their dimension, whereas the typical *nouvelle vague* film has little spatial location. Tavernier's characters move in space, they exist in three dimensions, whereas those of the *nouvelle vague*, as Deleuze has so perceptively pointed out,[9] tend to glide along walls, for all the world like the two-dimensional characters in cartoons or pulp fiction whom they sometimes, indeed, represent. In Godard's **Pierrot le fou**, for example, the protagonists read *La Bande des pieds nickelés* and cast themselves as heros of a cartoon strip or a Vietnam morality play while they are visually represented against a flat backdrop (a wall, the sea) without spatial or temporal landmarks. By contrast, Tavernier's characters, in **Le Juge et l'assassin**, in **La Passion Béatrice** or in **Coup de torchon** are precisely situated within the immensity of a landscape and are shown to be influenced by it.

Some of these contrasts can be illustrated by looking at Tavernier's first, and therefore to some extent programmatic, film, **L'Horloger de Saint Paul**, which takes the conflict of generations and the clash of old and new values as its central theme, and which pursues this theme in relation to society, politics and the cinema. The action takes place in Lyon, which is identified in a number of ways.[10] This city was Tavernier's birthplace, so the film represents to some extent a return to his roots. It also has a reputation for traditional gastronomy and for conservatism, both of which are explored in the film. The hero, Michel Descombes, is presented as a man pursuing the traditional craft of watchmaking in an old quarter of a conservative city and spending his leisure hours with a bunch of cronies who appreciate old-fashioned cooking. When they foregather in their regular meeting place the Restaurant Chauvin it is to defend the old against the new and the French against foreign imports (hence, perhaps, the xenophobic connotation of the restaurant's name). 'Hell, for me,' Descombes remarks, 'is paved with fast food restaurants, Wimpy Bars and self-service diners. Can you imagine, an eternity of hormone-injected chickens and grilled steak with "herbes de Provence" '.[11]

Craftsman that he is, Descombes is against mass production, which is seen as deleterious to health, against progress, which is seen as destructive of quality, and against

the inauthentically regional 'aux herbes de Provence'. However, his tranquil life is disrupted when he learns that his son
Bernard is being sought by the police for the murder of the
nightwatchman of a local factory, and a change in his attitude
then occurs. For it then turns out that although Bernard is
indeed a murderer he was defending his girlfriend against the
harassment of Razon, the nightwatchman who sought to take
sexual advantage of the women workers and to threaten them
with losing their jobs if they were not compliant. In the best
1968 tradition, Bernard strikes a blow against the oppressive
exercise of power which his father comes to understand.
Descombes realises that he knows virtually nothing of his
son and is completely out of touch with his generation.
Moreover, he strikes up a friendship with Commissaire
Guibout, who is investigating the case and discovers that he
suffers family difficulties similar to his own. Thus when
Bernard is tried and receives a long prison sentence, his
father stands by him and offers to take care of the child that
his girlfriend Liliane is expecting.

Politically, **L'Horloger de Saint Paul** clearly tries to
suggest that after the conflicts of the preceding years some
reconciliation and recognition of mutual benefit are possible.

The moral problematic is quintessentially Aurenche and Bost as Truffaut defined it, that of a conflict between individual conscience and public morality: murder is wrong but Bernard was right to kill Razon. Yet Descombes ends up subscribing neither to the conventional morality which prohibits fornication and murder nor to the new moral values ushered in by May 1968 and which rejected authoritarianism and the police as agents of it, for he is friendly with Commissaire Guibout and simultaneously reconciled with his son. However, the symbolic continuity of generations is not altogether convincingly carried through and Descombes's offer to look after Liliane's child seems contrived in the context, since the pregnancy had not previously been mentioned in the film. Nor is the film completely unified in tone and style and this may derive from the attempt to marry social and political concerns with those of an artistic or filmic nature.

The opening sequence, which shows a train rushing through the night carrying a little girl who looks out of the window at a car being burned, seems to suggest the film will be a thriller. It turns out that the burning car is a reference to the May Events, but these are not subsequently shown in scenes of violent action but as a minor source of irritation, as comic, or as a catalyst for moral enquiry. A similar attempt at naturalisation of the American film tradition is at work in the scenario, for the film is adapted from a Simenon novel, *L'Horloger d'Everton* which itself already married the French and American traditions. The novel has all the hallmarks of Simenon at his best – the setting in a small, conservative community, the depiction of a central character who by his work, as well as his inclination, is isolated and obsessive (*Les Fantômes du chapelier* is a comparable example), the creation of a relationship of dependency between the hunter and the hunted – but it is set in small town America.[12] **L'Horloger de Saint Paul** shows Tavernier attempting to synthesise the French and American film traditions of the 1950s. The characterisation of Commissaire Guibout is typically French – he is a distant descendant of Jouvet's Inspector Antoine in **Quai des orfèvres** – while that of the watchmaker owes something to the stage Frenchmen incarnated by Jean Gabin in the films of the 1950s (Descombes imitates Gabin's diction in his diatribe against fast food). But some of the film is shot in the style of a *film noir* while the political backdrop is reminiscent of the melodramatic scenarios of 1950s Hollywood. The synthesis is not altogether successful or coherent but it does point to a concern which has preoccupied Tavernier throughout his subsequent career.

## The Historian of French Society

After **L'Horloger de Saint Paul** Tavernier made two history films in quick succession, **Que la Fête commence** (1975) and **Le Juge et l'assassin** (1976). Despite the change of period, these films represent the continuation of the first in a number of ways. Both cast Phillipe Noiret in central roles and both were written by Jean Aurenche in collaboration with Tavernier himself. **Que la Fête commence** was inspired by Tavernier's reading of Alexandre Dumas's novel *La Fuïte du Régent*,[13] but it also bears some relation to the costume dramas popular in the cinema of the 1950s with films such as Sacha Guitry's **Si Versailles m'était conté**, as well as to the television history series popular in the 1960s which were, as we have seen, so brilliantly deconstructed by Raul Ruiz. Thus part of Tavernier's project is to reach back to the popular cinema of an earlier period and to attempt to update it thematically whilst retaining such things as the lush colour, the attention to period detail and the business of interaction between master and servant which fills much of such drama.

But there is also much in **Que la Fête commence** to differentiate it from earlier costume drama. The choice of period was not innocent. The Regency of Philippe d'Orléans, which lasted from the death of Louis XIV in 1715 to 1723 when Louis XV attained his majority, is described in conventional histories as 'characterised by unique effrontery, innovation and frivolous immorality',[14] exactly the material of costume drama. But it was also a period of change and instability following the death of a ruler of great power and influence, so that the parallel between the Regency and the post-Gaullist period (that of the making of the film) is inescapable. Indeed, the satirical newspaper, *Le Canard enchaîné*, dubbed this period 'La Régence'.

Why choose a historical rather than a modern subject if the subject was in reality modern society? First, undoubtedly, in an effort to make a film of wide popular appeal. Some of the more tiresome features of the film, such as girls in various states of undress, conform to the rules of the genre. But there were other reasons too. Political censorship was still strongly

Que la Fête commence
– Jean-Pierre Marielle as
the Marquis de Pontcalec
about to be deported to
Louisiana

practised in the French cinema and this simultaneously rendered historical topics attractive whilst stimulating film makers to make free with received opinions or versions of history. Tavernier himself quotes Michelet's dictum to the effect that in history 'you have to learn not to be respectful'.[15] There were also recent examples of disrespectful or frivolous treatments of the most solemn events of French history such as Bud Yorkin's comedy, **Start the Revolution without Me** (1970) banned, inevitably, in France. Second, Tavernier was influenced both in **Que la Fête commence** but even more in **Le Juge et l'assassin** by the 'new history', which tended to eschew traditional political and constitutional events in favour of social and economic history based on the exploitation of different archive sources. Thus the Regent, in the film, is shown almost entirely in his domestic character, much indeed as Saint-Simon had shown Louis XIV, while the political events which impinge on the tale all take place either in the provinces or even outside metropolitan France. Tavernier here joins forces with other film makers such as Allio or Techiné, who also attempted to tell history from a different point of view.

Like the watchmaker's son, the central characters in **Que la fête commence** are all in some way in revolt against the

159

old order. Though the Regent spends much of his time in debauchery he is presented as a reforming ruler who proposes to expropriate the church and provide free education. The Abbé Dubois is devoid of religious conviction, despite his calling, and has merely used the church as a means of social promotion, assisted in this by the Regent himself. The Marquis de Pontcalec is a Breton nationalist who attempts to mount a popular revolution in Brittany so as to free himself and his people from the oppression of Paris and, when this fails and he is arrested, he strongly resists deportation to Louisiana. Regional autonomist movements and the history of French colonialism are not often found in comedies of court life and they place it in an interesting perspective as well as providing another link with the politics of the 1970s: the 1968 movement had led to denunciations of colonialism of all kinds, beginning with the American presence in Vietnam and, in the name of self-determination, France had seen a large number of regional autonomist movements spring up. Moreover, it will be recalled that the pretext chosen by De Gaulle for his retirement from office in 1969 was his defeat in the referendum on the regions!

Like its predecessor, this film is a hybrid in which expressions of revolt against the established order are not always matched by aesthetic innovation. It is only in the Breton episodes that Tavernier comes close to the superb use of the natural environment that is to be found in some of his later films. Too much of **Que la Fête commence** is dull to look at and too many of its challenges to authority, particularly its conventional anti-clericalism, seem tame. There are symbolic episodes which are so clumsily integrated into the whole that they suggest the scriptwriters had difficulties in achieving an appropriate ideological resolution. The Regent, for example, has sudden intimations of mortality and, having shown a superb disregard for the death of others, including his own daughter, he now imagines that his hand is putrefying and requires it to be amputated forthwith. His party sets off at full speed in a carriage to see the doctor (called Chirac, perhaps after the Prime Minister of the day) and such is their haste that they run over a peasant boy who inadvertently stands in their way. The film closes on a group portrait of the dead boy, his sister and the Regent's mistress who attempts to comfort the girl while she declares, for all the world to hear, that the day will come when the peasants will have their revenge. This finale is highly embarrassing. But in this episode and in another in which the Regent's ward, Séverine, refuses to

160

come to Paris to be his mistress because, as a Breton, she sympathises with Pontcalec, the film does adumbrate a movement which gathers force in Tavernier's films and reaches full expression in **La Passion Béatrice**, by which the mantle of revolt gradually passes from the men to the women.

Le Juge et l'assassin (1976), by contrast, is set at the end of the nineteenth century and concerns a series of murders of shepherdesses and other young girls committed between 1893 and 1898 by Joseph Vachet (Bouvier in the film) an ex-army sergeant turned tramp. The Aurenche–Tavernier script was clearly influenced in two major respects by new approaches to the social sciences and, in particular, by Michel Foucault's work: first, the exploitation of 'popular history' in the use of hitherto unexplored archive material (it should be noted that René Allio's film version of **Moi Pierre Rivière** came out in the same year), in order to achieve a different perspective on a period; second, the critique of the French penal and judicial systems which raised questions about the definitions of madness and sanity by suggesting that these are as much social as clinical. Finally, in a manner characteristic both of Foucault and of post-1968 thinking in general, **Le Juge et l'assassin** questions the exercise of authority and power.

One of the ways in which this is most effectively done is by showing the similarities between the judge and the murderer and how a relationship of dependency is established between the two, similar to that set up between the watch maker and the policeman searching for his son. Both Bouvier and Judge Rousseau are anxious for the approval of women, both are victims of a similar innocence and enthusiasm, Rousseau placing his faith in the law and its workings, Bouvier in God's vengeance, and both carry rationalism to extremes and demonstrate its limits. Above all, in their search for fame and recognition, both depend on the murders that Bouvier commits, Bouvier himself to get his picture into the newspapers, Rousseau to contribute documentation to the essay he is writing on tramps which will, if he solves the case, establish him, he hopes, as a national expert on the subject. This relationship is brilliantly explored.

As with **Que la Fête commence** and **L'Horloger de Saint Paul** there is a political backdrop to this film which is not altogether successfully drawn, what Tavernier refers to as 'a whole social and historical background (...) Bouvier was active between the death of Van Gogh and the beginnings of Freud, Maurice Barrès was overcome by the execution of the

**161**

anarchist Emile Henry and wrote an unforgettable account of it. Ravochol killed as he played the accordeon.'[16] This takes specific shape in the sub-plot which concerns Rousscau's working class mistress Rose, whose family he supports and whom he visits secretly, precisely the kind of girl who is exploited not only by himself but also by Bouvier who kills young women on the pretext that they are prostitutes, having himself been jilted by his fiancée Louise. Rose's social and sexual exploitation is epitomised in a scene where the judge requires her to lie face downwards on her kitchen table while he rapes her. It is to this act of rape that we are invited to attribute Rose's participation in the socialist parade with which the film closes. Although such demonstrations were indeed a feature of the period, nothing in the portrait of Rose had shown her political interests up to that point, so that this episode seems a clumsy interpolation of crude feminism, while the equation between social and sexual oppression, economic exploitation and anal penetration seems a shallow approach to a subject explored at length in Godard's contemporaneous **Numéro deux**. As with **Que la Fête commence** the ending of this film seems to have been willed by its authors rather than motivated by the plot and it remains unconvincing for this reason.

However the portrait of Joseph Bouvier, as played by Michel Galabru, is masterly and it is this which gives the film its universal dimension. For Bouvier is the wise fool, the idiot who states uncomfortable truths about society with a licence that derives from his 'madness'. He exposes the mechanisms of power in two specific ways which are both comic and moving. First he takes contemporary fashions and movements such as the cult of Joan of Arc or anarchism and, by claiming them as his own, contrives to destroy their value as popular nostrums. 'I was struck,' he says to journalists visiting him in prison to report on his plight, 'by the similarity between my mission and that of that young girl [Joan]. She was a great martyr, like me, who came in another guise at another time to raise France from her slumber ... of course you will tell me I like her because she's a shepherdess.'[17] He also claims to be 'God's anarchist' which he defines as 'the great enemy of the real evil-doers'.[18] With this combination of pretension and incongruity, Bouvier shows how both the *fin de siècle* revival and its anti-clerical counterpart worked to oppress the poor. A similar mechanism operates in Bouvier's relationship to language. Like Frank Poupart in Corneau's **Série noire**, he works with clichés, slogans, aphorisms, maxims and the like, all of which are used by the educated to regiment the poor, whether through the church, the legal system or the education system, and he misinterprets them or interprets literally what are intended as metaphors, becoming in this way both a victim and a beneficiary of the spread of literacy.[19] His little learning is used both deliberately and involuntarily to subvert the order of things.

The conflict between education and ignorance and their representatives is only an instance of a wider conflict between nature and culture which is explored in a variety of ways in the film. Unlike the traditional costume drama or history film, **Le Juge et l'assassin** is shot in natural locations and it accords considerable importance and significance to the physical presence of the actors. The actors use their physical characteristics to denote moral qualities: Noiret relies on his imposing physique and sensual features to indicate the contrast between the public and the private sides to his character; Galabru transforms his body into spectacle by gestures, eye movements and diction and through his constant self-presentation as a religious fanatic, anarchist or epicurean to an audience of doctors, priests, nuns, journalists and magistrates. Here Tavernier has entirely assimilated the

Le Juge et l'assassin –
Michel Galabru in the
wild landscape of the
Vivarais

163

lesson of the American cinema which presents the physical and moral as a continuum.[20] The fact that the characters are both performers suggests that there is no discontinuity between body and mind, just as the relationship between man and his environment is seen as both physical and moral. Some of the most beautiful scenes of the film are when Bouvier is shown tramping the hills of the Vivarais where the savagery and immensity of the landscape are at one with the wildness of human impulses.

Yet both characters seek to explain their behaviour in terms of inadequate socialisation. Within the confines of home, court, asylum or prison, both Judge and Bouvier behave themselves. Outside these confines both become rapists. To the Judge's remark that he should have controlled his instincts, Bouvier replies: 'Your words are very fine, but Nature often speaks more loudly! Whatever the cost, I had to taste the fruits!'[21] This is a sentiment from which the Judge's aesthete friend the Procureur de Villedieu would not have dissented and although the Judge subscribes to the need to repress his instincts he is, of course, equally unable to do so.

The interesting disjunction here is not between public and private morality but between on the one hand the discourse of nature and culture to which the characters all subscribe and on the other the exploration of the relationship between the natural and the cultural contemporary with the making of the film. For the eighteenth-century debate had been revived by structural anthropology and popularised by writers such as Roland Barthes in his study of myths. The 'natural' in the 1970s was seen as a fiction, so that sanity and madness, for example, were seen as cultural not natural categories. Once again, in this film, Tavernier seems to be establishing an opposition between contemporary intellectual beliefs and the film practices of the 1950s. In **L'Enfant sauvage** (1970) Truffaut had cast the film maker as the agent of acculturation; in **Le Juge et l'assassin** Tavernier seems, at least in part, to be reaching back to something much more elemental, the valorisation of the physical and the exploration of its moral dimension.

## Rediscovering America

A third aspect of Tavernier's attempt to reach back to the 1950s consisted of an assimilation of the forms of American popular culture which first became widely appreciated in France in that decade – Hollywood genre films (especially the Western) through cinemas such as the MacMahon and the Cinémathèque, the thriller through the translations of the *série noire*, and jazz. Indeed, before venturing into directing films Tavernier had founded a film club called *Nickelodéon* devoted to showing the works of Boetticher, Fuller, Gordon Douglas, Sirk, André de Toth, King Vidor and Delmer Daves, with the last two as honorary presidents. He had also been an ardent defender of American genre films in the 'fiches' he wrote for the television guide *Télérama*, in the articles he contributed to *Positif*, in his contribution to studies of the Western and of Humphrey Bogart, and in the book *Trente Ans de Cinéma Américain*, which he published with Jean-Pierre Coursodon in 1970.[22] One of the things Tavernier admired in American popular culture was its capacity to give voice to the oppressed or to articulate sympathy for them. This is most obviously translated into his own films in **Round Midnight**, his tribute to saxophonist Dexter Gordon,[23] but it is also perceptible in his attitude towards young people in **L'Horloger de Saint Paul**, the Bretons in **Que la Fête commence**, the deranged in **Le Juge et l'assassin**, tenants in **Des Enfants gâtés**, black people in **Coup de torchon**, and so on. There are, indeed, few Tavernier films which do not defend in some way the interests of minorities or exploited groups. In American genre films such as the Western he consistently looks for the moral dimension and finds it, principally in the works of Delmer Daves:

> *the most noble, vigorous and least schematic of all those which tackled the problems of racism in the guise of the Western. Their high inspiration and refusal to see things in black and white terms (...) derived from the fact that the author was primarily concerned to praise nobility and beauty and to exalt certain gestures and sentiments.*[24]

Just as American genre films often focus on the figure of the lawgiver, whether the sheriff or the private detective, so too we find such characters recurring in Tavernier's films, in Commissaire Guibout, Judge Rousseau and even in the Regent himself. However, there is a marked shift from the official to the unofficial lawgiver, typified by Lucien Cordier in **Coup de torchon** (who is an official policeman employing criminal methods to achieve some form of rough justice), but also to be seen in the Pontcalec of **Que la**

La Passion Béatrice –
Christianity in the
landscape of the Aude

**Fête commence**, the Bouvier of **Le Juge et l'assassin** and above all in the François de Cortemart of **La Passion Béatrice**. This shift marks both a change in the interpretation of the nature of morality and in Tavernier's understanding of American cinema. For one of the things that Tavernier's generation of film makers shared with their *nouvelle vague* predecessors was an admiration for the capacity of Hollywood *mise en scène* to represent moral significance through spatial relationships. Hollywood cinema posits a continuity between man and his environment that cannot admit a distinction between the individual and the collective. The moral solitude of the typical genre film hero is created by and reflected in his physical isolation, the *locus classicus* being Ray's **In a Lonely Place**.[25] It might be argued that this is typical of a Protestant or non-conformist tradition which privileges acts of individual conscience over conformity to a moral code and where, to put it crudely, the individual's capacity to save himself needs to be physical as well as moral. Tavernier's own films, though perhaps influenced by a certain Protestantism, began by rehearsing what might be called the Resistance problematic, the 'shall I collaborate or shall I not' of Anouilh's *Antigone*, for example, and the dialectic of the public and private is still

166

central in **L'Horloger de Saint Paul**. Gradually, however, we see Tavernier moving away from this moral scheme and inserting man into his environment – almost it might be said abandoning him to it in **La Passion Béatrice** – so that progressively the drama and the tragedy of the film is invested in characters who crack under the strain of the moral and physical solitude to which they are condemned. For Cortemart and for Cordier the church and the law have ceased to serve as code or as comfort and they are entirely thrown back on their own resources. Thus the landscape which is briefly used in **Que la Fête commence** and more extensively in **Le Juge et l'assassin** to signify moral revolt (on the part of Pontcalec and Bouvier) becomes virtually an actor in **La Passion Béatrice** and **Coup de torchon**, imposing a new visual idiom on these films. In the former Tavernier adopts the sweeping camera movements he so much admired in Delmer Daves to suggest both the force of the natural environment and the frailty of man within it, while in **Coup de torchon** deep focus helps to isolate the individual within the immensity of the African plain that stretches behind him to infinity. The landscape becomes, as Tavernier wrote of Daves's **3.10 to Yuma** 'a moral locomotive of the action'.[26]

**La Passion Béatrice** might therefore be described as a Western set in mediaeval France 'around 1360'. It takes place at the confines of the kingdom on the borders, as it were, between civilisation and savagery. François de Cortemart, after many years in captivity following the French rout at Crécy, finally returns home to his ancestral castle in the Aude where he is awaited by the womenfolk, his daughter Béatrice and the mother whom he has hated ever since, as a boy, he discovered that she was unfaithful to his own father while *he* was away at war. The family has lived in increasing poverty since Cortemart's departure, selling lands and valuables to survive in the belief that he will return with the spoils of war. But Cortemart returns empty-handed and morally desperate, having seen ignominious defeat and his own son behave like a coward. Instead of conducting himself as a feudal lord should, he takes to marauding the countryside with other bandits, and instead of honouring the laws of God he rapes his own daughter and forces her to become his mistress thereby ensuring, of course, that he cannot benefit from either moral or economic salvation. The Church threatens excommunication and the no longer virgin Béatrice cannot be married to a rich landowner.

The film clearly shows that the old values, particularly the old code of military honour, are moribund. This is the period when the feudal system was beginning to break up and when, under Etienne Marcel, a primitive form of representative government was established. Both father and daughter, in their different ways, suffer from this collapse and from the lack of a new moral order with which to replace the old. Cortemart is in such moral despair that he believes he can descend no further into hell. He has degenerated from a noble representative of humanity into virtually an elemental being with his stocky body, unkempt beard and clothes, and violent actions assimilating him to the wild landscape. He hunts his own son across the countryside as if he were a wild animal and throws a peasant woman over his saddle as though she were a dead bird. Just as his fiefdom is on the edge of France so he marginalises himself with respect to the available jurisdictions of church and state. Tavernier has rightly talked of the 'almost organic relationship between character and landscape' in this film and of the wild sweep of the cameras as 'a way of expressing emotion'.[27] Béatrice too suffers from the moral expectations laid upon women and from her failure to conform to them. She knows she should love her father but in the end she murders him. The moral issue addressed in **La Passion Béatrice** is essentially that of **L'Horloger de Saint Paul**, but this time the film maker has found a visual idiom adequate to the expression of moral questions so that **La Passion** is much more emotionally convincing than the earlier film. This is a tale of the mental and physical frontier in which Tavernier succeeds in doing for French history what the Western did for the American by identifying individual struggle and the collective march of history.

**Coup de torchon**, similarly, is a frontier film, exploring the limits of legality and morality in an outpost of the French Empire in the 1930s. It is also a brilliant adaptation of Jim Thompson's thriller, *Pop 1280*, and thus represents a double assimilation of American popular culture. The story of sheriff Nick Corey who is trying to get himself re-elected in a small town in the Deep South is brilliantly transposed to French Africa.[28] The essential features of poor white corruption in an underdeveloped region and of the racism which was systematic in the American South are easily transposed from one context to another and what is dropped is the detail of Corey's election campaign, which is clearly inappropriate in the French context.

Thompson was a popular American author in the *série noire* and his books have frequently been adapted for the cinema.[29] He shares with Chandler and Hammett both a style of writing and a predicament, adopting the hard-boiled style (although less brilliantly than Chandler or Hammett) and placing the lonely protagonist at the centre of his stories. But in *mise en scène* and characterisation he is much closer to Faulkner than to the Californian authors, preferring the interior monologues of the Faulknerian simpleton or psychopath to the moral certainties of Philip Marlowe. *Pop 1280*, in fact, is a fascinating combination of Chandler and Faulkner, since it depicts a hero who is, theoretically at least, a lawgiver but who is in practice totally without morality.

Tavernier's film may be interestingly compared with Alain Corneau's **Série Noire**, also adapted from a Thompson novel.[30] The predicament of the hero is similar in both films since both Poupart and Cordier find themselves embarked on a course of action whose outcome must be criminal but without intending this and without any capacity to stop short. In **Série noire** the first-person narrative of the novel is replaced by play-acting or a form of self-objectivation by which Poupart casts himself in a variety of roles, most of them culled from American popular culture. His revolt is essentially linguistic.[31] In **Coup de torchon** the equivalent of Poupart is to be found in Huguette Cordier's idiot brother Nono who (as his name suggests) violates the laws of grammar as well as the incest prohibition. But the central character's interior monologue in *Pop 1280* is replaced in **Coup de torchon** not by linguistic violation but by landscape. Like François de Cortemart, Cordier is isolated in Nature in a world without limits regulated by laws which no-one obeys. He exists in both a moral and a physical vacuum and this is intensified by the visual style of the film 'which constantly situates people within a landscape' and which uses the Steadicam 'to give a great amount of freedom to the actors'.[32] As in **La Passion Béatrice**, a style adequate to the emotions of the film.


## Tavernier as a Radical Film Maker

There is a relatively clear qualitative division in Tavernier's work between those films which deal with contemporary life (**Des Enfants gâtés, La Mort en direct, Une Semaine de**

**vacances)** and those which do not. When he tackles contemporary subjects such as the housing crisis, the morale of the teaching profession or the way the media treat death, his style is unambitious, even though his sentiments are impeccably liberal – almost as though he imagines that, in order to be a radical film-maker, it is enough simply to display radical beliefs without any attempt to translate these into film practice. There is also more than a trace of sentimentality in Tavernier, detectable in the slightly nostalgic picture of Lyon in **L'Horloger de Saint Paul** and in the overwhelmingly nostalgic **Un Dimanche à la campagne**. Indeed, the latter film demonstrates all that is retrograde in Tavernier's approach to film making – his contrived painterliness, his simplistic belief in the reconciliation of generations, his liking for romanticised versions of French rural life. Progress in **L'Horloger de Saint Paul** was already an uncertain benefit; in **Un Dimanche à la campagne** it is unequivocally rejected. But the image of the past is, alas, inauthentic, lacking the ironic edge that Renoir, to whom the film pays tribute, always included even in his most lyrical evocations of the countryside.

This being so it might seem contradictory to see Tavernier as a radical film maker and, indeed, there is no radicalism at the level of plot or narrative, for his subjects are always easy to grasp and his exposition is often painstaking. But his great achievement is to have constructed in at least some of his films a visually innovative popular cinema able to approach French history and culture in much the same way as Hollywood approached American history and culture and so to have brought the cinema back to the centre of popular consciousness. It is in this sense that he is a radical.

170

# 7:

# In Search of the Popular Cinema: New French Comedy

Comedy is an important and highly profitable sector of the French film industry. Throughout the post-1968 period directors such as Jean Girault, Claude Zidi, André Hunebelle and Gérard Oury, with actors such as Louis de Funès, Bourvil or Les Charlots, have made large numbers of immensely popular films, often in series such as the **Gendarmes**. A comprehensive study of the industry would clearly find an immense amount of fascinating material in this corpus. However, although important from the point of view of the development of the film industry, the output of such directors and actors is often vulgar, repetitive and formulaic and it has contributed little that is original to the cinema in general. Comedy is a rich vein to study in order to learn about French society but often of less interest than other genres when examining how the cinema has developed.

On the other hand, comedy can occasionally be a genre chosen by *auteurs*. This is clearly the case with Jean Pierre Mocky, whose series of brilliant and personal satires on aspects of French society began with **Les Dragueurs** in 1959. The period after 1968 was particularly fertile for the development of comic art in a variety of forms and media – publishing and the theatre as well as the cinema. New subjects took account of the rapid social changes of the 1960s and a new audience was created in the aftermath of 1968 and the climate of freedom and irreverence that it generated. In the cinema the films of Jean Yanne exemplify the new subjects of satire, but his films are not innovative from the cinematic point of view. However, Bertrand Blier and Luc Moullet, both of whom began their careers in the 1960s, were two film makers who, in the period after 1968, used comedy as the means to pursue an *auteur* cinema broadening the conventional approach to comic subject matter and expanding the creative resources of the cinema.

# Bertrand Blier

Bertrand Blier's films are mordant and sometimes cruel comedies which combine a satirical view of aspects of French society with the classical comic repertoire. His films are often situated in identifiable and momentarily fashionable locations, such as the ski resort Courchevel in **La Femme de mon pote** or the high rise towers of La Défense in **Buffet froid**, but this represents the limit of their realism, for their characterisation depends heavily on the stereotyped assumptions of music hall and pantomime. Indeed, at the end of **Tenue de soirée**, Gérard Depardieu and Michel Blanc dress in drag like the ugly sisters in *Cinderella*. The structure of Blier's films is almost invariably picaresque in the classic comic tradition so that he often starts from an apparently realistic situation but proceeds through a series of episodes each more fantastic than the last to a resolution which is often equally improbable. Blier has said that the subject matter of his films is the 'ringard', what is outdated, the cliché or the conventional assumption, and this is applied to linguistic, physiological, psychological or social habits. His films are therefore explorations of language and styles of acting as well as social comedies and they require a new approach to *mise en scène* for this reason. The bedrock of Blier's comedy, however, is the mockery of the conventional in its cinematic and social forms, through the repeated and obsessive exploration of particular sexual configurations.

At the outset of his career Blier was, like all his contemporaries, strongly influenced by the *nouvelle vague*. His first film **Hitler connais pas**, (1963) was shot, or so he claimed, in the *cinéma vérité* style, 'cher à l'époque',[1] and it consisted of a montage of some thirty interviews with young people on their attitudes to life. However, in retrospect he perceived that the film's documentary realism had a surreal dimension to it since, at the editing stage, 'the monologues became completely fantastic'.[2] The same process is apparently at work in Blier's first major success, **Les Valseuses** (1973).[3] Its central characters are two young men, as they might have been in a *nouvelle vague* film, but the climate is one of physical and verbal violence. Blier explained this as a reaction to his failure to mount successful film projects: 'I conceived it as a deliberate affront to the public. It was the result of a huge amount of anger and the whole production is marked by this feeling'.[4] But it also translates to the screen, in memorable fashion, a completely changed perception of youth. Whereas in *nouvelle vague* films young people are almost always middle class and when they are not law-abiding their crimes consist of little more than stealing books and records,[5] by the 1970s urbanisation and the economic crisis had taken their toll and effected a shift in the perception of the juvenile delinquent from that of misguided adolescent to that of the psychopath exemplified in Stanley Kubrick's **A Clockwork Orange** (1971). Blier was one of the first film makers to depict the fauna of 'la zone', the outskirts of large towns dotted with high-rise buildings and patches of waste land, the home of discontented male representatives of the underprivileged classes.[6] The 'loubards' of **Les Valseuses** clearly belong to the fraction of the working class which verges on criminality and the film begins as a realistic portrait of a couple of delinquents who try to while away a Sunday afternoon by stealing a car. Instead of presenting these characters as problems or even as psychological specimens, however, Blier rapidly moves into picaresque mode, exploring the creative possibilities of delinquent language and behaviour so that the structure of the film might be seen as an expression of the imaginative energy of the two male protagonists, making the most of what comes to hand in a kind of delinquent serendipity, riding in a supermarket trolley or embarking the hairdresser's assistant in their crazy chase across the countryside. From its initial realist beginnings, therefore, **Les Valseuses** rapidly develops into an entirely non-realist film, even losing some of its physical and emotional violence along the way.

## The New Humour: From Café-Théâtre to Cinema

One of the most innovative features of **Les Valseuses** is to have placed on screen a style of acting that had been developed in the *café-théâtre*, where Miou-Miou and Patrick Dewaere had begun their careers. Indeed, Blier's films are all strongly influenced by the *café-théâtre* movement both in their satirical subject matter and in their ludic dimension, and the latter is particularly evident in **Les Valseuses**, which is a film about play and play-acting. Thanks to Blier's success, the vein of alternative comedy developed in the press and the theatre in the 1960s was brought to the film public and Blier's influence can be measured by the degree to which the dominant style of French film acting was altered after 1968 by the impact of the *café-théâtre*.

173

The *café-théâtre* movement was not a product of May 1968.[7] One of the foremost exponents of the post-1968 *café-théâtre*, Romain Bouteille, made his début in the mid-1960s, and its origins can be traced back to the cabarets at the turn of the century, while many of its theatrical routines and configurations derive from the Theatre of the Absurd and, especially, from Beckett. However, the movement was given a huge impetus by the May events and the social and political climate which they created, for the best known *café-théâtres*, the Café de la Gare, the Splendid and Le Vrai Chic Parisien, were set up after 1968 by young people with theatrical ambitions but no prospect of making a career in the straight theatre and little money to promote themselves or their own theatres. The names given to such venues, like 'Le Splendid', point in a mocking way to the gap between their owners' ambitions and their capacity to realise them, since instead of being luxurious they were often ad hoc and uncomfortable spaces without numbered seats, where the audience drew lots to discover how much they would pay.

Inspired to some extent by off-off-Broadway, these theatres created an intimacy and complicity between audience and performer which was reflected in the style and content of the material performed. The performance areas were often restricted, the number of actors was limited, as were their props and costumes, so the performances tended to concentrate strongly on routines and sketches in which social satire was predominant and where the actors were obliged to use their own physical resources to maximum effect. This is no doubt why Coluche, one of the most successful members of the *café-théâtre* movement, dressed as a clown, an attire indicating on the one hand, his marginal relationship to conventional or establishment society and, on the other, that his act, like that of a circus clown, would exploit his own physical resources. A similar attitude was evident towards language. Popular language and cliché were purposely used to comic effect: 'Je te le dis Jeanne c'est pas une vie la vie qu'on vit!' was the title of one show. Catch-phrases, clichés, slogans and aphorisms were all the stock-in-trade of the *café-théâtre*. In a situation where resources were limited, the success of the performance depended on the actor's physical and verbal ingenuity. Thus the *café-théâtre* was a happy conjunction of economic and theatrical imperatives allowing individuals to take charge of their own careers for a minimum financial outlay and, in so doing, introducing a new freedom and

174

inventiveness into styles of performance. Coluche, of whom it has been said that he was able to 'adapt the comedy which started life in the little laboratories of laughter to the scale of mass-production' with his appearances at the Olympia and at Bobino demonstrated how popular the style had become.[8]

The impact of the *café-théâtre* on the cinema has been of two kinds. First it has contributed to the establishment of a domain of social comedy which mocks the habits and mores of the petty bourgeoisie. The Splendid's *Amours Coquillages et Crustacés*, a satire on Club Méditerranée holidays, became Patrice Leconte's film **Les Bronzés** (1978) which spawned a sequel **Les Bronzés font du ski** (1979), while three further Splendid performances, **Les Hommes préfèrent les grosses** (1981), **Le Père Noël est une ordure** (1982) and **Papy fait de la Résistance** (1983) were directed for the cinema by Jean-Marie Poiré. It was probably inevitable that when these plays were produced for large audiences in the cinema, often a number of years after their first theatrical production, they lost some of their cutting edge. Nevertheless, it was characteristic of the 1970s to base the comic repertoire on the mockery of customs and traditions found in the 'new middle class' and similar satirical targets are to be found in Jean Yanne's films made in the same decade: **Tout le monde il est beau, tout le monde il est gentil** (1972), **Moi y en a vouloir des sous** (1973) and **Les Chinois à Paris** (1974). Some of this material was also to find its way into Blier's films.

However, Blier was more influenced by the particular type of humour affected in the *café-théâtre*, which is based on 'dérision', or the mockery of what most people take seriously through the exaggeration of its absurd or foolish aspects. A supreme example of an act of 'dérision' was Coluche's announcement in 1981 that he would be a candidate in the presidential elections. As Coluche's action also illustrates, such humour was consistently oppositional without necessarily being left-wing. Indeed, it had been developed in the contemporary publications *Hara-Kiri* and its successor *Charlie-Hebdo*, weekly newspapers or comic strips for young adults written in what was known as the 'bête et méchant' style,[9] which were characteristically anarchist but also sexist and racist and which used the simplifications implicit in the comic book format to get across gross simplifications of a political or social nature. *Hara-Kiri* and *Charlie-Hebdo* were often violent and sometimes infantile but they nevertheless mounted a political and social critique of the status quo, most effectively towards the end of the Gaullist period. Blier's exposure of 'ringardise' in all its manifestations is clearly very much of a piece with this vein of oppositional humour, and he is sometimes as voluntarily 'bête et méchant' as *Charlie-Hebdo*.[10]

On other occasions, however, episodes in his films can have the profound absurdity of a Beckett routine. Indeed, the typically picaresque structure of a Blier film lends itself to the use of sketches or routines which may be virtually self-contained or free-standing. The best example of this is **Buffet froid**, which has its logic and coherence but which is also a compilation of sketches, many of which might be considered anthology pieces. The opening sequence is a brilliant example. It shows Gérard Depardieu coming onto the platform of a metro station which is deserted except for one passenger waiting for a train. Depardieu chooses to sit next to this man, a perverse choice given the large number of empty seats, but the man proceeds to move around to avoid his company. A conversation ensues in which Depardieu accuses his fellow passenger of being afraid that he will be murdered and he produces a knife... Both characters wear long mackintoshes, both move within a confined space, the situation develops with no apparent motivation except Depardieu's imagination – the sketch could have been performed in the theatre, but instead it serves to motivate the rest of the film.

Styles of acting and performance constituted the second area where the *café-théâtre* influenced the cinema, thanks, first, to Blier. As we shall see, Blier's satirical agenda is highly idiosyncratic but he took the *café-théâtre* performance style and used it as the foundation of both a new kind of cinema and of a new kind of social analysis. Indeed, the one depended on the other. Blier turns on their head conventional notions of the relationship between the physical and the psychological which the cinema generally promotes. In the cinema, as a matter of course, the body expresses the mind and where it does not, that is to say where a character is disguised, this is made obvious. To a degree this is true of all acting and merely magnified or confirmed in the cinema, where physical characteristics are transformed into spectacle by amplification, close-up, repetition and all the other devices afforded by the camera. What Blier does, however, is systematically to confound the expectations we conventionally base on physical appearance and its relation to behaviour. The physical ease and versatility of Depardieu, Dewaere and Miou-Miou, their capacity to move within space and dominate it, their naturalistic comportment, lack of apparent narcissism or self-consciousness, were Blier's great discoveries. Although the *nouvelle vague* had introduced new styles of acting, and Jean-Paul Belmondo's naturalism in **A Bout de souffle** was considered revolutionary at the time, the *café-théâtre* actors took this further by positively exploiting their physical characteristics and their 'ordinariness'.[11] Neither Depardieu nor Dewaere, for example, is conventionally good-looking though both are physically compelling, while Blier is one of the few directors to allow women performers the freedom not to be beautiful, to employ exaggeration and caricature, and not to rely for their performance on physical attractiveness but to exploit their other physical resources.

In **Les Valseuses**, therefore, the actors are deliberately characterised against their physical type. Depardieu's height, heavy face and, more recently, weight seem to predestine him to heavily-coded masculine roles of the kind Belmondo traditionally plays, but Blier also detected in Depardieu a febrility, a sensuality and a vulnerability which apparently contradict or undermine his strongly masculine appearance. Conversely, Dewaere is fragile-looking and

**Les Valseuses** – design for living with Patrick Dewaere, Miou-Miou and Gérard Depardieu

slightly effeminate but turns out in the film to be aggressively heterosexual, and it is the injury inflicted on his testicles ('valseuses') by the owner of the car he tried to steal which inspires his desire for revenge that motivates the plot of the film. Similarly Miou-Miou is in appearance an uninhibited girl, complete with mini-skirt and contraceptives, yet she takes no pleasure whatsoever in sex and is not remotely preoccupied with her appearance. Thus much of the action of **Les Valseuses** depends on the disjunction – which is comic or tragic depending on one's point of view – between corporeal codes and psychology: Depardieu is the tough guy who makes love sensitively (or thinks he does) and who has homosexual leanings: 'it's normal between friends'. The *café-théâtre* had insisted on the deceptive nature of physical appearances and had, indeed, mocked modern society's investment in 'beauty' with **Les Hommes préfèrent les grosses**. Blier takes up and elaborates this vein with the addition of all the resources available in the cinema. In **Les Valseuses** his subversion of the physical also has a social dimension which renders the film extremely moving, for he contrives to suggest that the characters themselves are desperately attempting to live up to the expectations created by their appearance and failing. This is why the film is a brilliant critique of social and sexual conventions.

**Tenue de soirée** – design for living with Gérard Depardieu, Michel Blanc and Miou-Miou

In his later films, Blier becomes more exclusively preoccupied with the nature of our objects of desire to the exclusion of the social. Thus **Trop belle pour toi** (a distant remake of **Les Hommes préfèrent les grosses**) has a successful businessman prefer a dumpy secretary to a beautiful, elegant wife, **Tenue de soirée** has Gérard Depardieu prefer the ugly Michel Blanc to the beautiful Miou-Miou and **La Femme de mon pote** has the beautiful Isabelle Huppert prefer the self-confessedly unprepossessing Coluche to the attractive and successful Thierry Lhermitte. On one level, therefore, Blier's films subvert the gender stereotyping which the cinema conventionally promotes and which is represented in the French cinema by the careers of Catherine Deneuve and Jean-Paul Belmondo, to take but two examples. Blier's women are not necessarily beautiful and his men are not necessarily masculine. Moreover, this is a critique of both social and cinematic conventions, of the contribution cinema makes to the construction of gender identities and social identities. But he has also contributed to the expansion of the actor's physical repertoire, which was perhaps historically more constrained in France than elsewhere. The 1970s was the decade where, for the first time in French cinema, it became possible to exploit the resources of the body, and one only has to compare the ease and naturalness which became common at that time with the performance styles of the famous actors of earlier periods – Gabin or Arletty to take two examples – to see that this is so. After Blier, film makers knew how to exploit Depardieu, and in a series of roles in **La Dernière Femme, Le Camion, Mon Oncle d'Amérique** and even **Jean de Florette** he has laid bare the vulnerable aspects of his masculinity.

## On the Road

Like many French film makers of his generation (he was born in 1939) Blier is both a cinephile and an admirer of American popular culture. His films often adapt to the French context and circumstances ideas or situations taken from recent foreign films. The opening sequence of **Notre Histoire** (1984) for example has a man travelling in a train indulging in sexual fantasies about a woman who materialises in his compartment, much like the opening sequence of Fellini's **City of Women** (1980). Moreover, Stanley Kubrick has obviously been a particular influence. It has already been suggested that **Les Valseuses** took something of its portrayal of youth violence from **A Clockwork Orange**, but it should also be recalled that **Beau-père** (1981) depicts an older man's love for a very young girl which is comparable to that in Kubrick's **Lolita** (1962), while some of the military fantasies of **Calmos** (1975) bear similarities to those of Kubrick's **Dr Strangelove** (1964).[12]

However, Blier is also sensitive to the way the *nouvelle vague* reworked themes and tropes of the American cinema. Thus the seminal figure of the innocent couple on the run from persecution, to be found in Fritz Lang's **You Only Live Once** (1937), was taken up in both America and France in the 1960s but transformed, so that the innocent protagonists became guilty and self-destructive in Penn's **Bonnie and Clyde**, Truffaut's **La Sirène du Mississippi** and Godard's **Pierrot le fou**, while the nostalgic or elegiac tone of all three of these films, the period setting of **Bonnie and Clyde**, the reconstruction of the American South in **La Sirène**, and the tributes to the American cinema in **Pierrot le fou**, also suggest that this trope was felt to be prelapsarian, to represent somehow the innocence of the cinema as well as to demonstrate the injustices of society. In the 1960s, leaving civilised society, 'taking off' to use the title of the Milos Forman film released in 1971, became less a matter of necessity than of choice. Couples 'took off' not because they were guilty or suspected of being so, but in order to retain their purity and innocence. This was a utopianism not confined to the cinema but characteristic of youth culture in general and it is brilliantly identified and parodied in Georges Perec's novel *Les Choses* (1965) in which the heroic couple make a trip to Tunisia but return chastened and integrate into bourgeois society after all.[13] Blier exploits this tradition too in the themes and structure of his films, particularly in **Calmos** and in **Buffet froid**, both of which have strong utopian elements. Thus, although virtually all of Blier's films rely on the picaresque structure which, since *Don Quixote*, has supported the narrative of comic incident, they combine the classic picaresque with parodic references to the thriller on the one hand and to post-1960s utopianism on the other.

Blier's films often present a couple on the run, but it is never the romantic couple of **You Only Live Once** or **Pierrot le fou**. In **Les Valseuses** it is a couple of young men, in **Calmos** a couple of middle-aged men, in **Buffet froid** a policeman and a criminal. Similarly, the arcadian idyll which is momentarily achieved in some of the films, in the sequence in the country

**Buffet froid** – Bernard Blier, Gérard Depardieu and Jean Carmet as the assassins

cottage in **Les Valseuses** or **Trop belle pour toi**, in the mountains in **Buffet froid**, or in the houses of **Calmos**, **Notre Histoire** or **La Femme de mon pote**, is almost invariably violently disrupted, usually by a woman or women. Carole Bouquet shoots Depardieu at the end of **Buffet froid** and Josiane Balasko leaves him in **Trop belle pour toi**, while Miou-Miou and Isabelle Huppert in **Les Valseuses** and **La Femme de mon pote** find new partners. In other words Blier's reading both of the cinematic tradition and of the social aspirations of the 1960s and early 1970s is strongly coloured by his rejection of the heterosexual couple and his investigations of male identity.

## The Crisis of Masculinity

Like all satirical works, Blier's films have a profoundly serious side. They represent a challenge to the sexual and social identities constructed within the heterosexual couple and the family by proposing different and apparently more satisfactory configurations. To this extent they might be considered progressive. The trio (usually two men and a

181

woman) or the male couple are presented as a challenge to the family unit in virtually all Blier's films, and although the emphasis from film to film is different the repetition of this configuration is quite consistent, The major exception is obviously **Beau-père**, which does concern the relationship of a heterosexual couple but which nevertheless poses a considerable threat to the family institution since the couple in question is quasi-incestuous (a step-father and a step-daughter) and the girl is under the age of consent. The trio and the male couple are both present in **Les Valseuses**. Pierrot and Jean-Claude are first presented as a couple, companions in crime. They then meet Marie-Ange, whom they share with no apparent difficulty. Subsequently they encounter a nursing mother and Jeanne Moreau before returning to Marie-Ange with whom, at the end of the film, they appear to have established an idyllic relationship reminiscent of the three-some in Lubitsch's **Design for Living**. This is one of the few occasions in a Blier film where relationships between men and women appear to be remotely satisfactory.

Similar trios are to be found in **La Femme de mon pote** and **Tenue de soirée**, although presented very different-ly. In the former film Mickey (Coluche) resents the intrusion of Viviane (Isabelle Huppert) into his friendship with Pascal (Thierry Lhermitte). Whether or not the relationship between Mickey and Pascal is explicitly homosexual, it is clear that Mickey behaves like a jilted lover and compensates by falling in love with all Pascal's mistresses. Both men reiterate the superior importance of their friendship: 'Whatever happens, these two buddies are going to remain friends even if she's incredibly good in bed,' says Mickey. Pascal, meanwhile, opines: 'What's really good is having your woman and your best friend under the same roof', and when Viviane departs with another lover they remark: 'the main thing is that we've managed to preserve our friendship'. The tone of the film is sombre, with Coluche, in particular, playing the part of a depressed and unattractive hanger-on to Lhermitte's glamor-ous boutique owner. With **Tenue de soirée** the tone becomes more lighthearted and the plot less realistic. This film reprises the trio of **Les Valseuses** with Michel Blanc substituted in the Patrick Dewaere part,[14] and the homosexual relationship between the men, hinted at in **Les Valseuses**, is entirely explicit. In fact, Michel Blanc commences the film as Miou-Miou's husband and ends it as Gérard Depardieu's lover. Elsewhere in Blier films spontaneous male couples are created, sometimes of an improbable or comic kind, such as the alliance between the policeman and the criminal in **Buffet froid**, that between the two middle-aged renegades in **Calmos**, or between the husband and his wife's lover in **Préparez vos Mouchoirs**, while in **Notre Histoire** the men gang up against the central female character, Donatienne.

One of the reasons for the unsatisfactory heterosexual couple is that the sexual revolution has misfired. For Miou-Miou (**Les Valseuses**), for Nathalie Baye (**Notre Histoire**) and even for Isabelle Huppert (**La Femme de mon pote**) sexual freedom does not lead to sexual satisfaction. In **Les Valseuses** Pierrot and Jean-Claude spend hours trying to assist Marie-Ange to orgasm, without success; in **Notre Histoire** Donatienne, jilted by the man she loves, takes lover after lover in a desperate search for an adequate replacement, while in **La Femme de mon pote** Viviane leaves Pascal, who has failed to pay her enough attention, for someone who promises to be more sexually rewarding.

The other reason is that men in Blier's films are not quite sure if they are men and, if they are, what men should be. The uncertainty was already apparent in **Les Valseuses**, in which Jean-Claude/Dewaere fears for his virility after his testicles have been grazed by a bullet, fears for it even more when sucking the breasts of a nursing mother fails to give him an erection ('Why can't I get a hard-on?'), fears that Pierrot's homosexual advance has impaired his manhood ('I'm humiliated'), and cannot understand why another man rather than himself is able to satisfy Marie-Ange sexually. The title is obviously highly ironic. If **Tenue de soirée** is read in relation to **Les Valseuses**, of which is it virtually a remake, it might be interpreted as suggesting that happiness, for both men and women, is only achieved when men assume their femininity, that is to say when they no longer allow their sexual identities to be constrained by their social identities, and at the end of this film the male characters do indeed express their femininity by dressing as women and walking the streets with the approval of the female character.

The question of male identity is a theme which can be traced through many French films of the 1970s, marking them off clearly from the earlier period when gender did not seem to be an issue in film making. To a degree its emergence parallels the women's films which, as we have seen, became more numerous at the time and asserted the specificity of the feminine. Both must also be linked to the rise of the women's movement in the early 1970s and to debates over the construction of identity in general.[15]

But the women's films do not betray an anxiety about femininity in the same way as the films of Blier and others portray an anxiety about masculinity. Two virtually contemporary works, Ferreri's **La grande Bouffe** (1973) and Sautet's **Vincent, François, Paul et les autres** (1974) serve to illustrate the climate of the times as well as the degree to which Blier diverged from it. Both films concern groups of four men linked by professional or class interests. In the case of **La grande Bouffe** the men come together for a weekend of eating and drinking away from family and professional commitments; in the case of **Vincent, François**, the writer, doctor, small businessman and boxer are held together by a friendship which goes back to the 1950s.

Both films are interesting because they suggest that traditional bourgeois pursuits and traditional male camaraderie are inadequate to the times, and they point to a profound malaise with respect to the social and sexual status of men. Ferreri's film is a more general critique of bourgeois values. His protagonists commit suicide through self-indulgence and the film maker's attitude throughout is highly critical. Sautet's film, on the other hand, evinces a nostalgia for the 1950s, when life seemed simple and when individuals survived through solidarity and friendship, contrasting this period with the harsh climate of the 1970s, when even your friends refuse to lend you money. In the 1970s the collectivity, which was based on male solidarity, has disappeared, leaving a set of individuals who feel unprotected. In the same way, the creativity which is supposed to belong to the male, whether professionally or sexually, is shown to be lacking. François's wife claims that he is 'dead' sexually, takes a variety of lovers and finally leaves him; Paul cannot write the novel he wished to write and makes a living from third-rate journalism. In this way **Vincent, François, Paul et les autres** equates an economic and political change which had undoubtedly occurred, and which was ultimately reflected in the decline of the Communist Party and the rise of the belief in capitalist individualism, with a crisis of masculinity. This was well understood at the time since the film is seen playing on the background monitor during the introduction to Godard's **Numéro deux**, along with Bergman's **Scenes from a Marriage**.

Not all explorations of the subject explicitly relate the crisis of masculinity to the crisis of the family as Godard does in **Numéro deux**, but the common factor in the films of the decade is one of anxiety. As Jean-Luc Douillade pointed out, even a film maker as mainstream as Claude Berri in **Un Moment d'égarement** was affected by the climate of uncertainty: 'all men have left is friendship with other men and even that is now crumbling away'.[16] Sometimes, in fact, it appears as though the women film makers are better able to analyse the anxiety of the men than the men are themselves, if one is to judge from Claire Clouzot's sensitive father in **L'Homme fragile** (1983), or the homosexual *ménage à trois* in Coline Serreau's **Pourquoi Pas?** (1978), a film which certainly influenced Blier's **Tenue de soirée**. Nevertheless, one only has to look at the critical reception of **Vincent, François, Paul et les autres** to appreciate that it struck a chord with French audiences at the time because of what they perceived as its verisimilitude, its reflection of a situation which many men felt to be their own.[17]

Thus Blier reflects and elaborates on prevailing social concerns and anxieties, often with a felicitous degree of inventiveness, and part of the laughter his films provoke is that of relief. However, there is a darker side to his investigation of masculinity, for it is accompanied by a systematic and thoroughgoing misogyny. Mickey's heartfelt cry at the end of **La Femme de mon pote**, 'How can they be such bitches. Everything about women should make them angels', establishes the parameters within which Blier places his female characters – devils or angels, with little opportunity to be anything else.

Blier's films are peopled by very young or frankly middle-aged women. Indeed, Jeanne Moreau in **Les Valseuses** describes herself as 'an old woman' with no apparent irony. Whether young or old, the women are either frigid and unresponsive like Miou-Miou in **Les Valseuses** or Carole Laure in **Préparez vos Mouchoirs**, or they are impossibly sexually demanding, like Geneviève Page in **Buffet froid**, whose voracious sexuality drove her husband to suicide, or Nathalie Baye as the Sadeian Donatienne in **Notre Histoire**. Faced with such demands, the men take refuge in friendship with other men or in activities and occupations which exclude women. In **Notre Histoire** the elderly Michel Galabru opens his house to male refugees from women; in **Préparez vos Mouchoirs** and **La Femme de mon pote** the men dispose of the women by handing them on to another man and then settle down to more satisfactory male pursuits such as reading or drinking. In **Buffet froid** Gérard Depardieu murders his wife and thereafter frequents exclusively men.

However, it is **Calmos** which stands as the most extreme version of the elimination of women that occurs in one way or another in most of Blier's films. Indeed **Calmos** is a fantasy about how women might be eliminated. It concerns two middle-aged men, played by Jean-Pierre Marielle and Jean Rochefort, one of whom is a gynaecologist (that is, a specialist in women's problems), who decide that their wives are too demanding and that they will retreat to the country for a calmer existence and the more restful activities of eating and drinking well. The plot, as can be seen, bears some resemblance to that of **La grande Bouffe**, which preceded it by two years. However, Blier now imagines his two heroes pursued by women who demand their attention. They therefore take to the fields urging other men to join them in their resistance. A fantastic war of the sexes breaks out in which the two male protagonists are hunted down by marauding groups of excited women dressed in military uniform.

Of course, **Calmos** is not a realist film. As one of its most ardent defenders pointed out, 'it has the lyricism of excess, the broad brush of the fantastic worthy of the best Italian directors'.[18] But Blier, unlike Ferreri for example, is not obviously critical of his male protagonists. On the contrary, he positively invites the audience to sympathise and identify with them by casting two well-known comic actors in the central roles. When **Calmos** first opened the audience responded with laughter to the first appearances on screen of Marielle and Rochefort, reinforcing, as Claire Clouzot has shown, the complicity between their point of view and that of the audience, and preventing the film being read as a projection of the fantasies of these two characters.[19] Blier has said that **Calmos** was intended as a satire on the International Women's Year of 1975. This explains why women are seen as organised into a spoof army complete with uniforms and military drill. However, this is a film in which everything that happens apparently confirms the rectitude of the decision taken by the men in the first place, so that the audience has no choice but to acquiesce in the depiction of women acting collectively as militaristic, aggressive and above all sexually over-demanding. **Calmos** envisages Rochefort and Marielle hounded out of their tranquil male Eden into a cruel world in which a vagina-like engine of war threatens to engulf them.

186

Blier's humour, as has been said, often depends on the exploitation of stereotypical characters and behaviour. In **Calmos**, however, not all the characters are presented in equally simplistic or caricatural fashion. The male characters are not profoundly drawn, it is true, but they nevertheless function as human beings and are allowed a psychology, whereas the women are treated as a force of nature which is inexplicable and probably uncontrollable. Blier has imagined a pitched battle between the individual and an inhuman collectivity and has then foisted gender identities onto this unequal confrontation.

In general, women in Blier's films have not had the major roles, although there are signs that this is changing,[20] and they are often presented as enjoying humiliation and exploitation. However, there are positive female characters to be found and it is interesting to look at the virtues they embody. The adolescent Marion in **Beau-père** takes the initiative in the relationship with the older man and simultaneously defines herself as a sex object. Not only does this male fantasy have the advantage of exonerating the male partner from blame and responsibility, it also suggests the proper use of female action.[21] The middle-aged woman in **Les Valseuses** provides the two young men with the sex that they are seeking. Furthermore, she is extremely grateful to them because she has just emerged from a long prison sentence during which, as she tells Jean-Claude and Pierrot, she stopped menstruating. Fortunately her meeting with the pair enables her to regain her femininity, first through sex and then by shooting herself through the vagina, which causes blood to flow once again, an episode which it is tempting to read as symbolic incest followed by matricide. The mother kills herself after the 'sons' have made love to her, while her real son successfully makes love to Miou-Miou, whom her surrogate sons cannot satisfy. In this view, the woman's role is to be a good mother, she whom the sons desire, like the nursing mother the men encounter on the train, but one who is also capable of satisfying them. A refinement of this argument is offered in **Préparez vos Mouchoirs**, where the woman who desires to be a mother cannot find satisfaction except with a surrogate son (another adolescent) by whom, naturally, she then becomes pregnant. Even when he presents a woman in a positive light, therefore, Blier always places her in a situation where her role is to respond to the fantasies men create around her and to assume the consequences of such submissiveness.

Bertrand Blier's work is by his own account extremely uneven. He freely admits, for example, that **Calmos** is a 'failure', partly because the casting was 'wrong' and partly because he now considers it impossible to make fun of women: 'Today it is increasingly difficult to show a bum being pinched in the cinema.'[22] Indeed, he claims this is why his central characters are male: 'When I think of a story the comic characters that come to mind are always male. Because in life women are less funny.'[23] His least successful and interesting films are those which are most realistic or those which are based on the reversal of a conventionally farcical or romantic situation. **La Femme de mon pote**, for example, casts Coluche in a 'straight' role, which is of interest, but otherwise consists of a long-drawn-out complaint about the behaviour of women, while **Notre Histoire** opens with the brilliant debunking of a romantic encounter but rapidly degenerates into the depiction of drunken destructiveness. Blier's best and most interesting films are those in which the structure is most picaresque and the situations are fantastic, namely **Les Valseuses, Buffet froid** and, to some extent, **Tenue de soirée**. These films are inventive in their scripts, their performances and their structure and they are also free from the pessimism which often informs Blier's films, allowing his humour to manifest its creative side.


## Luc Moullet

The second major director of comedy in the post-1968 period, Luc Moullet, has a career that stretches back to the 1950s – a fact that it is important to bear in mind when considering his intellectual and cinematic influences. Moullet is a contemporary of the *nouvelle vague* directors and, like them, worked as a critic on *Cahiers du cinéma* before turning his hand to directing in 1960 with a short film entitled **Un Steack trop cuit**. Moullet has subsequently produced films and acted in them as well as continuing to direct. Where Bertrand Blier's preferred subjects are sexual habits and the construction of gender identities, Moullet is interested primarily in the world of work and in the cinema. He is closely allied with the *nouvelle vague* generation, both in the documentary basis of some of his comedies and in his liking for making films whose inspiration and raison d'être are other films or film genres. But he shares with Blier and other directors like Doillon and Tavernier a utopianism which is characteristic of the post-1968 period, and which in Moullet's case can be linked to the thinking of the Situationists.

Moullet's films can best be approached through **Les Sièges de l'Alcazar** (1989), a 'comedy about film lovers and their sexuality', which explains some of Moullet's own history in a wittingly self-deprecating manner. According to this film the Alcazar was a cinema that was demolished in 1963, but the action of the film takes place during the mid-1950s, as we can tell from one of the newsreels it screens and which shows the war in Algeria. The cinema is situated in a suburban district and presents double bills as well as newsreels. It is run by a middle-aged couple, the husband acting as projectionist and the wife, by turns, as box office clerk, usherette and ice-cream vendor. It is also a cinema which, at the time the action is situated, has lost most of its audience, so that it is virtually empty for a great deal of the time except for the front rows, the *premières*, which are cheaper and less comfortable than the other seats and which children and film buffs compete to occupy. Some of the film consists of the detached and amused observation, with voice-over commentary, of the life of the cinema. We see the wife complaining as the hero purchases a seat in the *premières*, we see the children complaining that all the *premières* are occupied, we see the hero complaining, one Sunday night when the proprietors want nothing better than to shut up shop and go to bed, that the projectionist has failed to screen one of the reels of the advertised film and threatening to report him to the trading standards office, we see the wife hurriedly clipping a red bow into her hair in order to transform herself from usherette to ice-cream vendor and, at the end of the evening, we see her walking down the rows of seats, picking up ticket halves so that she can stick them together with sellotape. This is an affectionately nostalgic portrait as well as an amusing one for, like so many other film lovers, Moullet owes his film culture to the rich and random programming of the less than salubrious cinemas which still operated in most cities in the 1950s.

When the story opens, our hero is pursuing his research on the Italian director Vittorio Cottafavi, celebrated as the director of **Hercules Conquers Atlantis** and a film maker considered to be a major *auteur* by several critics in France.[24] He clearly subscribes to those aspects of the *politique des auteurs* which require critics to seek out obscure directors and to claim that they are better than well-known film makers, so that for the hero Antonioni is merely 'the poor man's Cottafavi'. As a result of these activities, the film critic is hired by *Cahiers du cinéma*, whose distinctive yellow cover can be glimpsed poking out of his jacket pocket, and acquires his critic's card – much to the disgust of the cinema owner's wife for whom this represents, naturally, considerable loss of revenue.

The pursuit of Cottafavi is one strand in the film; the other is the pursuit of love. For one day the hero notices a famous and glamorous woman sitting in a seat towards the back of the cinema and recognises her as the senior critic of *Cahiers du cinéma*'s great rival, *Positif*. He wonders whether *Positif* has also discovered Cottafavi or whether she is just keeping an eye on *Cahiers* and when, by dint of feigning an exit from the cinema, he discovers that it is the latter, he decides to lay siege to her, attempting to impress her with his knowledge of the Italian cinema, which she undermines by correcting his pronunciation of the Italian language. However, despite the shaky and confrontational start to this relationship, their romance ends as happily as all romances should. The opus on Cottafavi is published, the *premières* at the Alcazar are full of cinephiles who have come to sample the glories of this new discovery, and the *Cahiers* and *Positif* critics manage to sink their intellectual, political and aesthetic differences, at least for a while.

**Les Sièges de l'Alcazar** parodies, in an affectionate manner, the filmic and other mores of the 1950s. The hero sports a short haircut and suit when going to the cinema (Moullet himself, in later films, appears bearded and rather unkempt); *Positif*'s critic wears a suit and high heels, full make up, and her hair in an elaborate chignon, while the friend she persuades to date the *Cahiers* critic, just to see what he is like, wears evening dress and fur stole for an outing to the movies. As well as parodying the formality of the 1950s Moullet is also acknowledging, in this film, that for directors with his background the distinction between life and film is extremely blurred. The spectatorial position adopted in **Les Sièges de l'Alcazar**, with the camera placed slightly above the seats of the cinema so that the viewers' entrances and exits appear to take place as though they were themselves on a stage, lends fictional quality to what purports to be a presentation of life. Thus the viewer of **Les Sièges** believes that the hero may have imagined his encounter with the *Positif* critic, who comes and goes like a figure in a dream and who is dressed like a creature of fantasy. Part of the comic effect of **Les Sièges**, therefore, depends on a gentle mockery of the notion that life and the cinema are a continuum. But although Moullet makes fun of the fanaticism of his youthful cinephilia, he still subscribes in a variety of ways to the principle of Godard's famous dictum to the effect that 'les travellings sont affaire de morale'.[25] The world, for Moullet, might be said to exist in order to end up in a film, with the result that his films often take their inspiration from the world of work, as can be seen in **La Comédie du travail** (1987) or from the banal events or situations of his own life, as exemplified by **Anatomie d'un rapport** (1975) or **Genèse d'un repas** (1979).

The typical structure of a Moullet film can best be seen in **La Comédie du travail**. This involves a cast of several characters who accidentally come together when they pass through the labour exchange. Though the characters are all fictional, the detail of their activities is observed with documentary precision so that the film could almost pass for a study of the habits of the unemployed. The tenacious and hardworking Françoise Duru works in the department which helps to place the unemployed in jobs. She encounters the mild-mannered but slightly dim bank clerk, Benoît Constant, when he is made redundant after having been promoted to the loans department of his bank with strict instructions to lend to no-one; hence the disappearance of his job. Benoît attempts to chat up Françoise but she does not welcome his advances. Meanwhile Sylvain Berg, lover of nature and of mountains, signs on every month and draws benefits on the strength of the forged pay slips he purchases from a company which specialises in such things, but uses his dole to finance his mountain-climbing expeditions. Françoise falls in love with Sylvain just by looking at him queuing outside the labour exchange and resolves to do him a favour. She is an expert in finding jobs for unlikely candidates, so she summons Sylvain for an interview and accompanies him to see his prospective employer Ducroq, who is about to take on the recently sacked Benoît. When Françoise reminds Ducroq that he has fiddled his employer's social security contributions he agrees to take Sylvain instead, even though the latter does all he can not to get the job, including reading the newspaper *Rouge* in an ostentatious fashion. As Françoise and Sylvain emerge from Ducroq's office, she is attacked by her colleagues, who fear that her Stakhanovite success in placing the unemployed in jobs will soon put all the employees of the labour exchange out of work. Sylvain feels so sorry for Françoise that he takes her home and explains that the last thing he wants is a job. They then make love.

Until the attack on Françoise the plot of the film is entirely realistic, the more so, indeed, for apparently revealing abuses in the allocation of unemployment benefit. We are even prepared to accept that an elderly man whom Sylvain meets on the train when returning to sign on might assume a disguise so elaborate as to render him unrecognisable in order to sign on for a friend who cannot be present. The observation of the way a labour exchange works and of the people who frequent it seems to have required little authorial intervention. However, the attack on Françoise marks a shift of gear. The plot becomes fantastic and, in so doing, makes us see earlier events in the film in a new light. Françoise goes climbing with Sylvain, collapses under the strain and is hospitalised. She tells Sylvain to go to Nepal without her. He hitch-hikes to Brussels Airport and is picked up by Benoît who is on his way to a secluded spot where he can compose his job applications away from his wife's prying gaze. Benoît recognises Sylvain as the man who stole the job he wanted and who seduced Françoise, and he kills him. When sentenced to twenty years in prison he refuses to appeal on the grounds that prison will protect him from job-hunting. Françoise, meanwhile, takes to filling out false pay slips in honour of Sylvain's memory and so ensures that her colleagues in the labour exchange will never be out of a job.

As can be seen, Moullet enjoys pushing situations to their logical conclusions, to the point at which they become illogical or fantastic, and he is sometimes called a pataphysicist because he pursues the 'science of imaginary solutions'.[26] It is typical of his view of the world that an organisation dedicated to keeping people in work should in fact turn out to keep them out of work in order to keep itself in work, or that a man who commits a crime because he has no work should choose to remain in prison so as not to have to work again. This is a critique of the constraints of bureaucracy, and a hymn to human creativity, an attack on the perverted morality of capitalism which does not wish to recognise the immense creativity involved in not working. It is also a paradigm of Moullet's own creative processes.

Moullet refers to his 'modest origins' – his father was a post office sorter, his mother a typist – as having influenced his approach to film making:

*I am used to living and working in an economical fashion. I can make films much more easily than a bourgeois film maker (...) because I don't need much money to live on or to make films. I can count. If another film maker can make a film for sixty million francs, I can make the same film for thirty million (...) For example, I try to avoid anything elaborate (...) Things which are purely decorative but contribute nothing to the subject or to the value of the film. I also avoid gentrifying actors or situations, or complicated exteriors which are of no interest at all.*[27]

The 'modesty' that is typical of Moullet's works derives, however, from choice as well as necessity and is an aesthetic principle as well as a thematic preference.

Frequently, Moullet chooses subjects from his own life and casts himself in his own films. In the short film, **Terres noires** (1961), for example, 'most people are unaware of the fact that I myself play the part of the roadmender'. This is both an exercise in frugality and a way of recalling his personal trajectory: 'my presence indicates a documentary aspect of the film. I almost stayed in the farming community and I might have become a roadmender'.[28] Similarly, the 'documentary' **Genèse d'un repas** opens with Moullet and his partner, face to an immobile camera, eating a frugal meal composed of omelette, tuna fish and a banana, so that personal history and ordinary, daily activities serve as the pretext or stimulus for the film, which goes on to investigate in some detail the origins of the foodstuffs consumed. But the film in which the director is most present is **Anatomie d'un rapport**, a portrait of his sexual relations, or absence of them, with his partner Antonietta Pizzorno, in which the topic is stripped of all possible romanticism and explored in its physiological and almost technical detail. Economy of means is a thematic constant in Moullet's films, therefore, and whether he is creating a film or making a meal he is able to work with a limited number of ingredients, so that the contrast between the modesty of the origins of the film and the often elaborate construction put upon them, as in **Les Sièges de l'Alcazar**, or in **Genèse d'un repas**, is an integral part of the pleasure of his work and is often highly comic in its effect.

Economy is also translated into an aesthetic principle. The fixed camera is one of the cheapest forms of filming but it is also associated with the documentary and, more especially, the ethnographic film, for which the classic situation is provided by a camera which is positioned slightly above a

**193**

point of intersection or interaction (such as a crossroads) and which observes and records what occurs. Many writers have stressed, of course, how such ultra-realism and lack of 'intervention' can lend what is filmed a fantastic quality,[29] and this is undoubtedly why some avant-garde film makers have favoured this aesthetic approach, which allows the absence of authorial intervention to generate fiction and art. Moullet has, at times, appeared or pretended to adopt this position too, most notably in the short film **Barres** (1984). This required Moullet to position his camera at the Quai de la Rapée métro station in Paris and to film, in spoof documentary manner, with intertitles in stead of voice-over commentary, the different ticket barriers installed at the station over a period of six months and the ever more inventive means of avoiding them (the latter, in fact, mostly invented for the purposes of the film). In other words, Moullet takes the common, everyday occurrence of fare-dodging, and renders it comic through the combination of apparently dispassionate authorial distance and a massive investment in fantastic action. He adopts a particular position and role for his camera which is that of the deadpan observer merely recording the extravagance of everyday life, but this, in its detail at least, is invented. It is Moullet, for example, who is the author of the idea that an excellent way to get through the barrier without a ticket is by lying flat on a skateboard and sliding underneath the bar. In this way the poverty of aesthetic means becomes a source of creation, the lack of intervention, paradoxically, a source of exuberance, and the limitation of the subject a stimulus to physical as well as verbal intervention. The tongue-in-cheek quotation from Pascal which figures on one of the intertitles of the film – 'the more obstacles there are, the more man wishes to overcome them' – could be a paradigm of Moullet's aesthetics as well as his morals, the aesthetic equivalent of Sylvain Berg's determination, in **La Comédie du travail**, to scale mountains despite, or because of, his very limited resources.

Moullet differs from most ethnographic or conventional documentary film makers, however, in making explicit not just the fantastic nature of the real but the role of the camera in an economy of desire. It has already been suggested that the camera position in **Les Sièges de l'Alcazar** is used to blur the distinction between reality and the cinema and to point to a continuum between life and film which is enacted in the hero's life. The camera succeeds in eroticising what it films, so that what it shows may be a projection of our desire. A similar process is at work in **La Comédie du travail**, for it is when Françoise gazes down from the first floor windows of the labour exchange, from the position the camera so often occupies in documentary films, that she perceives Sylvain in the queue and invests him with her desire. Thus in Moullet's films the cinema is the eroticisation of the look, explicitly so when objects of desire are gazed upon, and implicitly when any act of filming or camera position can transform reality into fantasy.

Does this mean that Moullet is a film maker divorced from social realities? He said of his spoof western, **Une Aventure de Billy le Kid** (1971): 'I didn't make a realist film because I didn't have the means to do so.'[30] If economic constraints force Moullet into the comic and the fantastic, it is also true that when setting out to make a documentary he cannot resist focusing on the fantastic or surreal aspects of the subject. In **Barres**, as we have seen, everyday life serves as a pretext for an excursion into the imaginary. Even in **La Valse des médias** (1987), a study of various different libraries and their readers in Paris, Nantes and Rabat, which was commissioned from Moullet by the Ministry of Culture and Communication, he turns the film into a study of the foibles and eccentricities of human behaviour, on which he himself dryly comments in voice-over. 'There is no censorship at the Pompidou Centre' he says, as the image shows a reader with a pornographic magazine concealed inside a scientific textbook. Another shot shows an athlete in shorts, completely out of place in a library, running up the down escalator to get to the Bibliothèque publique d'information.

Nevertheless, there is a political constant in Moullet's films which is partly revealed in the subversiveness that **Barres**, **La Valse des médias** and **La Comédie du travail** all celebrate. Despite the presentation of himself in **Les Sièges de l'Alcazar** as a clean-cut youth, bored with political questions such as the Algerian war (the hero is impatient for the newsreels to finish so that the Cottafavi can begin) and despite the fact that historically the *Cahiers* on which he was employed was much further to the right politically than was *Positif*, there is little, except a lack of respect for authority, that links Moullet with the right-wing anarchism espoused by *Cahiers's* critics in the 1950s. First, Moullet is at pains to stress both his sympathies and his identification with the poor, and whenever he shows his own circumstances on film they would seem to confirm his relative lack of wealth. Second, he is sceptical of institutions and agencies set up to defend the poor, and in his merciless attack on bureaucracies Moullet might be considered an advocate of permanent revolution. Thus if **La Comédie du travail** has a serious message it must reside in the revelation that the labour exchange has no interest in helping the unemployed. Third, he has a highly developed consciousness that, however poor the poor in the First World may be, they still benefit from a relative affluence procured by the exploitation of the Third World. **Genèse d'un repas** systematically traces the origins of tuna fish and banana, which bear the names of their French retailers, back to Africa and the Caribbean and, through the juxtaposition of interviews with workers in those regions and workers in the processing and packaging plants in France, shows that labour in France, and the trade union movement in general, are more concerned with the protection of their own privileges than with the plight of the Third World. All operate according to a cynical self-centredness, just like the labour exchange employees in **La Comédie du travail** or the ticket clerks in **Barres**, who watch fare-dodging with perfect equanimity on the grounds that it 'isn't their job' to try and stop it.

There are other political strands in Moullet's works. **Terres noires** and **Une Aventure de Billy le Kid** suggest his concern for the preservation of rural sites; **Anatomie d'un rapport**, as Louis Skorecki percipiently suggested,[31] shows the influence of the women's movement in its extraordinarily honest portrayal of male sexual anxiety, which is then challenged by Moullet's female partner. However, in order to define Moullet's political position somewhat more closely, it is helpful to compare his stance with that of the Situationists who were, it will be recalled, extremely active in France throughout the 1960s and who, it is sometimes claimed, had a subterranean influence on the Events of May 1968. The subject matter of Moullet's films frequently matches central Situationist concerns such as preoccupation with everyday life, the nature of the urban environment and what, today, would be called the question of the 'quality of life', the way human beings are or are not enriched by their environment. Their thinking was thus closely linked with that of Henri Lefebvre and the *Socialisme ou Barbarie* group which criticised Soviet Marxism for not having produced the 'new man' precisely because of lack of attention to qualititative modernisation.[32] Typical of this wish to link the material with the intellectual and the aesthetic is the famous Situationist pamphlet *De la Misère en milieu étudiant* (1966) which denounced both the material and intellectual poverty of French student life and saw the movement of protest against it, in premonitory fashion, as 'the prelude to the next revolutionary period'.[33] Moullet's films are not utopian in the sense that they do not prescribe or prefigure an ideal community, but they are utopian in their stress on the fantastic dimension of life, which means that his preoccupations are consistently close to those of the Situationists. Hence his first feature, **Brigitte et Brigitte** (1966), recapitulates, in its depiction of the difficulties encountered by two girls from the provinces who come to Paris to study, many of the themes of the pamphlet, *De la Misère en milieu étudiant*.

**Brigitte et Brigitte –** Françoise Vatel prays to her household gods

However, the originality of Situationism was that it was an attempt to update the Marxist revolutionary tenets by aesthetic means and that it insisted on the unity of the practical, ideological and cultural spheres. In their considerations of the urban environment, the Situationists imagined 'an experimental city', a far cry from the kind of new town that had sprung up all over Europe in the 1950s and 1960s, which would be a ludic space, a 'city of play' in which the conventional division between work and leisure would disappear: 'the essential value will be that of play (...) overcoming the old division between work that is imposed and passive leisure'.[34] Furthermore, the way in which this would happen was by a process of *détournement* defined as 'the reuse of pre-existing artistic elements in a new unity'.[35] If one compares these theses with Moullet's approach to film making, his preoccupation with the world of work and his vision of the ludic potential of virtually any situation, his relation with Situationist thinking becomes clear. In this he resembled many intellectuals of his generation who were similarly inspired to mistrust established agencies of revolution such as the French Communist Party, but he is probably the only film maker, apart from the Situationist Guy Debord, to have enacted these ideas so literally on film.[36] For what is

Genèse d'un repas – Luc Moullet and Antonietta Pizzorno eating omelette and tuna fish

**198**

**La Comédie du travail** if not a fantastic *détournement*, an exercise in how to go beyond the conventional divisions between work and leisure, and thus in turn a reworking of the central thesis of **Les Sièges de l'Alcazar** that life and the cinema are a continuum.

# 8:

# The Family in Question

## Jacques Doillon

Jacques Doillon has become one of the most productive and widely admired film makers of the post-1968 period. Although he made his first feature, **L'An 01**, in 1972 it was not until the late 1970s that he began to direct the films which would be considered characteristic of his style and preoccupations today. Doillon is now held to be an 'intimist' director whose works focus on the emotional and sexual interactions of small groups of people, depicting the difficulties of the heterosexual couple and the violence often engendered within it. Like André Techiné he might be considered a poet of the alternative family, but unlike Techiné his style combines austerity and excess in a surprising and sometimes frightening manner, emphasising the human face, through the extensive use of close-ups and a style of acting which is a *mise en scène* of the human body. Doillon has acknowledged both Bergman and Cassavetes as major influences and he shares with these masters not only the quest for physical expressivity but also the capacity to render the anxieties of the bourgeoisie of universal concern.[1]

## From Utopia to Neo-Naturalism

At the outset of his film-making career, however, it might have been difficult to predict that this is how Doillon would develop. With the cartoonist Gébé, a member of the *Hara-Kiri* and the *Charlie-Hebdo* teams,[2] he collaborated on a short film, **On ne se dit pas tout entre époux** (1971) and then joined Jean Rouch and Alain Resnais in filming **L'An 01** (1972) adapted from Gébé's original comic strip of the same name. For Doillon 'L'An 01 is an *auteur* film, but it's Gébé's film (...) I wasn't yet ready to say anything on my own account.'[3] But it was also a collaborative effort very much in keeping with the spirit of the times, which brought together several film makers (in much the same way as the compilation films popular in the 1960s, notably **Loin du Vietnam**) as well as many actors from the *café théâtre* who were shortly to become well known in the cinema, such as Miou-Miou, Gérard Depardieu and Thierry Lhermitte, together with Gébé's fellow contributors to the magazines *Hara-Kiri* and *Charlie-Hebdo*, Cavanna, Cabu, Delfeil de Ton and the Professor Choron.[4] Financially, the film was put together from candle ends, with funds from those involved in making it: 'This film has not been granted an *avance sur recettes* (...) it has been produced (with too little money) by a small team of film makers.' This meant that demarcation rules disappeared in the general enthusiasm: 'one camera with everyone behind it and everyone in front of it'.[5] **L'An 01** is a film whose poverty of means contrasts with its extraordinary exuberance of spirit, a contrast which Doillon later in his career, although in a different register, was to exploit in a systematic fashion. It consists of a series of sketches or situations designed to illustrate, praise or promote the transgression of bureaucratic rules and the liberation from all forms of repression. One marvellous and typical scene, for example, shows a group of people standing by a notice which reads 'pelouse interdite' (keep off the grass). They look at each other and then at the lawn in an interrogatory manner and then, very slowly, as though dipping a toe into a cold swimming pool, first one and then another steps onto the grass until a great rush of people suddenly bursts onto the lawn in joy and ecstasy, leaping, shouting and laughing at the feel of the grass beneath their feet.

Just like the eighteenth century revolutionaries whose new calendar was intended to mark a radical break with the traditions of the past, **L'An 01** puts forward the idea that with May 1968 a new world had been ushered in. However, this is not a film about conventional party politics or even alternative political groups, but about the quality of life, about the way people relate to one another and about what would happen if they acted upon the May 1968 slogan and 'took their desires for reality'. It mocks consumerism and those aspects of the affluent society that are forms of alienation: 'Wearing a tie in the middle of July is really the quality of life. Pure silk!';[6] it is anarchist in its rejection of all organisations, and it practises the kind of wit that had become the hallmark of *Charlie-Hebdo*, the 'dérision' or mocking of conventional views which Blier also incorporated into his films. Indeed, the very practice of making the film was to be illustrative of the new social order in its collective and tentative aspects:

*A great film. The only film that is to be made. There won't be any more after this, there won't need to be any more for a long time because when it is finished we'll start it again. While we're shooting it we have to live it so as to make it accurate. And when it's finished we'll show it to other people so that they want to experience the same things (...) and start making it all over again.*[7]

In **L'An 01** we can see how the ideas of the Situationists and the humour of the *Hara-Kiri/Charlie-Hebdo* teams came together for a brief and wonderful moment in a film showing youthful exuberance, transgression and anarchy. When asked, somewhat later, if it accurately translated his own views, Doillon replied:

*Yes, my position is with people who don't belong to any political party, who cannot tolerate what previous generations tolerated in their idiotic belief in a society (...) I wanted to support the kind of liberation movement which was mobilising people at the time. But I am much more pessimistic than Comrade Gébé. His ideas pleased me but the film wasn't in any way my political manifesto.*[8]

Indeed, for Doillon it becomes increasingly apparent that life is a form of tragedy and that politics, or even public affairs, are inimical to his film making concerns: 'I don't want to express my opinions through the cinema. I don't believe in the language of politics and because I am without such belief I tell myself that whatever happens nothing will alter the tragedy of our lives.'[9] It is not surprising, therefore, that the broad canvas, the public arenas and the large crowds to be found in **L'An 01** rapidly disappear from Doillon's films even though the concern with the quality of life and with the alternative society remains. **L'An 01** equates the end of repression with the disappearance of the authoritarian state. In Doillon's subsequent films, however, introspection gradually replaces politics and private lives are substituted for public actions so that the exploration of desire, which was already strongly present in **L'An 01**, is increasingly seen in interpersonal and psychoanalytical terms.

Doillon's second feature film, **Les Doigts dans la tête** (1974), was praised when it opened as an example of the 'new naturalism'. François Truffaut, for example, described it in an influential article as 'a film that is witty and true, a film whose tone is exactly right, a film of extreme simplicity', and praised it for being 'designed to film real slices of life'.[10] For Truffaut this is a film whose strength lies in its apparent artlessness, whose story appears to belong to a tradition which Truffaut himself created, since it concerns the professional and emotional difficulties of a group of young people. Chris, employed as an assistant in a baker's shop, befriends a young Swedish tourist, Liv, and allows her to sleep in his room. This intrigues his friend Léon and upsets his girlfriend Rosette, who has been counting on marrying Chris. After the boss has sacked him for turning up late to work Chris and his friend 'occupy' his room over the baker's shop and it is here that the four young people learn to come to terms with their lives.[11]

These adolescents are away from home, cut off (unwillingly in the case of Rosette) from their families, obliged to live in lodgings provided by their employers or in a 'hostel for young workers', short of money and trying to make their way in a hostile world of work. Thus far, their situation may appear to resemble that of Truffaut's Antoine Doinel in **Baisers volés**. Yet in describing this film as 'a comedy' Truffaut suggests that it is more comparable to his own approach to film making than is really justified, for **Les Doigts dans la tête** is both political and tragic in a way that is entirely uncharacteristic of Truffaut. Like other post-1968 works, such as Claude Faraldo's **Bof** (1971) or Alain Tanner's **La Salamandre** (1971), Doillon's film depicts the working lives of young people in terms of exploitation and alienation, and their fierce resistance to such situations. Chris is prevented from having any kind of social life because his job requires him to get up at two in the morning. When he does decide to go out in the evening he oversleeps and is sacked. Having been persuaded to consult the trade union on his next move, he discovers that he has been underpaid and that his boss, when dismissing him, did not give the requisite period of notice or follow the required procedures. This is why Chris decides to 'occupy' the room over the baker's shop until the boss gives him the money he is owed, and he is supported in this not just by his friends Léon, Rosette and Liv, but also by François, who has been recruited to replace him! The benign trade unionist, the solidarity among the exploited classes, and the recourse to occupation are all activities characteristic of industrial relations in the early 1970s and suggest that for Doillon the 'lessons of May' are still positive.

However, the dominant tone of **Les Doigts dans la
tête** is not optimistic. Despite the apparently positive nature of
political action, despite what Truffaut wrote and the immediate charm of naturalistic scenes such as Chris at work in the
*boulangerie* or the visit to Rosette's mother, the story is
ultimately tragic and its atmosphere claustrophobic. For the
fact is that Chris falls in love with Liv and hurts both himself
and Rosette in the process. Liv is doubly 'foreign' in this
environment since she is both Swedish and middle class. She
behaves in a maternal manner towards Chris and Léon
although they are the same age as she. She lectures them on
the corrupting nature of formal education, initiates them into
yoga and calmly tells both Chris and Rosette that her relationship with Chris cannot last.[12] Her horizons are in every way
broader than Chris's and she treats their meeting as an
interesting but necessarily short-lived experience. Her lucidity is fascinating to young people who have not been brought
up to discuss their emotions or to consider life as a series of
endless possibilities. Thus, although **Les Doigts dans la tête** is
a film about the aftermath of 1968, featuring spoof organisations such as the GRAT (Groupe de résistance au travail)
which could have come straight out of **L'An 01**, it is also a
film about class and social opportunity whose conclusions are
profoundly pessimistic. Unlike Truffaut, who is implicitly

criticised here, Doillon does not see comedy as a refuge from the inexorable pressure of the class system. Instead, like Tanner, Faraldo and Eustache, he presents his young protagonists' brief attempts to explore their feelings as doomed to extinction.

François Truffaut was instrumental in procuring Doillon the commission for his third feature film, **Un Sac de billes** (1975), recommending him to the producer Claude Berri on the strength of **Les Doigts dans la tête**. This is Doillon's only excursion to date into history and it is an adaptation of the Joseph Joffo novel about two Jewish boys under the Occupation (the title of the film refers to their habit of swapping the star of David that they are forced to wear for marbles). In this film there is an undoubted contradiction between the producer's intentions and what Doillon wanted to do: 'I wanted to stick to the children with a lot of close-ups of the boys' faces. But what I was commissioned to provide was a historical drama for the Christmas holidays.'[13] He considers the film a failure: 'I found all the adventure film and the history film side, all the period reconstruction rather distasteful and I just couldn't do it. What did interest me was the last part in the village when virtually nothing happens.'[14] Doillon stresses that he accepted the commission in order to gain experience within the film industry, 'to get to know how the profession worked and (...) to have a regular income'.[15] This was not a positive experience and in fact did Doillon a disservice with the film industry in France, but from the point of view of his personal development it was crucial.[16] **Un Sac de billes** enabled him, on the one hand, to affirm his thematic distance from Truffaut: from this point he ceases to be considered 'naturalist' and the young people in his films are henceforth completely devoid of the artlessness which Truffaut so admired.[17] On the other hand, it allowed him to state his vocation as an *auteur*: 'I prefer making a low-budget film which I have written, directed and edited myself. At the end of the day something exists which I feel responsible for.'[18]

## Behind Closed Doors

Looking back over Doillon's career it can be seen that **Les Doigts dans la tête** introduced an important figure which has subsequently recurred in his films. Though inspired by a newspaper report of an event which really took place, praised for its naturalism and noted for its use of ideas which were

205

generated by May 1968, **Les Doigts dans la tête** also depends on the 'huis clos', the closed room or confined space. Traditionally the 'huis clos' may be a dramatic or legal device. In classical drama it is a means of securing the unity of time, place and action required to generate tragedy, and in legal proceedings it is the term used for the judge's private chamber where testimonies of the most secret kind are heard 'in camera' and are privately resolved. Although in **Les Doigts dans la tête** the young people voluntarily barricade themselves inside a room, here, as elsewhere in Doillon's films, the confined space is psychological as well as physical, involuntary as well as voluntary, and designates both the limited and limiting set of relationships to which Chris has access, the confines of his personal and professional horizons. As has been suggested, this film is unusual in the context of Doillon's *œuvre* for having a strongly developed social dimension and for equating psychological limitations with those of class or even nationality, but it nevertheless points forward to what was to become a systematic psychological and dramatic principle.

Thus in many of Doillon's subsequent films the arena of 'action' is a physically confined space. This is true of the hideaway in **La Drôlesse** (1979), of the family house and the daughter's apartment in **La Fille prodigue** (1980), of the hotel rooms in **La Pirate** (1984), **La Vie de famille** (1985) and **La Vengeance d'une femme** (1989). But whereas in **Les Doigts dans la tête** it is implied that the young people are willing to emerge from their room just as soon as their conditions are met, in **La Fille prodigue** and **La Drôlesse** the room is a retreat from the world and even a psychological regression: the daughter in **La Fille prodigue** is experiencing a depression during which she reverts to her childhood, while the twenty-year-old François in **La Drôlesse** kidnaps the eleven-year-old Mado and hides her from the world in an attempt to arrest time. In **La Vie de famille** and **La Vengeance d'une femme** some of the action takes place out of doors, but the intense moments of confrontation, explanation and dénouement all occur in hotel rooms.

Thus the 'huis clos' in Doillon's films has a psychological as much as, or more than, a physical dimension and is transformed from the scene of political action to that of private theatre. In accepting that this figure has become fundamental to his cinema – 'all my films depend on the "huis clos" '[19] – Doillon naturally invites reference to the most famous modern theatrical exploitation of the figure, Sartre's one-act play, *Huis clos*. This, it will be recalled, opens with three characters, a man and two women, finding themselves locked up together in a windowless, mirrorless and airless room. They realise that they are all dead and that this is hell, and they proceed to recount what acts of emotional torture or moral cowardice have led them to their present predicament, and then to reproduce within this room the patterns of seduction and jealousy which they practised before death.

In *Huis clos*, Sartre played on the metaphorical implications of the term in combining the processes of self-examination and cross-examination, analysis and interrogation. Doillon takes this process still further. His theatre takes place behind closed doors in the sense that it is entirely devoted to the private rather than the public domain and almost always to the emotional nexus of the family. Like Sartre, he chooses locations which are characterised by their impersonality, such as hotel rooms, and which therefore resemble the institutional environment of investigation, the police cell or the padded cell of the psychiatric hospital. In **La Pirate**, for example, some of the rooms are made to resemble those of a hospital, so that the neutral greyness of their decor magnifies the violence of the physical and emotional suffering experienced within them. Doillon also explicitly acknowledges the comparison between his films and the procedures of legal enquiry. For example, when discussing the scene between the father and daughter at the end of **La Vie de famille**, he remarked: 'We call this *finale* "the trial": the father asks the child's forgiveness and his request can only take the form of a series of accusations levelled at the child.'[20] Finally, in Doillon as in Sartre, the 'huis clos' is pre-eminently theatrical, partly because of its reference to the classical tradition but also because of the various ways physical behaviour is voluntarily or involuntarily heightened in the courtroom or the psychiatric hospital. Doillon uses this tradition to structure the action of his films. Unconsciously or deliberately, Doillon's characters set scenes or play out roles rehearsed previously. In **La Drôlesse**, François deliberately sets the scene for Mado and the couple enact a variety of roles on the stage he has created.[21] In **La Fille prodigue**, the daughter (Jane Birkin) attempts to stage a seduction scene between her father and the young woman he is in love with, whom she intends as a surrogate for herself, at the same time as re-enacting her childhood relationship with her father.

Often in Doillon's films the distinction between roles played in life and in art is elided. Thus in **La Femme qui pleure** he and his daughter Lola play out the roles of father and daughter, while in **La Vie de famille** one of the wives is called Mara, the real name of the girl who plays Elise, and the fictional father and daughter, Emmanuel and Elise, use the device of video film to record and explore their relationship. In this way Doillon's films suggest that because of its frame the cinema is an ideal 'huis clos', the perfect medium for the process of psychological exposure and for the treatment of the emotions as theatre.

## The Geometry of Desire

After **Un Sac de billes**, which was not well received by the French film industry, Doillon had difficulty in financing his next projects either through the *avance sur recettes* or from television.[22] His lack of success undoubtedly pushed him into being more personal and idiosyncratic than might otherwise have been the case and led him to affirm his identity as an *auteur*. **La Femme qui pleure**, which followed, was begun as a 'Sunday film' which only later acquired commercial producers,[23] and the degree of Doillon's personal invest-ment, indicated by the presence of himself and his daughter as actors in the film, may go some way towards accounting for the paradigmatic nature of the subject and the style.

Doillon has stated that his interest is in the elemental passions – 'What exists are ultra-familiar feelings such as desire or jealousy' – and that he wishes to expose the unconscious motives of action and passion: 'The cinema is a fantasy. It is worth absolutely nothing unless it recounts the images which come into one's head between six and eight in the morning.'[24] He is deeply interested in psychoanalysis and sees it as an important source of fiction because it exposes our desires and lays bare the bedrock of the emotions: 'I can't understand psychoanalytical jargon but I read psychiatric literature when I am looking for stories: some of these people are fantastic raconteurs (...) It's the detective side of it that I find interesting. There's always a crime, the criminal has to be found and the analysis searches for the clues.'[25] Whatever the pretext for Doillon's films, therefore, he typically seeks out the tragic dimension of a situation, the fundamental patterns of human behaviour, the unspoken motivations of desire, and attempts to place these on screen. Though he makes low-

budget films, with a small number of actors whom he films in essentially domestic situations, his films are immensely ambitious in examining the constants of human behaviour and in their view of man as tragic.

La Femme qui pleure, which inaugurated Doillon's tragic manner, is a banal tale of a triangular relationship. Jacques is married to Dominique but falls in love with Haydée. Dominique cannot come to terms with this betrayal. This is the stuff of innumerable fictions, many of them moral fables or farces. Doillon's treatment of the theme, however, is remarkable for its lack of complicity with any of the characters and, indeed, for its lack of moral dimension. As the title of the film clearly indicates, it is Dominique who is the subject of study, but Dominique in her physical as much as her emotional existence. Doillon is interested in the bodily effects of emotions such as jealousy on an individual. Thus the film is composed as a series of scenes of remarkable intensity, linked by dissolves, which provide the viewer with welcome respite, during most of which Dominique cries or otherwise behaves in an hysterical manner, whilst both the performances and the editing of the film remove narrative progression and substitute immediacy of experience. In this way Dominique's final solution, to offer herself as a sexual partner to Haydée along with her husband, seems an entirely logical outcome of her physical suffering and the physical impact of her emotions.

Certain motifs, however, recur with great regularity in Doillon's films. One is the relationship between father and daughter, what might be considered as a basic oedipal structure, which is seen as a source of fiction. It is present in **La Femme qui pleure**, with Doillon himself acting the father and his daughter Lola the daughter, and is central to **La Fille prodigue** and **La Vie de famille**. The relationship between fiction and the unconscious in this structure is made explicit in both **La Fille prodigue** and **La Drôlesse**. In the first, as has been said, the daughter Jane Birkin tries to promote what is a fictional relationship between her father and another woman as a way of realising her own fantasy of an oedipal relationship with her father. In **La Drôlesse**, similarly, the oedipal relationship is seen as a compelling model for that between men and women generally when Mado, who is unrelated to François, says that she has no father and elects François, her kidnapper, to fulfil that role.[26] The second motif is that of the man who is torn between two (or sometimes more) women. This is obviously central to **La Femme qui pleure** and is present in sublimated form in **La Fille prodigue** and **La Vie de famille**. In the former, Jane Birkin's father has fallen in love with another woman with whom he has been conducting a mainly imaginary relationship. In the latter, Emmanuel is torn between his former and his present wife, as well as his own daughter and the daughter of his second wife whom he makes an attempt to seduce. Doillon is far from pursuing the indulgent moralising which characterises popular treatments of this topic in films such as **Fatal Attraction**. He explores passion and pain rather than right and wrong, so much so that the gender of the individual who suffers is immaterial. Thus in **La Pirate**, perhaps his most disturbing and painful film to date, Alma is torn between her husband and another woman, Carole, with whom she has fallen in love. However, as **La Drôlesse** illustrated with respect to the oedipal relationship, Doillon again sees such structures as a powerful source of fiction. Hence in **La Vengeance d'une femme** (1989) a man's widow strikes up a relationship with her dead husband's mistress in order to kill her. The detection of this crime then creates the fiction which the film narrates.

Among his prolific output two films stand out as *summa* of Doillon's *oeuvre*, **La Pirate** and **La Vie de famille**, the former dismissed as exaggerated and virtually unwatchable, the latter praised for its sureness of touch and its verisimilitude. **La Pirate** is a film which plays entirely on the physical expression of the emotions, attempting to give physical expression to an emotional configuration. This, as Doillon stressed, runs counter to the traditions of the French cinema which is

> *not generally very physical. It does not like dealing with the violence and emotions within us. In France we always try to be clever, we have to think about everything and comment on the images. We always insert a point of view between the actor and the spectator. I hate it (...) I am not yet satisfied with my films but I do try to get straight to the emotions.*[27]

**La Pirate** is shot in grey tones and in Cinemascope, which in Doillon's view breaks the implicitly cosy relationship of the shot/reverse shot and the standard format, allowing the image to be elongated horizontally to include the third party which is inevitable to the geometry of desire as Doillon sees it. And in the best Shakespearean tradition, the triangular drama played out between Alma, her husband Andrew, and her lover Carole is observed by two 'innocent' parties, a clown and a child, a

**La Pirate** – Jane Birkin and Maruschka Detmers

device both for heightening the emotional impact of the film and for providing its dramatic dénouement when the child kills Alma. **La Pirate** is difficult to follow as a narrative because, as has been pointed out, no temporal context is provided. At some point in the past Alma must have met Carole, but Doillon does not show us their encounter, only allowing access to the group at the point where passion becomes insupportable. The result is an extraordinarily emotional investment in corporeal presence in the poignant contrast between the bodies of the two women, and in the suffering Jane Birkin expresses in her writhing and contortions.[28]

    **La Vie de famille** begins as a much sunnier film. Emmanuel takes Elise, the daughter of his first marriage, away for a weekend and they end up in a hotel in Spain. The light of the South where the film is set, the many exterior scenes, and the unselfconscious acting of the child all contribute to an immense sense of liberation. Indeed, this is a feeling experienced by both Emmanuel and Elise as they slip away for a weekend on their own away from the implied recriminations of Emmanuel's wives, present and former. However, Emma-

La Vie de famille –
Emmanuel (Sami Frey)
filming his daughter Elise
(Mara Goyet)

La Vie de Famille

nuel is not a sympathetic character. He is described by Doillon as: ' impatient, demanding (. . .) a very idealistic character who finds everyday life difficult (. . .) twisted, complicated, malicious, disappointing, sarcastic'.[29] Because of her father's volatility Elise appears more poised, more mature and more stable than she might otherwise be, so that the normal relation between parents and children appears to be reversed, with the parent becoming ever more importunate and the child refusing to cede to his emotional demands. Shut up in a hotel room the pair judge each other, not in a face-to-face confrontation but addressing each other through video recordings. The father, who feels guilty towards his daughter, asks for her forgiveness but typically does so in the form of an accusation. This is a condensation of the thematics of Doillon's cinema: 'The strange thing is that we had always imagined the scene of the final accusation as a face-to-face confrontation, but the video camera gave us the idea of separating them and making them confess one after the other (. . .) so that the video recorder becomes the successor to the confession box.'[30]

## The Aesthetics of Austerity

Such remarks should not be held to imply that Doillon is a Catholic film maker. In reality, the austerity of Protestantism has made an important contribution both to his iconography and to his investigation of the emotions. Doillon was brought up in the non-conformist tradition and confesses to a liking for Protestant churches where 'nothing distracts the eye, there are no superfluous details'.[31] Part of the intimism of his films and their often austere decor comes from a dislike of visual excess and physical promiscuity, so that he attempts to shoot in 'the most impersonal places I can find' and avoids public places such as cafes and restaurants.[32] This, indeed, might form a further element of comparison with *Huis clos*, from which mirrors, or any of the myriad devices for reflection which are typical of cafes, are totally absent. Part of Doillon's admiration for the directors he refers to as 'les Nordiques', such as Dreyer and Bergman, can be traced to their use of the contrast between decorative restraint and emotional excess. But the Protestant tradition also encourages self-examination, concentration on the individual and his or her emotional resources and, on occasions, the act of testimony. Though historically a Catholic, Joan of Arc, as filmed by Dreyer, might be held typical of this kind of inspirational self-examination and

**213**

suffering. Thus, although Doillon's more recent films, in particular **La Vie de famille**, have been literally sunnier, it remains the case that his aesthetic principles combine emotional extravagance with visual austerity, an austerity which extends beyond the sets and decor to the way in which his films are composed and edited. Dreyer's androgynous Joan belies in appearance the exquisite torture she is suffering, and in this she has many affinities with Doillon's heroines. Such principles, therefore, allow Doillon to make the transition from deviant or criminal behaviour, considered as a form of liberation, which was typical of the early 1970s and is treated in jocular mode in **L'An 01**, to homosexuality, incest, kidnapping or murder considered as a sign of emotional stress, a necessary part of Doillon's tragic vision of the world.

Doillon has suggested that **La Pirate** is a partial remake of Bergman's **The Silence** and a comparison between the two films is useful in attempting to define Doillon's aesthetics. **The Silence** portrays two sisters, Anna and Ester, together with Anna's son, who arrive at a hotel in a city of a country whose language they cannot understand. Ester is dying, probably from lung cancer. Anna is sexually hungry, picks up a man in the street and brings him back to the hotel to make love. This makes Ester angry and jealous. The child, meanwhile, is expelled into the hotel corridor and comes across a group of circus dwarfs who entertain him. Thematically, **The Silence** with its consideration of homosexuality, incest, jealousy and the family, is clearly very close to **La Pirate**. The film is chiefly remarkable, however, for its depiction of pain, for which Bergman uses close-ups of the women's faces, for example in the sequence where Anna suffers such excruciating physical pain that she has to hold on to the bedstead, or in the acrimonious discussions between the sisters which explode the convention of the shot/reverse shot and instead place the two heads at different angles but held within the same frame. It becomes clear that Doillon was particularly impressed by Bergman's capacity to exploit the expressivity of the human face and to use physical contrast as a form of characterisation. Thus the difference between the ailing Ester and robust Anna is mirrored in the deliberate contrast between the bodies of Jane Birkin and Maruschka Detmers in **La Pirate**, the one tall and thin, the other plump and feline.

Like Bergman, Doillon is a director of women and, like him, uses children to emphasise the suffering of his

214

female characters. Doillon's children are like the dwarfs in **The Silence**, small in stature but adult in comportment, clowns with a serious message, the focus of stability, like Elise in **La Vie de famille** or Lola in **La Femme qui pleure**, in a world in which the adults have gone mad. Moreover an examination of his filmography suggests that after shooting films whose subject is extreme passion, such as **La Femme qui pleure** and **La Pirate**, he returns to the fundamentals of childhood, as in **La Drôlesse** and **La Vie de famille**. Doillon has said that he has repressed most memories of his childhood and therefore attempts to reconstruct it through his films,[33] so that the constant return to the origins of life is also a renewal of the sources of his inspiration. Life, for Doillon, continues, but it is constantly perverted.

## Maurice Pialat

Pialat is a film maker who is difficult to classify and describe because his career has followed an unusual pattern and he has devoted considerable energy to promoting a view of himself and his works as maverick. In public Pialat often appears aggressive and hostile; he frequently claims in interviews that financial constraints have ruined his films, and he cultivates the image of someone difficult for actors and writers to work with.[34] Above all his attitude is that of a person who refuses to attempt to please and consequently an artist who will not make compromises to attract the audience. However, whatever its 'real-life' truth, this picture is assiduously constructed and must be read off against the characters in the films, some of which are strongly autobiographical and some of which are played by Pialat himself. Pialat wishes himself to be seen as a film maker who cannot be pigeonholed, as an individual and an *auteur* whose original, eccentric and difficult personality match a political, social and above all aesthetic position.

The progress of Pialat's career illustrates his resistance to classification. He was born in 1925, trained as a painter at the Ecole des Arts Décoratifs and the Ecole des Beaux-Arts and held several exhibitions of his work in the late 1940s. After this he discovered the cinema and during the 1950s made a number of amateur films whilst beginning a second career as an actor, appearing on stage in *Julius Caesar*, *Coriolanus* and *Marie Stuart* and, in 1955, joining Michel

Vitold as assistant. He subsequently had some success as a film actor and can be seen in Chabrol's **Que la Bête meure** (1969) and Eustache's **Mes petites Amoureuses** (1975) as well as his own films, **La Maison des bois** (1971), **A nos Amours** (1983) and **Sous le Soleil de Satan** (1987). It was therefore not until he was well into his thirties that Pialat started making films professionally, with the short films **L'Amour existe** dating from 1960 and **Janine** dating from 1961,[35] and he did not shoot his first full-length film until the age of forty-four, when he made **L'Enfance nue** (1969).

In terms of his film making career, therefore, Pialat clearly belongs with the post-1968 film makers, but in terms of his age and generation he belongs with film makers such as Resnais, Varda and Marker who, like him, were born in the 1920s. This generational displacement gives rise to a series of textual disjunctions in Pialat's films which are the product of the longevity of his apprenticeship, his early film influences, the artistic climate of the 1950s and the impact of the *nouvelle vague*. Pialat claims Renoir as his earliest mentor: 'I think the film which started it all for me was **La Bête humaine** (...) I went to see it five or six times in a row.'[36] This is an admiration, along with that of Dreyer, which Pialat shares with the *nouvelle vague*, and Renoir's influence can sometimes be seen in the construction of his shots and the way he uses actors. However, Pialat appreciates other aspects of Renoir's films which are also typical of French cinema of the 1930s, such as the stress on individuality and eccentricity, on a France riddled with particularisms and regional interests, on the family as the microcosm in this sense of the nation and, therefore, on family rituals as particularly psychological and socially significant. Thus the famous meal scenes in Pialat's films **A nos Amours** and **Loulou** (1980) recall those – convivial in Pagnol, bitter-sweet in Renoir – of the populist cinema. Pialat has claimed that his own experience of family life was typically that of 'prewar France as described by Phillippe Ariès' and he has long cherished a project for a film on the Popular Front years.[37]

Another important influence on Pialat's films was the non-fiction cinema of the 1950s, both the ethnographical film movement and the poetic documentaries of the Left Bank School. The sweeping shots of working class districts of outer Paris in **L'Amour existe**, the documentary detail of **L'Enfance nue**, the authentic locations and characters of **Passe ton Bac d'abord** (1979) all recall the urban studies of Rouch and his followers. Pialat has been attracted by the virtues of direct cinema, the spontaneity and realism of the language and behaviour of non-professional actors, especially young people, and the cinema's capacity to reveal little-known parts of the country, such as the mining town of Lens in which **Passe ton Bac d'abord** is set. Conversely, his first professional short film, **L'Amour existe**, resembles (to judge from the script) the documentary as practised by Varda and Resnais, that is to say the montage of shots of Paris districts, most of which are poor or run-down, is juxtaposed with a soundtrack on which Pialat speaks or recites a poetic text which is inspired by or is a reflection on the images. This text bears little relation to those Pialat has written subsequently and he has repudiated it,[38] but the technique of combining the real and the imaginary, the everyday and the poetic is one which he continued to explore (as did Varda), although in a different form.

The third major influence on Pialat, as on all post-1968 film makers, was that of the *nouvelle vague*, although in Pialat's case the relationship with this group of film makers, who were almost all younger than he, has always been extremely tense, for one of the things Pialat most disliked about the group was its clannishness: 'It was a bit like the hare and the tortoise: they were making films and I wasn't. The *nouvelle vague* was made up of a bunch of friends and if you weren't one of them you found it difficult to make films.'[39] There are many things which differentiate Pialat's films from those of the *nouvelle vague*: they do not have a metropolitan focus, they are without the playful intellectualism characteristic of the *nouvelle vague*, they do not privilege montage, they do not seek the lush colours typical of later Truffaut. When Pialat began to make films the *nouvelle vague* represented the modernist orthodoxy and he therefore stressed how different he was. Yet **L'Enfance nue** was made with the help of Truffaut, who no doubt saw in it echoes of his own unhappy childhood and thematic similarities with **L'Enfant sauvage** which he was himself to make the following year.

Although Pialat depicts a different class milieu from that to be found in Truffaut or Chabrol films, he shares the *nouvelle vague*'s interest in young people. The older generation rarely figures in Pialat's films, and when it does, as in **Nous ne vieillirons pas ensemble** (1972) or **La Gueule ouverte** (1973), it is presented as passive and impotent in relation to the younger characters. Even though he himself has aged, Pialat has continued to depict young people, from the maladjusted child in **L'Enfance nue**, to the final-year lycée students in **Passe ton Bac d'abord**, to the gangs of young people in **Loulou** and **Police** (1985) or the fifteen-year-old Suzanne and her boyfriends in **A nos Amours**. Pialat's young people come from less well-heeled or establishment backgrounds than Chabrol's children of provincial notables or Godard's revolutionary students. They are the children of miners, of Jewish traders, or they belong to the immigrant and/or the semi-criminal sub-culture. Pialat denies that this is a political statement and his attitude is certainly different from that of the post-1968 political film makers who sought to give the people a voice. His relation to these youngsters is best characterised by the role he himself plays in **A nos Amours**, that of the father who is complicit with his daughter and indulgent towards her without identifying with her. There is no sense in Pialat's films, unlike those of the *nouvelle vague*, of a director making films for his own generation. Pialat's look combines both warmth and dispassion; it is simultaneously that of participant and observer, the progenitor who, as in **A nos Amours**, is both present and absent.

Thus if we consider the evolution of Pialat's career, at least up to the point at which he made **Police**, we receive a curious sense that it has failed to observe the normal flow of time and that he has frequently made films whose affinity appears not to be with those that are contemporary but with those made up to a decade earlier. Hence it is tempting to compare **L'Enfance nue** (1969) with **Les 400 Coups** (1959), **Nous ne vieillirons pas ensemble** (1972) to **L'Amour fou** (1968) and **Passe ton Bac d'abord** (1979) to **Adieu Philippine** (1962). However, this interplay of influences and rejections is not confined to *nouvelle vague* films or their subject matter: it is, as we shall see, an important principle of Pialat's film making.[40]

## The Pialat Aesthetic

Pialat's earlier films impressed by what was held to be their realism. The documentary elements in **L'Enfance nue** and **Passe ton Bac d'abord**, the use of non-professional actors which is also to be found, to a limited extent, in **Loulou** and **A nos Amours**, the physical and emotional violence of **Nous ne vieillirons pas ensemble** and **La Gueule ouverte** have all contributed to this impression. If by 'realism' it is meant that Pialat does not shrink from tackling sensitive or difficult

subjects then clearly he is a realist. The maladjusted child in
**L'Enfance nue** is painfully unable to communicate, Jean the
lover in **Nous ne vieillirons pas ensemble** is physically and
verbally violent towards his mistress Catherine, the son in **La
Gueule ouverte** behaves callously towards his dying mother.
Pialat is celebrated for the apparently uncontrived recording of
non-standard speech and behaviour, leading *Ecran* to describe
**Passe ton Bac d'abord** as 'a delightful new example of the
new naturalism which Jacques Doillon and Daniel Duval
launched some years ago'.[41] Pialat also displays a remarkable
insouciance about plot construction, basing the structure of his
film on his own observations at the Assistance Sociale for
**L'Enfance nue**, and plot, characterisation and casting on the
unstructured interviews carried out with teenagers in Lens in
**Passe ton Bac d'abord**.[42] Moreover, the chance events of
'real life' figure in an important way in **A nos Amours** when,
for example, the father who had left his family returns
unexpectedly to the family flat.

 But whatever the naturalism of Pialat's films he is
only partly a realist and his realism has more to do with a
rejection of Bressonian formalism and aestheticism than with a
political or social project.[43] Pialat has said: 'I loathe beautiful

photography in the cinema' and 'perhaps because of my early career as a painter I refused for many years to try to make my films pictorially interesting'.[44] However, he claims to have obliged the cameraman Pierre-William Glenn, well-known for his 'fine photography' in Truffaut and Tavernier films, to use a much cruder palette than usual in **Passe ton Bac d'abord**, so that the bright red of the brick walls strikes a particularly jarring note. Clearly Pialat is not above the odd plastic intervention. In **A nos Amours**, in the role of Suzanne's father, he engineers a discussion of aesthetics which is useful in elucidating his compositional idiom. Over the family meal which takes place towards the end of the film, Suzanne, the heroine, claims that her favourite painter is Bonnard, 'because he's sensual'. This might be one reason for the failure of her short-lived relationship with Luc, the art student who spends much of his time copying academic nudes, or her marriage to Jean-Pierre, who is a 'chromiste' by trade, that is, someone who corrects the colours on reproductions of paintings. Jean-Pierre, meanwhile, engages in a discussion with Jacques, director of an intellectual and implicitly pretentious art magazine, on the relative merits of Picasso and Rousseau. Jacques states that Picasso is overrated and over-intellectual, that he sees life in a distorted manner and that Rousseau is the greater painter; Jean-Pierre defends Picasso as the recognised father of modern painting. When interviewed, Pialat claimed that he was expressing his own opinion of Picasso, whose view of the world he disliked and, as important, whose 'myth' he made Jacques reject: 'The myth of the priapic old man, still sexually active at the age of ninety, with all his canvases piled up . . .'.[45] It is not simply Picasso's painting but his status that is irritating, as is the corresponding view of Rousseau as a 'Sunday painter'. For Pialat, Rousseau is undervalued because 'in France (. . .) the University dictates taste everywhere'.[46]

It is perhaps characteristic of Pialat that his aesthetic position includes a perception of the social status of the artist. Rousseau should not be treated as an amateur any more, no doubt, than Pialat should have failed to have been taken seriously as a film maker. Human endeavour and human diversity are to be respected whatever the attempt of academic or cinematic 'cliques' to prevent this happening. Here Pialat elides the canons of beauty, good taste and good behaviour into a middle class orthodoxy against which he presents himself as rebelling. He respects the psychologically damaged (**L'Enfance nue**) and the physically lame (**Loulou**), the minor enthusiasms of the poor (**Passe ton Bac d'abord**) and the obsessions of the fanatic (**Sous le Soleil de Satan**). He contrasts the pretentiousness of the academic and the intellectual with the solid values of the craftsman and has twice cast himself in the latter role, wearing the overalls that are the symbol of this status as the primary school teacher in **La Maison des bois** and the artisan/father in **A nos Amours**. What Pialat admires in Rousseau, perhaps, is the combination of simplicity with a rejection of hierarchies of value. Picasso's perspective may have been new but it was still hierarchised; Rousseau treats man and the natural world, it might be argued, without the conventional distinctions, composing his paintings of materials chosen without respect for the existing canons.

Pialat is careful to avoid pushing this thesis beyond the limits at which it can be sustained and it is an indication, but no more, of the way he goes about composing his films. It should be stressed, however, that neither Picasso nor Rousseau are realists in the conventional sense and that Rousseau may also appeal to Pialat because his paintings are magical transformations of the real world. If we return briefly to Pialat's account of the making of **L'Enfance nue** we can see the basis on which his cinema has developed. This film was commissioned by the Assistance Sociale and before filming Pialat spent several months in documentary research. But when he actually came to make the film he had in the front of his mind a recent viewing of Louis Lumière's **Le Goûter de bébé**: 'What I understand by realism goes beyond reality (...) Did Lumière film reality? I don't think so (...) Lumière is a more fantastic film maker than Méliès (...) The cinema creates a dream world (...) it transforms what is sordid into something marvellous, it makes the ordinary exceptional, and turns what is filmed into a moment of death. That's what I understand by realism.'[47]

Admiration for Rousseau may also be helpful in elucidating Pialat's attitude to the subject matter of his films, to narrative structure and ultimately to the passage of time. Just as in painting Pialat apparently admires Rousseau's refusal of conventional hierarchies and perspectives, so in the structure of his films he does not necessarily order events into a hierarchy of significance. He has frequently run short of money when shooting or found finance difficult to raise. This has had an effect on films such as **Passe ton Bac d'abord**, which was hurriedly made as a substitute for a more ambitious film **Les Meutrières**, which ran out of money, and on **A nos**

**Amours**, in which all that remains of a more ambitious and expensive earlier version is the prologue set in a holiday camp. But whether or not he has adequate resources Pialat is nonchalant about narrative. He has only recently begun to use a storyboard again,[48] and when editing he retains much that other film makers would eliminate for the sake of consistency or coherence. In the hands of a director such as Godard traces of earlier versions of a film would stress the materiality of the cinema, but in Pialat's case they serve to underline the fact that, though his films sometimes resemble a bricolage and are sometimes elliptical, this is because he seeks emotional intensity and immediacy above all else.

His nonchalance also affects the depiction of the passage of time and this is best exemplified by **A nos Amours**. The script for this film was written by Arlette Langmann. Originally entitled **Les Filles du faubourg**, it was an autobiographical account of her own adolescence in the 1960s as the daughter of a Polish, Jewish furrier, documenting her relationship with her family and particularly her father who was to die at the end of the film.[49] This early version might be compared to Diane Kurys's account of a Jewish girlhood in **Diabolo menthe** (1977) or to the Nicole Garcia episode in Resnais's **Mon Oncle d'Amérique** (1980). But because nearly ten years elapsed between the writing of **Les Filles du faubourg** and the making of **A nos Amours** there is a curious discrepancy, which Pialat freely admits, between the parents' attempts to prevent their daughter Suzanne going out with her boyfriends and the more liberal behaviour of the 1980s which allows Suzanne short-lived sexual adventures and frequent changes of partner. The partial but not total recasting of the script is matched by strange temporal disjunctions within the film itself. It opens with a scene in a *colonie de vacances* in which Suzanne is rehearsing for a part in Musset's *On ne badine pas avec l'amour* (in real life she does, of course, trifle with love). We know that this episode was to have had a narrative function. Now it has none except, perhaps, to show that Suzanne's brother Robert finds his sister beautiful. But when Suzanne is shown wearing a short white dress, standing with her back to the camera in the prow of a boat to the accompaniment of Purcell's 'The Cold Song' we have a moment of intensity which explains why Pialat retained the sequence. Suzanne's changes of boyfriend are extremely rapid but made to seem more so because the various characters are not properly introduced, and by the time we reach the meal scene, towards the end of the film, it would appear that some time has elapsed. The father who left home returns unexpectedly to show the flat to a potential purchaser. Suzanne, whom we briefly saw preparing for her marriage, now appears to be married, as does her brother. There are, in other words, many gaps in our knowledge which Pialat makes no attempt to fill and it must be concluded that he is not interested in doing so.

Similar lacunae are apparent in **Loulou**, which opens in a fairly conventional manner with the break-up of a marriage but quickly ceases to exist in identifiable time or space, with much of the action taking place in beds in which time is by definition suspended.[50] Once again the meal scene towards the end of the film serves as a catalyst and yet is curiously timeless. It is shot out of doors with the actors visibly improvising some of their lines, so that the scene which should have been central to the dramatic denouement appears divorced from the remainder of the film. **Police** is constructed as a series of tense moments of interrogation and seduction with virtually no establishing set or decor, so that the viewer is left to deduce a milieu and a social situation, while **Sous le Soleil de Satan** recounts the mystical experience of the Abbé Donissan's encounter with the devil after which his ministry on earth takes on an unreal quality, existing almost in the kind of semi-hallucinatory state procured by fasting or self-immolation.

Pialat's disregard for time and its effects is interestingly illustrated in the opening lines of his novel, **Nous ne vieillirons pas ensemble**, from which the film was adapted: 'I have never known,' says the central character, 'where I was going in life and I have absolutely no notion of time passing. I am like that today and if I go back several years I was still like that and even further back I was still as I am today . . . Is this a way of not growing old? Time has little influence on someone who does not feel it passing.'[51] This approach to time is typical of all his films and it accounts for his lack of concern with conventional narrative, in which events are unfolded as a linear time sequence, as well as his refusal to make films that echo the concern of his own generation. It also explains aspects of his visual style in which sequence shots are often used to signify the passage of time.[52]

## Sex and Family Life

Pialat's major interest might be described as the exploration of sexual relations between men and women on the one hand, and

the study of the family on the other, sometimes although not always in one and the same film. Both **Nous ne vieillirons pas ensemble** and **Loulou** chart the disintegration of a relationship, **A nos Amours** and **Police** each describe the sex life of a young girl, while **Sous le Soleil de Satan** explores the sexual temptation of a devout Catholic priest. Pialat's films attach great importance to women, especially to young women, towards whom he displays a degree of ambivalence. Sometimes, as with Suzanne in the opening sequence of **A nos Amours**, Pialat films women so as to exaggerate their visual function as an object of desire; at other times, as with Nelly in **Loulou,** he attributes actions to women which fulfil the worst male fantasies of jealousy. On these occasions Pialat apparently restricts women to a conventional object function and indeed makes much of the drama of his films turn on male anxiety that women will revolt. But in Pialat's films the women always do so. They are creatures of flesh and blood whose feelings and emotions are presented as important and are treated seriously. At the same time as sympathising with the male predicament, therefore, Pialat also encourages rebelliousness among women. The father figure in **A nos Amours** does not disapprove of his daughter. The husband,

**Nous ne vieillirons pas ensemble** – Jean Yanne and Marlène Jobert making a documentary film

Jean, in **Nous ne vieillirons pas ensemble** complains about Catherine precisely because she has preferred a dull and conventional marriage to life with himself. Thus, exceptionally among directors, Pialat has created a series of splendid roles for women, foremost among which is that of Suzanne, played by Sandrine Bonnaire in **A nos Amours**.

Pialat's women tend to be sexually adventurous. In **Nous ne vieillirons pas ensemble**, Jean fears that Catherine may leave him but tries to lay the blame for this on her parents. They deny that they have encouraged her and say that Catherine makes her own decisions – something which, of course, Jean fears. In **Loulou** the deserted husband André asks Nelly his wife what attracts her to Loulou and she replies, in a way calculated to hurt André's pride, 'If you really want to know, he never stops.' In **A nos Amours** Suzanne flits from boyfriend to boyfriend because, she claims, her heart is 'dry' and unfeeling. She is so apparently detached that she cannot be provoked by a former boyfriend taking up with one of her girlfriends. She causes protective and incestuous jealousy in her brother and to a lesser degree her father, but again apparently remains unmoved and, having been married for only six months, leaves for America with a young man who is not her husband. The men in this film all revolve round Suzanne, who is perceived as charming, attractive but also dangerous because of her inability to settle down.

In **Police** the detective who falls in love with the gangster's moll, Noria, hopes she will abandon her loyalty to her drug-dealing lover as a result. Instead she happily serves two men until forced to choose between them. In **Sous le Soleil de Satan** Mouchette (Sandrine Bonnaire again) is a youthful seductress who has already threatened to ruin a local politician and who now tempts the Abbé Donissan. In its various permutations we can see Pialat pursuing a modern version of the myth of the femme fatale, originally encountered in **La Bête humaine**, the woman who enjoys sex for its own sake, without being attached, who is prepared to leave her husband and abandon her social class for her lover and who then betrays him. Unlike the femme fatale of the 1930s and 1940s, however, Pialat's women assert their intellectual as well as their sexual freedom. Catherine, Suzanne and Nelly all make rational life choices which hurt the men they love but are entirely logical within their own terms; Catherine decides to marry a safe but dull man, Suzanne leaves her husband and goes to America, Nelly decides to have an abortion, so that it might be argued that Pialat gives his women a superior lucidity.

Unlike his more misogynist contemporaries, Pialat does not blame his women, but he does show his men suffering. Indeed, Pialat is highly typical of the post-1968 generation in showing the fragile side of apparently robust males. Pialat's men often have a psychological vulnerability which contrasts with their strongly virile appearance, or they combine acts of violence, which are coded as masculine, with exaggeratedly feminine traits. The deserted males in **Nous ne vieillirons pas ensemble** and **Loulou** played, respectively by Jean Yanne and Guy Marchand, are both strongly virile in appearance. Yanne is stocky, dark, looks as though he needs a shave and displays the hair on his chest; Marchand is also dark and slightly unshaven and the emphatic masculinity of his appearance renders his performance as a well-heeled advertising executive less convincing, a fact which again illustrates how Pialat is prepared to trade one form of verisimilitude for another. But both of these characters have an emotional vulnerability which is at odds with their physical appear-

**Loulou** – Nelly (Isabelle Huppert) eats Sunday lunch with Loulou's family

226

ance. In **Loulou** the eponymous hero (Gérard Depardieu) hangs out with a bunch of thugs, thinks nothing of starting a brawl in a cafe, moves in a male culture of leather jackets, gangs, flick-knives and violence. And yet when Nelly becomes pregnant his reaction is extremely sentimental, and when she decides, without consulting him, to have an abortion, he experiences an immense sense of betrayal. In **A nos Amours** Suzanne's brother Robert is both protective of his sister and violent towards her (he beats her from time to time), aggressive in his personal relations but of marked homosexual inclination. Pialat's men have raw nerves, they are outwardly violent and inwardly vulnerable; they are also frequently masochistic, either because they torture themselves psychologically like Jean or André or because, like the priest in **Sous le Soleil de Satan**, they punish themselves physically. The epigraph of **A nos Amours** might be a quotation attributed to Van Gogh and spoken in the film, 'Unhappiness will last for ever' and for Pialat, no doubt, Van Gogh (on whom he wished to make a film) serves as the exemplary tortured artist whose suicide represents the climax of his self-immolation.

## Family Life and the Class Structure

Despite the fact that he has a reputation for portraying working class milieux in an authentic manner, Pialat's lack of concern for certain kinds of verisimilitude means that his films offer a weak sense of social structure. Parts of his films may ring true as class portraits – **Passe ton Bac d'abord** was praised for its depiction of the mining community, **Police** for its portrait of the immigrant community.[53] Yet a closer examination of his major films, **A nos Amours**, **Loulou** and **Police**, reveals considerable uncertainties about class and, at the same time, the promotion of the family as opposed to the class structure.

　　The clearest instance of this is, perhaps, **Loulou**. The film is apparently structured round a contrast between the milieu of the middle class Nelly and the working class Loulou. This contrast is pursued at the level of set and decor, with Nelly's spacious and well-furnished apartment juxtaposed with Loulou's environment of seedy bars, cheap hotels and run-down flats. It is less clear at the level of casting since Guy Marchand, as we have seen, does not conform to the middle class physical or sartorial stereotype, while Isabelle Huppert as Nelly is not dressed, even at the beginning of the film, in the kind of clothes that her background would have led us to expect. On closer inspection, indeed, the viewer is struck by the similarities rather than the differences between the two milieux. Nelly, it is implied, has moved from one extended family to another and has as a result of the move become preoccupied with flat-hunting, that is to say with a place in which to recreate the familial structure. The scene in which Nelly's brother comes for a meal with Loulou and Nelly, in order to enquire after Loulou's intentions towards his sister and his employment prospects, is mirrored therefore by a scene in which Nelly is similarly inspected by Loulou's family over Sunday lunch, and in both cases the family meal, whatever its difference of scale, provides a point of psychological and social concentration. Arguably, therefore, what is wrong with Nelly's marriage to André is not, as she implied, the inadequacy of their sex life, but the failure of the relationship to be transformed into the supportive and creative family environment which Nelly comes from and which she seeks.

A similar analysis might be applied to **A nos Amours**. The script started life as the portrait of a Jewish family and some elements of this remain.[54] As in **Loulou**, this

A nos Amours –
Sandrine Bonnaire and
Dominique Besnehard at
the family gathering

is an extended family in which the children do not move away from home but, instead, incorporate their partners into the existing structure. The family is a physical and emotional nexus and, again as in **Loulou**, much concern focuses on the family apartment, which is here a place for working as well as living. Indeed, it is his preoccupation with the future of the family apartment which brings Suzanne's father back to the flat and which precipitates the dramatic dénouement of the film. It is within this structure, round the meal table at which the family foregather, that the crucial discussions about art and life take place, where Rousseau is preferred to Picasso, where Suzanne decides to leave her husband, and so on.

It is significant, however, that in **A nos Amours** the family is an economic as well as a psychological unit. This confirms, on the one hand, Pialat's implicit preference for the authenticity of the artisan, already discussed, but on the other hand his belief that art and life are a continuum, a position which can, for example, also be seen in the shading of the distinction in his work between fiction and autobiography. The scriptwriter Arlette Langmann's own family network also contributed a considerable amount to the making of **A nos Amours**. Langmann is the sister of Claude Berri, who wrote

Police – Gérard Depardieu enmeshed by Sophie Marceau

and acted in Pialat's early film, **Janine** (1961). Evelyne Ker, who plays the mother in **A nos Amours**, had acted the prostitute to Berri's punter in **Janine** and, in addition, believed she was cast in **A nos Amours** because she was well acquainted with Langmann's real family background and had frequently visited her parents.[55] Dominique Besnehard, likewise, claims long acquaintance with the Langmann family.[56] In this way, film, family and the film business are all superposed in **A nos Amours** in a way that renders the distinction between truth and fiction virtually impossible to draw.

Pialat has sometimes been accused of anti-semitism,[57] and it is true that he sometimes caricatures Jewish people. However, he is also fascinated by the immigrant family, no doubt because it is often more tightly-knit than the non-immigrant family and therefore, in some sense, more expressive of the qualities he wishes to attribute to this structure. Nowhere is this more interestingly revealed than in **Police**, in which the group of young drug-dealers form a mafia-style, unofficial family which is just the kind of support network provided by official families, but which also, as Depardieu finds to his cost, is the locus for the erosion or the elision of distinctions between truth and fiction, the family serving in this case, as in others, to generate fictions.

In his films, therefore, Pialat takes the family, which is one of the central themes of French cinema in the 1970s, explored by directors as disparate as Godard, Téchiné and Doillon, and makes it the source of his art. The family, for Pialat as for Doillon, is the origin of suffering and the generator of fictions. Pialat's actors all emphasise the creative role the film maker attributes to stress and suffering,[58] a creative role which is confirmed by Pialat's reinvention of his own upbringing: 'I got it into my head that I had had an unhappy childhood. Perhaps I really did.'[59] The remark might stand as an epigraph to all his work.

# 9:

# The New History Film

## René Allio

## The People's War

The 1970s saw the production of a new kind of history film which, unlike those made in the studios of Hollywood, Rome or France in the 1940s and 1950s, was neither costume drama, cloak and dagger intrigue nor epic.[1] Although the revival of the history film came after a period in the 1960s when the present day seemed to preoccupy film makers to the exclusion of almost everything else, its cinematic antecedents are comparable to those of the *nouvelle vague*, for in its regionalism, its use of authentic locations and of non-professional actors the new history film clearly had affinities with Italian neo-realism and the French ethnographic film movement. But its intellectual inspiration derived ultimately from the work of the *Annales* school which, during the 1960s, thanks to historians such as Emmanuel Le Roy Ladurie, had become widely known outside the confines of the university and the milieux of professional historians.[2] The shift that had taken place in the historian's field of enquiry,[3] encouraging the study of the lives of ordinary people rather than kings and queens, of the region and the locality rather than the capital city and the court, and of structures rather than events, was reflected in the films made in the 1970s, such as René Allio's **Les Camisards** and **Moi Pierre Rivière**, Betrand Tavernier's **Que la Fête commence** and **Le Juge et l'assassin**, Frank Cassenti's **L'Affiche rouge** and **La Chanson de Roland**, Louis Malle's **Lacombe Lucien** and André Techiné's **Souvenirs d'en France**. Moreover, the Events of 1968 gave a new relevance to the shift of emphasis and in the case of Allio these history films were clearly inspired by the political and intellectual project of rediscovering and rendering interesting to the present day episodes in French history which had been hidden or forgotten, and particularly of giving a 'voice' to oppressed sections of society. As with the documentaries made in the early 1970s, Allio's films are animated by the belief that, for the first time, an alternative version of history could be promoted.

**Les Camisards**, which was Allio's fourth film, was made in 1970 but not released until 1972, by which time it had acquired an underground reputation. It tells a story of a Protestant revolt in the Cévennes in 1702, in other words shortly after the revocation of the Edict of Nantes (1685) had deprived Protestants of their civil rights. The inspiration for the film was partly personal and partly intellectual. Though not a Protestant himself,[4] Allio was born and brought up in the south (in Marseilles) and had spent holidays in the Cévennes as a child, and he stressed the 'libidinal pleasure' he took in returning to his childhood haunts to work. He also read with immense interest Le Roy Ladurie's study, *Les Paysans du Languedoc*, and, perhaps most important of all, came across a collection of authentic Camisard texts edited by Philippe Joutard in 1965.[5] In addition Allio viewed the subject as highly political. Although he acknowledged that it is difficult to lend the Camisard revolt an ideology other than religious, unlike, for example, the Roundhead side in the English revolution, he nevertheless wished to see the Camisard revolt as premonitory in a number of ways.

The leaders of the revolt were all extremely young (in their early twenties) and their choice of resistance, rather than the emigration or conversion which was the strategy adopted by most Protestants, could be interpreted as a revolt of the generations. They then engaged in a guerilla war in which, thanks both to their intelligence and to their superior knowledge of difficult terrain, they managed to inflict defeats on the King's armies. Finally, the Protestants represented a sub-group within the state which claimed the right to cultural and religious self-determination against the centralising tendencies of the King in Versailles: '[It is not] so much a religious problem for me (...) as a moment in history when a community, a minority community was subjected to oppression and therefore was uprooted from its own culture. The Protestant ideology at that time played a revolutionary role which prefigured the bourgeois revolution of 1789.'[6] In all his comments on the film when it was released, Allio continued to stress modern political comparisons with the Camisards, especially with colonial wars of independence in Algeria

232

and, of course, Vietnam, where a peasant army was, at the time the film was made, opposing a large and well-equipped force. From a political point of view, therefore, the story of the Camisards had the advantage in his view of being simultaneously popular, regional and youthful and therefore of embodying not only the principles of 1789 but also those of May 1968.

If part of the significance of **Les Camisards**, and later of Tavernier's **Que la Fête commence**, was to use the past to criticise the present, and especially the Gaullist regime's attempts to impose what was felt to be a stultifying uniformity and consensus, nevertheless the popularity of the 'new history' and the films it generated also derived from a great public desire for knowledge of different national origins, which should be linked to the anxieties of modernisation rather than to any systematic anti-Gaullism. The attachment to local and familial roots was a very important counterpart to the rapid urbanisation of the postwar period; indeed, Allio remarked that **Les Camisards** represented for him a return to 'the land'! However, the celebration of the rural as against the urban and the nostalgia for peasant origins also links **Les Camisards** to a tradition of representation on which it reflects and to which it contributes.

Before turning to film making in 1963, Allio had pursued a career as a painter and as a stage designer, and **Les Camisards** is a contribution to his reflection on the dramatic and plastic representations of history. In the theatre he saw the dramatic tradition as that of the

> *historical romantic melodrama. There is a hero who is none other than the viewer himself projected into the part by means of identification, who finds himself, as though by accident, close to the people who are 'making history'. He is caught up in the lives of the great of this world in exactly the same way as the readers of* France Dimanche *and* Ici Paris. *This dramatic device which comes straight from boulevard theatre creates a gallery of characters desperately lacking inspiration and it masks our historical heritage.*[7]

In **Les Camisards**, therefore, he attempted to broaden the spectrum of the 'representable' and to disturb the processes of spectatorial identification normally associated with the dramatisation of history. Brecht is obviously Allio's mentor here and the narrative structure of **Les Camisards**, which sets up a constant juxtaposition between the two camps, the Royalist and the Protestant, and which distances the action through the use of the voice-over in order for characters to articulate the rationale of their actions, or for the texts of the period to be read, obviously owes much to Brechtian principles. Brecht's influence is also apparent in the treatment of the subject, *Mother Courage* being the obvious example of how a war can be looked at from the people's point of view, and in the reference to English eighteenth-century drama, which Brecht knew and adapted and which was familiar to Allio through his spell at the Royal Court Theatre in London, where he had worked on Gaskell's production of Farquhar's *The Recruiting Officer*, another oblique and popular view of war and of history.

The use of the voice-over and of authentic contemporary texts also functions to emphasise the 'truth' of what is said. Historically based characters such as Mazel may have styled themselves 'prophets' inspired by God, and may have been subject to fits of enthusiasm but, it is implied, they also have a superior lucidity and rationality. Whatever their performance style they are the opposite of melodramatic. This is in turn linked to the tradition of pictorial representations of 'the people' to which Allio refers in this film. In his discussions of the film he stressed how his own training as a painter and work as a stage designer had contributed to the visual idiom adopted, and that the iconography of the film derived from the representation of peasants by the painters of the Barbizon school such as Millet and Courbet.[8] Costume also seems to have been of immense concern to Allio in this film and he claims to have used it to establish the distinction between the Royalists and the Protestants,[9] yet to the viewer it is clear that what Allio took, from Millet in particular, was not the realistic portrayal of rural life, but a poetic simplicity of gesture and a sense of dignity which is lent to the peasant figures in some of Millet's most famous paintings. It is the capacity of gesture and costume to signify the immemorial activities of rural life such as gleaning or threshing or the irruption of the divine into the material landscape which is paralleled in the film in the delivery of inspirational texts on the part of Mazel and his companions. Allio places himself squarely in the pictorial tradition which celebrated ordinary people and the work that they perform.

**Les Camisards** therefore proposed a different elaboration and representation of history from both the literary and the visual point of view by using material deriving from a

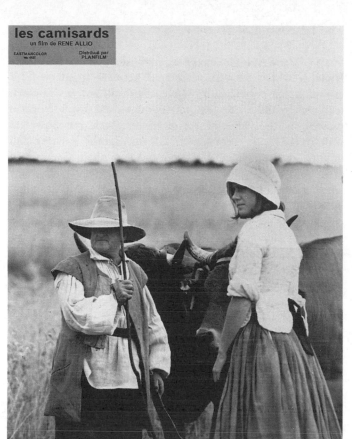

les camisards
un film de RENE ALLIO
EASTMANCOLOR    Distribué par
no 448        PLANFILM

**Les Camisards** – Allio as an admirer of nineteenth century realist painting

tradition which had not, conventionally, contributed much to the cinema. What it did not do, on the other hand, was exploit an alternative linguistic tradition. The Camisards are interesting to the linguist since their native language was Occitan, the 'langue d'oc', but when preaching, prophesying or writing their memoirs they used French, that is the vernacular in which their bibles were written. The language of oppression was also, in their case, the language of liberation. However, Allio makes no attempt in this film to draw these linguistic distinctions and does not even attempt to signify them by the use of regional accents as he did in later films such as **L'Heure exquise** or **Le Matelot 512**. This is the one aspect of **Les Camisards** which Allio chose to criticise in later discussions of the function of the history film and it was clearly central to his preoccupations when returning to the genre for a second time.[10]

## The Discourse of History

In 1976, René Allio directed a second history film, **Moi Pierre Rivière**, which became celebrated because it adapted for cinema a text published by Michel Foucault and his research team in 1973.[11] The text itself, composed by a Norman peasant by the name of Pierre Rivière, sets out how and why in 1835 he decided to kill his mother, sister and brother. It was written in prison and was cited as evidence at Rivière's trial where it was used to attempt to determine whether or not he was insane. It is clear why Michel Foucault, who had devoted much of his career to analysing the development of the penal system and to studying madness and sanity, should have been interested in this text: 'I systematically called up all the records of medico-legal expert opinions delivered in criminal cases during the first half of the nineteenth century (...) and I simply selected the largest file.'[12] Foucault's original concern was to explore the point at which psychiatric opinion began to have some influence on legal judgments but it was the literary quality of Rivière's text which encouraged him to publish it.

In his commentary on the text Foucault illuminates the nature of the document and the way in which it could contribute to the examination of the 'discourse of history'.[13] For although the extant text was written while he was in prison, Rivière states in it that his original intention had been to write an account of the murders first and place it in the post, then to commit the murders, and then to kill himself. In other words the account would have preceded the murders and not vice versa.[14] For Rivière, it might be said, narrating the murders was as important as committing them, so that the discourse of history is performative here[15] and chronological time is deliberately complicated in order, no doubt, to give the act the quality of 'history'. Foucault draws attention, in a fascinating manner, to Rivière's literary sources, especially the 'canards' or popular newspapers of the period.[16] In such publications the emphasis on 'detail, circumstance, explanation, event' enabled daily life to accede to the status of history by stressing its extraordinary nature, and precisely because it was extraordinary and horrible, murder was the point at which crime, as it were, became history: 'Hence, no doubt, the fact that for the popular memory (...) murder is the event par excellence.'[17] Thus in the popular press of the period two voices, or two discourses, were heard, that of the 'objective' narration of events and that of the criminal, and these two discourses are mixed together in Rivière's text where they have a single author.

For Allio *Moi Pierre Rivière* shared some of the attractive features of the story of the Camisard revolt. First, it is a regional subject satisfying his desire to work outside Paris 'where I thought I would encounter real life'.[18] Secondly, as with **Les Camisards**, only to a much greater extent, Allio was able to make use of an authentically 'popular' text – authentic in the sense that it was written by a peasant. This does not mean that Rivière's text is devoid of literary qualities – far from it – but it did mean that the people were able to regain their voice: 'I was convinced that if one talked about the peasants it was important to do so with the peasants.'[19] Thirdly, its hero in Allio's view is the kind of person 'who is usually refused the status of hero in History'.[20]

If the popular memory, ironically described by *Cahiers du cinéma* in 1985 as the 'pillar of the Left in the 1970s', appeared to Allio at the time he made the film as one of his source text's principal virtues, the film itself turns out to be more complex and more interesting that his comments would imply.[21] His approach to filming might be compared to that of Marin Karmitz in **Coup pour coup**, that is to say that he and his team went to stay in the area in Normandy where Rivière had committed his crime, talked to the local people about the project and selected local inhabitants to play the principal roles in the film. The advantage of this procedure – akin to that of community theatre today – is that in both accent and comportment the principals emanate a difference, held to be both authentic and unattainable by professional actors. This difference is then exploited to establish class differences within the film so that in **Coup pour coup** the bosses and their allies were played by professional actors and the workers by non-professionals, and in **Moi Pierre Rivière** the legal and medical officials are played by professionals and the peasants by non-professionals.[22] Of course, the unacknowledged source of this division is the view that the regional is more authentic than the metropolitan and thus it has more to do with nostalgia than the class war,[23] but it is a separation well understood and well received by the French viewing public. On the other hand, what Allio does achieve in his use of non-professional actors, which links this film to **Les Camisards** and to the nineteenth-century iconographical tradition discussed above, is an adequacy of gesture and comportment to the natural world, the physical equivalent of the regional accent, and this gives his film an extraordinary physical beauty.

**Moi Pierre Rivière** is a structurally complex film as befits an adaptation of a discursively complex text. Considerable time is given to the voice-over reading of Rivière's text, which itself contains two different kinds of narrative – an account of his parents' life since their marriage, on the one hand, and a statement of his own action and the reasons for it, on the other. Allio constantly shifts between the text read voice-over and dialogue, and between the present of the narrative (Rivière shown writing his text) and the enactment of the events narrated, creating the discursive uncertainties arising from what Barthes called 'two moments in time rubbing against each other: the time of utterance and the time when what is spoken of occurred' which is characteristic of all historical narratives.[24] In fact there are more than two 'times' at work in this film, since Pierre Rivière's family history extends over time, as does his trial. Furthermore, the text itself is dramatic in two different registers. On the one hand, Rivière presents the relationship of his parents, who spent very little time together, as a kind of boulevard theatre with dramatic entrances, demands, ultimatums and exits, the modern avatar of which, of course, would be a soap opera such as **Dallas**.[25] On the other hand, there is the metaphorical dimension of Rivière's narrative, his recourse to comparisons with popular heroes and popular histories: 'The example of De la Rochejaquelain seemed to me to have a close relation to what concerned me. he died in the twenty-first year of his life for having supported the King's side, saying to his soldiers: ''If I advance, follow me, if I retreat, kill me, if I die, avenge me''.'[26] In order to render this complexity Allio punctuates the film with other texts from other discourses such as the prosecutor's statements and the reports from the local papers, as well as the 'images d'Epinal' from the kinds of books that Rivière might have had access to, such as catechisms and popular moralities. For, despite what Allio appeared to believe, Rivière was not an unsung hero but became, at least momentarily, the subject of popular ballads in the 'littérature de colportage'[27] and achieved the status he sought by his crime. Like the character of Joseph Bouvier in Tavernier's **Le Juge et l'assassin** he was the beneficiary of the development of popular education and, like him, to some extent a victim of it.

In this way Allio's film achieves a brilliant juxtaposition of images and discourses which provokes a constant interrogation of both. This is simultaneously a reminder – if one were now needed – of a view popularised at the time that 'the discourse of history is essentially an ideological (...) or imaginary construction'[28] and a questioning, in the most subtle and interesting manner, of the relationship between sound and image and the work of the imagination in generating both text and picture, which, as Barthes again said, confirms 'narration as a privileged signifier of the real'.[29] Telling the story was the means by which Rivière tried to authenticate his actions and succeeded. **Moi Pierre Rivière** has been criticised for its needless complication of chronology, its fastidious reading of texts as a substitute for action and for a ponderous visual style deriving from over-respect for the written word.[30] These criticisms, however, do not do justice to the film, to its probing investigation of the nature of history, to the beauty of the images and to the beauty of Rivière's text. It is an intellectual film but also the work of a painter.

By an extraordinary paradox, however, the contemporary discussions of both the text and the film of **Moi Pierre Rivière** remain silent on the aspect of the crime which today seems most significant and most likely to have appealed to the concerns of readers and viewers in the 1970s, namely the way in which Pierre Rivière attempts to call into question the social, legal and sexual status of women. It is true that Foucault emphasised that the Rivière murders demonstrated 'the Code Civil beginning to be applied in rural areas, introducing new property relations',[31] creating contention over the husband's conjugal rights – whether his wife was his 'property' – and over his right, or otherwise, to acquire ownership of what she had brought to the marriage. In the view of *Cahiers du cinéma* this also explains the similarity between the relationship of Rivière *père* and *mère* and the boulevard theatre since the latter embodies 'the typical conflict to be found exercising the bourgeois family cell, the debate about property and about the essential item of merchandise, the wife'.[32] These critics were apparently more assiduous readers of Engels than of Freud, however, since none of them when referring to this as a case of parricide stresses that the central victim was Rivière's mother. Yet Rivière said that he hated his mother and that he blamed her for his father's miserable life and for his own actions: 'I looked on my father as being in the hands of mad dogs or barbarians against whom I had to take up arms.'[33] This state of affairs is to be blamed upon women: 'Women are in charge at the present time. This great century which calls itself a century of enlightenment, this nation which seems to have a great taste for freedom and glory, obeys women. The Romans were much more civilised.'[34] More particularly, it is his own mother who is guilty:

> *In my family this tyrant is my mother; she makes all contracts void of meaning; she lowers my father's standing and heaps burdens on him. In doing so she leads her son astray; I desire her all the time perhaps because of the empty space in her bed where, right from the beginning, she refused to allow my father and which he was not able to occupy.*[35]

In other words, Rivière is obliged to kill his mother because of his incestuous feelings towards her.

Rivière's tirade against women, the emotions which mix hatred and desire, and even the inadequacy of the father to whom he longs to be a substitute, were all more or less direct topics of debate in the early 1970s, so much so that one can find enacted on the symbolic level in films such as Bertrand Blier's **Les Valseuses** (1973) the incest and parricide that Pierre Rivière committed in his life. When **Moi Pierre Rivière** was

Moi Pierre Rivière – Pierre composing his testament

first released it was acclaimed as a major contribution to the recovery of popular memory and for this reason it is important to stress today what the sexual politics of the Rivière text have in common with those fiction films contemporary with its publication, as well as the fact that Rivière like his modern counterparts also sought an artistic resolution to his most uncontrollable desires.

## Back to Marseilles

The new history film was an episode in Allio's career as it was in the careers of the other directors who contributed to the genre and it would be right to conclude, from this, that it flourished and died in a particular social and ideological climate, with the election of a Socialist President and government in 1981 contributing to the final deflation of a movement that was in any case running out of steam. But it was far from being an aberration or a detour in Allio's already varied career. The preoccupations of the history films are to a greater or lesser extent present in those he directed both before and afterwards. Thus his first film, **La vieille Dame indigne** (1965), a hugely successful comedy which a little to Allio's surprise gave him an international reputation, is an adaptation of a Brecht novella, which is set in Marseilles and depicts the 'ordinary' life of an 'ordinary' person (it is, or was, unusual to find an old woman cast as the heroine of a successful film) but it establishes a double discourse or double point of view, the one real, the other fantastic or imaginary. In the same way **L'Une et l'autre** (1967) takes place in the theatre milieu well known to Allio for professional reasons and plays on the relationship between reality and the theatre in portraying an actress who, during the rehearsals for a performance of *Uncle Vanya*, decides to leave the man she lives with and attempts to disguise herself as her sister in order to tell him so. **Pierre et Paul** (1968) and **Rude Journée pour la reine** (1974) both criticise mass culture and its damaging psychological effects. Indeed, in addition to being a brilliant portrait of a cleaning lady and of a working class household, **Rude Journée pour la reine** is also extremely Brechtian, since Jeanne/La Reine, its heroine, leads a double fantasy life, inspired by her reading of the popular press, which parodies that of the 'beau monde' she reads about.[36] There is a clear link here with **Moi Pierre Rivière**, whose imagination was likewise conditioned by his reading of the popular press.

In 1980, Allio made **Retour à Marseille**, a fictionalised account of his real return to the south in 1978. The film
revolves round the Bertini family, who provide the link with
his earlier works, having already figured in both **La vieille
Dame Indigne** and **Pierre et Paul**.[37] Its drama is provided by
the juxtaposition of generational contrasts and the changes in
the city of Marseilles, a topographical exploration pursued
more thoroughly in the documentary **L'Heure exquise** (1982).
For in 1978, Allio finally succeeded in setting up a project
which he had been attempting to promote for several years, the
creation in Vitrolles, just outside Marseilles, of a Centre
Méditerranéen de Création Cinématographique (CMCC), the
object of which was to provide production facilities for local
film makers, to work with local television and to exploit local
subjects.[38] Allio thus became the producer of the films of
others as well as the director of his own, most notably **Le
Matelot 512** (1984). In this film he returns to the use of the
authentic popular sources already exploited in **Les Camisards**,
**Moi Pierre Rivière** and, although ironically, **Rude Journée
pour la reine**. The film is based on the autobiographical
account of the roving life of a sailor called Max who joined
the navy in 1907 and sailed the world. Though the document
was authentic it is doubtful whether the events recounted in it
were. Indeed, like Pierre Rivière or Jeanne, Max seems to have
been blessed with an extraordinary imagination which allowed
him to narrate and perhaps invent two passionate love affairs
which he pursued across the years.[39]

In setting up a film production company in Marseilles,
René Allio ran the risk of inviting unfavourable comparison
with Marcel Pagnol, whose success had been based on a
thriving regional popular entertainment industry[40] (with indigenous singers, cabaret artistes and the like) and whose
national and international reputation established an image of
the city of Marseilles and its inhabitants which it is virtually
impossible to eradicate even today. To date, the production
activities of Allio and his team have had little impact on this
traditionally held view.

On the other hand, Allio's use of popular and regional
sources from **Les Camisards** to **Matelot 512** charts, in a
fascinating way, the evolution of the notion of popular history
in the cinema. One of the most important lessons to be drawn
from Allio's use of authentic popular sources is precisely that
history is a discourse and that popular authors themselves write
within the available tradition. Thus the Camisard leaders use

the language of the Bible, Pierre Rivière the imagery of the 'littérature de colportage' and the moral schema of the catechism, and Max the sailor the language of romantic literature, while Jeanne in **Rude Journée pour la reine** has her imagination structured by the magazines that she reads. In this way history and fiction are always intertwined in the 'popular memory'. In the early part of the 1970s this perception served to denounce the 'lies' of offical history so that Marcel Ophüls, as we have seen, juxtaposed the often faulty memories of his witnesses with what really happened as recorded on film at the time. At the time of **Les Camisards**, Allio was sympathetic to this approach, believing that by promoting the story of their revolt to, as it were, the centre stage he could create a counter-history. But **Moi Pierre Rivière** was a revelation in the sense that it was the most authentic of the popular texts that he used but also the most fictionalised in form and function, thus demonstrating above all the perennial creativity of the popular imagination.

## Recovering the 'Popular Memory'

The perception of this continual and necessary relationship between history, the imagination and fiction places what was known as the 'popular memory' debate in a new light. The early 1970s saw the passionate discussion of the presentation of history not only in documentary films, such as **Le Chagrin et la pitié**, as we have seen, but also in fiction films such as Louis Malle's **Lacombe Lucien** (1974). This, it will be recalled, tells the story of a teenage peasant boy living in the Lot during the German occupation who attempts to join the Resistance but is turned away and who then succeeds in joining the Gestapo. He falls in love with the daughter of a family of Jewish refugees; she tries to use him to help her father escape to Spain and he ends up by being shot. What attracted viewers at the time, as it attracted them to **Le Chagrin et la pitié**, was the film's moral ambiguity. Louis Malle stressed the implicit collaboration of many French people during the war ('a number of Gestapo archives have been found and people have realised that in France 90 per cent of the people working for the Gestapo were French') as well as the fact that Lucien was a youngster who simply enjoyed wielding a gun.[41] The film suggests other possible reasons for his behaviour such as the fact that his father is absent and his mother has taken a lover, but essentially Lucien is depicted as not very intelligent, politically naive but nevertheless redeemed by his death.

For Michel Foucault and other commentators it was the end of Gaullism, signified by the election of Giscard d'Estaing to the French Presidency in 1974, that allowed the whole topic of the Occupation to be addressed in the cinema. For as long as De Gaulle or his political inheritors ruled France, or so the argument ran, the war was always presented in terms of Resistance, since this was 'the only way of writing this particular history in terms of an honourable nationalism'.[42]

But perhaps more important, although more insidious, than the end of nationalist narratives was the disappearance of heroes of history and, more important, of the popular struggles that made it up. The Foucaldian thesis was that the early 1970s saw a concerted attempt to 'recode' the popular memory by showing people 'not what they were but what they are supposed to remember having been'.[43] This thesis depends, in part, on a belief in the existence of a vivacious oral and popular tradition which institutions such as the education system and television have conspired to stifle,[44] so that by dispossessing the people of their cultural heritage they also neutralise their capacity to struggle.

The significance of **Lacombe Lucien** and no doubt the source of its public success, was that it valorised history as an individual and not a collective experience, as it were atomising public events. Lucien's individuality is stressed by the film's title, which presents his name as though he were identifying himself for inspection or as a specimen, and it is reinforced by his evident lack of comprehension of what is going on around him. His desire to 'have a good time' is at odds with the collective pursuit of politics, so much so that he is indifferent as to whether he signs up with the Resistance or the Gestapo, just as his affair with the Jewish girl is entirely self-regarding and takes place in ignorance of the ironic conflict of interests. Lucien is presented as alone, not part of any collectivity, carrying no mark of exemplarity. He is almost the anti-Brechtian hero par excellence, moving through a war, even camp-following like Mother Courage, but, unlike Brecht's character, unable either to understand, or to teach us about, the collective processes at work.

Although Foucault and other commentators wished to link the popularity of films such as **Lacombe Lucien** with the political and ideological situation in France, the revision of history, whether in a positive or a negative manner, was characteristic of British and German cinema after the 1960s as well. In other words, it did not just depend on the particular circumstances of France but was the expression of anxiety about the profound social changes in European societies since the war, symbolised by the disappearance of the traditional working class. Television series such as **Days of Hope** and films such as **Winstanley** testify to a comparable attempt, outside France, to promote alternative history. Thus some scepticism may be permitted in the face of statements such as 'the people constitute their own archives',[45] since part of the difficulty, for film makers and historians, was that the people per se were rapidly disappearing. Conversely, both Louis Malle and René Allio, although from different political and cinematic perspectives, suggest that it is the relationship between subjectivity and history that had a particular significance in the cinema.

## André Techiné

## The Petty Bourgeois Consciousness

André Techiné's second feature film, **Souvenirs d'en France** (1975) is a brilliant exploration of the relationship between history and the imagination or of the twin senses of 'histoire' in French,[46] and the pun contained in its title, **Souvenirs d'en France/Souvenirs d'enfance**, suggests that the relationship between the individual and the collective, between history and subjectivity will be at the centre of the film.

Rather in the manner of the 'chronique familiale', the family sagas such as *Les Thibault* or *The Forsyte Saga* popular in Europe in the interwar years, when the action of the film opens, these 'memories' focus on the Pédret family and its fortunes from the 1930s to the 1970s, when the film was made, with a flashback to the period of the First World War. Old Pédret is a Spanish immigrant who settled in the south west of France, married Augustine the baker's daughter and had three sons – Victor who marries the school teacher Lucie, Prosper who marries the flighty and imaginative Regina and Hector who, not without some opposition from his mother, marries the laundress Berthe. After the Second World War, during which Berthe joins the Resistance alongside Pierre,

245

husband of her best friend, Pierrette, and himself one of Pédret's employees, Berthe takes over the running of the Pédret factory, exploiting her Gaullist connexions to good effect. Meanwhile Regina abandons Prosper for an American officer she meets at the Liberation and with whom she leaves for the United States, but at the beginning of the 1970s she returns to seek her legal divorce from Prosper so as to marry her American, and offers in exchange to put money into the family business which, with the end of Gaullism and the economic crisis of the early 1970s, is no longer profitable. After some hesitation the offer is accepted.

Several histories and stories are combined in this narrative, each of which reinforces and complements the others. There is, first, the political history of France from the First World War to the present day. This is seen in 'condensed' form as a series of high points or moments of tension: the First World War, the Popular Front, the Occupation and Resistance, May 1968, a set of notations and significant encounters from which the political history of the country may be deduced. Thus the First World War leaves the old aristocracy, embodied in the Marquis de Valnoble, destitute in every way, with his sons killed and the fortune dissipated, while it assists the petty bourgeoisie such as the Pédret family, whose business flourishes in its aftermath. This process is indicated by a scene in which Pédret proposes a business partnership to Valnoble and the latter refuses, where-upon Pédret proceeds to make on his own the agricultural machinery which will modernise farming. The Resistance equally creates useful opportunities for Berthe, but it is depicted in a mere couple of scenes, where she discusses the placing of a bomb with her friend Pierre and where she is decorated with a medal for heroism. The Popular Front is signified by some posters on the factory wall, the singing of the *Internationale*, and a discussion between Regina and her sisters-in-law about the strikes, while May 1968 is sketched with similar economy in the form of a demonstration in the factory yard followed by a discussion between Berthe and Pierre. In this way political events, however momentous they may be, are constantly represented through their impact on individuals within this single family and within the spatial confines that this family commands.

The second history narrated in this film is the economic history of France. Although this might be described as a process of modernisation it is again seen in its impact on individuals and their interactions as expressed in labour relations. Thus in the 1920s Pédret is a model employer: 'I will put up wages (...) they will come and work for me (...) the land needs my techniques so it can be changed' (p. 24).[47] The depression of the 1930s is represented as an encounter between Berthe and Pierre, who arrives in the village seeking work; the wage increases and management changes resulting from May 1968 take the form of a dialogue between Berthe and Pierre: 'I accept all your conditions,' says Berthe, 'your struggle is right', to which Pierre replies, 'this day takes our own romance (*histoire*) forwards' (p. 38). Finally, the American takeover of the 1970s is represented as a dialogue between Berthe and Regina.

It should not be thought that Techiné's presentation of economic and political history is reductive or trivialising, for the point of the procedure resides not in the accuracy of the history but in the narrative form espoused. Techiné adopts the manner of organising and presenting history already available in popular works of economics or in the official statements put out by political parties. The narrative technique is that of the Left in France after the great *rapprochement* of 1972 and the publication of the *Programme commun*, which posited the continuity between 1936 and the new Popular Front, jumping decades of history in the process; and it is also that of Jean Fourastié, one of the most successful popularisers of economic history, who in his bestseller, *Les Trente glorieuses*, the title of which indicates that the enterprise of modernisation is heroic, presents two 'snapshots' of French villages, the one modern the other old-fashioned, and then explains that it is the same village 'photographed' at an interval of thirty years. [48] What Techiné has done to establish the background for his film is to take his material from the accounts available to him in the public domain and already popular.

The structure within which these events take place is the small family business. But in **Souvenirs d'en France** the family is a romantic nexus as well as an economic unit and, indeed, the two are intimately and necessarily connected. Thus when Pédret senior explains the history of the factory he does so in terms of a *roman des origines*,[49] itemising his arrival from Spain, his encounter with Augustine, the foundation of the Pédret dynasty, and the transformation of his forge into a factory (pp. 19–24). This is narrated as a genesis myth for which Techiné has found a cinematic equivalent in his use of flashback, of heightened colour and in the stylised, non-naturalistic manner of the actors' performances. Pédret's memories, however, were triggered by a photograph, the enormous portrait of himself as a young man which hangs on the living room wall and which bears no resemblance to him now (p. 19) but whose function is to perpetuate the memory of his heroic itinerary. The film is punctuated by such photographs, which serve a variety of purposes: to trigger memories, to encapsulate the significance of an occasion, a rite of passage in the family chronicle such as the wedding of Regina and Prosper or Hector and Berthe, and to foretell the future, as when Berthe inadvertently gets caught in the frame of Prosper and Regina's wedding photograph.[50] Above all, perhaps, the photograph which is both snapshot and commonplace (the 'cliché' in French) serves to structure both film and life, distributing social and cinematic roles in a manner which is underlined when Regina, looking through the family photograph album with Berthe, remarks as she contemplates the photographs: 'Here every son has his function. Look, that's Victor . . . he reigns. See, there's Prosper, he governs . . . Hector, he carries out decisions' (p. 18). Thanks to photography, or the cliché, these men are acting their part.

Souvenirs d'en France – Berthe (Jeanne Moreau) has taken over the factory

But even more than photographs or snapshots it is the cinema which offers the frame of reference for **Souvenirs d'en France**. The film is, as it were, framed by the cinema. The opening shot shows a brick wall running alongside the factory on which are plastered posters advertising Cukor's film **Camille** ('Le Roman de Marguerite Gautier') starring Greta Garbo and Robert Taylor, an adaptation of *La Dame aux camélias* by Dumas fils.[51] In the closing shot the camera tracks back from the Pédret family house as Berthe speaks lines evoking her memories of the cinema and suggesting that the house itself has been the theatre or the scene of a film:

> *When I was a child, I sometimes used to hide behind the iron gates at the entrance watching for hours this house that fascinated me (. . .) I was hypnotised as I watched people coming and going on the other side of the window panes. I took them for ghosts . . . and then I used to go home late at night . . . just as one goes home after the cinema when all the lights are out. (p. 42)*

Souvenirs d'en France –
Marie-France Pisier as
Regina escaping from the
Pédret mansion

The reference to the shadow-play and to Berthe's spectatorial position as a child point to the link the film wishes to make between cinema, history and subjectivity. Berthe is

both outside and inside, participant and observer, doubly privileged by her class and her gender. She and Regina are the heroines of the family romance in which the action has passed to the women and both have romantic destinies. Berthe's is a rags-to-riches story of an improbable and improbably successful marriage; Regina's life is based on her taste for romance, for the extravagant gesture and for the cliché. Regina sees America entirely in clichéd terms – 'You want to write a novel about the war. Your advertising agency is on the 34th floor of the Chrysler Building. Charlie Parker and Dizzy Gillespie play on 52nd Street. The Staten Island Ferry costs a nickel' (p. 33) – and yet she realises her romantic fiction.

Téchiné's film therefore has a second centre, topographically and psychologically parallel and equivalent to the family house. This is the local cinema, where all these images are generated and where all these fortuitous and fortunate encounters take place. For the cinema has the advantage of bringing together all classes of society so that this is where Pierre finds his job, where Berthe meets Hector as well as where Regina absorbs romantic fiction. In this way family history, family memories and the cinema are all linked. The bourgeois romance in its various forms has, of course, always centred on women and Téchiné refers to this tradition by making two women the centre of his film. This is done partly by recalling Marguerite Gautier, the mistress who gives up her lover for the good of his family and dies of consumption; it is partly done by reference to Hollywood 1950s melodrama, exemplified by Douglas Sirk, with its strong women, doomed men and tragic destinies; and it is partly done by reference to *Othello*, both as a tragedy of jealousy (the woman as property) and as the reference point for French romantic theatre. Thus when towards the beginning of the film Augustine summons Berthe to return the handkerchief whose discovery has revealed Berthe's liaison with Hector, we recall the nineteenth-century theatrical battle in which Desdemona's handkerchief became a symbol both of the possibility of betrayal and of the transition from classicism to romanticism.[52] However, unlike their literary and cinematic precursors, the women in **Souvenirs d'en France** experience a 'happy end', itself no doubt a fiction but nevertheless a source of immense pleasure and satisfaction to the viewer. For in making Berthe a 'hero' of the Resistance Téchiné is also exploring the heroism that derives from her structural role in the narrative, the fact that we have a libidinal investment in Berthe and we want her to succeed.

For 'common sense' and 'romance' are complementary petty bourgeois values in Techiné's view, and Berthe, Regina and indeed Pédret see themselves as heroic as well as being seen by us as heroes. In this way, although apparently a very different kind of history film from **Les Camisards** or **Moi Pierre Rivière**, **Souvenirs d'en France** resembles Allio's works in its attempt to question the discourse of history. But instead of focusing on the peasants, it takes as its centre the petty bourgeois consciousness and the petty bourgeois narrative, asking 'why does the viewer wish to project his desires onto the families as they are represented on screen?'.[53]

## The Exploration of Spectacle

**Souvenirs d'en France** is a film which sets out to procure for its viewers the kind of pleasure traditionally associated with filmgoing because it is, in Techiné's words: 'a sort of imitation of the spectacle based on classical narrative'.[54] It is, perhaps, an attempt to reconstruct the 'mixture of escapism and the more-than-true-to-life life (...) which constitutes the magic of the cinema' that Techiné recalls having experienced as a child.[55] This 'cinéma de spectacle' is to be contrasted, for Techiné, with the 'cinéma d'écriture' in accordance with Bresson's classic distinction. However, although there is no difficulty in identifying the avant-garde cinema ('a whole radical cinema (...) which runs from Straub to Duras, is based on the rejection of spectacle. Because it is true that the spectacle is dangerous')[56] the question for Techiné is whether it is possible to achieve a 'cinéma de spectacle' whilst remaining resolutely modern, to make the viewer question his aesthetic habits at the same time as satisfying his desire for cinema.

Techiné's first approach was 'to work with a form of exaggeration and theatricality',[57] together with the recourse to popular genres like the family saga. Hence the non-naturalistic acting, sets and lighting in **Souvenirs d'en France** side by side with the appeal to a film tradition its viewers knew well, that of the *théâtre social* of Renoir, Carné or Duvivier, in order to represent periods such as the Popular Front or the Resistance. Anti-naturalism was pursued and even exaggerated in Techiné's two subsequent films, **Barocco** (1976) and

251

**Les Soeurs Brontë** (1979). The first is a pastiche *film noir* set in a labyrinthine city, a kind of utopia peopled by underworld characters engaged in desperate love affairs and crime; the second takes a close-knit but doomed family and places its members in an isolated house in which they can give rein to their creative fantasies. **Barocco** has many affinities with the post-modern thriller which it preceded by almost a decade, and its performance, sets, lighting and cinephilic references make it a compelling film, but its fluctuations of register ultimately defeat comprehension of the narrative since the viewer lacks the supportive chronological framework of **Souvenirs d'en France**. Similarly, **Les Soeurs Brontë** fails to explore the relationship between life and imagination in a way that the subject demanded because it relies too heavily on a previous knowledge of the Brontë biographies.

Techiné recalls that his introduction to the cinema came by means of the theatre company run by Marc'O, for whom he acted as assistant on **Les Idoles** (1968) after using members of the company in his own film, **Paulina s'en va**, the preceding year,[58] and theatricality and performance have remained identifiable interests in his films. Thus in **Souvenirs d'en France** Regina saw herself as a star and modelled her behaviour on what she had seen in the cinema, a performance parodied in **Barocco** where the same actress, Marie-France Pisier, now even more heavily made up, plays a prostitute who displays herself in a shop window. Performance is the subject of the documentary, **L'Atelier** (1984), Techiné made with Patrice Chéreau's company at the Théâtre des Amandiers, showing the actors rehearsing scenes from several plays, including Dostoievsky's *The Possessed*. Performance is also central to the feature film **Rendez-vous** (1985), inspired by that experience, in which most of the principal characters work in the theatre. Performers are also to be encountered elsewhere in Techiné's films, often unsuccessful ones, like the failed conductor played by Jean-Claude Brialy in **Les Innocents** (1987) or the guitarist and would-be pop singer played by Etienne Chicot in **Hôtel des Amériques** (1981). However, in the films Techiné made in the 1980s spectacle has been used somewhat differently, as a plot element in more realist dramas, and this is most apparent in his use of the star system.

In **Les Soeurs Brontë** it was evident that Techiné was attempting to put together a film which, by casting Marie-France Pisier, Isabelle Adjani and Isabelle Huppert, would in part depend for its appeal on the combined performances of three of the most successful young actresses in the French cinema at the time. But in the two films he has made with Catherine Deneuve, **Hôtel des Amériques** and **Le Lieu du crime** (1986), the star system is made to function as a form of narrative expectation which can also be playfully denied. Thus the opening of **Hôtel des Amériques** is shot like a *film noir* with the rain beating on the windscreen of a car being driven towards a deserted city in whose streets there waits a man. The driver, however, is Deneuve and the man is Patrick Dewaere, so that the viewer's hope and desire, agonisingly postponed by the film maker, is that the two will meet and the question posed is how.[59] Conversely, the ending of **Le Lieu du crime** has Deneuve driven away in a police van, a scene which Techiné admits gave him particular satisfaction because it did not correspond to her 'star' image.[60]

The narrative exploitation of the star system underlines the differences between Techiné's works in the 1970s and 1980s: 'From **Hôtel des Amériques** onwards my films are no longer genre films. My inspiration is no longer drawn from the cinema.'[61] The central concerns of family and place remain but it is as though the *topoi* of the 1970s were redistributed in the films of the 1980s, giving an apparently more naturalist cinema and one in which concerns are more immediate. Techiné ceases to explore the relationship between memory, imagination and spectacle but now sees imagination as a function of desire and a projection towards the future rather than into the past. This is perhaps why, after Regina had said in **Souvenirs d'en France**: 'I won't have children here' (p. 25), children begin to figure for the first time in Techiné's films, and in **Le Lieu du crime** the structure of the film is that of the family romance as a child might invent it.[62] This is also why Techiné says that love 'is the thread linking all my films',[63] for love and the imagination are necessarily linked and culturally determined: 'There is no such thing as spontaneous desire, it is always structured by culture and the imagination'.[64]

The changing significance of place in Techiné's films is an excellent illustration of his different approach. Thus although **Souvenirs** was set in the south west of France its real location was a house and a cinema between which comparisons were drawn, as we have seen, just as the setting of **Les Soeurs Brontë** was a mansion worthy of a Gothic novel and that of **Barocco** an 'unreal city'. **Hôtel des Amériques** provides an interesting transition between the topography of the mind and that of social distinctions, for it opens with a montage of black and white stock shots of old Biarritz, evoking the fashionable seaside resort that it once was, making it as unreal as Amsterdam had been in **Barocco**, and only then settles into the principal locations of the action, the hotel which is owned by the mother of Gilles (Dewaere) and in which he lives, and the Café de la Gare where much of his interaction with Hélène (Deneuve) takes place. Nostalgia is used to conjure up memories of a certain social climate which is part contrast with the seediness of the present and part confirmation of the fact that the characters are not firmly rooted in an environment – all are momentarily in Biarritz but are, or would like to be, en route for somewhere else. **Hôtel des Amériques** also refers back to the utopian topography of **Barocco** and **Les Soeurs Brontë** in the architect's model of an ideal city contained in the loft of the empty mansion Hélène has inherited from her dead lover. The model itself, reminding us of the ambitious and occasionally totalitarian fantasies of architects active when Biarritz was in its heyday, such as Le Corbusier, and recalling the cinema's critique of the idea of a link between psychology and the physical environment in Lang's **Metropolis**, is a structure *en abîme*: the city is but a model, the house is empty, the lover is dead, and with these observations Téchiné seems to wrench himself away from the past and to turn towards the future.

Thereafter provincial France figures in his films in both a realistic and fantastic manner. In **Rendez-vous** the heroine leaves her rapidly evoked province to come to Paris, while in **La Matiouette** (1983) the young man who left his province to become an actor in the capital goes back to his village to pay a brief visit to the brother who stayed behind, and through the thick regional accents in which their discussion of relative values takes place the provincial is evoked in all its materiality. The setting of **Les Innocents** is in some ways a more realist version of that of **Hôtel des Amériques** (although the town has changed from the resort of Biarritz to the port of Toulon), yet the film opens with the classic fictional introit: 'Once upon a time in a city in the south of France . . .' and goes on to show that it is literally a place of transit for the brother and sister who are attending a family wedding, but a mythical point of transit for the Algerian immigrants who have come to seek work and even more for those children of immigrants like Saïd who have been born in France, never set foot in North Africa, but who nevertheless refer to Algeria as 'my country'. Finally, **Le Lieu du crime** focuses on a place which is both entirely real and entirely imaginary, a stuffy provincial village portrayed in all its ritualistic detail and the scene of fantastic criminal events which may or may not have come straight out of the mind of a child. Whereas in **Barocco** and **Les Soeurs Brontë** topography served to demonstrate that the real was fantastic, in **Le Lieu du crime** it might be said that the fantastic has become real and, as with the architect's model in **Hôtel des Amériques**, a structure *en abîme* is provided here in the dance hall built on stilts over water which shimmers enticingly at night and which forms an entirely self-contained world of pleasure and distraction, a real place which is made to seem unreal, like Amsterdam in **Barocco**.

Some of these locations undoubtedly represent auto-biographical transpositions – indeed, **Souvenirs d'en France** was shot in Techiné's native village.[65] But for all that the south is remembered as a provincial backwater,[66] its cities, in particular, have social characteristics which allow Techiné to mix social realism and the structure of desire. For the southern coastal cities – Marseilles is the most obvious example – are nowadays places of transit where the mixing of classes and races takes place and this is reflected in the changing role of the immigrant in Techiné's films. **Souvenirs d'en France** might be thought of as enacting the myth of integration and assimilation, with Pédret, Berthe and Regina all successfully becoming part of a different milieu, changing status, class or country in the process. Similarly, **La Matiouette** and **Rendez-vous** also figure protagonists who, at least in their professional lives, have successfully left behind one identity and gone north to play another or others. This is the French equivalent of the melting pot, the immigrant who makes good in the new world. But in **Hôtel des Amériques**, **Le Lieu du crime** and **Les Innocents**, differences of race, class and sex are only too apparent and they serve to undermine or render impossible the romantic structure of **Souvenirs d'en France**.

In **Hôtel des Amériques** the love between the heterosexual couple is impossible for both social and sexual reasons. Hélène is an anaesthetist whose social contacts are among the grande bourgeoisie to which her deceased lover belonged, while Gilles is an unemployed layabout with a set of disreputable friends, including the guitarist Bernard with whom he has an implicitly homosexual relationship. In **Le Lieu du crime**, Lili is the daughter of a stiflingly repressive and conformist provincial family (the father is deaf, the mother short-sighted) and is married to a dull and conven-

tional man, but she falls in love with Martin who is a criminal
on the run. However, this socially impossible relationship is
brought to an end by their arrest and separation. In **Les
Innocents** love is almost always one-sided: Maité is marrying
an Algerian not for love but because she wants children; Klotz
loves the Algerian Saïd but is rejected by him; Jeanne loves
Stéphane but he is killed; Alain loves Saïd who leaves him to
return to Algeria; Stéphane claims to hate immigrants but
finds himself compellingly attracted to Saïd.

If the romantic heterosexual couple is impossible, so
is the bourgeois family represented in **Souvenirs d'en France**
and with it, of course, the representational structure, the star
system, which figures it and which is the focus of petty
bourgeois investment. However, Techiné's later films create
parallel or unofficial families which are represented as
alternative and more enticing poles of attraction. Thus Gilles
in **Hôtel des Amériques** has an alternative family based in the
hotel run by his mother and sister but which includes his male
friend Bernard. In **Le Lieu du crime**, Lili, Martin and her son
Thomas (who bears an uncanny resemblance to Martin)
regroup into an alternative and highly romantic family,
conceived in the whirlwind of the storm, perhaps a figure of

LES
INNOCENTS
ANDRÉ TÉCHINÉ

Thomas's romantic imagination, a family which is 'mainly incestuous and doomed to ruin, the monstrous repetition on a different stage of what was once a united family'.[67] Finally, in **Les Innocents** there are two official families, each of which is manifestly unsatisfactory, that of the homosexual composer Klotz, his hysterical wife and their son Stéphane, and that formed by Jeanne, her teenage brother Alain who is deaf and dumb, and their sister Maité whose wedding opens the film. However, Klotz's Algerian friend Saïd creates an alternative family in the hotel he inhabits when Alain goes to stay with him and is later joined by Jeanne, and this is seen, at least by Alain, as a haven of happiness and source of hope.

In **Les Innocents** the immigrant Saïd becomes the focus of virtually every character's desire: that of Klotz, that of Alain whom he promises to take with him to Algeria, that of Stéphane whom he knifed in a racial attack, and that of Jeanne who thinks herself attracted by Stéphane and only discovers too late, when both Stéphane and Saïd have been shot, that it was Saïd she loved. With his sexual ambiguity, his dual nationality and his ill-defined social status, Saïd undermines the fixed identities that the cinema conventionally projects and explodes our belief in the ideal romantic couple. Viewers are

257

no longer allowed to project themselves into the families they see on the screen or if they do those families have themselves changed. The most telling and moving symbol of Techiné's films in the 1980s is the image of the handicapped Alain setting out, in a supreme gesture of desperation, to swim the Mediterranean in order to find Saïd.

In André Techiné's *œuvre* we can detect a movement similar to that already described in René Allio's, from an initial concern to explore the history of the nation to a renewed emphasis on personal history with, in Techiné's case even more than in Allio's, a consciousness of how the two are inevitably intertwined. Techiné is concerned with the way a culture represents its own history and how individuals within a culture represent theirs and in this his great teacher, like Allio's, was Brecht. Both Allio and Techiné came to the cinema from an involvement with the theatre, where Brecht was an enormous influence in the 1950s and 1960s, an influence charted by Roland Barthes in the review, *Théâtre Populaire*. In addition to acknowledging how important Barthes had been to him, Techiné later explained that Brecht allowed him to overcome the impasse affecting many other film makers as well as himself, caused by the encounter between the *nouvelle vague* and *gauchisme*: 'It was at that point that a writer like Brecht became extremely valuable and important for all of us I believe, because he seemed to have asked himself all the new questions to which we had to find answers. His was just about the only aesthetic and therefore practical way forward for a film maker.'[68] Techiné stresses that it was not only in France that new solutions had to be found:'Fassbinder, Angelopolous, Bellocchio or Bertolucci were also faced with this momentous change.'[69] Nevertheless, his example has proved particularly influential in France, where his particular manner of overcoming the aesthetico-ideological rupture of 1968 set an example for the practitioners of the so-called 'cinéma du look'. In Carax, Beineix and Besson, Techiné has his disciples, even if their films are far from being as accomplished or as visually or thematically interesting as his own. And what is certain is that in Techiné's own films the opposition between naturalism and aestheticism has been rendered obsolete.[70]

# Conclusion

In two special issues entitled 'Situation du cinéma Français' published in 1981, *Cahiers du cinéma* described the 1970s as having been the '*post* decade' – 'post-*nouvelle vague*, post-68, post-modern' – with no animating school or movement.[1] Nearly ten years later it is possible to see that the remark is true in a positive sense but untrue in a negative sense. The French cinema after 1968 did, indeed, come to terms with the *nouvelle vague*, but it used this process as a springboard for the creation of a new cinema. The *auteur* film continued to be a distinctive category within the French cinema and this was a trend which, it anything, was exaggerated after 1968. The benevolent sponsor of the 1960s, such as Pierre Braunberger or Georges de Beauregard, gave way to the more anonymous television company prepared to contribute only part of the budget to any one film. In response, French film makers increasingly tended to make films much as one would run a small family business, acting frequently as their own producers, using the same group of technicians, having recourse to family and friends as actors, and specialising in particular 'lines' – themes or preoccupations which they make their own. A glance at the credits of most of the *auteurs* discussed here will confirm the strength of this trend. There is therefore a recognisable economy of the *auteur* cinema in France which is constituted by the marriage of specific production practices with the pursuit of thematic continuities.

The *auteur* cinema is different from the popular cinema, on the one hand, and from the avant-garde cinema, on the other, but it engages with both these traditions in a self-conscious manner. As far as the popular cinema is concerned, Tavernier, Corneau, Blier and Techiné have all, in their different ways, attempted to come to terms with the American popular cinema as the *nouvelle vague* did before them and, in their contribution to the renewal of the spectacle, of the thriller, or of the Western, have attempted to recreate a version of American popular cinema in France. In addition, Blier takes much from the French popular tradition, performing a kind of Situationist *détournement* by borrowing actors

259

and situations from French popular entertainment and employing them differently. Jean Rochefort and Jean-Pierre Marielle in **Calmos** and Coluche in **La Femme de mon pote** are used in this way.

At the other end of the spectrum, Marguerite Duras and Philippe Garrel in their films, and Godard and Raul Ruiz in their television work, all illustrate the fact that in France, unlike America and, perhaps, Britain, there is no extreme compartmentalisation, no hard and fast distinction, between avant-garde film making and the rest, and that the more mainstream and accessible film makers are attentive to the experiments with sound and image to be found in avant-garde films. Several French film makers, like Agnès Varda and Jean-Luc Godard, have experience of working in the American independent cinema and, as Dominique Noguez has shown,[2] French avant-garde film makers tend to take their inspiration from America, as much for political as for aesthetic reasons. Nevertheless, this does not prevent them from, in turn, influencing their compatriots. Thus the American cinema, in both its popular and its experimental forms, has assisted the French *auteur* cinema to achieve its specificity, either through the naturalisation of American film techniques and genres or by inspiring it to make a different kind of cinema.

My reference to the popular and the avant-garde cinema in France serves as a reminder of the richness and variety of French cinema, only a very small proportion of which ever finds its way abroad. Three categories of film makers which lie outside the scope of this book deserve a mention as having made an important contribution to the industry in the post-1968 period. First, there are those *Cahiers du cinema* refers to as the 'ancestors', the contemporaries of the *nouvelle vague* or earlier, who continued to make films of greater or lesser interest but invariably of high quality – Tati and Demy, Bresson and Resnais, Rivette, Rohmer and Chabrol. Second, there are those film makers who are not French but who position themselves in relation to French cinema – the Belgian Chantal Akerman, the Frenchman Jean-Marie Straub who left for Germany in 1958 and who makes films mainly in German in collaboration with his French partner Danièle Huillet, the Swiss Alain Tanner, and the Argentinian exiles Eduardo de Gregorio and Hugo Santiago. The latter, unlike the Chilean exile Raul Ruiz, who has worked extensively for French television and who was employed for a brief period as the Director of the Maison de la Culture in Le

Havre, derive the tone of their films from the juxtaposition of recognisably European and Latin American themes. Finally, there are all the *auteurs* who have not yet made many films, either because they are still very young or because they have been unlucky. Every critic will have his or her choice. Philippe Garrel, when asked to organise a season for the Cinémathèque in 1983, included Danielle Dubroux (**Soeur Anne, ne vois-tu rien venir?** 1982), Juliet Berto (**Neige,** 1981), Pascal Laperrousaz (**Le Petite déjeuner, La Jeune Fille à la rose, L'Odalisque** 1974), and Patrick Bokanowski (**La Femme qui se poudre,** 1972). My own list would include Luc Béraud's **La Tortue sur le dos** (1978), Jacques Bral's **Extérieur nuit** (1980), Benoît Jacquot's **Les Enfants du placard** (1977), Claire Clouzot's **L'Homme fragile** (1983), Aline Issermann's **Le Destin de Juliette** (1982) and Jean-François Stevenin's **Le Passe-montagne** (1978). If these names are unfamiliar to English-speaking readers it is because film distributors have become increasingly conservative over the last twenty years and have been unwilling, or unable, to extend the range of French films shown outside France. The loss to film viewers is inestimable.

If we review the French cinema of the last twenty years from a comparative perspective it has one characteristic which French critics rarely mention, perhaps because they feel it to be self-evident, but which is nevertheless distinctive. The first concern of all the film makers discussed in this book, even the political and documentary film makers, is not to change society but to change the cinema. To take up the popular post-1968 slogan, their impetus is always to film in a different way rather than to film different things. This means that French *auteur* cinema is without the didacticism that is virtually obligatory in British independent films and that it must be appreciated and judged without necessarily considering the rectitude of the message. This is perhaps most obvious from my study of the women's cinema but it is, in fact, characteristic of the *auteur* cinema as a whole. The lesson may be hard for those educated to value cinema for its capacity to change the world rather than our ways of seeing the world. It is nevertheless in its ability to change our ways of seeing that the value of the French *auteur* cinema resides, and if this book has any success at all it will be judged by the extent to which is can persuade conservative viewers and, above all, distributors of the value and interest of the undeservedly unfamiliar.

# Notes

Unless otherwise indicated, all books in English are published in London and all books in French are published in Paris.

## Introduction

1. See 'La Fréquentation et l'image du cinéma en 1970', in *Bulletin du CNC* (126) déc. 1970.
2. Gilles Deleuze, *Cinéma 1: l'Image-Mouvement* (Eds. de Minuit, 1983), *Cinéma 2: L'Image-Temps* (Eds. de Minuit, 1985).
3. See, for example, Roland Barthes 'La mort de l'auteur' (1968) reprinted in *Le Bruissement de la langue* (Eds. du Seuil, 1984) pp. 61–7.
4. The best account of the 'politique des auteurs' remains Peter Wollen's in *Signs and Meaning in the Cinema* (Secker and Warburg, 1969).

## The French Film Industry Since the War: A Very Brief History

1. Cf. Jacques Portes, 'La légende noire des Accords Blum–Byrnes sur le cinéma', in *Revue d'histoire moderne et contemporaine*, XXXIII avril–juin 1986, pp. 314–29.
2. Cf. Michel Margairaz, 'Autour des accords Blum–Byrnes: Jean Monnet entre le consensus national et le consensus atlantique'. With respect to television, see Jill Forbes, 'Everyone needs Standards', in *Screen*, vol. 24, no. 1, pp. 28–39.
3. Paul Léglise, 'La Politique du cinéma français depuis 1946', in *Cinéma d'aujourd'hui*, nos. 12–13, printemps 1977, p.20.
4. The most scathing criticism remains François Truffaut's in 'Une certaine tendance du cinéma français', in *Cahiers du cinéma*, janvier 1954, pp. 15–29.
5. Léglise, 'La Politique du cinéma', p. 20.
6. Ibid., p. 21.
7. See Léglise, 'La Politique du cinéma', pp. 22–3. See also Michael Wilson, 'Défense et illustration du système français des avances sur recettes', in *Film Echange* no. 5, hiver 1979, pp. 53–70 for a list of beneficiaries of support.
8. David Bordwell 'The Art Cinema as a Mode of Film Practice', in *Film Criticism*, vol. 4, no. 1, Fall 1979, pp. 56–64.
9. Fellini, Godard and Truffaut might be examples with **8½** (and others), **Le Mépris** and **La Nuit américaine**.

10. Contemporary studies of the *nouvelle vague* emphasised how they utilised elements of the nascent youth culture and suggested that their success was due to the fact that they were in step with their times. It was only outside France that the *nouvelle vague* films were seen as avant-garde. Cf. Edgar Morin 'Conditions d'apparition de la "Nouvelle Vague"', in *Communications* 1 (1961) pp. 139–41 and C. Brémond et al. 'Les Héros de films dits "de la Nouvelle Vague"', ibid., pp. 142–77.
11. Bordwell 'The Art Cinema' p.59, is wrong when he says 'the *politique des auteurs* arose in the wake of art cinema'. The *auteur* film, which he correctly characterises, only derives from the *politique des auteurs* in its attitude to *mise en scène*. Otherwise, the *politique des auteurs* was developed in the 1950s in *Cahiers du cinéma* as a way of reading Hollywood cinema. Cf. Jill Forbes 'French Film Culture and British Cinema' in C. Crossley and I. Small (eds.), *Imagining France* (Macmillan, 1988) pp. 163–5.
12. Wilson, 'Defense et illustration'.
13. René Bonnell, *Le Cinéma exploité* (Ramsay, 1986), p. 253.
14. Quoted in Francis Courtade, *Les Malédictions du cinéma français* (Eds. A. Moreau, 1978) p.344. See also 'Spécial Porno', in *Le Film Français*, 19 sept. 1975, pp. 64–7.
15. See Augustin Girard (ed.). *Des Chiffres Pour la Culture* (La Documentation Française, 1980) pp. 259–75 and *passim*.
16. Cf. Michael Wilson 'Les Rapports Cinéma–Télévision en France', in *Film Echange*, 12 automne 1980, p.53.
17. Cf. Jill Forbes, *INA French for Innovation* (BFI, 1984) pp. 41–4.
18. Cf. *The Bredin Report* (BFI, 1983) p. 31.
19. Ibid.
20. Cf. Jean Roux and René Thévenet, *Industrie et commerce du film français* (Eds. scientifiques et juridiques, 1979) p.134, and 'L'Activité Cinématographique en 1984', in *Information CNC*, 206, juin 1985, pp. 2–3.

# 1 Political and Documentary Cinema

1. *Monthly Film Bulletin*, vol. 54 no. 640, pp. 132–5.
2. See Jacques Leenhardt and Barbara Maj, *La Force des mots* (Megrelis, 1982) pp. 123–35.
3. Celia Britton's analysis of Resnais's **Muriel** in *French Cultural Studies*, vol. 1, no. pp. 37–46, brings out the political references in this film.
4. Marker's own collective changed its name to ISKRA.
5. But in 'Enquête sur une image', in *Tel Quel* 51, hiver 1972, pp. 74–90, Jean-Luc Godard and Jean-Pierre Gorin stress that the Vietnamese are helping the war rather than vice versa.
6. For 'youth culture in France' see Françoise Giroud, *La Nouvelle vague. Portraits de jeunesse* (Gallimard, 1958).
7. See Jean Fourastié, *Les Trente Glorieuses* (Fayard, 1979).
8. This film, whose title refers to the revolutionary calendar, is inspired by Situationist writing and attempts to give practical

illustration to some of the utopian slogans, such as 'sous le pavé la plage', invented in May 1968.

9. See Michel de Certeau, *La Prise de parole* (Desclée de Brouwer, 1968)
10. See *Cahiers du cinéma* nos. 200–1, avril–mai 1968, p. 63.
11. See Sylvia Harvey, *May '68 and Film Culture* (BFI, 1978) and Christian Zimmer *Cinéma et politique* (Seghers, 1974).
12. *Cahiers du cinéma*, no. 218, mars 1970, p. 46. Cf. p. 47. 'We should recall Renoir's own remarks about the director's job being to receive, consume and digest all the advice, help and demands of others.'
13. Ibid., p. 47
14. Ibid., p. 48
15. Ibid., p. 48
16. *Cahiers du cinéma* nos. 238–9, mai–juin 1972, p. 15.
17. Jean-Louis Comolli, '**L'Aveu**: 15 Propositions', in *Cahiers du cinéma*, no. 224, oct 1970, pp.48–51.
18. See Groupe Lou Sin, 'Quelles sont nos tâches sur le front culturel?', in *Cahiers du cinéma*, nos. 242–3, nov.–déc. 1972, janvier 1973, pp. 5–6.
19. 'Entretien avec Marin Karmitz', in *Ecran* 3, mars 1972, p. 5.
20. Jacques Demare, 'Une fête de notre temps', in *Positif*, 138, mai 1972, p. 2.
21. See, for example, Pierre Dubois and Renaud Dulong, *Grèves revendicatives ou grèves politiques* (Eds. Anthropos, 1971).
22. See, for example, E. Morin, C. Lefort, and J.-M. Coudray, *Mai 68 La brèche suivi de 20 ans après* (Fayard, 1988).
23. For an extensive account of the preparation for filming of *Coup pour coup*, see *Positif*, 138, mai 1972, pp. 4–17.
24. 'Entretien avec Martin Karmitz', p. 6.
25. However, this guarantee is called into question by Comolli's investigation of the 'effet de réel' discussed below, p. 44.
26. *Positif*, 138, p. 7.
27. 'Polémique sur **Coup pour coup**', in *Ecran*, avril 1972, p. 43. Leblanc was the editor of *Cinéthique*.
28. *Cahiers du cinéma*, nos. 238–9, mai–juin 1972, p. 8.
29. Ibid.
30. Jan Dawson in *Monthly Film Bulletin*, Feb. 1974, p. 25.
31. Ibid.
32. See 'Ces femmes au-delà du plaisir', in *Art Press Spécial Godard*, Hors Série no. 4, Dec 1984–jan./fév. 1985, pp. 28–31.
33. Godard's use of the 'tricolour palette' is brilliantly discussed in Jean-Louis Leutrat *Kaléidoscope* (Lyon: Presses Universitaires de Lyon, 1988) pp. 89–91.
34. See 'Spécial Godard' in *Avant-scène cinéma* nos. 171–2, juillet–sept 1976. Also Godard's discussion of **La Chinoise** in *Cahiers du Cinéma*, pp. 13–26.
35. As is claimed in Colin MacCabe, *Godard: Images, Sounds, Politics* (BFI/Macmillan, 1980) p. 71.
36. For the Dziga Vertov group, see *Cinéma 70* no. 151, déc. 1970, pp. 82–7 and *Cahiers du Cinéma*, nos. 238–9 mai–juin 1972, pp. 10–15. 'It was an attempt to construct new unity from two opposites, according to the Marxist idea, and thus to create a

new cell which would make political films but would try to make political films politically, which was rather different from what other militant film makers were doing.' The group, which by 1972 consisted almost exclusively of Godard and Gorin, operated under the slogan 'faire politiquement les films politiques'.

37. Cf. 'Enquête sur une image', in *Tel Quel* no. 51, hiver 1977, pp. 74–90.
38. Ibid.
39. Cf. Guy Debord, *La Société du spectacle* (Eds. Champ Libre, 1983) first published in 1967.
40. See, for example, D Mascolo, *Le Communisme. Révolution et Communication ou la Dialectique des valeurs et des besoins* (Gallimard, 1953).
41. See Robert Linhart, *L'Etabli* (Eds. de Minuit, 1978).
42. Exemplified in Simone Weil's essays and taken up particularly by the CFDT trade union in volumes such as *Les Dégâts du Progrès* (Eds. du Seuil, 1972).
43. Interview in *Cahiers du cinéma*, nos. 268–9, juillet–août 1976 : 'Here the Gaullist *doxa* is closely dependent on the modes of commercial fiction, its fetishism and its illusion of spontaneity.'
44. Debord, *La Société du spectacle* .
45. Interview with Marin Kamitz in *Cinématographe*, 100, mai 1984, p. 70.
46. Ibid.
47. 'Le Groupe Dziga Vertov', in *Cinéma 70*, no. 151, déc. 1970, p. 82.
48. Interview with Marcel Ophüls in *Cinéma 71*, 157, juin 1971.
49. Marc Ferro, 'De l'interview chez Ophüls, Harris et Sédouy', in *Cinéma et histoire* (Denoël/Gonthier, 1977) pp. 53–7, p. 56
50. *Jeune Cinéma*, 55, mars 1971 p. 11.
51. Itemised by Marc Ferro, 'De l'interview'.
52. Interview with Michel Foucault in *Cahiers du cinéma*, 251–2, 1974, reprinted in *Edinburgh Magazine no.2* 1977, *History/Production/Memory*, pp. 20–5. For a feminist critique of the film see also Sian Reynolds, 'The Sorrow and the Pity Revisited', in *French Cultural Studies*, vol. 1, no. 2. June 1990, pp. 149–59.
53. *Jeune cinéma*, 55, mars 1971 p .8.
54. Quoted in Guy Hennebelle 'La Traversée de la Mer Rouge', in *Cinémas d'avant-garde*, *CinémAction* 10–11, printemps–été 1980, p. 243.
55. *Jeune cinéma*, 55, mars 1971, p. 17.
56. Foucault, *Edinburgh Magazine*. p. 21.
57. Ibid., p. 22.
58. Stephen Heath, 'Contexts', in *Edinburgh Magazine*, no. 2 1977, p. 37.
59. Francis Denel, Director of the INA Archive, interviewed in J. Forbes, *INAFrench for Innovation* (BFI, 1984) p. 17.
60. J. Rancière, interviewed in *Edinburgh Magazine*, no. 2, 1977, p. 26.
61. See J. Forbes, *INAFrench for Innovation* (BFI, 1984) pp. 6–8.
62. Francis Denel, Director of the Archive, in J. Forbes, *INA*.

63. Thierry Garrel and Louisette Neil, in J. Forbes, *INA*, p. 19.
64. Ibid., p. 20.
65. Ibid., p. 19.
66. Stellio Lorenzi quoted in Jacqueline Beaulieu, *La Télévision des réalisateurs* (La Documentation française, 1984) p. 99.
67. For example, Cozarinsky shows the celebrated image of a woman drawing a line up the back of her legs to imitate stocking seams. This is reprised in F. Truffaut's fiction film, **Le dernier Métro**.
68. 'I knew that I wanted the harsh, arrogant and sentimental voices of the newsreels alternating with the voice of Niels Arestrup reading Jünger; I like Niels's delivery (...) it was recorded very close to the microphone so that you can feel his presence in the small breathing noises that are usually removed from the sound track. It's an intimate 'bedroom' voice, speaking directly into the viewer's ear' ('Entretien avec Edgardo Cozarinsky', in *Cahiers du Cinéma*, no. 333, mars 1982, p. 16).
69. Ibid., p. 15.
70. Ibid.
71. Ibid.
72. See J. Forbes and R. Nice, 'Pandora's Box: Television and the 1978 French general elections', in *Media Culture and Society*, vol. 1, no. 1, Jan. 1979, p. 39.
73. Roland Barthes, 'L'Effet de réel' in *Communications*, 11, 1968 reprinted in G. Genette and T. Todorov (eds.) *Littérature et réalité* (Eds. du Seuil, 1982) p. 87.
74. The key essays in Barthes's discussion are 'Le message photographique', in *Communications*, 1, 1961; 'Rhétorique de l'image', in *Communications*, 4, 1964; 'Le troisième sens: notes de recherche sur quelques photogrammes de S. M. Eisenstein', in *Cahiers du cinéma*, no. 222, 1970. All are translated into English in S. Heath (ed.) *Roland Barthes Image Music Text* (Fontana, 1977). The remark cited is taken from 'Le Message photographique'.
75. See 'Rhétorique de l'image'.
76. J.-L. Comolli, 'Le détour par le direct', in *Cahiers du cinéma* no. 209, Février 1969, p. 49.
77. Ibid., p. 51.
78. Ibid., p. 49.
79. André Bazin, in essays on Orson Welles and William Wyler, had developed the notion that deep focus and the sequence shot were more 'authentic', closer to reality, because they restored ambiguity and left the viewer free to take decisions, unlike montage which was overtly manipulative. For a detailed discussion of Bazin's views see J.-L. Comolli.
80. *Cahiers du cinéma*, no. 220–1, mai-juin 1970; no. 222 juillet 1970.
81. 'Montage', in *Cahiers du cinéma*, no. 210, mars 1969, pp. 17–35. The debate included Jacques Rivette, Jean Narboni and Sylvie Pierre.
82. T. Todorov (ed.) *Théorie de la littérature Textes des formalistes russes* (Eds. du Seuil, 1965). This contained texts by Schlovsky, Jakobson, Brik, Eichenbaum, Propp and others.

83. 'Montage' p. 29.
84. Ibid.
85. Michel Marie quoted in J. Hillier (ed.) *Cahiers du cinéma*, vol. 2 (Routledge and Kegan Paul, 1986) p. 231.

## 2 Hollywood–France: America as Influence and Intertext

1. See Jacques Portes, 'Les Origines de la légende noire des Accords Blum–Byrnes sur le cinéma', in *La Revue d'histoire moderne et contemporaine*, xxiii, avril–juin 1986, pp. 314–29. This contains a useful analysis of the CNC statistics.
2. For example, Raymond Borde and Etienne Chaumeton, *Panorama du film noir américain* (Eds. de Minuit, 1955) or André Bazin's essays on the Western published in the early 1950s and reprinted in *Qu'est-ce que le cinéma?* (Eds. du Cerf, 1975).
3. See for example, Luc Boltanski, 'America, America. Le Plan Marshall et l'importation du "management" en France', in *Actes de la recherche en sciences sociales*, 38, mai 1981, pp. 19–41.
4. For a fascinating overview see Michel Winock, 'L'Antiaméricanisme français', in *Nationalisme, antisémitisme et fascisme en France* (Eds. du Seuil, 1990) pp. 50–76.
5. See J. Forbes, 'The *Série noire*', in N. Hewett and B. Rigby (eds.), *The Mass Media in France* (Macmillan, 1991).
6. Ibid.
7. See François Guérif, *Le Cinéma policier français* (Eds. Artefact, 1981) pp. 123–6.
8. Eric Rohmer, in *Cahiers du cinéma*, mai 1957, p. 19.
9. J.-L. Godard, 'Défense et illustration du découpage classique', in *Cahiers du cinéma*, sept. 1952, reprinted in Jean Narboni (ed.), *Jean-Luc Godard par Jean-luc Godard* (Belfond, 1968) pp. 29, 33.
10. Cf. Claude Chabrol, 'Petits sujets, grands sujets', in *Cahiers du cinéma* oct. 1959, translated in Peter Graham (ed.), *The New Wave* (Secker & Warburg, 1968) pp. 73–8.
11. See *Film Comment*, Sept.–Oct. 1984, pp. 12–13.
12. Quoted in Annette Insdorf, *François Truffaut* (Macmillan, 1981) p. 26.
13. Quoted in Guérif, *Le Cinéma policier français*, p. 139.
14. Pierre Sorlin, in 'The Dark Mirror', in *L'Avant-scène cinéma*, 329/330, juin 1984, pp. 7–14, points out that this was part of the secret of the success of the American *film noir*.
15. Perhaps for this reason one of his most successful performances was as the Baron de Charlus in **Un Amour de Swann**. Blier also draws on Delon's capacity to appear vulnerable in **Notre Histoire**.
16. At the time when the first *Programme commun de gouvernement* was signed in 1972 there was much talk of a new 'popular front' and much discussion of why the 1936 Popular Front had failed. Resnais's **Stavisky** (1974) reflects these discussions.
17. I am indebted to Jean-Pierre Jeancolas for this observation.
18. Guérif, *Le Cinéma policier français*, pp. 143–67.

19. Jean-Pierre Jeancolas, *Le Cinéma des Français: La V<sup>e</sup> République 1958–78* (Stock, 1979) pp. 228–9.
20. In *New Left Review*, 146, July–Aug. 1984, pp. 53–92.
21. Fredric Jameson, 'Postmodernism and Consumer Society', in Hal Foster (ed.) *Postmodern Culture* (Pluto Press, 1985) p. 112.
22. See his review in *Monthly Film Bulletin*.
23. A 'Jules' in French is a 'man' or a 'boyfriend' as, for example, in the title of Godard's film, **Charlotte et son Jules**.
24. *Positif*, 160, juin 1974, p. 5.
25. *Ecran*, juin 1974, p. 70.
26. See Guérif, *Le Cinéma policier français*, pp. 143ff. Films featuring anarchist groups include Mocky's **Solo** (1970) and Chabrol's **Nada** (1973).
27. Cf. the interview with Corneau in *Positif*, 219, juin 1979, p. 41.
28. Cf. *Positif*, mai 1986, p. 81.
29. Interview with Corneau in *La Revue du Cinéma/Image et son*, 306, mai 1976, p. 41.
30. Cf. *Ecran*, mars 1976, p. 63.
31. J. Forbes, 'The *Série noire*'.
32. The script was published in *L'Avant-scène cinéma*, 233, oct. 1979.
33. See *Polar*, no. 2, 1979, p. 53: 'His job leads him to lend great importance to language which is, in fact, the tool of his trade.'
34. This is confirmed by the nature of Poupart's relationship with Mona: 'Don't leave me alone,' he says, 'Speak! Talk' (p. 22), as well as the emphasis throughout the film on various sources of sound such as radios and the juke box.
35. *Positif*, 219, juin 1979.
36. Exemplified, respectively, in his books *Les Choses*, *Espèces d'espaces* and *La Vie mode d'emploi*.
37. *Polar*, no. 2, 1979, p. 20.
38. Ibid. pp. 21–2.
39. Michel Sineux in *Positif*, 219, juin 1979, pp. 37–8.
40. See Henriette Walter, *Le Français dans tous les sens* (Robert Laffont, 1988) pp. 281–93.
41. *L'Avant-scène cinéma*, 233, p. 48.
42. Ibid., p. 40.
43. Ibid., p. 49.
44. *Positif*, 219, p. 41.
45. *Cahiers de la Cinémathèque*, 25.
46. Discussed by J. Forbes in '*Série noire*'. See also Pascal Ory, 'Mister Blum goes to Hollywood', in *Europe Hollywood et retour*, *Autrement*, avril 1986, pp. 91–8.

## 3  Women Film Makers in France

1. Charles Ford, *Femmes cinéastes ou le triomphe de la volonté* (Denoël Gonthier, 1972).
2. See, for example, Françoise Audé, *Cinémodèles – Cinéma d'elles* (Lausanne: Eds. de l'Age d'homme, 1981); Claire Clouzot, 'Spécial femmes', in *Ecran*, 28 août–sept. 1974;

Charles Ford, *Femmes cinéastes*, counted under a hundred women film makers.

3. For example, Teresa de Lauretis, *Alice Doesn't* (Macmillan, 1984); Claire Johnston, (ed.), *Notes on Women's Cinema* (S.E.F.T., n.d.); E. Ann Kaplan, *Women and Film: Both Sides of the Camera* (Methuen, 1983); Annette Kuhn, *Women's Pictures: Femminism and Cinema* (Routledge & Kegan Paul, 1982); Molly Haskell, *From Reverence to Rape* (New York: Rinehart & Winston, 1973).
4. *Women and Film*, pp. 23–35.
5. For accounts in English see Elaine Marks and Isabelle de Courtivron, *New French Feminisms* (Brighton: Harvester, 1980); Claire Duchen, *French Connections* (Hutchinson, 1987).
6. Duchen, *French Connections*, p. 11.
7. M. Merleau-Ponty, 'Le cinéma et la nouvelle psychologie', in *Sens et non-sens* (Nagel, 1966) pp. 104–5. This text was originally delivered as a lecture to IDHEC in 1947.
8. See J. Forbes, ' French Film Culture and British Cinema', in C. Crossley and I. Small (eds.) (Macmillan, 1988) pp. 154–86.
9. *Notes* pp. 28–9.
10. Jacqueline Rose, *Sexuality in the Field of Vision* (Verso, 1986) pp. 227–8.
11. *Alice Doesn't*, p. 4.
12. There is also the polemical counterpart. For example, *Sorcières*, no. 10, devoted to 'L'Art et les femmes', has as its cover illustration a reproduction of Jeanne Soquet's painting, *Le Silence*.
13. H. Cixous, 'Le Sexe ou la tête', *Les Cahiers du grif*, 13 oct. 1976, pp. 5–15.
14. Ibid., p. 16, 'Quelques questions à Hélène Cixous'.
15. This hotly debated issue and the position of Cixous are usefully summarised and discussed by Barbara Freeman, 'Plus corps donc plus écriture: Hélène Cixous and the body-mind problem', in *Paragraph*, vol. 11, no. 1, pp. 58–70.
16. H. Cixous, 'Le Rire de la Méduse', in *L'Arc*, 61, 1975, p. 48.
17. Ibid., p. 43.
18. *Les Cahiers de grif*, 13, p. 16.
19. Cf. the interview with Marin Karmitz in *Positif*, 138, mai 1972, p. 16; 'What they [the women from the MLF] said to the women workers was that their enemy was their husband and their boss in that order. The women workers said that on the contrary their enemy was the boss and not their husbands. Their film is a film about the class struggle and about the women's struggle against the bosses who oppress them (...) I want to say something else as well. It was as a result of their struggle against their bosses that the women in Troyes for example became conscious of their condition and of their dignity as women.'
20. See Claire Clouzot's useful catalogue of women's films in 'Le Cinéma au féminisme', *CinémAction*, 9, automne 1979, pp. 176–202, especially p. 188.
21. Audé, *Cinémodèles*, p. 167.
22. Akerman constructs women's marginality through recourse to her own biography as a Belgian Jewish lesbian.

23. See 'Spécial femmes', in *Ecran*, août–sept. 1974.
24. Clouzot, ibid. p. 77. This is entirely confirmed by Henri Agel's preface to René Prédal, *Le Cinéma français contemporain* (Eds. du Cerf, 1984) pp. 7–8 in which he recalls his former students who had succeeded in gaining admission to IDHEC, all of whom were men.
25. Quoted in J. Beaulieu, *La Télévision des réalisateurs* (La Documentation française, 1984) p. 90.
26. Cf. the interview with Schiffman in M. Ciment et al. (eds.), 'Les 400 coups de François Truffaut', *Cahiers du 7ᵉ Art*, no. 6, 1988, pp. 21–5.
27. Cf. 'Regards sur Agnès Varda, cinéaste français', in *Visuelles: Des femmes et des images*, no. 2, sept. 1980, p. 21: 'I produced my films myself when I couldn't find a producer or else they were produced by a distributor I was able to find. This means that there has been no continuity, no contract, no stability of employment which would have allowed me to relax and think that all I had to do was to write my next film and it would get made.' See also Varda's interview in *Les Nouvelles littéraires*, 2636, 18 mai 1976: 'French cinema remains super chic and super selective. That is why it's the most bourgeois cinema in the world.' Marguerite Duras's films have been made in conditions of even greater austerity. See Benoît Jacquot in M. Duras *et. al.* (eds.), *Marguerite Duras* (Albatros, 1975) pp.123–8.
28. F. Flamant, 'Des Femmes organisent un festival', in *La Revue du cinéma/Image et son*, 283, avril 1974, pp. 70–1.
29. M. Amiel, '*Musidora* Arrête ton cinéma', in *Cinéma 75*, 199, juin 1975, p.28.
30. Femmes de Musidora, *Paroles. . .elles tournent* (Des Femmes, 1976). The title is a pun – 'tourner' meaning both to 'shoot' a film and to go round and round.
31. Flamant, 'Des Femmes organisent un festival'.
32. *Catalogue du 10ᵉ Festival de films de femmes* (Créteil: Maison des Arts, 1988) p. 10.
33. Audé, *Cinémodèles*, p. 140.
34. Quoted in ibid.
35. Ibid., p. 141. See also Monique Martineau's summary of the famous debate about Varda in 'Le Cinéma au Féminisme', *CinemAction*, 9, pp. 53–8.
36. Interview with Varda in *La Revue du cinéma*, 436, mars 1988, p. 58.
37. *Cinéma 75*, 204, déc. 1975, p.39.
38. *Cahiers du cinéma*, 276, mai 1977, p. 23.
39. Cf. *Visuelles*, no. 2, sept. 1980, p. 28. For example, **Histoires d'A** shows documentary footage of the Bobigny demonstration which is reprised in **L'Une chante** with the participation of the lawyer Gisèle Halimi who acted for the defendants in the trial.
40. Ibid.
41. *Cinéma 85*, 332, déc. 1985, p. 2.
42. Cf. E. Ann Kaplan (ed.), *Women in Film Noir* (BFI, 1978) pp. 35–67.
43. A. Astruc, 'Naissance d'une nouvelle avant-garde', in *L'Ecran français*, 30 mars 1948, pp. 236–40.

44. M.A. Doane, 'The Voice in the Cinema: The Articulation of Body and Space', in *Cinema/Sound*, *Yale French Studies*, 60, 1980, pp. 33–50.
45. *Cinéma 65*, 92, jan. 1965, quoted in Claire Clouzot, *Le Cinéma français depuis la nouvelle vage* (Nathan/Alliance Française, 1972).
46. See M. Duras, *Hiroshima mon amour: Scénario du film d'Alain Resnais* (Gallimard, 1959).
47. For a fascinating discussion of Duras's rhetoric see D. Noguez, 'Les India Songs de Marguerite Duras', in *Cahiers du 20e siècle: Spécial Cinéma et littérature*, no. 9, 1978, pp. 31–48, reprinted in D. Noguez, *Eloge du cinéma expérimental* (Centre G. Pompidou, 1979) pp. 141–9.
48. M. Duras and M. Porte, *Les Lieux de Marguerite Duras* (Minuit, 1977) p. 94: 'In the cinema, as I was virtually disgusted with the films that had been made, or at least the great majority of them, I wanted to start from scratch with a very primitive grammar.' See also Duras, quoted in M. Borgomano, *L'Ecriture filmique de Marguerite Duras* (Albatros, 1985) p. 137: 'For forty years I think the cinema has been ashamed of speech in the same way as it has been ashamed of being intelligent.'
49. Duras and Porte, *Les Lieux*, p. 108.
50. Ibid., p. 109.
51. See E. Ann Kaplan, *Women and Film Both Sides of the Camera*, pp. 91–103.
52. *Les Cahiers du grif*, 13, p. 16.
53. M. Duras, *Le Camion* (Gallimard, 1977).
54. See Noguez, *Eloge*, p. 45.
55. See M. Borgomano, 'Une Ecriture féminine. A propos de Marguerite Duras', in *Littérature*, 53, février 1984, p. 60.
56. Ibid., p. 67.
57. Duras and Porte, *Les Lieux*, p. 110.

## 4  Truffaut and Godard in the 1970s

1. The cycle consists of **Les 400 coups** (1959), **Antoine et Colette** (1962), **Baisers volés** (1968), **Domicile conjugal** (1970) and **L'Amour en fuite** (1979).
2. See below, p. 217.
3. See below, p. 205.
4. See *L'Avant-scène cinéma*, 168, avril 1976, for the script of this film. This film marked the beginning of Miller's extremely successful collaboration with Luc Béraud, who was assistant director and co-scriptwriter.
5. See the excellent discussion of **Numéro deux** by Laura Mulvey in Colin MacCabe, Mick Eaton and Laura Mulvey, *Godard: Images, Sounds, Politics* (Macmillan, 1980) pp. 96–101.
6. Mulvey, *Godard*, p. 98, perceptively notes that 'the repression of homosexuality' is one of the founding moments of male sexuality. The fear of homosexuality and the compensating investment in aggressively male pursuits like boxing is well

depicted in Sautet's film, which plays on the monitor at the beginning of **Numéro deux.**

7. See *Cahiers du cinéma*, nos. 262–3, janvier 1976, pp. 10–39 for a series of articles on **Numéro deux**, several of which stress how Godard is reacting to the wave of sex films produced in France. See also above, p. 10.
8. See Jill Forbes, *INA French for Innovation* (BFI, 1984) especially pp. 41–4 for details of INA's production output. The investment in experimental television was brought to an end in 1979 when INA lost its semi-monopoly of film production for television.
9. The titles are: **Y a personne/Louison, Leçons de choses/Jean-Luc, Photos et cie/Marcel, Pas d'histoires/Nanas, Nous trois/René(e)s, Avant et après/Jacqueline et Ludovic.**
10. Gilles Deleuze, 'Trois question sur **Six fois deux**', in *Cahiers du cinéma'*, 271, nov. 1976, pp. 5–12.
11. 'Number one, number two, finally number three, me finally.'
12. See, for example, Chrisian Metz, 'La grande syntagmatique du film narratif', in *Communications*, 8, 1966, pp. 120–4.
13. This, of course, refers to the constitution of the sign as signifier plus signified, elaborated by Saussure and popularised by Barthes among others.

## 5 The Heritage of the *Nouvelle Vague*

1. *Cahiers du cinéma*, no. 204, sept. 1968, p. 47.
2. Ibid.
3. Ibid., p. 54.
4. Ibid., p. 49.
5. Ibid., p. 47.
6. Ibid., p. 53.
7. Ibid., p. 44.
8. *Cahiers du cinéma*, no. 287, avril 1978, p. 61.
9. Ibid., p. 62.
10. See *CinémAction*, nos. 10–11, printemps–été 1980, p. 727.
11. See *La Revue belge du cinéma*, 10, hiver, 1984, pp. 96–7.
12. *Cahiers du cinéma*, no. 287, avril 1978, p. 62.
13. Ibid.
14. See *Cinéma 72*, no. 169, sept.–oct. 1972, pp. 87–8: 'I contrast the industrialist and the futurist. The futurist moves closer and closer to the ceremony which leaves no trail whereas the industrialist continues to enrich the medium because he is suffering from the psychosis of the material world.'
15. See *Cahiers du cinéma*, no. 344, février 1983, p. 23.
16. *Cahiers du cinéma*, no. 344, février 1983, p. 23.
17. See *Cahiers du cinéma*, no. 204, sept. 1968, p. 48.
18. Philippe Garrel, interviewed in *Cahiers du cinéma*, 344, février 1983, p. 26.
19. Ibid.
20. He edited in particular **Jean Renoir le patron** (1966) – three films in the series **Cinéastes de notre temps**. See B. Amengual,

*Jean Eustache. Etudes Cinématographiques*, 152–5 (Lettres Modernes/Minard 1986) pp. 125–9.

21. See *Image et son*, 244, 1970, pp. 143–7 for an account of the filming of **La Rosière de Pessac**.
22. *Image et son*, 250, mai 1971, p. 144.
23. Ibid.
24. Ibid., p. 87.
25. Ibid., p. 85.
26. See *Image et son*, 244, 1970, p. 144.
27. Ibid., p. 146.
28. See Serge Daney, 'D'une Rosière à l'autre', in *Cahiers du cinéma*, no. 306, déc. 1976, pp. 39–40.
29. *Image et son*, 244, 1970, p. 145.
30. Ibid.
31. See, for example, C. Brémond, E. Sullerot, S. Berton, 'Les Héros des film dits "de la nouvelle vague"', in *Communications I* (1961) pp. 142–77.
32. J. Eustache, *La Maman et la putain – Scénario* (Cahiers du cinéma, 1986) p. 53.
33. Ibid., p. 27.
34. Ibid., p. 65. 'I am convinced that everything that's happened to the world in the past few years has happened in order to spite me,' says Alexandre in the same breath.
35. 'Draguer': to try to pick up or seduce. Much of **A bout de souffle** is directed to this activity.
36. See *Scénario*, p. 17: 'She was smoking Gauloises. She was wearing a Moroccan-style dress and no bra.' See also p. 33: '[The MLF] Don't you know what it is? It's the Women's Liberation Movement. It's for women who are fed up with taking their husbands breakfast in bed. So they've rebelled. They've got a slogan, "We don't need men under our eiderdowns", something like that.' Interestingly their conversation continues with a discussion of a 'friend of Alexandre's' who seduced a girl by talking about his grandmother 'who spent her time doing the housework, looking after her children, her family and her grandchildren'.
37. Ibid., p. 119.
38. Ibid., p. 120.
39. Ibid., p. 120.
40. Ibid., p. 119.
41. 'There are no whores. Just cunts and cocks. It isn't depressing, it's fantastic,' says Veronika, p. 119.
42. Ibid.
43. Léaud does not play in **Mes petites amoureuses** since, by the time Eustache managed to raise money for this project, which he had nursed for a decade, Léaud was clearly too old for the part. See the discussion of this film in B. Amengual *et al.*, 'Jean Eustache', *Etudes Cinématographiques*, 153–5 (Lettres Modernes/Minard, 1986).
44. *Scénario*, p. 45. This episode figures in Truffaut's **Les 400 coups** and was, as Truffaut's letters reveal, a habit of the film maker's adolescence, and in the introduction to *Les Aventures d'Antoine Doinel* (Mercure de France, 1970) Truffaut stated that

the Doinel character 'is the synthesis of two real people, Jean-Pierre Léaud and myself' (p. 9).

45. The mother in **Mes petites Amoureuses** has, like the mother in **Les 400 coups**, taken a lover and the pair treat the child badly; the mother in **Du côté de Robinson** has abandoned her children; the 'mother' in **La Maman et la putain**, frankly, is not maternal enough.

46. As well as **Jules et Jim**, Eustache was clearly influenced by Lubitsch's **Design for Living** (adapted from the Noel Coward play). The latter, set in Paris in the 1920s, depicts a threesome of bohemian Americans attempting to be artists. The tone is as lighthearted as Eustache's is pessimistic and, in addition, the woman having 'married well' like Gilberte, decides she is bored by her earnest, businessman husband and is delighted to be rescued by here two artist lovers. By contrast, in Eustache the 'bohemians' seem obliged to revert to a more conventional design for living. It is also interesting that Eustache now makes a single man the object of two women's affections, whereas in both **Jules et Jim** and **Design for Living** the reverse was the case.

47. Eustache, interviewed in *Cahiers du cinéma*, 284, janvier 1978, p. 23.

48. 'I believe in Renoir more and more strongly,' he said in 1967. See also B. Amengual's analysis of Eustache's debt to Renoir in **Mes petites Amoureuses** and **Du côté de Robinson**, in *Jean Eustache*, pp. 92–3, 107–8.

49. *Cahiers du cinéma*, no. 187, février 1967, pp. 50–1.

50. Ibid.

51. See S. Bernard (ed.), *Oeuvres de Rimbaud* (Garnier, 1960) pp. 90–2, 392. The title may well contain a private joke since the film maker M. Pialat plays the role of Henri in the film, while the Rimbaud poem contains the lines:

Blancs de lunes particulières
Aux pialats ronds.

Bernard cannot elucidate 'pialat'.

52. See M. Foucault, *La Volonté de savoir* (Gallimard, 1978) p. 155.

53. *Jean Eustache*, pp. 32–3.

54. Interviewed on *France Culture*, 4 June 1985, quoted in *Jean Eustache*, p. 122.

55. See Freud's essay 'Instincts and their vicissitudes' (1915) reprinted in J. Strachey (ed.), *The Standard Edition of the Complete Psychological Works of S. Freud* (Hogarth Press, 1957) vol. XIV, pp. 109–40.

56. See Chantal Labre, 'Un cinéma de la cruauté', in *Positif*, 204, mars 1978, pp. 66–8.


## 6   In Search of the Popular Cinema: Bertrand Tavernier and the Return to the 'Tradition de Qualité'

1. F. Truffaut, 'Une certaine tendance du cinéma français' (1954) reprinted in *Le Plaisir des yeux* (Cahiers du cinéma, 1987) pp. 192–207.

2. J. Eustache interviewed in *Cahiers du cinéma*, 284, janvier 1978 p. 24.
3. See *L'Avant-scène cinéma*, 147, mai 1974, and J.-L. Douin, *Bertrand Tavernier* (Edilig, 1988).
4. 'L'influence d'Aurenche et Bost est immense', in 'Une certaine tendance du cinéma français', pp. 200ff.
5. Pierre Bost died in 1975.
6. See Jacqueline Beaulieu, *La Télévision des réalisateurs* (La Documentation française, 1984) p.99.
7. Michel Mitrani, quoted in Beaulieu, p.99.
8. Ibid., p. 90.
9. G. Deleuze, *L'Image-Temps* (Eds. de Minuit, 1985) pp. 251–2.
10. For example, the train in the opening sequence hurtles past a sign which reads 'Lyon 15km'. Other scenes are shot in identifiable locations such as the Quai de la ficelle.
11. *L'Avant-Scène cinéma*, 147, p. 10.
12. Simenon's perverse dialectics – one thinks of *Monsieur Hire* – were perhaps responsible for his renewed popularity at this time.
13. See *Image et son/Ecran*, 352 juill–août 1980, p. 108. Another obvious source of Dumas as of costume dramas is, of course, Saint-Simon's memoirs. Cf. Douin, *Bertrand Tavernier*, P. 88.
14. *Encyclopaedia Britannica*, 1949 edition, will serve as an example.
15. *Image et son/Ecran*, 325, p.110.
16. *L'Avant-scène cinéma*, 176, juin 1976, p. 5.
17. Ibid., p. 34.
18. Ibid.
19. Cf. *L'Avant-scène cinéma*, 176, p. 24: 'What a liberation to be able to read a newspaper. Especially the articles about perverted priests that come out on Wednesdays,' says Bouvier.
20. See Douin, *Bertrand Tavernier*, p. 97: 'I am not trying to emphasise the landscape but rather the reverse: I am trying not to separate character and landscape. I am sure this is because of my past as a film critic. Like the MacMahonians I learned to be sensitive to the way Walsh's or Losey's characters fit into their locations.'
21. *L'Avant-scène cinéma*, 176, p. 38.
22. See Douin, *Bertrand Tavernier*, pp. 76–9 and *Films in Review*, vol. 34, no. 4. April 1983, pp. 230–7. See also J.-P. Coursodon and B. Tavernier, *Trente Ans de cinéma américain* (Ed. CIB, 1970); B. Eisenschitz (ed.) *Humphrey Bogart* (E. Losfeld, 1967).
23. Tavernier published a tribute to Dexter Gordon in *Le Monde*, 28 avril 1990, p. 16. The obituary (*Le Monde* 27.4.90, p. 15) emphasised the power of Gordon's voice: 'He is not playing a character in **Round Midnight**, he's incarnating my idea of a jazz musician.'
24. 'Delmer Daves' in *Positif*, 50/51/52, mars 1963, p. 114.
25. See J. Forbes 'French Film Culture and British Cinema', in C. Crossley and I. Small (eds.), *Imagining France* (Macmillan, 1988) p. 165.
26. See Coursodon and Tavernier p. 148.
27. *Première*, nov. 1987, p. 159.

28. See *Cinématographe*, 71, october 1981, pp. 27–30 where Tavernier states that his reading of Céline, particularly *L'Eglise* but also, no doubt, the African interlude of *Voyage au bout de la nuit*, suggested not just Africa but the 1930s as well. Céline's vision is one of total corruption and the character of Nono, in particular, borrows some of his verbal extravagance from Céline as well as from Queneau.

29. *Pop 1280* was translated by Marcel Duhamel and published as *1275 Ames* (Gallimard, 1966).

30. **Série noire** was an adaptation of Thompson's *A Hell of a Woman*, scripted by Georges Perec. Tavernier recalls that he had thought of asking Perec to script his film as well but that the novelist had refused because the book 'frightened him' (Douin, *Bertrand Tavernier*, p. 119).

31. Tavernier emphasises how much the hero of **Série noire** is motivated by words (in much the same way as the Bouvier of **Le Juge et l'assassin**) 'the character is chasing after the sentences he has just uttered and (...) he catches them with gestures. The nights urge him on.' *Cinématographe*, 71, p. 28.

32. Ibid., p. 30

## 7 In Search of the Popular Cinema: New French Comedy

1. See *Cinéma 81*, nos 271–2 août 1981, p. 108.
2. Ibid., p. 109.
3. His second film, **Même si j'étais un espion** (1967), was extremely unsuccessful.
4. *Cinéma 81*, p. 110.
5. In *nouvelle vague* films crime is always implicitly condoned as a form of self-development or self-protection.
6. See Henriette Walter, 'L'innovation lexicale chez les jeunes Parisiens', in *La Linguistique*, xx (1984). See also *Cités Cinés* (Editions Ramsay, 1987) pp. 61–117.
7. This account is dependent on Pierre Merle, *Le Café-Théâtre* (PUF, 1985). See also *Positif*, 300, féb 1986, pp. 52–3 for a discussion of the impact of the *café-théâtre* on the cinema.
8. Merle, *Le café-théâtre*, pp. 45–7.
9. *Hara-Kiri* was subtitled 'journal bête et méchant'. For an account of its foundation and development see F. Cavanna, *Bête et méchant* (Belfond, 1981).
10. In an interview with the author Blier stated that his technique consisted of exploiting what he called the 'ringard', which might be translated as 'naff'. See *City Limits*, 1 March 1990, pp. 29–30. Elsewhere he has said: 'J'adore les poncifs (...) Ce qui m'amuse c'est de retourner complètement le poncif' (*La Revue du cinéma*, 417, June 1986).
11. Merle, *Le café-théâtre*.
12. See *Image et son/Ecran* 364, sept. 1981, for a discussion of Kubrick's influence. Blier is only one illustration – although perhaps an extreme one – of the fact that French film makers clearly go to the cinema for inspiration.

13. For an analysis of *Les Choses* see J. Leenhardt and P. Jozsa, *Lire la Lecture* (Le Sycomore, 1982).
14. Dewaere died in 1982.
15. There is an extensive literature on this subject, well summarised in Jane Jensen, 'Representations of Difference', in *NLR* (180) 1990, pp. 127–60.
16. See *Positif*, 204, mars 1978, pp. 13–17.
17. For an overview of the almost entirely favourable reviews of **Vincent, François, Paul et les autres** see *Ecran*, 33, février 1975, pp. 78–80. As is pointed out in this article the term of commendation which constantly recurs is 'true'. The film was above all credited with being 'true to life'.
18. *Image et son*, 304, mars 1976, p. 61.
19. Claire Clouzot, 'Le point de vue de Vénus' (*sic*) in *Image et son*, 304, mars 1976, pp. 61–2.
20. He confided to this author a project for a road movie in which the protagonists would be girls. See *City Limits*, 1 March 1990.
21. See *Cahiers du cinéma*, 329, nov. 1981, pp. 63–4 .
22. In *City Limits*, 1 March 1990.
23. Ibid.
24. See, for example, The special number of *Présence du Cinéma*, déc. 1961.
25. The remark was made in *Cahiers du cinéma* in July 1959 and is discussed in J. Forbes, 'French Film Culture and British Cinema' in C. Crossley and I. Small (eds.), *Imagining France*, pp. 164 and 183.
26. This is the definition of the pseudo-science invented by the playwright Alfred Jarry in 1911.
27. *Cinéma 80*, no. 255, mars 1980, p. 40.
28. Ibid., p. 41.
29. This point was stressed by Jean-Louis Comolli, for example, in 'Le détour par le direct', in *Cahiers du cinéma*, no. 209, février 1969, pp. 48–53.
30. *Image et son*, 265, 1972, p. 53.
31. *Cahiers du cinéma*, no. 270, sept.–oct. 1976 pp. 61–2.
32. For a useful account of the intellectual origins of Situationism see Jean-François Martos *Histoire de l'Internationale Situationniste* (Eds. Gérard Lebovici, 1989) and Peter Wollen, 'Bitter Victory', in *An Endless Adventure, An Endless Passion, An Endless Banquet* (ICA/Verso, 1989) pp. 9–16.
33. Quoted in Martos, *Historie de l'Internationale Situationniste*, p. 227.
34. Ibid., p. 135.
35. Ibid., p. 115.
36. Debord himself made a number of short films but he is nowhere near as talented as Moullet and his writing remains much more influential than his film making.

## 8 The Family in Question

1. See the interview with Doillon in *Cahiers du cinéma*, nos. 360–1 été 1984, pp. 23–8, *La Revue du cinéma*, 395, juin 1984, p. 75 and *Positif*, 220–1 juillet–août. 1979, p. 40.

2. See Gébé, *L'An 01* (Eds. du Square, 1975) and *L'An 01 Plaquette de présentation*, 1972: 'in **L'An 01** you find the whole *Hara-Kiri* team (minus Reiser who's got a contract with Les Charlots). They play the only unpleasant roles in the film.'
3. *La Revue du cinéma*, 395, juin 1984, p. 71. Resnais and Rouch contributed moral support but very little to the actual direction of the film, see *Positif*, juillet 1979, p. 38.
4. *Plaquette de présentation* (1972).
5. Ibid.
6. Gébé, *L'An 01* p. 8.
7. Ibid.
8. *La Revue du cinéma*, 395, p. 71.
9. Ibid.
10. François Truffaut, *Les Films de ma vie* (Flammarion, 1975) pp. 357–60.
11. The scenario is printed in *L'Avant-scène cinéma*, 157, avril 1975.
12. Ibid., pp. 38 and 40.
13. *La Revue du cinéma*, 395, juin 1984, p. 73.
14. *Positif*, 220–1, juillet–août, 1979, p. 40.
15. Ibid., p.37.
16. Ibid.
17. *La Revue du cinéma*, 395, juin 1984, p. 75. Doillon was criticised, for example, for making his children talk like adults, to which he replied: 'I don't waylay children as they are coming out of school. I'm not a specialist in the way they talk.'
18. Ibid., p. 73.
19. *La Revue du cinéma*, 396, juillet 1984, p. 67.
20. Cf. *Cinématographe*, 108, mars 1985, pp. 67–70, where Doillon discusses his Protestant origins.
21. Doillon himself remarked of **La Drôlesse**: 'it's about a guy who kidnaps a child. He sets the whole scene up' (*La Revue du cinéma* 395, p. 74).
22. See *Cinématographe*, 100, mai 1984, p. 24.
23. *La Revue du cinéma*, 395, juin 1984, p. 71: 'We shot it in my house, with me and my child acting in it and my car. Plus a few technicians whom I could trust. All this to make the most expensive Sunday film ever.'
24. Ibid., p.73.
25. *Cinéma 85*, no. 34 février 1985, p. 44.
26. See *Positif*, 220–1, juillet–août 1979, p. 30: 'I've got something to tell you. I've no father. So I've decided to call you Daddy.'
27. *La Revue du cinéma*, 395, juin 1984, p. 74.
28. Cf. *Cahiers du cinéma*, été 1984, p. 23: 'Despite everything, the beauty and seductive quality of Maruschka's body had to count for Jane. The difficult thing was to film in such a way that the audience would be moved by the contrast between Jane's body and that of another woman!' Doillon's procedure might be compared with that of Agnès Varda, who in **Jane B par Agnès V**, discusses with Birkin the latter's somewhat androgynous physical presence. In **La Pirate**, as in Varda's **Kung Fu Master**, Birkin's physical similarity to her brother Andrew (they are both tall and thin) who appears in both films also

foregrounds her androgynous qualities and underlines her contrast with Detmers.

29. *Cinéma 85*, no. 314, février 1985, p. 43.
30. *Cinématographe*, 108, mars 1985, p. 70.
31. Ibid.
32. Ibid.
33. *Cinéma 85*, no. 314, février 1985, p.43.
34. See, for example, *Cinématographe*, 94, nov. 1983, pp. 3–6; *Positif*, 235, oct. 1980, pp. 18–30. The topic recurs in virtually every interview Pialat has given.
35. For details see *L'Avant-scène cinéma*, 134, mars 1973 p. 39 (where **L'Enfance nue** is wrongly dated) and *Positif*, 159, mai 1974, p. 21. The script of **L'Amour existe** was published in *L'Avant-scène cinéma*, 12, février 1962, pp. 47–52, and **Janine** is summarised in an interview with Evelyne Ker in M. Pialat, *A nos Amours* (Lherminier, 1984) pp. 150–2.
36. *Cahiers du cinéma*, no. 304, oct. 1979, p. 9.
37. Quoted in *La Revue du cinéma*, 408, sept. 1985, p. 77. See also *Cinématographe*, 94, nov. 1983, p. 4. For the Popular Front project see *Positif*, 275, janvier 1984, p. 7.
38. *Positif*, 159, mai 1974, p. 3, 'L'Amour existe suffers from being vulgar and naive. I made it after having spent ten years in the depressing trade of commercial traveller. The film shows it. The commentary is particularly insufferable.'
39. *Cahiers du cinéma*, 304, oct. 1979, p. 14. See also the extended interview in *Positif*, 159, mai 1974 pp. 2–21 in which Pialat refers to the 'nullity of the *nouvelle vague*' and suggests that Godard 'est le type même de faux talent qui s'est écroulé'.
40. Cf. *Cahiers du cinéma*, 304, oct. 1979, p. 5.
41. *Ecran*, 83, sept. 1979, p. 63.
42. *Cahiers du cinéma*, 304, oct. 1979, p. 11 and *Cinéma 79*, 250, oct. 1979, p. 60.
43. See *Ecran*, 83, sept. 1979, p. 62.
44. *Cinéma 79*, oct. 1979, p. 62 and *Cinématographe*, 94, nov. 1983, p. 6.
45. See M. Pialat, *A nos Amours*, p. 114.
46. *Cinématographe*, 94, p. 6.
47. *Positif*, 159, mai 1974, pp. 4–5.
48. See *Cinématographe*, 113, sept. 1985, p. 16 and *Cinématographe*, 94, p. 19.
49. See the interview with Arlette Langmann in M. Pialat, *A nos Amours*, pp. 134–5. 'When Pialat decided to play the role himself he realised that the father's death would be read symbolically and in the final version, therefore, the father moves out of the family apartment and is absent from the screen for a while'.
50. This was pointed out in *Positif*, 235, oct. 1980, p. 18.
51. *L'Avant-scène cinéma*, 134, p. 7.
52. See *Positif*, 235, oct. 1980, p. 52.
53. *Cinématographe*, 113, sept. 1985, p. 18.
54. See M. Pialat, *A nos Amours*, pp. 134–5.
55. Ibid., p. 150.
56. Ibid., p. 152.

57. This accusation is based on a scene in **Passe ton Bac d'abord**, in which two Jewish theatrical agents arrive by Rolls Royce in Lens to search for film extras, and a scene in **Loulou** in which André implicitly refers to Nelly's Jewish background. See *Cahiers du cinéma*, 316, oct. 1980, p. 46.
58. See, for example, Jacques Fieschi in *Cinématographe*, 94, pp. 18–19.
59. Ibid., p. 9.

# 9  The New History Film

1. This classification of earlier history films proposed by François Regnault, 'Les Camisards et le film d'histoire', in *Cahiers du cinéma*, 238–9, mai–juin 1972, pp. 71–4, seems essentially accurate.
2. Cf. Regnault, 'Les Camisards', p. 72. Le Roy Ladurie's *Montaillou, village occitan* (Gallimard, 1975) became a bestseller.
3. See, for example, E. Le Roy Ladurie, *Le Territoire de l'historien* (Gallimard, 1973) pp. 169–86 and *passim*.
4. See *Jeune cinéma*, 58, nov. 1971, p. 15 'I am not a Protestant but I lived for a long time in Nîmes.'
5. Philippe Joutard (ed.), *Journaux camisards* (U.G.E. 1965); E. Le Roy Ladurie, *Les Paysans du Languedoc* (Flammarion, 1969).
6. *Jeune cinéma*, 58, nov. 1971, p. 16. This was wishful thinking. Joutard, *Journaux camisards*, p. 10., stresses that the revolt should not be seen in this way.
7. *La Revue de cinéma/Image et son*, 258, mars 1972, p. 88.
8. For example, *Les Glaneuses, L'Angélus, L'Enterrement à Ornans.*
9. See *L'Avant-scène cinéma*, 122, février 1972, p. 9. Compare, too, R. Barthes, 'Les Maladies du costume de théâtre' (1955) reprinted in *Essais critiques* (Seuil, 1971) pp. 53–62.
10. See the round-table discussion of the history film in *Positif*, 189, janvier 1977, p. 7.
11. M. Foucault (ed.) *Moi Pierre Rivière ayant égorgé ma mère, ma sœur, mon frère* (Gallimard/Juillard, 1973).
12. Interview with Foucault in *La Revue du cinéma/Image et son*, 312, déc. 1976, p. 39.
13. R. Barthes, 'Le Discours de l'histoire' (1967) reprinted in *Le Bruissement de la langue* (Seuil, 1984) pp. 153–66.
14. See M. Foucault (ed.) *Moi Pierre Rivière*, pp. 130–1.
15. In the sense defined by Barthes, 'Le Discours de l'histoire', p. 156: 'what one might call the performative overture, for the word is a solemn founding action: the model is poetic, it is the poet's "I sing"'.
16. Foucault, *Moi Pierre Rivière*, p. 272.
17. Ibid., pp. 269–70.
18. *Cinéma 76*, 215, nov. 1976, p. 76.
19. Ibid., p. 74.
20. Ibid.
21. See *Cahiers du cinéma*, no. 367, jan. 1985, pp. 38–40.

22. *Cinéma 76*, 215, nov. 1976, p. 77: 'There are two main schools of thought about non-professionals, the Bressonian, in which the non-professional is an empty vessel completely filled up by the director – or the documentary, *cinéma vérité* school.' **Moi Pierre Rivière** clearly belongs to the latter school.
23. It has been pointed out that at that time, if not today, most of the lawyers and doctors involved in the trial would have had regional accents too.
24. Barthes, 'Le Discours de l'histoire', p. 155.
25. See *Cahiers du cinéma*, no. 271, nov. 1976, p. 52.
26. *L'Avant-scène cinéma*, 183, mars 1977, p. 55.
27. Foucault, *Moi Pierre Rivière*, p. 272.
28. Barthes, 'Le Discours de l'histoire', p. 164.
29. Ibid., p. 166.
30. See *Positif*, 189, janvier 1977, pp. 69–70.
31. Foucault in *La Revue du cinéma/Image et son*, 312, déc. 1976, p. 40.
32. *Cahiers du cinéma*, no. 271, nov. 1976, p. 52.
33. Foucault, *Moi Pierre Rivière*, p. 132.
34. Ibid.
35. Ibid. and p. 258.
36. See *L'Avant-scène cinéma*, 143/144, janvier–février 1974.
37. See 'Images d'en France', *CinémAction* 18/19 1982, pp. 16–23.
38. See 'Cinémas des régions', *CinémAction* 12, automne 1980, pp. 119–23.
39. See *Cinématographe*, 106, janvier 1985, p. 52; *Cahiers du cinéma*, no. 367, janvier 1985, pp. 38–40.
40. See C. Peyrusse, *Le Cinéma méridional* (Toulouse: Eché, 1986).
41. Interview with Louis Malle in *Positif*, 157, mars 1974, p. 29.
42. Interview with Michel Foucault in *Cahiers du cinéma*, juillet–août 1974, p. 6.
43. Ibid., p. 7.
44. This, of course, is also the message of works like Richard Hoggart's *The Uses of Literacy*.
45. Foucault, *Cahiers du cinéma* 1974, p. 14.
46. *Cinéma 75*, nos 201–2, sept.–oct. 1975, p. 190: 'I don't make politically militant films so all I can do is ask a few questions about History and the imagination.'
47. Quotations are from the script published in *L'Avant-scène cinéma*, 166, février 1976, to which page numbers refer.
48. Jean Fourastié, *Les Trente glorieuses* (Fayard, 1979) ch. I.
49. Marthe Robert, *Roman des origines et origines du roman* (Grasset, 1972) especially pp. 52–3: The hero is 'the person who creates himself'.
50. This is an interesting amalgamation of two genres. Usually, as in Clouzot's **Les Diaboliques** or Antonioni's **Blow Up**, the accidental inclusion of a figure in the photograph serves to elucidate a mystery.
51. Cf. Roland Barthes, 'La Dame aux camélias', in *Mythologies* (Eds. du Seuil, 1970) pp. 179–81. Techiné acknowledged the influence of Barthes's writing and the compliment was returned with Barthes publishing a favourable article on **Souvenirs** in *Le Monde*, 18 sept. 1975, partially reprinted in *L'Avant-scène*

*cinéma*, 166, and playing the role of Thackeray in **Les Soeurs Brontë**.

52. See 'Lettre à Lord X', in A. De Vigny (trans.), *Le More de Venise Othello* (Levasseur, 1830) pp. xxiv–vi.
53. *Cinéma 75*, p. 188.
54. *Cinéma 77*, no. 217, janvier 1977, p. 54.
55. See interview with Techiné in A. Philippon, *André Techiné* (Cahiers du cinéma, 1988) p. 117. See also *Cinéma 75*, 201–2, pp. 190–1.
56. *Cinéma 77*, no. 217, p. 54.
57. Ibid.
58. Philippon, *André Techiné*, p. 118.
59. *Cinématographe*, déc. 1981, p. 46.
60. *Cinématographe*, 118, avril 1986, p. 17: 'I was excited by the idea of Catherine being driven off by the police. It offends the image that people usually have of her.'
61. Philippon, *André Techiné*, p. 121.
62. Cf. Marthe Robert, *Roman des origines*. See also *Cinéma 86*, no. 354, mai 1986, pp. 14–20.
63. Philippon, *André Techiné*, p. 121.
64. *Cahiers du cinéma*, no. 373, juin 1985, p. 59.
65. That is, Valence d'Agen. See Philippon, *André Techiné*, p. 121.
66. Ibid., p. 117.
67. *Positif*, 304, juin 1986, p. 78.
68. Philippon, *André Techiné*, p. 120.
69. Ibid.
70. *Cinématographe*, 118, avril 1986, p. 20.

## Conclusion

1. 'Situation du cinéma français', in *Cahiers du cinéma*, nos. 323–4, mai 1981; no. 325, juin 1981.
2. Dominique Noguez, *Eloge du cinéma expérimental* (Centre Georges Pompidou, 1979); *Trente Ans de cinéma expérimental en France* (A.R.C.E.F., 1982).

# Bibliography

This bibliography is not a complete list of all the works referred to in the text. Such references will be found in the notes. Instead, it is an attempt to indicate works which will be of most interest and use to those who wish to pursue further their study of the contemporary French cinema.

There is no comprehensive history of the contemporary French cinema and very few monographs on contemporary French film makers. Most analysis and discussion is to be found not in books but in periodicals. Those I have referred to most frequently are: *Cahiers du cinéma*, *CinémAction*, *Cinématographe* (which has, alas, ceased publication), *Positif* and *La Revue du cinéma*, all of which are published in Paris, and *Monthly Film Bulletin* and *Sight and Sound*, both of which are published in London. In addition, the monthly review *L'Avant-scène cinéma* regularly publishes scripts of French films and many of those it selects are contemporary.

Virtually nothing in English can be recommended. Of the available literature Roy Armes's *French Cinema* (Secker and Warburg, 1985) covers this period very superficially, while Keith Reader's *Cultures on Celluloid* (Quartet Books, 1981) is mainly concerned with earlier periods of French cinema. The exception is Susan Hayward and Ginette Vincendeau's *French Film: Texts and Contexts* (Routledge and Kegan Paul, 1990) a collection of essays by various authors, only three of which are devoted to the post-1968 period, which nevertheless does contain useful bibliographical and filmographical material.

Unless otherwise stated, all books in French are published in Paris and all books in English in London.

## 1 Works of General Relevance

Françoise Audé, *Cinémodèles – Cinéma d'elles* (Lausanne: Editions de L'Age d'homme, 1981).

Raymond Borde and Etienne Chaumeton, *Panorama du film noir américain* (Editions de Minuit, 1955).

Jean-Pierre Coursodon and Bertrand Tavernier, *Trente Ans de cinéma américain* (Editions CIB, 1970).

Gilles Deleuze, *Cinéma I: L'Image mouvement* (Editions de Minuit, 1983).

Gilles Deleuze, *Cinéma II: L'Image temps* (Editions de Minuit, 1985).

Marguerite Duras et al., *Marguerite Duras* (Albatros, 1975).

Marguerite Duras and Michèle Porte, *Les Lieux de Marguerite Duras* (Editions de Minuit, 1977).

Femmes de Musidora, *Paroles... Elles tournent* (Des Femmes, 1976).

Marc Ferro, *Cinéma et histoire* (Denoël/Gonthier, 1977).

Charles Ford, *Femmes cinéastes ou le triomphe de la volonté* (Denoël/Gonthier, 1972).

Michel Foucault (ed.), *Moi Pierre Rivière, ayant égorgé ma mère, ma soeur, mon frère* (Gallimard/Juillard, 1973).

Gébé, *L'An 01* (Editions du square, 1975).

Lise Grenier (ed.), *Cités-Cinés* (Ramsay, 1987).

François Guérif, *Le Cinéma policier français* (Editions Artefact, 1981).

Sylvia Harvey, *May 68 and Film Culture* (BFI, 1978).

Molly Haskell, *From Reverence to Rape* (New York: Rinehart and Winston, 1973).

Susan Hayward and Ginette Vincendeau (eds.), *French Film: Texts and Contexts* (Routledge, 1990).

Youssef Ishaghpour, *Cinéma contemporain de ce côté du miroir* (Editions de la différence, 1986).

E. Ann Kaplan, *Women in Film Noir* (BFI, 1978).

E. Ann Kaplan, *Women and Film Both Sides of the Camera* (Methuen, 1983).

Annette Kuhn, *Women's Pictures* (Routledge and Kegan Paul, 1982).

Teresa de Lauretis, *Alice Doesn't* (Macmillan, 1984).

Jean-Louis Leutrat, *Kaléidoscope* (Lyon: Presses universitaires de Lyon, 1988).

Pierre Merle, *Le Café-théâtre* (PUF, 1985).

Dominique Noguez, *Eloge du cinéma expérimental* (Centre Georges Pompidou, 1979).

Claudine Peyrusse, *Le Cinéma méridional* (Toulouse: Eché, 1986).

Jacqueline Rose, *Sexuality in the Field of Vision* (Verso, 1986).

François Truffaut, *Les Films de ma vie* (Flammarion, 1975).

François Truffaut, *Le Plaisir des yeux* (Cahiers du cinéma, 1987).

Christian Zimmer, *Cinéma et politique* (Seghers, 1974).

## 2  Histories

Jacqueline Beaulieu, *La Télévision des réalisateurs* (La Documentation française, 1984).

René Bonnell, *Le Cinéma exploité* (Ramsay, 1986).

Freddy Buache, *Le Cinéma français des années 70* (Hatier, 1990).

Claire Clouzot, *Le Cinéma français depuis la nouvelle vague* (Nathan/ Alliance Française, 1972).

Francis Courtade, *Les Malédictions du cinéma français* (Editions A. Moreau, 1978).

Jill Forbes, *INA: French for Innovation* (BFI, 1984).

Jean-Pierre Jeancolas, *Le Cinéma des Français. La V$^e$ République 1958–78* (Stock, 1979).

René Prédal, *Le Cinéma français contemporain* (Editions du Cerf, 1984).

Jean Roux and René Thévenet, *Industrie et commerce du film français* (Editions scientifiques et juridiques, 1979).

## 3  Monographs

Barthélemy Amengual, *Jean Eustache* (Les Lettres modernes/ Minard, 1986).

Madeleine Borgomano, *L'Ecriture filmique de Marguerite Duras* (Albatros, 1985).
Gérard Courant, *Philippe Garrel* (Studio 43, 1983).
Jean-Louis Douin, *Bertrand Tavernier* (Edilig, 1988).
Colin MacCabe *et al.*, *Godard: Images, Sounds, Politics* (BFI/Macmillan, 1980).
Alain Philippon, *André Techiné* (Cahiers du cinéma, 1988).

## 4  Scripts

Marguerite Duras, *Hiroshima mon amour. Scénario du film de Alain Resnais* (Gallimard, 1959).
Marguerite Duras, *Le Camion* (Gallimard, 1977).
Jean Eustache, *La Maman et la putain* (Cahiers du cinéma, 1986).
Gébé, *L'An 01* (Edition du square, 1975).
Louis Malle and Patrick Modiano, *Lacombe Lucien* (Gallimard, 1974).
Maurice Pialat, *A nos Amours* (Lherminier, 1984).
François Truffaut, *Les Aventures d'Antoine Doinel* (Mercure de France, 1970).

## 5  Special Issues

'Special Godard', *Art Press*, hors série, no. 4, déc. 1984, janvier février 1985.
'Europe Hollywood et retour', *Autrement*, avril 1986.
'Situation de cinéma français', *Cahiers du cinéma*, nos. 323–4, mai 1981; no. 325, juin 1981.
'Cinéma et littérature', *Cahiers du 20ᵉ siècle*, no. 9, 1978.
'Le Cinéma au féminisme', *CinémAction*, no. 9, automne 1979.
'Cinémas d'avant-garde', *CinémAction*, nos. 10–11, printemps–été 1980.
'Cinémas des régions', *CinémAction*, no. 12, 1980.
'Images d'en France', *CinémAction*, nos. 18–19, 1982.
'Le Cinéma français au présent', *Cinéma d'aujourd'hui*, printemps–été 1977.
'Les nouveaux cinémas français', *Cinématographe*, juillet 1979.
'Cinema/Sound', *Yale French Studies*, no. 60, 1980.

## 6  Reference

Jean Mitry, *Histoire du cinéma, art et industrie*, 5 vols (Editions Universitaires, 1967–80).
Jean Mitry, *Filmographie universelle*, 26 vols (Service des Archives du film, Bois d'Arcy, 1980–2).
Jean Tulard, *Dictionnaire de cinéma*, 2 vols (Robert Laffont, 1982–4).

# Filmography

## Abbreviations

*d*: director      *sc*: script      *c*: camera
*l.p.*: leading players      *r*: running time      *p*: producer.

This filmography is as full as it is possible to make it in the present state of knowledge but complete information is not available for all films listed. No leading players are listed for documentary films.

**Chantal AKERMAN**
Born in Brussels in 1950. Attended film school for four months. Discovered American experimental cinema on a visit to New York in 1971. Also acts in some of her films (**Je tu il elle, L'Homme à la valise**). Appears in Philippe Garrel's **Elle a passé trop d'heures sous les sunlights**.

**Saute ma ville**
*d*: Chantal Akerman – *sc*: Chantal Akerman – *r*: 13 min, b/w, 1968

**L'Enfant aimé (ou je joue à être une femme mariée)**
*d*: Chantal Akerman – *sc*: Chantal Akerman – *l.p.*: Claire Wauthin – *r*: 35 min, b/w, 1971

**Hôtel Monterey**
*d*: Chantal Akerman – *sc*: Chantal Akerman – *c*: Babette Mangolte – *r*: 65 min, col, 16mm, 1972

**La Chambre**
*d*: Chantal Akerman – *sc*: Chantal Akerman – *c*: Babette Mangolte – *r*: 11 min, col, 16mm, 1972

**Le 15/18**
*d*: Chantal Akerman, Samy Szlingerbaum – *sc*: Chantal Akerman – *r*: 42 min, b/w, 16mm, 1972

**Hanging out Yonkers**
*d*: Chantal Akerman – *sc*: Chantal Akerman – *c*: Babette Mangolte – *r*: 90 min, col, 16mm, 1973

**Je, tu, il, elle**
*d*: Chantal Akerman – *sc*: Chantal Akerman – *c*: Bénédicte Delsalle –

*l*.p.: Chantal Akerman, Niels Arestrup, Claire Wauthin – *r*: 90 min, b/w, 16mm – p: Paradise Films 1974

**Jeanne Dielman, 23 Quai du Commerce 1080 Bruxelles**
*d*: Chantal Akerman – *sc*: Chantal Akerman – *c*: Babette Mangolte – *l*.p.: Delphine Seyrig, Henri Storck, Jacques Doniol-Valcroze, Yves Bical – *r*: 225 min, col, – *p*: Paradise Films/Unité Trois 1975

**News from Home**
*d*: Chantal Akerman – *sc*: Chantal Akerman – *c*: Babette Mangolte – *l*.p.: narrated by Chantal Akerman in English – *r*: 90 min, col, 16mm – *p*: Paradise Films/Unité Trois/INA 1976

**Les Rendez-vous d'Anna**
*d*: Chantal Akerman – *sc*: Chantal Akerman – *c*: Jean Penzer – *l*.p.: Aurore Clément, Magali Noël, Léa Massari, Hans Zischler, Jean-Pierre Cassel – *r*: 127 min, col, – *p*: Hélène Films/Paradise Films/Unité Trois/ZDF 1978

**Hôtel des Acacias**
*d*: Chantal Akerman, Michèle Blondeel – *sc*: Chantal Akerman, Michèle Blondeel – *p*: Institut National Supérieur des Arts du Spectacle, Brussels 1982

**Toute une nuit**
*d*: Chantal Akerman – *sc*: Chantal Akerman – *c*: Caroline Champetier – *l*.p.: Natalia Akerman, Paul Allio, Aurore Clément, Matthieu Schiffman, Jacques Vidla – *r*: 89 min, col, – *p*: Paradise Films/Avidia Films 1982

**J'ai faim, j'ai froid** (an episode of **Paris vu par … vingt ans après**) *d*: Chantal Akerman – *sc*: Chantal Akerman – *c*: Luc Benhamou – *l*.p.: Maria de Medeiros, Pascale Salkin, Esmoris Hanibal – *r*: 13 min, b/w, – *p*: JM Productions/Antenne 2 1984

**L'Homme à la valise**
*d*: Chantal Akerman – *sc*: Chantal Akerman – *c*: Caroline Champetier – *l*.p.: Chantal Akerman, Jeffry Kime – *r*: 60 min, col, 16mm – *p*: INA 1984

**Golden Eighties**
*d*: Chantal Akerman – *sc*: Chantal Akerman, Leora Barish, Henry Bean, Pascal Bonitzer, Jean Gruault – *c*: Gilberto Azevedo, Luc Benhamou – *l*.p.: Delphine Seyrig, Myriam Boyer, Fanny Cottençon, Lio, Pascale Salkin, Charles Denner – *r*: 96 min, col, – *p*: Paradise Films/La Cecilia/Limbo Films 1986

**American Stories (Food, Family and Philosophy)**
*d*: Chantal Akerman – *sc*: Chantal Akerman – *c*: Luc Benhamou – *l*.p.: Eszter Balint, Stefan Balint, Bill Bastiani, Jacob Becker, Rosalind Harris, Dean Jackson, Judith Malina, Roy Nathanson, Deborah Offner – *r*: 95 min, col, – *p*: Bertrand van Effenterre/La Sept/Le Centre Pompidou/RTBF 1989

**René ALLIO**
Born in Marseilles in 1924. At first painter and stage designer.
Exhibited in Paris in 1957 and 1962. From 1957 worked with Roger
Planchon at the Théâtre de la Cité as well as at the Comédie Française
and the TNP. Also worked with William Gaskell at the Royal Court
Theatre in London. In 1978 set up the Centre Méditerranéen de
Creation Cinématographique in Marseilles.

**La Meule**
*d*: René Allio – *sc*: René Allio – *c*: Denys Clerval – *l.p.*: Henri Serre,
Malka Ribowska, Jean Bouise – *r*: 15 min, b/w, – *p*: René Allio 1963

**Le vieille Dame indigne**
*d*: René Allio from the short story by Brecht, *Die unwürdige Greisin*
– *c*: Denys Clerval – *l.p.*: Sylvie, Malka Ribowska, Victor Lanoux,
Etienne Bierry, François Maistre, Lena Delanne, Jean Bouise, André
Thorrent – *r*: 88 min, col, – *p*: SPAC Cinéma 1965

**L'Une et l'autre**
*d*: René Allio – *sc*: René Allio – *c*: Jean Badal – *l.p.*: Malka
Ribowska, Philippe Noiret, Claude Dauphin, Françoise Prévost – *r*:
140 min, col, – *p*: Ancinex 1967

**Pierre et Paul**
*d*: René Allio – *sc*: René Allio, Serge Ganz – *c*: Georges Leclerc –
*l.p.*: Pierre Mondy, Bulle Ogier, Madeleine Barbulée, Robert Juillard,
Pierre Santini – *r*: 100 min, col, – *p*: Productions de la Gréville/
Madeleine Films/Films de la Colombe/Polsim Films 1969

**Les Camisards**
*d*: René Allio – *sc*: René Allio, Jean Jourdheuil – *c*: Denys Clerval –
*l.p.*: Philippe Chevenot, Gérard Desarthe, Dominique Labourier,
François Marthouret, Rufus, Jean Bouise – *r*: 100 min, b/w – *p*:
Polsim/ORTF 1972

**Rude Journée pour la reine**
*d*: René Allio – *sc*: René Allio – *c*: Denys Clerval – *l.p.*: Simone
Signoret, Jacques Debary, Olivier Perrier, Orane Demazis, Alice
Reichen, André Valtier, Michel Pereylon, Arlette Chosson – *r*: 105
min, col, – *p*: Polsim/Citel Films/ORTF 1973

**Moi, Pierre Rivière, ayant égorgé ma mère, ma sœur, mon frère**
*d*: René Allio – *sc*: René Allio, Pascal Bonitzer, Jean Jourdheuil,
Serge Toubiana, adapted from a text edited by Michel Foucault – *c*:
Nurith Aviv – *l.p.*: Claude Hébert, Jacqueline Millière, Joseph
Leportier, Annick Gehan, Nicole Gehan, Emilie Lihou, Antoine
Bourseiller, Michel Amphoux – *r*: 125 min, col, – *p*: René Feret/
Les Films Arquebuse 1976

**Retour à Marseille**
*d*: René Allio – *sc*: René Allio, Janine Peyre – *c*: Renato Berta – *l.p.*:
Raf Vallone, Andréa Ferréol, Jean Maurel, Gilberte Pinet, Paul Allio,

René Fontanarava, Danielle Durand, Marie Cecora, Roger Crouzet, Yvonne Gamy – *r*: 117 min, col, – *p*: Action Films/Film Producktion Janus 1980

**L'Heure exquise**
*d*: René Allio – *sc*: René Allio – *c*: Denis Gheerbrant, Claude Michaud – *l.p.*: René Allio in voice-over – *r*: 60 min, col, 16 mm - *p*: Laura Production/INA/Centre Mediterranéen de Création Cinématographique 1981

**Le Matelot 512**
*d*: René Allio – *sc*: René Allio – *c*: Emmanuel Machmel – *l.p.*: Dominique Sanda, Jacques Perot, Bruno Cremer, Laure Duthilleul, Michel Piccoli – *r*: 100 min, col – *p*: Centre Mediterranéen de Création Cinématographique/FR3 1984

**Jean-Jacques BEINEIX**
Born 1946 in Paris. First medical student. Then assistant to Gérard Brach, **Le Bâteau sur l'herbe** (1971), René Clément, **La Maison sous les arbres** (1971) and **La Course du lièvre à travers les champs** (1973); Jean-Louis Trintignant, **Une Journée bien remplie** (1972).

**Diva**
*d*: Jean-Jacques Beineix – *sc*: Jean-Jacques Beineix, Jean Van Hamme, from the novel by Delacorta – *c*: Philippe Rousselot – *l.p.*: Wilhelmina Higgins Fernandez, Frédéric Andrei, Richard Bohringer, Thuy An Luu, Jacques Fabbri, Chantal Dermaz – *r*: 115 min, col, – *p*: Irène Silberman/Films Galaxic/Greenwich Film Production 1981

**La Lune dans le caniveau**
*d*: Jean-Jacques Beineix – *sc*: Jean-Jacques Beineix, Ollvier Mergault, from the novel by David Goodis – *c*: Philippe Rousselot – *l.p.*: Gérard Depardieu, Natassia Kinski, Victoria Abril, Vittorio Mezzogiorno, Dominique Pinon – *r*: 137 min, col – *p*: Gaumont/TFI Films 1983

**Trente-sept deux Degrés le matin**
*d*: Jean-Jacques Beineix – *sc*: Jean-Jacques Beineix, based on the novel by Philippe Djian – *c*: Jean-François Robin – *l.p.*: Béatrice Dalle, Jean-Hugues Anglade, Consuelo de Haviland – *r*: 121 min, col, – *p*: Constellation Production/Cargo Films 1986

**Roselyne et les lions**
*d*: Jean-Jacques Beineix – *sc*: Jean-Jacques Beineix, Jacques Forgeas, Thierry le Portier – *c*: Jean-François Robin – *l.p.*: Isabelle Pasco, Gérard Sandez, Philippe Clévenot – *r*: 130 min, col – *p*: Caro Films/ Gaumont 1988

**Yannick BELLON**
Born in Biarritz in 1924. Sister of actress Loleh Bellon who often appears in her films. At first editor, in particular for Nicole Vedrès,

Paris 1900 (1948) and for **Le bel Age** (1959), **La morte saison des amours** (1960) both directed by Pierre Kast. Also worked extensively for television.

**Goémons**
*d*: Yannick Bellon – *sc*: Yannick Bellon – *c*: André Dumaître – *l.p.*: commentary spoken by Michel Vitold – *r*: 28 min, b/w, 16mm and 35mm – *p*: Etienne Lallier 1947

**Colette**
*d*: Yannick Bellon – *sc*: Yannick Bellon – *l.p.*: Colette, Jean Cocteau – *r*: 30 min, b/w, 16mm and 35mm – *p*: Les Films Jacqueline Jacoupy 1951

**Tourisme**
*d*: Yannick Bellon – *sc*: Max Champion – *c*: Picon Borel – *l.p.*: commentary spoken by Claude Dauphin – *p*: Atlantic Films 1951

**Varsovie quand-même**
*d*: Yannick Bellon – *sc*: Henri Magnan – *r*: 20 min, b/w, – *p*: Procinex/Films Polski 1954

**Un Matin comme les autres**
*d*: Yannick Bellon – *sc*: Henri Magnan – *c*: Henri Alekan – *l.p.*: Simone Signoret, Yves Montand, Loleh Bellon – *r*: 79 min, b/w, – *p*: Procinex 1956

**Hommes oubliés**
*d*: Yannick Bellon, Jacques Villeminot – *sc*: Yannick Bellon – *r*: 27 min, col – *p*: Les Ecrans modernes 1959

**Le second souffle**
*d*: Yannick Bellon – *sc*: Henri Magnan – *c*: M. Barry, M. Joulin – *l.p.*: M. Biraud, Françoise Prévost, André Cellier, Pierre Sabbagh – *p*: F. Tavano 1960

**Zaa le petit chameau blanc**
*d*: Yannick Bellon – *sc*: Claude Roy – *c*: André Dumaître – *l.p.*: commentary spoken by François Perier – *r*: 20 min, col – *p*: COFERC/Jean Salvy 1960

**Le Bureau des mariages**
*d*: Yannick Bellon – *sc*: Henri Magnan from the text by Hervé Bazin – *c*: Bernard Taquet – *l.p.*: Michel Lonsdale. François Perrot, Pierre de Boysson – *p*: Pathé Cinéma 1962

**Bagatelle pour un centenaire**
*d*: Yannick Bellon, Jean Salvy – *sc*: Jacques Lanzmann – *c*: Jean Boffety – *l.p.*: Alain Cuny, Michel Robin – *p*: Court-métrage Sélection 1964

**Quelque part, quelqu'un**
*d*: Yannick Bellon – *sc*: Yannick Bellon – *c*: Georges Barsky – *l.p.*: Loleh Bellon, Roland Dubillard, Hugues Quester, Hélène Dieudonné,

Paul Ville, Hélène Bernardin – *r*: 100 min, b/w – *p*: Films de l'Equinoxe 1972

**Le Femme de Jean**
*d*: Yannick Bellon – *sc*: Yannick Bellon – *c*: Georges Barsky – *l.p.*: France Lambiotte, Claude Rich, Hippolyte, James Mitchell – *r*: 103 min, col – *p*: Films de l'Equinoxe 1974

**Jamais plus toujours**
*d*: Yannick Bellon – *sc*: Yannick Bellon – *c*: Georges Barsky – *l.p.*: Bulle Ogier, Jean-Marc Bory, Loleh Bellon, Anne-Marie Descot – *r*: 90 min, col – *p*: Films de l'Equinoxe/FR3/SNC 1976

**L'Amour violé**
*d*: Yannick Bellon – *sc*: Yannick Bellon – *c*: Georges Barsky, Pierre-William Glenn – *l.p.*: Nathalie Nelle, Alain Fourès, Michèle Simonnet, Daniel Auteuil, Bernard Granger, Alain Marcel, Gilles Tamitz – *r*: 133 min, col, – *l.p.*: Les Films de l'Equinoxe/MK2/Les Films du Dragon 1978

**L'Amour nu**
*d*: Yannick Bellon – *sc*: Yannick Bellon – *c*: Jean Charvein – *l.p.*: Marlène Jobert, Jean-Michel Folon, Georges Rouquier, Michèle Simonnet – *r*: 95 min, col – *p*: Les Films de la tour/Antenne 2 1981

**La Triche**
*d*: Yannick Bellon – *sc*: Yannick Bellon – *c*: Houchang Baharlou – *l.p.*: Victor Lanoux, Annie Duperey, Xavier Deluc, Valérie Mairesse, Michel Galabru, Michèle Simonnet – *r*: 100 min, col – *p*: Les Productions du Daunou/Les Films de l'Equinoxe 1984

**Les Enfants du désordre**
*d*: Yannick Bellon – *sc*: Yannick Bellon Loleh Bellon, Rémi Waterhouse – *c*: Pierre-William Glenn – *l.p.*: Emmanuelle Béart, Robert Hossein, Patrick Catalifo, Mona Bausson, Pierre Bergez, Thierry Miroux – *r*: 98 min, col – *p*: Les Films de l'Equinoxe/Les Films de la Cadence/Sofica/Coficiné/Canal Plus 1989


**Bertrand BLIER**
Born in Paris in 1939. Son of the actor Bernard Blier. Novelist as well as film maker.

**Hitler connais pas**
*d*: Bertrand Blier – *sc*: Bertrand Blier, from an idea by Gérard Hédin – *c*: Jean-Louis Picavet – *r*: 100 min. b/w – *p*: Chaumiane Productions 1963

**Même si j'étais un espion**
*d*: Bertrand Blier – *sc*: Antoine Tudal, Bertrand Blier – *c*: Jean-Louis Picavet – *l.p.*: Bernard Blier, Bruno Cremer, Suzanne Flon, Patricia Scot, Claude Piéplu – *r*: 95 min, col – *p*: SN Pathé Cinéma/UGC/Sirius 1967

**Les Valseuses**
*d*: Bertrand Blier – *sc*: Bertrand Blier, from his novel of the same title
– *c*: Bruno Nuytten – *l.p.*: Gérard Depardieu, Patrick Dewaere. Miou-
Miou, Jeanne Moreau, Brigitte Fossey, Isabelle Huppert – *r*: 117 min,
col – *p*: CAPAC/Uranus/UPF/Prodis 1974

**Calmos**
*d*: Bertrand Blier – *sc*: Bertrand Blier, Philippe Dumarçay – *c*: Claude
Renoir – *l.p.*: Jean-Pierre Marielle, Jean Rochefort, Bernard Blier,
Claude Piéplu, Brigitte Fossey, Dora Doll, Valérie Mairesse – *r*: 107
min, col – *p*: Films Christian Fechner/Renn Productions 1976

**Préparez vos mouchoirs**
*d*: Bertrand Blier – *sc*: Bertrand Blier – *c*: Jean Penzer – *l.p.*: Carole
Laure, Gérard Depardieu, Patrick Dewaere, Michel Serrault, Jean
Rougerie – *r*: 108 min, col – *p*: Films Ariane – CAPAC/Belga Films
1978

**Buffet froid**
*d*: Bertrand Blier – *sc*: Bertrand Blier – *c*: Jean Penzer – *l.p.*: Gérard
Depardieu, Bernard Blier, Jean Carmet, Geneviève Page, Michel
Serrault, Jean Rougerie – *r*: 95 min, col – *p*: Sara Films/Antenne 2
1979

**Beau-père**
*d*: Bertrand Blier – *sc*: Bertrand Blier, from his novel of the same title
– *c*: Sacha Vierny – *l.p.*: Patrick Dewaere, Ariel Besse, Maurice
Ronet, Nicole Garcia, Nathalie Baye, Macha Méril – *r*: 122 min, col –
*p*: Sara Films/Antenne 2 1981

**La Femme de mon pote**
*d*: Bertrand Blier – *sc*: Bertrand Blier, Gérard Brach – *c*: Jean Penzer
– *l.p.*: Coluche, Isabelle Huppert, Thierry Lhermitte, François Perrot
– *r*: 99 min, col – *p*: Sara Films/Renn Productions 1983

**Notre Histoire**
*d*: Bertrand Blier – *sc*: Bertrand Blier, – *c*: Jean Penzer – *l.p.*: Alain
Delon, Nathalie Baye, Michel Galabru, Sabine Haudepin – *r*: 110
min, col – *p*: Adel Productions/Sara Films/Films A2 1984

**Tenue de soirée**
*d*: Bertrand Blier – *sc*: Bertrand Blier – *c*: Jean Penzer – *l.p.*: Gérard
Depardieu, Michel Blanc, Miou-Miou, Bruno Cremer, Jean-Pierre
Marielle, Jean-François Stevenin, Mylène Demongeot – *r*: 84 min.
col – *p*: Hachette Première/DD Productions Ciné-Valse/Philippe
Dussart 1986

**Trop belle pour toi**
*d*: Bertrand Blier – *sc*: Bertrand Blier – *c*: Philippe Rousselot – *l.p.*:
Gérard Depardieu, Josiane Balasko, Carole Bouquet – *r*: 91 min, col –
*p*: CinéValse/DD Production/Orly Films/Sedef/TFI 1989

## Alain CORNEAU

Born in Orléans in 1943. Studied at IDHEC, after which worked in America. Assistant to Roger Corman, Marcel Camus, Costa-Gavras, José Giovanni, Michel Drach.

### France S.A.

*d*: Alain Corneau – *sc*: Jean-Claude Carrière – *c*: Pierre-William Glenn – *l.p.*: Michel Bouquet, Roland Dubillard, Michel Vitold, Anne Zacharias, Daniel Ceccaldi – *r*: 95 min, col – *p*: Albina Productions/ W.M. Productions 1974

### Police python 357

*d*: Alain Corneau – *sc*: Daniel Boulanger, Alain Corneau – *c*: Etienne Becker – *l.p.*: Yves Montand, François Perier, Simone Signoret, Stefania Sandrinelli, Mathieu Carrière – *r*: 125 min, b/w – *p*: Albina Productions 1976

### La Menace

*d*: Alain Corneau - *sc*: Daniel Boulanger, Alain Corneau – *c*: Pierre-William Glenn – *l.p.*: Yves Montand, Carole Laure, Marie Dubois – *r*: 112 min, col – *p*: Les Productions du Daunou 1977

### Série noire

*d*: Alain Corneau – *sc*: Georges Perec, from the novel *A Hell of a Woman* by Jim Thompson – *c*: Pierre-William Glenn – *l.p.*: Patrick Dewaere, Myriam Boyer, Marie Trintignant, Bernard Blier – *r*: 110 min, col – *p*: Prospectacle/Gaumont 1979

### Le Choix des armes

*d*: Alain Corneau – *sc*: Alain Corneau, Michel Grisola – *c*: Pierre-William Glenn – *l.p.*: Yves Montand, Gérard Depardieu, Catherine Deneuve, Michel Galabru, Gérard Lanvin – *r*: 133 min, col – *p*: Sara Films/A2/Parafrance 1981

### Fort Saganne

*d*: Alain Corneau – *sc*: Henri de Turenne, Louis Garde, Alain Corneau – *c*: Bruno Nuytten – *l.p.*: Gérard Depardieu, Philippe Noiret, Catherine Deneuve, Sophie Marceau – *r*: 180 min, col – *p*: Albina Productions/Films A2/SFPC 1984

### Le Môme

*d*: Alain Corneau – *sc*: Alain Corneau, Christian Clavier – *c*: Jean-Francis Gondre – *l.p.*: Richard Anconina, Ambre, Michel Dechaussoy, Yan Epstein – *r*: 99 min, col – *p*: Alain Sarde/Sara Films 1986

### Nocturne indien

*d*: Alain Corneau – *sc*: Alain Corneau, Louis Garde – *c*: Yves Angelo – *l.p.*: Jean-Hugues Anglade, Clémentine Celané, Otto Tausig, T.P. Jain, Ratna Bhooshan – *r*: 110 min, col – *p*: Sara Films/AFC/Ciné Cinq/Christian Bourgois Productions/Sofinergie 1989

**Edgardo COZARINSKY**
Born in Argentina. At first journalist. Came to France in 1974 to
escape Argentine censorship.

**Puntos Suspensivos (Dot Dot Dot)**
*d*: Edgardo Cozarinsky – *sc*: Edgardo Cozarinsky – *c*: Carlos Sorin –
*l.p.*: Jorge Alvarez, Marcia Moretto, Roberto Villanueva, Marilu
Marini, Nina Gomez, Nestor Paternostro, Diana Zermoglio – *r*: 89
min, col – *p*: Edgardo Cozarinsky 1971

**Les Apprentis sorciers**
*d*: Edgardo Cozarinsky – *sc*: A. Tauman, Edgardo Cozarinsky – *c*:
Jean-Claude Rivière – *l.p.*: Zouzou, Peter Chatel, Marie-France
Pisier, Christian Marquand, Niels Arestrup, Jean-Pierre Kalfon,
Pierre Clémenti, Carlos Clarens – *r*: 91 min, col – *p*: Buffalo Film/
INA/ZDF 1977

**La Guerre d'un seul homme**
*d*: Edgardo Cozarinsky, with material from the *Paris Journal* of Ernst
Jünger and archive film footage – *l.p.*: the voice of Niels Arestrup *r*:
105 min, b/w – *p*: INA/ZDF 1982

**Jean Cocteau: Autoportrait d'un inconnu**
*d*: Edgardo Cozarinsky – *sc*: Edgardo Cozarinsky, Carole Weisweiller
– *c*: Jean-Louis Léon, Dominique Antoine – *r*: 66 min, col and b/w –
*p*: JC Production/Antenne 2/ Ministère de la Culture 1983

**Volle Zee**
*d*: Edgardo Cozarinsky – *sc*: Edgardo Cozarinsky – *l.p.*: Willeke Van
Ammelrooy, Cristina Hoving, Andrzej Seweryn – *p*: La Production
du Tigre 1984 (unfinished)

**Guerriers et captives**
*d*: Edgardo Cozarinsky – *sc*: Edgardo Cozarinsky – *c*: Hector
Collodoro – *l.p.* Dominique Sanda, Lesley Caron, China Zorilla,
Gabriella Toscana – *r*: 97 min, col – *p*: Les Films du Phare/La Sept/
La TV Susisse-Romande/Jorge Estrada Mora Producciones 1990


**Jacques DOILLON**
Born in Paris in 1944. After leaving school was postman, insurance
salesman, soldier, before training as a film editor. Assistant editor for
Robbe-Grillet's **Trans-Europ Express** (1966). 1969-73 made several
shorts for the Ministry of Agriculture (including **Les demi-jours** and
**Les Laissés pour compte**) on the conditions of farm workers as well
as several films on sport.

**On ne se dit pas tout entre époux**
*d*: Jacques Doillon – *sc*: Gébé – *r*: 20 min, 1972

**L'An 01**
*d*: Jacques Doillon, with Alain Resnais and Jean Rouch – *sc*: Gébé –
*c*: Renan Pollès – *l.p.*: Gérard Depardieu, Paul Panel, Romain

Bouteille, Gérard Jugnot, Coluche, Marcel Gassouk, Cavanna, Delfeil de Ton – *r*: 90 min, b/w – *p*: UZ Productions 1973

**Les Doigts dans la tête**
*d*: Jacques Doillon – *sc*: Jacques Doillon, Philippe Defrance – *c*: Yves Lafaye – *l.p.*: Christophe Soto, Olivier Bousquet, Roselyne Vuillame, Ann Zacharias, Martin Trevières – *r*: 104 min, b/w – *p*: UZ Productions 1974

**Un Sac de billes**
*d*: Jacques Doillon – *sc*: Jacques Doillon, Denis Ferraris, from the novel by Joseph Joffo – *l.p.*: Paul-Eric Schulmann, Richard Constantini, Joseph Goldenberg, Reine Bartève, Hubert Drac, Gilles Laurent, Dominique Ducros – *r*: 105 min, col – *p*: Films C Fechner/Renn Productions 1975

**La Drôlesse**
*d*: Jacques Doillon – *sc*: Jacques Doillon – *c*: Philippe Rousselot – *l.p.*: Madeleine Desdevises, Claude Hébert, Paulette Lahaye, Juliette Le Cauchois, Fernand Decaen, Dominique Besnehard – *r*: 90 min, col – *p*: Lola Films/Productions de la Guéville 1979

**La Femme qui pleure**
*d*: Jacques Doillon – *sc*: Jacques Doillon – *c*: Yves Lafaye – *l.p.*: Dominique Laffin, Haydée Politoff, Jacques Doillon, Lola Doillon, Jean-Denis Robert, Michel Vivian – *r*: 90 min, col – *p*: Lola Films/ Renn Productions/Productions de la Guéville 1979

**La Fille prodigue**
*d*: Jacques Doillon – *sc*: Jacques Doillon – *c*: Pierre Lhomme – *l.p.*: Jane Birkin, Michel Piccoli, René Féret, Natasha Parry, Eva Renzi, Audrey Marson – *r*: 95 min, b/w – *p*: Productions de la Guéville/ Gaumont 1981

**La Pirate**
*d*: Jacques Doillon – *sc*: Jacques Doillon – *c*: Bruno Nuytten – *l.p.*: Jane Birkin, Philippe Léotard, Maruschka Detmers, Andrew Birkin, Laure Marsac, Michael Stevens – *r*: 90 min, col – *p*: FLF/Tango Films/Lola Films 1984

**La Vie de famille**
*d*: Jacques Doillon – *sc*: Jean-François Goyet, Jacques Doillon – *c*: Michel Carré – *l.p.*: Sami Frey, Mara Goyet, Juliet Berto, Juliette Binoche, Simon de la Brosse – *r*: 98 min, col – *p*: TFI/Flach Films 1985

**La Tentation d'Isabelle**
*d*: Jacques Doillon – *sc*: Jean-François Goyet, Jacques Doillon – *c*: William Lubtchansky – *l.p.*: Fanny Bastien, Ann-Gisel Glass, Jacques Bonnafé, Xavier Deluc, Françoise Brion, Charlotte Gainsbourg – *r*: 90 min, col – *p*: MK2/Films A2/Strada Films/CNC/TV Suisse-Romande 1985

**La Puritaine**
d: Jacques Doillon – sc: Jean-François Goyet, Jacques Doillon – c: William Lubtchansky – l.p.: Michel Piccoli, Sabine Azéma, Sandrine Bonnaire, Laurent Malet – r: 84 min, col – p: Philippe Dussart/Man's Films/La Sept/CNC 1986

**Comédie**
d: Jacques Doillon – sc: Jacques Doillon, Jean-François Goyet, Denis Ferraris – c: William Lubtchansky – l.p.: Jean Birkin, Alain Souchon – r: 82 min, col – p: Sara Films 1987

**La Fille de 15 ans**
d: Jacques Doillon – sc: Jean-François Goyet, Jacques Doillon, Arlette Langmann – c: Caroline Champetier – l.p.: Judith Godèche, Melvil Poupaud, Jacques Doillon – r: 87 min, col – p: Odessa Films 1989

**La Vengeance d'une femme**
d: Jacques Doillon – sc: Jacques Doillon – c: Patrick Blossier – l.p.: Isabelle Huppert, Béatrice Dalle, Jean-Louis Murat, Laurence Cote – r: 133 min, col - p: Sara Films 1990

**Marguerite DURAS**
Born in Indochina in 1914. Active in the Resistance during the Second World War. Novelist, playwright and author of film scripts for Alain Resnais's **Hiroshima mon amour** (1959) and Henri Colpi's **Une aussi longue Absence** (1961). Four of her works have been filmed by other directors: **Barrage contre le Pacifique** (René Clément, 1958), **Le Marin de Gibraltar/The Sailor from Gibraltar** (Tony Richardson, 1967), **Moderato Cantabile** (Peter Brook, 1960), **Dix heures et demie du soir en été/10 30 pm Summer** (Jules Dassin, 1966). She appears in **Le Camion** and her voice is to be heard in **Le Navire Night**, **Aurelia Steiner**, **L'Homme atlantique** and **Dialogue de Rome**.

**La Musica**
d: Marguerite Duras, Paul Seban – sc: Marguerite Duras – c: Sacha Vierny – l.p.: Delphine Seyrig, Robert Hossein, Julie Dassin – r: 80 min, b/w – p: Films Raoul Ploquin 1966

**Détruire dit-elle**
d: Marguerite Duras – sc: Marguerite Duras – c: Sacha Vierny – l.p.: Michel Lonsdale, Catherine Sellers, Henri Garcin, Daniel Gélin, Nicole Hiss – r: 90 min, b/w – p: Marguerite Duras/Anicex Films/ Madeleine Films 1969

**Jaune le soleil**
d: Marguerite Duras – sc: Marguerite Duras – c: Ghislain Cloquet – l.p.: Sami Frey, Catherine Sellers, Michel Lonsdale, Gérard Desarthe – r: 16 min, b.w – p: Marguerite Duras 1971

**Nathalie Granger**
*d*: Marguerite Duras – *sc*: Marguerite Duras – *c*: Ghislain Cloquet – *l.p.*: Lucia Bose, Jeanne Moreau, Gérard Depardieu, Nathalie Bourgeois, Dionys Mascolo, Valérie Mascolo – *r*: 83 min, b/w – *p*: Luc Moullet 1973

**La Femme du Gange**
*d*: Marguerite Duras – *sc*: Marguerite Duras, from her own novel *L'Amour* – *c*: Ghislain Cloquet – *l.p.*: Catherine Sellers, Nicole Hiss, Dionys Mascolo, Gérard Depardieu – *r*: 90 min, b/w – *p*: ORTF 1974

**India Song**
*d*: Marguerite Duras – *sc*: Marguerite Duras – *c*: Bruno Nuytten – *l.p.*: Delphine Seyrig, Michel Lonsdale, Mathieu Carrière, Didier Flamand, Claude Mann, and the voices of Nicole Hiss, Monique Simonet, Viviane Forrester, Dionys Mascolo, Marguerite Duras, Françoise Lebrun, Benoît Jacquot, Nicole-Lise Bernheim, Kevork Kutudjan, Daniel Dobbels, Jean-Claude Biette, Pascal Kané, Marie-Odile Briot – *r*: 120 min, col – *p*: Sunchild/Armorial 1975

**Son nom de Venise dans Calcutta désert**
*d*: Marguerite Duras – *sc*: Marguerite Duras from her novel, *Le Vice Consul* – *c*: Bruno Nuytten – *l.p.*: Delphine Seyrig, Nicole Hiss, Sylvie Nuytten, Marie-Pierre Thiebault – *r*: 115 min, col – *p*: Cinéma 9/Albatros/Pipa 1976

**Baxter, Vera Baxter**
*d*: Marguerite Duras – *sc*: Marguerite Duras – *c*: Sacha Vierny – *l.p.*: Claudine Gabay, Delphine Seyrig, Noëlle Châtelet, Gérard Depardieu, Claude Aufort, Nathalie Nell – *r*: 90 min, col - *p*: Sunchild/INA 1977

**Le Camion**
*d*: Marguerite Duras – *sc*: Marguerite Duras – *c*: Bruno Nuytten – *l.p.*: Marguerite Duras, Gérard Depardieu – *r*: 80 min, col – *p*: Cinéma 9/Auditel 1977

**Des Journées entières dans les arbres**
*d*: Marguerite Duras – *sc*: Marguerite Duras – *c*: Nestor Almendros – *l.p.*: Madeleine Renaud, Bulle Ogier, Jean-Pierre Aumont, Yves Gasq – *r*: 95 min, col – *p*: SFP/Gaumont 1977

**Le Navire Night**
*d*: Marguerite Duras – *sc*: Marguerite Duras – *c*: Pierre Lhomme – *l.p.*: Bulle Ogier, Dominique Sanda, Mathieu Carrière, and the voices of Marguerite Duras and Benoît Jacquot – *r*: 94 min, col – *p*: Films du Losange 1978

**Aurelia Steiner**
*d*: Marguerite Duras – *sc*: Marguerite Duras – *c*: Pierre Lhomme – *l.p.*: Voice of Marguerite Duras – *r*: 97 min (4 films: **Césarée**, 11 min; **Les mains négatives**, 16 min; **Aurélia Steiner Melbourne**, 30

min; **Aurelia Steiner Vancouver**, 40 min), col – *p*: Films du Losange/Branco 1979

**Agatha et les lectures illimitées**
*d*: Marguerite Duras – *sc*: Marguerite Duras – *c*: Dominique le Rigoleur – *l.p.*: Bulle Ogier, Yann Andréa – *r*: 90 min, col – *p*: Berthemont Productions/INA 1980

**L'Homme atlantique**
*d*: Marguerite Duras – *sc*: Marguerite Duras – *c*: Dominique le Rigoleur – *l.p.*: Yann Andréa, voice of Marguerite Duras – *r*: 45 min, col – *p*: Berthemont Productions/INA 1981

**Dialogue de Rome**
*d*: Marguerite Duras – *sc*: Marguerite Duras – *c*: Dario di Palma – *l.p.*: Voices of Yann Andréa and Marguerite Duras – *r*: 65 min, col – *p*: RAI/RTV Italiana/Lunga 1983

**Les Enfants**
*d*: Marguerite Duras – *sc*: Marguerite Duras – *c*: Bruno Nuytten – *l.p.*: Alexandre Bougoslavsky, Daniel Gélin, Tatiana Moukhine, Martine Chevalier, André Dussolier, Pierre Arditi – *r*: 104 min, col – *p*: Berthemont Productions 1985


**Jean EUSTACHE**
Born 1938 in Pessac. Assistant to Paul Vecchiali, then editor of **Dedans Paris** (d. Philippe Théaudière, 1964), **Jean Renior le patron** (d. Jacques Rivette, 1968) **Les Idoles** (d. Marc'O, 1967) **Une Adventure de Billy le Kid** (d. Luc Moullet, 1970). Acted in some of his own films as well as **The American Friend** (W. Wenders, 1977), **La Tortue sur le dos** (Luc Béraud, 1978). Died Paris 1981.

**Du Côté de Robinson**
*d*: Jean Eustache – *sc*: Jean Eustache – *c*: Philippe Théaudière – ; *l.p.*: Aristide, Daniel Bart, Dominique Jayr, Jean Eustache – *r*: 42 min, b/w, 16 mm – *p*: Anouchka Films (J.-L. Godard) 1963

**Le Père Noël a les yeux bleus**
*d*: Jean Eustache – *sc*: Jean Eustache – *c*: Nestor Almendros, Philippe Théaudière – *l.p.*: Jean-Pierre Léaud, Gérard Zimmermann, Henri Martinez, René Gilson, Carmen Ripou, Jean Eustache – *r*: 47 min, b/w – *p*: Anouchka Films (J.-L. Godard) 1966

**Les mauvaises Fréquentations**
Title of double bill consisting of *Du Côté de Robinson* and *Le Père Noël a les veux bleus*, when programmed in 1967

**Série 'Rencontres' Le dernier des hommes** de Murnau and **La Petite Marchande d'allumettes** de Renoir
*d*: Jean Eustache – presented by Jean-Pierre Escande and Jean Paul Török – *p*: George Gaudin for the Centre National de la Documentation Pédagogique 1968-69

## La Rosière de Pessac

*d*: Jean Eustache – *sc*: Jean Eustache – *c*: Philippe Théaudière – *l.p.*: the inhabitants of Pessac – *r*: 65 min, b/w, 16 mm blown up to 35 mm – *p*: Jean Eustache/Les Films Luc Moullet 1968

## Le Cochon

*d*: Jean Eustache and Jean-Michel Barjol – *sc*: Jean Eustache and Jean-Michel Barjol – *c*: Philippe Théaudière and Renan Polles – *r*: 52 min, b/w, 16 mm – *p*: Luc Moullet and Françoise Lebrun 1970

## Numéro zéro

*d*: Jean Eustache – *sc*: Jean Eustache 1971. This film has never been released.

## La Maman et la putain

*d*: Jean Eustache – *sc*: Jean Eustache – *c*: Pierre Lhomme – *l.p.*: Françoise Lebrun, Bernadette Lafont, Jean-Pierre Léaud, Isabelle Weingarten, Jean Douchet, Jean-Noël Picq – *r*: 209 min, b/w, 16 mm blown up to 35 mm – *p*: Elite Films/Cine-Qua-Non/Les Films do Losange/Simar-Films/V.M. Productions 1973

## Mes petites Amoureuses

*d*: Jean Eustache – *sc*: Jean Eustache – *c*: Nestor Almendros – *l.p.*: Martin Loeb, Ingrid Caven, Jacqueline Dufranne, Dionys Mascolo, Henri Martinez, Maurice Pialat, Jean-Noël Picq, Pierre Edelman, Marie-Paule Fernandez – *r*: 123 min, col – *p*: Elite Films 1974

## Une sale Histoire I

*d*: Jean Eustache – *sc*: Jean Eustache, Jean-Noël Picq – *c*: Jacques Renard – *l.p.*: Michel Lonsdale, Jean Douchet, Douchka, Laura Fianning, Josée Yann, Jacques Bruloux – *r*: 28 min, col – *p*: Les Films du Losange 1977

## Une sale Histoire II

*d*: Jean Eustache – *sc*: Jean Eustache, Jean-Noël Picq – *c*: Pierre Lhomme – *l.p.*: Jean-Noël Picq, Elisabeth Lanchener, Françoise Lebrun, Virginie Thévenet, Annette Wademant – *r*: 22 min, col, 16 mm – *p*: Les Films du Losange 1977

## La Rosière de Pessac II

*d*: Jean Eustache – *sc*: Jean Eustache – *c*: Robert Alazraki, Jean-Yves Coic, Armand Marco, Philippe Théaudière – *l.p.*: the inhabitants of Pessac – *r*: 67 min, col, 16 mm – *p*: INA/ZDF/Médiane Films 1979

## Odette Robert

*d*: Jean Eustache – *sc*: Jean Eustache – *c*: Philippe Théaudière, Adolfo Arrietta – *l.p.*: Odette Robert, Jean Eustache, Boris Eustache – *r*: 54 min, b/w, 16 mm – *p*: INA for TFI 1980 This film is a shortened version of **Numéro Zéro** (1971)

## Avec passion Bosch ou Le Jardin des délices de Jérome Bosch

*d*: Jean Eustache – *sc*: Jean Eustache – *c*: Philippe Théaudière – *l.p.*: Jean-Noël Picq, Sylvie Blum, Catherine Nadaud, Jérôme Prieur – *r*: 34 min, col, 16 mm – *p*: INA for Antenne 2 1980

**Offre d'emploi**
*d*: Jean Eustache – *sc*: Jean Eustache – *c*: Philippe Théaudière – *l.p.*:
Michel Delahaye, Michèle Moretti, Rosine Young, Bertrand van
Effenterre, Jean Douchet, Noël Simsolo – *r*: 19 min, col, 16 mm –
*p*: INA for Antenne 2 1980

**Les Photos d'Alix**
*d*: Jean Eustache – *sc*: Jean Eustache – *c*: Robert Alazraki – *l.p.*: Alix
Cléo-Roubaud, Boris Eustache – *r*: 17 min, col – *p*: Médiane Films
1980

**Philippe GARREL**
Born in 1947. Son of actor Maurice Garrel and brother of producer
Thierry Garrel. Began his career as a technician with ORTF (French
television) before directing feature films.

**Anémone**
*d*: Philippe Garrel – *sc*: Philippe Garrel – *c*: Francisco Espresale –
*l.p.*: Maurice Garrel, Anémone Bourguignon, Pascal Laperrousaz – *r*:
60 min, col, 16 mm – *p*: ORTF 1967

**Droit de visite**
*d*: Philippe Garrel – *sc*: Philippe Garrel – *c*: André Weinfeld – *l.p.*:
Maurice Garrel – *r*: 15 min, b/w – *p*: Garrel Production 1967

**Les Enfants désaccordés**
*d*: Philippe Garrel – *sc*: Philippe Garrel – *c*: André Weinfeld – *l.p.*:
Christine Pérez, Pascal Laperrousaz, Maurice Garrel – *r*: 15 min, b/w
– *p*: Philippe Garrel 1967

**Marie pour mémoire**
*d*: Philippe Garrel – *sc*: Philippe Garrel – *c*: Michel Fournier – *l.p.*:
Zouzou, Didier Léon, Nicole Laguigner, Thierry Garrel, Maurice
Garrel – *r*: 80 min, b/w – *p*: Garrel Production/ORTF 1968

**Actualités revolutionnaires**
*d*: Philippe Garrel – *sc*: Philippe Garrel – *c*: Philippe Garrel – *r*: 20
min, b/w – *p*: Garrel Production 1968

**La Concentration**
*d*: Philippe Garrel – *sc*: Philippe Garrel – *c*: Michel Fournier – *l.p.*:
Jean-Pierre Léaud, Zouzou – *r*: 90 min, col – *p*: Sylvina Boissonnas
1968

**Le Révélateur**
*d*: Philippe Garrel – *sc*: Philippe Garrel – *c*: Michel Fournier – *l.p.*:
Bernadette Lafont, Laurent Terzieff, Stanislas Robiolles – *r*: 68 min,
b/w – *p*: Zanzibar 1968

**Le Lit de la Vierge**
*d*: Philippe Garrel – *sc*: Philippe Garrel – *c*: Michel Fournier – *l.p.*:
Pierre Clémenti, Zouzou, Jean-Pierre Kalfon, Frédérico Parado, Nico
– *r*: 100 min, b/w – *p*: Sylvina Boissonnas 1970

**La Cicatrice intérieure**
*d*: Philippe Garrel – *sc*: Philippe Garrel – *c*: Michel Fournier – *l.p.*:
Pierre Clémenti, Nico – *r*: 60 min, col – *p*: Zanzibar 1972

**Athanor**
*d*: Philippe Garrel – *sc*: Philippe Garrel – *c*: André Weinfeld and
Michel Fournier – *l.p.*: Nico, Musky – *r*: 20 min, col – *p*: Philippe
Garrel 1973

**Les hautes solitudes**
*d*: Philippe Garrel – *sc*: Philippe Garrel – *c*: Philippe Garrel – *l.p.*:
Jean Seberg, Laurent Terzieff, Tina Aumont, Nico – *r*: 75 min – *p*:
Garrel Production 1974

**Un Ange passe**
*d*: Philippe Garrel – *sc*: Philippe Garrel – *c*: Philippe Garrel – *l.p.*:
Maurice Garrel, Laurent Terzieff, Bulle Ogier, Nico, Jean-Pierre
Kalfon – *r*: 90 min, b/w – *p*: Philippe Garrel 1975

**Le Berceau de cristal**
*d*: Philippe Garrel – *sc*: Philippe Garrel/Nico – *c*: Philippe Garrel –
*l.p.*: Nico, Dominique Sanda, Anita Pallenberg, Margareth Clémenti –
*r*: 80 min, col – *p*: Philippe Garrel 1976

**Voyage au jardin des morts**
*d*: Philippe Garrel – *sc*: Philippe Garrel – *c*: Philippe Garrel – *l.p.*:
Laurent Terzieff, Maria Schneider, Nico – *r*: 53 min, col – *p*: Philippe
Garrel 1978

**Le Bleu des origines**
*d*: Philippe Garrel – *sc*: Philippe Garrel –*c*: Philippe Garrel – *l.p.*:
Nico, Zouzou, Philippe Garrel – *r*: 45 min, b/w – *p*: Philippe Garrel
1979

**L'Enfant secret**
*d*: Philippe Garrel – *sc*: Philippe Garrel/Annette Wademant – *c*:
Pascal Laperrousaz – *l.p.*: Anne Wiazemsky, Henri de Maublanc,
Ellie Maderos, Edwige Gruss – *r*: 95 min, b/w – *p*: Philippe Garrel
G.I.E. 1983

**Liberté le nuit**
*d*: Philippe Garrel – *sc*: Philippe Garrel – *c*: Pascal Laperrousaz – *l.p.*:
Maurice Garrel, Emmanuelle Riva, Christine Boisson, Lazio Szabo,
Brigitte Sy – *r*: 90 min, b/w – *p*: INA Productions 1984

**Rue Fontaine** (Part of **Paris Vu Par (. . .) 20 Ans après**)
*d*: Philippe Garrel – *sc*: Philippe Garrel – *c*: Pascal Laperrousaz – *l.p.*:
Christine Boisson, Jean-Pierre Léaud, Philippe Garrel – *r*: 17 min, col
– *p*: JM Production/Films A2. 1984

**Elle a passé tant d'heures sous les sunlights**
*d*: Philippe Garrel – *sc*: Philippe Garrel – *c*: Pascal Lapérousaz – *l.p.*:
Mireille Perrier, Jacques Bonnaffé, Anne Wiazemsky, Lou Castel,
Chantal Akerman, Jacques Doillon, Philippe Garrel – *r*: 130 min, b/w
– *p*: Garrel Production 1985

**Les Ministères de l'art**
*d*: Philippe Garrel – *sc*: Philippe Garrel – *c*: Jacques Loiseleux – *l.p.*:
Chantal Akerman, Juliet Berto, Léos Carax, Jacques Doillon, Philippe
Garrel, Hélène Garidon, Benoît Jacquot, Jean-Pierre Léaud, Werner
Schroeter, Brigitte Sy, André Techiné – *r*: 52 min, b/w – *p*: Lasa
Films/La Sept/CNC 1988

**Les Baisers de secours**
*d*: Philippe Garrel – *sc*: Philippe Garrel, Marc Cholodenko – *c*:
Jacques Loiseleux – *l.p.*: Philippe Garrel, Brigitte Sy, Louis Garrel,
Anémone, Maurice Garrel, Yvette Etievant, Jacques Kébadian,
Valérie Dréville – *r*: 83 min, b/w – *p*: Les Films de L'Atalante/La
Sept/Planète et Compagnie 1989


**Jean-Luc GODARD**
Born in 1930 in Paris to a family of Swiss bankers. At first film critic
for *Arts* and *Cahiers du cinéma*. After May 1968 founded the Dziga
Vertov group with Jean-Pierre Gorin and since 1974 has worked with
Anne-Marie Miéville.

**Opération Béton**
*d*: Jean-Luc Godard – *sc*: Jean-Luc Godard – *c*: Adrien Porchet – *r*:
20 min, b/w – *p*: Actua Film 1954

**Une Femme coquette**
*d*: Jean-Luc Godard – *sc*: Jean-Luc Godard, from the story *Le Signe*,
by Guy de Maupassant – *c*: Hans Lucas (Godard) – *l.p.*: Maria
Lysandre, Roland Tolma, Jean-Luc Godard – *r*: 10 min, b/w, 16 mm
– *p*: Jean-Luc Godard 1955

**Tous les Garçons s'appellent Patrick**
*d*: Jean-Luc Godard – *sc*: Eric Rohmer – *c*: Michel Latouche – *l.p.*:
Jean-Claude Brialy, Nicole Berger, Anne Colette – *r*: 21 min, b/w –
*p*: Les Films de la Pléiade 1957

**Charlotte et son Jules**
*d*: Jean-Luc Godard – *sc*: Jean-Luc Godard – *c*: Michel Latouche –
*l.p.*: Jean-Paul Belmondo, Anne Colette, Gérard Blain – *r*: 20 min, b/
w – *p*: Les Films de la Pléiade 1958

**Une Histoire d'eau**
*d*: Jean-Luc Godard, François Truffaut – *sc*: Jean-Luc Godard – *c*:
Michel Latouche – *l.p.*: Jean-Claude Brialy, Caroline Dim – *r*: 18
min, b/w – *p*: Pierre Braunberger/Les Films de la Pléiade 1958

**A Bout de souffle**
*d*: Jean-Luc Godard – *sc*: Jean-Luc Godard, from an idea by François Truffaut – *c*: Raoul Coutard – *l.p.*: Jean-Paul Belmondo, Jean Seberg, Daniel Boulanger, Jean-Pierre Melville – *r*: 90 min, b/w – *p*: Georges de Beauregard 1959

**Le petit Soldat**
*d*: Jean-Luc Godard – *sc*: Jean-Luc Godard – *c*: Raoul Coutard – *l.p.*: Michel Subor, Anna Karina, Henri-Jacques Huet – *r*: 88 min, b/w – *p*: Georges de Beauregard 1960

**Une Femme est une femme**
*d*: Jean-Luc Godard – *sc*: Jean-Luc Godard – *c*: Raoul Coutard – *l.p.*: Jean-Paul Belmondo, Anna Karina, Jean-Claude Brialy, Marie Dubois – *r*: 84 min, col – *p*: Rome-Paris Films 1961

**La Paresse** (one episode in **Les sept Péchés capitaux**)
*d*: Jean-Luc Godard – *sc*: Jean-Luc Godard – *c*: Henri Decaë – *l.p.*: Eddie Constantine, Nicole Mirel – b/w – *p*: Films Gibé/Franco-London Films 1961

**Vivre sa vie**
*d*: Jean-Luc Godard – *sc*: Jean-Luc Godard – *c*: Raoul Coutard – *l.p.*: Anna Karina, Saddy Rebot, André S. Labarthe, Guylaine Schlumberger, Brice Parain – *r*: 85 min, b/w – *p*: Les Films de la Pléiade 1962

**La nouveau Monde** (one episode in **RoGoPaG**)
*d*: Jean-Luc Godard – *sc*: Jean-Luc Godard – *c*: Jean Rabier – *l.p.*: Alexandra Stewart, Jean-Marc Bory, Michel Delahaye – *r*: 20 min, b/w – *p*: Arco Films/Cineriz/Lyre Films 1962

**Les Carabiniers**
*d*: Jean-Luc Godard – *sc*: Jean-Luc Godard, Jean Gruault, Roberto Rossellini, based on the play by Benjamino Joppolo – *l.p.*: Marino Masé, Albert Juross, Geneviève Galéa, Catherine Ribéro, Gérard Poirot – *r*: 80 min, b/w – *p*: Rome-Paris Films/Laetitia 1963

**Le Mépris**
*d*: Jean-Luc Godard – *sc*: Jean-Luc Godard, from the novel by Alberto Moravia – *c*: Raoul Coutard – *l.p.*: Brigitte Bardot, Michel Piccoli, Jack Palance, Fritz Lang – *r*: 100 min, col – *p*: Rome-Paris Films/Films Concordia/Compagnia Cinematografica 1963

**Le grand escroc** (one episode in **Les plus belles Escroqueries du monde**)
*d*: Jean-Luc Godard – *sc*: Jean-Luc Godard – *c*: Raoul Coutard – *l.p.*: Jean Seberg, Charles Denner, Laszlo Szabo – *r*: 20 min, b/w – *p*: Ulysse Productions/Primex Films/Vides/Toho/Caesar Film 1963

**Montparnasse-Levallois** (one episode in **Paris vu par. . .**)
*d*: Jean-Luc Godard – *sc*: Jean-Luc Godard – *c*: Albert Maysles – *l.p.*: Johanna Shimkus, Philippe Hiquilly, Serge Davri – *r*: 20 min, col, 16 mm – *p*: Les Films du Losange/Barbet Schroeder 1963

**Bande à part**
*d*: Jean-Luc Godard – *sc*: Jean-Luc Godard, based on the novel *Fool's Gold*, by Dolores Hitchens – *c*: Raoul Coutard – *l.p.*: Anna Karina, Claude Brasseur, Sami Frey – *r*: 95 min, b/w – *p*: Anouchka Films/ Orsay Films 1964

**Une Femme mariée**
*d*: Jean-Luc Godard - *sc*: Jean-Luc Godard – *c*: Raoul Coutard – *l.p.*: Macha Méril, Bernard Noël, Philippe Leroy, Roger Leenhardt – *r*: 95 min, b/w – *p*: Anouchka Films/Orsay Films 1964

**Alphaville**
*d*: Jean-Luc Godard – *sc*: Jean-Luc Godard – *c*: Raoul Coutard – *l.p.*: Eddie Constantine, Anna Karina, Akim Tamiroff, Howard Vernon – *r*: 98 min, b/w – *p*: Chaumiane/Filmstudio 1965

**Pierrot le fou**
*d*: Jean-Luc Godard – *sc*: Jean-Luc Godard, from the novel *Obsession* by Lionel White – *c*: Raoul Coutard – *l.p.*: Jean-Paul Belmondo, Anna Karina – *r*: 110 min, col – *p*: Rome-Paris Films/Dino de Laurentis 1965

**Masculin feminin**
*d*: Jean-Luc Godard – *sc*: Jean-Luc Godard, based on *Le Signe* and *La Femme de Paul*, by Guy de Maupassant – *c*: Willy Kurant – *l.p.*: Jean-Pierre Léaud, Chantal Goya, Marlène Jobert, Brigitte Bardot, Antoine Bourseiller, Françoise Hardy – *r*: 110 min, b/w – *p*: Anouchka Films/ Argos Films/Svensk Filmindustri/Sandrews 1966

**Made in U.S.A.**
*d*: Jean-Luc Godard – *sc*: Jean-Luc Godard, based on the novel *Rien dans le coffre*, by Richard Stark – *c*: Raoul Coutard – *l.p.*: Anna Karina, Laszlo Szabo, Jean-Pierre Léaud, Marianne Faithfull – *r*: 90 min, col – *p*: Rome-Paris Films 1966

**Deux ou trois Choses que je sais d'elle**
*d*: Jean-Luc Godard – *sc*: Jean-Luc Godard – *c*: Raoul Coutard – *l.p.*: Marina Vlady, Annie Duperey, Roger Montsoret – *r*: 95 min, col – *p*: Anouchka Films/Argos Films/Les Films du Carrosse/Parc Film 1966

**La Chinoise**
*d*: Jean-Luc Godard – *sc*: Jean-Luc Godard – *c*: Raoul Coutard – *l.p.*: Anne Wiazemsky, Jean-Pierre Léaud, Michel Sémeniako, Juliet Berto – *r*: 90 min, col – *p*: Productions de la Guéville/Parc Film/ Athos Films/Simar Films/Anouchka Films 1967

**L'Anticipation ou l'An 2000** (one episode in **Le plus vieux Métier du monde)**
*d*: Jean-Luc Godard – *sc*: Jean-Luc Godard – *c*: Pierre Lhomme – *l.p.*: Jacques Charrier, Marilu Tolo, Anna Karina, Jean-Pierre Léaud – *r*: 20 min, col – *p*: Les Films Gibé/Francoriz/Rialto Films 1967

**Loin du Vietnam** (one episode)
*d*: Jean-Luc Godard, William Klein, Joris Ivens, Claude Lelouch, Alain Resnais, Agnès Varda – *sc*: by the same directors – *c*: Bernard Ziterman, Théo Robiche – *l.p.*: contributions from Michel Ray, Roger Pic, Marcelin Loridan, François Maspéro, Chris Marker, Jacques Sternberg, Jean Lacouture – *r*: 120 min, col and b/w – *p*: SLON 1967

**L'Amour** (one episode in **Vangelo 70**)
*d*: Jean-Luc Godard – *sc*: Jean-Luc Godard – *c*: Alain Levent – *l.p.*: Christine Guého, Nino Castelnuovo, Catherine Jourdan – *r*: 26 min, b/w – *p*: Anouchka Films/Castoro Films 1967

**Weekend**
*d*: Jean-Luc Godard – *sc*: Jean-Luc Godard – *c*: Raoul Coutard – *l.p.*: Jean Yanne, Mireille Darc – *r*: 95 min, col – *p*: Comacico Films/Films Copernic/Ascot/Cineraid 1967

**Le gai Savoir**
*d*: Jean-Luc Godard – *sc*: Jean-Luc Godard – *c*: Jean Leclerc – *l.p.*: Juliet Berto, Jean-Pierre Léaud – *r*: 95 min, col – *p*: ORTF/Anouchka Films/Bavaria Atelier 1968

**Un Film comme les autres**
*d*: Jean-Luc Godard and the Dziga Vertov Group – *l.p.*: workers and students – *r*: 100/120 min, 16 mm 1968

**One plus one**
*d*: Jean-Luc Godard – *c*: Tony Richardson – *l.p.*: The Rolling Stones, Anne Wiazemsky, Iain Quarrier - *r*: 99 min, col – *p*: Cupid Productions 1968

**One American Movie (One AM)**
d: Jean-Luc Godard – *sc*: Jean-Luc Godard – *c*: D.A. Pennebaker, Richard Leacock – *l.p.*: Rip Thorn, Jefferson Airplane, Eldrige Cleaver, Tom Hayden, Le Roi Jones – *p*: Leacock/Pennebaker 1968 (unfinished)

**British Sounds**
*d*: Jean-Luc Godard, Jean-Henri Roger – *sc*: Jean-Luc Godard, Jean-Henri Roger – *c*: Charles Stewart – *l.p.*: Michel Lonsdale – *r*: 52 min, col, 16 mm – *p*: Kestrel Productions/LWT 1969

**Pravda**
*d*: Dziga Vertov Group, with Jean-Henri Roger, Paul Burron – *r*: 50 min, col, 16 mm – *p*: CERT 1969

**Vent d'est**
*d*: Dziga Vertov Group – *sc*: Jean-Luc Godard, Daniel Cohn Bendit, Sergio Bassini – *c*: Mario Vulpiani – *l.p.*: Gian Maria Volonte, Anne Wiazemsky, Paolo Pozzesi, Christiana Tullio, Daniel Cohn-Bendit, Glauba Rocha – *r*: 100 min, col, 16 mm – *p*: Kuntz Film/Poli Film/Anouchka Films 1969

**Luttes en Italie**
*d*: Dziga Vertov Group – *l.p.*: Christiana Tullio, Anne Wiazemsky.
Jérôme Hinstin – *r*: 76 min, col, 16 mm – *p*: Cosmoseion/RAI 1969

**Jusqu'à la victoire**
*d*: Dziga Vertov Group – col, 1970 (unfinished)

**Vladimir et Rosa**
*d*: Dziga Vertov Group – *sc*: Dziga Vertov Group – *c*: Dziga Vertov
Group – *l.p.*: Anne Wiazemsky, Jean-Pierre Gorin, Jean-Luc Godard,
Juliet Berto – *r*: 103 min, b/w – *p*: Télépool/Grove Press 1971

**Tout va bien**
*d*: Jean-Luc Godard, Jean-Pierre Gorin – *sc*: Jean-Luc Godard – *c*:
Armand Marco – *l.p.*: Yves Montand, Jane Fonda, Vittorio Caprioli,
Jean Pignol, Huguette Miéville, Anne Wiazemsky – *r*: 95 min, col –
*p*: Anouchka Films/Vicco Film/Empire Films 1972

**Letter to Jane**
*d*: Jean-Luc Godard, Jean-Pierre Gorin – *sc*: Jean-Luc Godard, Jean-
Pierre Gorin – *r*: 60 min, col, 16 mm – *p*: Jean-Luc Godard, Jean-
Pierre Gorin 1972

**Ici et ailleurs**
*d*: Jean-Luc Godard, Anne-Marie Miéville – *sc*: Jean-Luc Godard,
Anne-Marie Miéville – *c*: William Lubtchansky – *r*: 50 min, col, 16
mm – *p*: Sonimage/INA 1974

**Numéro deux**
*d*: Jean-Luc Godard – *sc*: Jean-Luc Godard, Anne-Marie Miéville – *c*:
William Lubtchansky (film) Gérard Teissèdre (video) – *l.p.*: Sandrine
Battistella, Pierre Oudry, Alexandre Rignault, Rachel Stefanopoli – *r*:
88 min, col – *p*: Sonimage/Bela/SNC 1975

**Comment ça va?**
*d*: Jean-Luc Godard – *sc*: Anne-Marie Miéville, Jean-Luc Godard –
*l.p.*: M. Marot, Anne-Marie Miéville – *r*: 78 min – *p*: Sonimage/Bela/
SNC 1975

**Six fois deux/Sur et sous la communication**
*d*: Jean-Luc Godard – *sc*: Jean-Luc Godard, Anne-Marie Miéville – *c*:
William Lubtchansky, Dominique Chapuis, Gérard Teissèdre – *r*: 6 x
100 min, col, film and video – *p*: Sonimage/INA 1976

**France/Tour/Détour/Deux Enfants**
*d*: Jean-Luc Godard – *sc*: Anne-Marie Miéville, Jean-Luc Godard – *c*:
Pierre Binggeli, William Lubtchansky, Dominique Chapuis, Philippe
Rony – *l.p.*: Camille Virolleaud, Arnaud Martin, Betty Berr, Albert
Dray – *r*: 12 x 26 min, video, col – *p*: Sonimage/INA 1978

**Sauve qui peut (la Vie)**
*d*: Jean-Luc Godard – *sc*: Anne-Marie Miéville, Jean-Claude Carrière
– *c*: William Lubtchansky – *l.p.*: Jacques Dutronc, Nathalie Baye,

Isabelle Huppert, Roland Amstutz – *r*: 87 min, col – *p*: Sara Films/ MK2/Saga Productions/Sonimage/CNC/ZDF/SSR/ORF 1979

**Passion**
*d*: Jean-Luc Godard – *sc*: Jean-Luc Godard – *c*: Raoul Coutard – *l.p.*: Isabelle Huppert, Hanna Schygulla, Michel Piccoli, Jerzy Radziwilowicz, Laszlo Szabo – *r*: 87 min, col – *p*: Sara Films/Sonimage/ Films A2/Vidéo Production SA 1981

**Scénario du film Passion**
*d*: Jean-Luc Godard, Anne-Marie Miéville – *r*: 52 min, col – *p*: J.L.G. Films/Télévision Romande 1982

**Lettre à Freddy Buache**
*d*: Jean-Luc Godard – *sc*: Jean-Luc Godard – *c*: Jean-Bernard Menoud, François Musy, Pierre Binggeli, Gérard Ruey – *r*: 11 min video – *p*: Films et vidéo production Lausanne 1982

**Changer d'image (lettre à la bien-aimée)**
*d*: Jean-Luc Godard – *sc*: Jean-Luc Godard – *r*: 9 min – *p*: INA 1982

**Prénom Carmen**
*d*: Jean-Luc Godard – *sc*: Anne-Marie Miéville – *c*: Raoul Coutard – *l.p.*: Maruschka Detmers, Jacques Bonnaffé, Myriem Roussel, Hippolyte Girardot – *r*: 85 min, col – *p*: Alain Sarde 1982

**Je vous salue Marie**
*d*: Jean-Luc Godard – *sc*: Jean-Luc Godard – *c*: Jean-Bernard Menoud, Jacques Firmann – *l.p.*: Myriem Roussel, Thierry Rode, Philippe Lacoste, Juliette Binoche – *r*: 72 min, col – *p*: Sara Films/ Channel 4 1983

**Détective**
*d*: Jean-Luc Godard – *sc*: Alain Sarde, Philippe Setbon – *c*: Bruno Nuytten – *l.p.*: Nathalie Baye, Claude Brasseur, Johnny Halliday – *r*: 95 min, col – *p*: Sara Films/JLG Films 1984

**Soft and Hard (Soft Talk on a Hard Subject between Two Friends)**
*d*: Jean-Luc Godard – *sc*: Jean-Luc Godard, Anne-Marie Miéville – *r*: 52 min – *p*: Channel 4 1986

**Grandeur et décadence d'un petit commerce de cinéma**
*d*: Jean-Luc Godard – *sc*: Jean-Luc Godard, from a novel by James Hadley Chase – *c*: Caroline Champetier – *l.p.*: Jean-Pierre Léaud, Jean-Pierre Mocky, Maria Valéra – *p*: Hamster Production/TFI 1986

**Meeting W.A.**
*d*: Jean-Luc Godard – *sc*: Jean-Luc Godard – *l.p.*: Woody Allen – *r*: 26 min – *p*: Festival International de Film/Jean-Luc Godard 1986

**Soigne ta droite**
*d*: Jean-Luc Godard – *sc*: Jean-Luc Godard – *c*: Caroline Champetier – *l.p.*: Jean-Luc Godard, Jacques Villeret, François Perier, Jane

Birkin, Michel Galabru – *r*: 81 min, col – *p*: Gaumont/Xanadu/RTSR/ JLG Film 1987

**King Lear**
*d*: Jean-Luc Godard – *sc*: Jean-Luc Godard – *c*: Sophie Maintigneux – *l.p.*: Burgess Meredith, Peter Sellars, Molly Ringwald, Jean-Luc Godard, Woody Allen, Norman Mailer, Kate Miller, Léos Carax – *r*: 90 min, col – *p*: Cannon International 1987

**Enfin il est en ma puissance** (one episode of **Aria**)
*d*: Jean-Luc Godard – *sc*: Jean-Luc Godard – *c*: Caroline Champetier – *l.p.*: Marion Petersen, Valérie Allain – *p*: RVP Productions/Virgin Vision 1987

**On s'est tous défilé**
*d*: Jean-Luc Godard – *sc*: Jean-Luc Godard – *c*: Caroline Champetier – *r*: 13 min, col – *p*: Marithé and François Girbaud 1988

**Puissance de la parole**
*d*: Jean-Luc Godard – *sc*: Jean-Luc Godard – *c*: Caroline Champetier – *l.p.*: Jean Bouise, Lydia Andrei, Jean-Michel Irribarren, Laurence Cote – *r*: 25 min, col – *p*: France Télécom. 1988

**Le dernier Mot** (one episode of **Les Français vu par. . .**)
*d*: Jean-Luc Godard – *sc*: Jean-Luc Godard – *c*: Pierre Binggeli, Pierre-Alain Besse – *l.p.*: André Marcon, Hans Zischler, Catherine Aymerie, Pierre Amoyal, Michel Radic, Luc Briffod – *r*: 12 min, col – *p*: Erato Films/Sopresse 1988

**Histoire(s) du cinéma**
*d*: Jean-Luc Godard – *sc*: Jean-Luc Godard – *c*: Jean-Luc Godard, Pierre Binggeli (video) – *p*: Canal Plus/La Sept/FR3/Gaumont/JLG Films 1989

**Marin KARMITZ.**
Born in Bucharest in 1938. Fled Romania in 1947 and came to Paris in 1950. Studied at IDHEC and became assistant to Godard (**La Paresse**), Varda (**Cléo de 5 à 7**) and Rozier (**Adieu Philippine**). Since 1972 has ceased direction to concentrate on film distribution and more recently production. Karmitz is now one of the most influential producers of independent films in France.

**Nuit noire à Calcutta**
*d*: Marin Karmitz – *sc*: Marguerite Duras – *c*: Willy Kurant – *l.p.*: Maurice Garrel, Natacha Parry, Nicole Hiss – *r*: 26 min, b/w – *p*: MK Productions 1964

**Comédie**
*d*: Marin Karmitz with Samuel Beckett, Jean-Marie Serreau – *sc*: Samuel Beckett – *c*: Pierre Lhomme – *r*: 5 min, b/w – *p*: MK Productions 1966

**Sept Jours ailleurs**
*d*: Marin Karmitz – *sc*: Marin Karmitz – *c*: Willy Kurant – *l.p.*:
Jacques Higelin, Catherine Martin, Michèle Moretti – *r*: 100 min, b/w
– *p*: MK Productions 1968

**Camarades**
*d*: Marin Karmitz – *sc*: Marin Karmitz, Jean-Paul Giquel, Lia Wajntal
– *c*: Pierre-William Glenn – *l.p.*: Jean-Paul Giquel, Juliet Berto,
Dominique Labourier, André Julien – *r*: 90 min, col – *p*: MK2
Productions/Reggane Films/Films 13/Les Productions de la Guénille
1970

**Coup pour coup**
*d*: Marin Karmitz – *sc*: Marin Karmitz and 100 workers and film crew
– *c*: André Dubreuil – *l.p.*: workers, actors, students, teachers – *r*: 90
min, col – *p*: MK2 Productions/Cinéma Services/WDR 1972

**Claude MILLER**
Born in Paris in 1942. Studied at IDHEC, after which assistant to
Carné (**Trois Chambres à Manhattan**), Demy (**Les Demoiselles de
Rochefort**) and Pirès (**Elle court, elle court la banlieue**). Worked
frequently with both Godard and Truffaut (production manager for all
Truffaut's films between 1966 and 1975). Acted in Luc Béraud's **La
Tortue sur le dos** (1978) and in Jean-Patrick Lebel's **Notes pour
Debussy** (**Lettre ouverte à Jean-Luc Godard**) (1987).

**Juliet dans Paris**
*d*: Claude Miller – *sc*: Claude Miller – *c*: Pierre-William Glenn – *l.p.*:
Juliet Berto – *r*: 18 min, b/w – *p*: Claude Miller 1967

**La Question ordinaire**
*d*: Claude Miller – *sc*: Claude Miller – *c*: Pierre-William Glenn – *l.p.*:
Guy Héron, Gérard Desarthe, Victor Tazartesse, Sofia Torkelli, Juliet
Berto – *r*: 9 min, b/w – *p*: Claude Miller 1969

**Camille ou la comédie catastrophique**
*d*: Claude Miller – *sc*: Claude Miller – *c*: Pierre-William Glenn – *l.p.*:
Juliet Berto, Philippe Léotard, Marc Chapiteau, Michel Delahaye,
Viviane Gosset, Jeanne Goupil, François Girod – *r*: 36 min, b/w – *p*:
Claude Miller 1971

**La meilleure Façon de marcher**
*d*: Claude Miller – *sc*: Claude Miller, Luc Béraud – *c*: Bruno Nuytten
– *l.p.*: Patrick Dewaere, Patrick Bouchitey, Christine Pascal, Claude
Piéplu, Michel Blanc, Marc Chapiteau – *r*: 90 min, col – *p*: Filmoblic
1976

**Dites-lui que je l'aime**
*d*: Claude Miller – *sc*: Claude Miller, Luc Béraud, from the novel *This
Sweet Sickness*, by Patricia Highsmith – *c*: Pierre Lhomme – *l.p.*:

Miou-Miou, Gérard Depardieu, Claude Piéplu, Jacques Denis – *r*: 107 min, col – *p*: Prospectacle/Filmoblic/FR3 1977

**Garde à vue**
*d*: Claude Miller – *sc*: Claude Miller, Jean Hermann, from the novel by John Wainwright – *c*: Bruno Nuytten – *l.p.*: Lino Ventura, Michel Serrault, Romy Schneider, Guy Marchand – *r*: 85 min, col – *p*: Films Ariane/TFI 1981

**Mortelle Randonnée**
*d*: Claude Miller – *sc*: Michel Audiard, Jacques Audiard – *c*: Pierre Lhomme – *l.p.*: Michel Serrault, Isabelle Adjani, Guy Marchand, Stéphane Audran, Geneviève Page, Sami Frey, Macha Méril, Jean-Claude Brialy – *r*: 120 min, col – *p*: Telema/TFI Film Production 1983

**L'Effrontée**
*d*: Claude Miller – *sc*: Claude Miller, Luc Béraud – *c*: Dominique Chapuis – *l.p.*: Charlotte Gainsbourg, Bernadette Lafont, Jean-Claude Brialy – *r*: 90 min, col – *p*: Oliane Productions/Films A2/Telema/ Monthyon Films 1985

**La petite Voleuse**
*d*: Claude Miller – *sc*: François Truffaut, Claude de Givray, adapted by Claude Miller, Luc Béraud, Anne Miller – *c*: Dominique Chapuis – *l.p.*: Charlotte Gainsbourg, Didier Bezace, Simon de la Brosse, Raoul Billerey, Chantal Banlier, Nathalie Cardone, Catherine Arditi, Dominique Besnehard – *r*: 110 min, col – *p*: Claude Berri/Orly Films/ Ciné Cinq/Les Films du Carosse 1988

**Luc MOULLET**
Born in Paris in 1937. In 1956 became film critic for *Télérama*, *Arts*, *Cahiers du Cinéma*. Author of *Luis Bunuel* (Brussels: Club du livre de cinéma, 1957) and *Fritz Lang* (Editions Seghers, 1963). Acts in his own films and in **Le Cabot** (Letellier, 1971). **L'interminable Chevauchée** (M.C. Questerbert, 1972), **Une Baleine qui avait mal aux dents** (Jacques Bral, 1973). Producer of his own films and of **Nathalie Granger** (Marguerite Duras, 1972), **Du Côté de Robinson**, **La Rosière de Pessac**, **Le Cochon** (all by Jean Eustache), **La Peau dure** (Jean-Michel Barjol).

**Un Steack trop cuit**
*d*: Luc Moullet – *sc*: Luc Moullet – *c*: André Murgalski – *l.p.*: Françoise Vatel, Albert Jurose – *r*: 19 min, b/w – *p*: Luc Moullet 1961

**Terres noires**
*d*: Luc Moullet – *sc*: Luc Moullet – *c*: Bernard Davidson – *r*: 19 min, col, 16 mm and 35 mm – *p*: Les Films du Carosse 1962

**Capito?**
*d*: Luc Moullet – *sc*: Luc Moullet – *c*: Pietro Morbidelli – *l.p.*: Françoise Vatel, Alessandro Ninchi – *r*: 8 min, col – *p*: Luc Moullet 1962

**Brigitte et Brigitte**
*d*: Luc Moullet – *sc*: Luc Moullet – *c*: Claude Croton – *l.p.*: Françoise
Vatel, Colette Descombes, Claude Melki, Michel Gonzales, Claude
Chabrol, Samuel Fuller – *r*: 85 min, b/w – *p*: Luc Moullet 1966

**Les Contrabandières**
*d*: Luc Moullet – *sc*: Luc Moullet – *c*: Philippe Théaudière – *l.p.*:
Françoise Vatel, Monique Thiriet, Johnny Monteilhet, Luc Moullet,
Paul Martin, Bernard Carassus – *r*: 80 min, b/w – *p*: Moullet et cie
1968

**Une Aventure de Billy le Kid**
*d*: Luc Moullet – *sc*: Luc Moullet – *c*: Jean-Jacques Flori, Jean
Gonnot – *l.p.*: Jean-Pierre Léaud, Rachel Kesterber, Jean Valmont –
*r*: 100 min, col – *p*: Luc Moullet 1971

**Anatomie d'un rapport**
*d*: Luc Moullet – *sc*: Luc Moullet, Antonietta Pizzorno – *c*: Michel
Fournier – *l.p.*: Luc Moullet, Christine Hébert, Antonietta Pizzorno –
*r*: 82 min, b/w, 16 mm – *p*: Moullet et cie 1976

**Genèse d'un repas**
*d*: Luc Moullet – *sc*: Luc Moullet – *c*: Richard Copans – *l.p.*: Luc
Moullet, Antonietta Pizzorno – *r*: 117 min, b/w, 16 mm – *p*: Luc
Moullet 1978

**Ma première Brasse**
*d*: Luc Moullet – *sc*: Luc Moullet – *c*: Richard Copans – *l.p.*: Luc
Moullet – *r*: 43 min, b/w, 16 mm – *p*: INA 1981

**Introduction**
*d*: Luc Moullet – *sc*: Luc Moullet – *c*: Jacques Bouquin – *l.p.*: Michel
Delahaye – *r*: 8 min, col, 16 mm – *p*: INA 1982

**Les Minutes d'un faiseur de films**
*d*: Luc Moullet – *sc*: Luc Moullet – *c*: Richard Copans – *l.p.*: Luc
Moullet – *r*: 13 min, b/w, 16 mm – *p*: Télé Europe 1983

**Les Hâvres**
*d*: Luc Moullet – *sc*: Luc Moullet – *c*: Renato Berta – *r*: 12 min, col,
16 mm – *p*: Unité Cinéma Normandie 1983

**Barres**
*d*: Luc Moullet – *sc*: Luc Moullet – *c*: Richard Copans – *l.p.*: Jean
Abeille – *r*: 14 min, col, 16 mm – *p*: Les Films d'ici 1984

**L'Empire de Médor**
*d*: Luc Moullet – *sc*: Luc Moullet – *c*: Richard Copans – *r*: 13 min,
col, 16 mm – *p*: Les Films d'ici 1986

**La Valse des médias**
*d*: Luc Moullet – *sc*: Luc Moullet – *c*: Richard Copans – *r*: 29 min,
col, 16 mm – *p*: Les Films d'ici 1987

**La Comédie du travail**
d: Luc Moullet – sc: Luc Moullet – c: Richard Copans – l.p.: Roland
Blanche, Sabine Haudepin, Henri Deus – r: 88 min, col – p: Vidéo 13/
La Sept/Les Films d'ici 1987

**Les Sièges de l'Alcazar**
d: Luc Moullet – sc: Luc Moullet – c: Richard Copans – l.p.: Sabine
Haudepin, Olivier Mattinti – r: 58 min, col – p: Les Films d'ici 1989

**Marcel OPHÜLS**
Born in Frankfurt (Main) in 1927. Son of director Max Ophüls.
Family fled Germany for France and the USA, where Marcel attended
University of California and served in the American army (1944–5).
Returned to France in 1950 and worked as an assistant for John
Huston (**Moulin Rouge**) and Julien Duvivier (**Marianne de ma
jeunesse**). Subsequently worked extensively for French television
with such programmes as **Les dernières Élections en Allemagne**
(1966), **Munich ou la paix pour cent ans** (1967), **La Moisson de
My Lai, Faisons un Rêve**.

**Matisse ou le talent du bonheur**
d: Marcel Ophüls – sc: Max-Pol Fouchet, Marcel Ophüls – c: Henri
Martin – l.p.: commentary spoken by Jeanne Moreau and Claude
Dauphin – r: 15 min, col – p: Franco-London Films 1960

**L'Amour à vingt ans** (one episode)
d: Marcel Ophüls – sc: Marcel Ophüls – c: Wolfgang Wirth – l.p.: C.
Doermer – r: 18 min, col – p: Pierre Roustang 1962

**Peau de banane**
d: Marcel Ophüls – sc: Marcel Ophüls, Claude Sautet, Daniel
Boulanger – c: Jean Rabier – l.p.: Jeanne Moreau, Jean-Paul
Belmondo, Alain Cuny, Gert Frobe, Jean-Pierre Marielle, Claude
Brasseur – r: 90 min, col – p: Sud Pacific Films/Capitole Films/CCM
1963

**Feu à volonté**
d: Marcel Ophüls – sc: Marcel Ophüls – c: Jean Tournier – l.p. Eddie
Constantine, Daniel Ceccaldi, Nelly Benedetti – r: 90 min, col – p:
Henri Baum 1964

**Le Chagrin et la pitié (Chronique d'une ville française sous
l'occupation)**
d: Marcel Ophüls – sc: Marcel Ophüls, André Harris – c: André
Gazut, Jurgen Thieme – l.p.: interviews with E. d'Astier de la
Vigerie, G. Bidault, Emile Coulandon, R. de Chambrun, Jacques
Duclos, M. Fouchet-Degliame, G. Laminaud, Charles de la Mazière,
Pierre Mendès-France, Anthony Eden, M. Buckmaster, General
Spears, D. Rock, Dr. Michel, Général Marlimont, Dr. Schmidt, H.
Tausend, H. Bleibinger – r: 250 min, b/w, 16 mm – p: SSR/TV
Rencontre/NDR 1971

**Memory of Justice**
*d*: Marcel Ophüls – *sc*: Marcel Ophüls – *c*: Mike Davis – *l.p.*: interviews with the principals at the Nuremberg Trials – *r*: 278 min, col and b/w – *p*: Marcel Ophüls 1975

**Hôtel Terminus (Klaus Barbie, His Life and Times)**
*d*: Marcel Ophüls – *sc*: Marcel Ophüls – *c*: Reuben Aaronson, Pierre Boffety, Daniel Chabert, Mike Davis, Paul Goron, Lionel Legros, Wilhelm Rosing – *r*: 267 min, col – *p*: Marcel Ophüls/Memory Pictures 1988

**Maurice PIALAT**
Born 1925 in the Puy-de-Dôme. Trained as a painter at the Ecole des Arts Décoratifs and the Ecole des Beaux Arts, Paris. Several exhibitions in the 1940s. Then worked as an actor on stage (*Julius Caesar, Coriolanus, Marie Stuart*) and in the cinema (**Que la Bête meure**, Chabrol, 1969; **Mes petites Amoureuses**, Eustache, 1975). Appeared in his own films, **A nos Amours** and **Sous le Soleil de Satan**.

**L'Amour existe**
*d*: Maurice Pialat – *sc*: Maurice Pialat – *c*: Gilbert Sarthe – *l.p.*: commentary by Pialat – *r*: 21 min, b/w – *p*: Films de la Pléiade 1960

**Janine**
*d*: Maurice Pialat – *sc*: Claude Berri – *c*: Jean-Marc Ripert – *l.p.*: Claude Berri, Evelyne Ker – *r*: 19 min, b/w – *p*: France Opera Films 1962

**Jardins d'Arabie**
*d*: Maurice Pialat – *sc*: Maurice Pialat – *c*: Gilbert Sarthe – *r*: 23 min, col – *p*: Tony Adès 1963

**Pehlivan**
*d*: Maurice Pialat – *sc*: Maurice Pialat – *c*: Willy Kurant – *r*: 13 min, b/w – *p*: Como Films 1963

**Istanbul**
*d*: Maurice Pialat – *sc*: A. Falk – *c*: Willy Kurant – *r*: 13 min, b/w – *p*: Como Films 1963

**Byzance**
*d*: Maurice Pialat – *sc*: Stefan Zweig – *c*: Willy Kurant – *r*: 11 min, b/w – *p*: Como Films 1964

**Maître Galip**
*d*: Maurice Pialat – *sc*: Nazim Hikmet – *c*: Willy Kurant – *r*: 11 min, b/w – *p*: Como Films 1964

**L'Enfance nue**
*d*: Maurice Pialat – *sc*: Maurice Pialat, Arlette Langmann – *c*: Claude Beausoleil – *l.p.*: Michel Tarrazon, Marie-Louise Thierry, Marie

Marc, Henri Ruff – *r*: 90 min, col – *p*: Parc Films/Films du Carosse/ Renn Production/Parafrance Film 1969

**La Maison des bois**
*d*: Maurice Pialat *sc*: René Wheeler, Maurice Pialat, Arlette Langmann – *c*: Roger Duculot – *l.p.*: Pierre Doris, Jacqueline Dufranne, Agathe Natanson, Fernand Gravey, Ovila Legare, Maurice Pialat – *r*: 360 min (7 episodes), col – *p*: ORTF/RAI/Son et Lumière 1971

**Nous ne vieillirons pas ensemble**
*d*: Maurice Pialat – *sc*: Maurice Pialat – *c*: Luciano Toroli – *l.p.*: Marlène Jobert, Jean Yanne, Macha Méril – *r*: 110 min, b/w – *p*: Lido Films/Empire Films 1972

**La Gueule ouverte**
*d*: Maurice Pialat – *sc*: Maurice Pialat – *c*: Nestor Almendros – *l.p.*: Philippe Léotard, Nathalie Baye, Hubert Deschamps, Monique Mélinand – *r*: 90 min, col – *p*: Les Films de la Boétie 1974

**Passe ton Bac d'abord**
*d*: Maurice Pialat – *sc*: Maurice Pialat – *c*: Pierre-William Glenn – *l.p.*: Sabine Haudepin, Philippe Marlaud, Annick Alane, Michel Caron, Christian Bouillette – *r*: 105 min, col – *p*: Les Films du Livardois/Renn Production/FR3/INA 1979

**Loulou**
*d*: Maurice Pialat – *sc*: Arlette Langmann, Maurice Pialat – *c*: Pierre-William Glenn – *l.p.*: Isabelle Huppert, Gérard Depardieu, Guy Marchand – *r*: 100 min, col – *p*: Klaus Hellwig/Yves Gasser/Yves Peyrot 1980

**A nos Amours**
*d*: Maurice Pialat – *sc*: Arlette Langmann, Maurice Pialat –*c*: Jacques Loiseleux – *l.p.*: Sandrine Bonnaire, Dominique Besnehard, Evelyne Ker, Maurice Pialat – *r*: 102 min, col – *p*: Les Films du Livardois/ Gaumont/FR3 1983

**Police**
*d*: Maurice Pialat – *sc*: Catherine Breillat, Maurice Pialat – *c*: Luciano Tovoli – *l.p.*: Gérard Depardieu, Sophie Marceau, Richard Anconina, Pascale Rocard, Sandrine Bonnaire – *r*: 113 min, col – *p*: Gaumont/ TFI Film Productions 1985

**Sous le Soleil de Satan**
*d*: Maurice Pialat – *sc*: Maurice Pialat, from the novel by Georges Bernanos – *c*: Willy Kurant – *l.p.*: Gérard Depardieu, Sandrine Bonnaire, Maurice Pialat, Yann Dedet – *r*: 103 min, col – *p*: Erato Films/Films A2/Flack Films/CNC/SOFICA 1987

**Raul RUIZ**
Born 1941 in Chile. Playwright and film adviser to the Allende government. After the latter's fall took refuge in France where he has

worked extensively for television as well as in cinema. Briefly
Director of the Maison de la Culture du Havre and, more recently,
has left France for the United States.

### El Tango del Vuido
d: Raul Ruiz – sc: Raul Ruiz – c: Diego Bonacina – l.p.: Ruben
Sotoconil, Claudia Paz, Luis Alarcon, Shenda Roman – r: 70 min, b/
w – p: Cine Club Vina del mar 1967

### Los Tres Tristes Tigres/Trois tristes tigres
d: Raul Ruiz – sc: Raul Ruiz – c: Diego Bonacina – l.p.: Nelson
Villagra, Shenda Roman, Luis Alarcon, Jaime Vadell, Delfina
Guszman – r: 95 min, b/w – p: Enrique Reimann 1969

### Que Hacer?
d: Raul Ruiz, Saul Landau, James Becket, Nina Serrano, Bill Yahraus
– sc: collective – c: Gustavo Moris – l.p.: Luis Alarcon, Sandy
Archer, Anibal Reyna, Richard Stahl, Monica Echeverria, Country
Joe McDonald – r: 90 min, b/w – p: Lobo Films 1970

### La Colonia Penal
d: Raul Ruiz – sc: Raul Ruiz, from the novel by Katka – c: Hector
Rios – l p : Monica Echeverria, Luis Alarcon, Anibal Reyna, Nelson
Villagra, Dario Pulgar, Sergio Meza – r: 75 min, b/w – p: Alcaman
1970

### Ahora Te Vamos a Llamar Hermano
d: Raul Ruiz – sc: Raul Ruiz – c: Mario Handler – r: 20 min, col, 16
mm – p: Citelco 1971

### Nadie dijo Nada
d: Raul Ruiz – sc: Raul Ruiz, from the story by Max Beerbohm,
Enoch Soames – c: Silvio Caiozzi – l.p.: Carlos Solanos, Jaime
Vadell, Luis Vilches, Luis Alarcon, Nelson Villagra – r: 90 min, b/w
– p: RAI TV 1971

### L'Expropriacion
d: Raul Ruiz – sc: Raul Ruiz – c: Jorge Müller – l.p.: Jaime Vadell,
Nemesio Antunez, Delfina Guzman, Luis Alarcon – r: 60 min, b/w –
p: Raul Ruiz 1971

### Los Minuteros
d: Raul Ruiz, Valeria Sarmiento – sc: Raul Ruiz – c: Adrian Cooper –
r: 15 min, b/w, 16 mm – p: Quimandu-Canal 7 1972

### Poesia Popular La Teoria y la Pratica
d: Raul Ruiz, Valeria Sarmiento – sc: Raul Ruiz – c: Adrian Cooper –
r: 20 min, b/w, 16 mm – p: Quimandu-Canal 7 1972

### Nueva Cancion (Chilena)
d: Raul Ruiz, Valeria Sarmiento – sc: Raul Ruiz – c: Adrian Cooper –
r: 20 min, b/w, 16 mm – p: Quimandu-Canal 7 1973

**El Realismo Socialisto**
*d*: Raul Ruiz – *sc*: Raul Ruiz – *c*: Jorge Müller – *l.p.*: Jaime Vadell, Javier Maldonado, Juan Carlos Moraga – *r*: 270 min, col, 16 mm – *p*: Raul Ruiz, Dario Pulgar 1973

**Palomita Brava**
*d*: Raul Ruiz – *sc*: Raul Ruiz – *c*: Jorge Müller – *r*: 60 min, b/w, 16 mm – *p*: Chile Films 1973

**Palomita Blanca**
*d*: Raul Ruiz – *sc*: Raul Ruiz – *c*: Silvio Caiozzi – *l.p.*: Beatriz Lapido, Rodrigo Ureta, Belgica Castro, Luis Alarcon, Monica Echeverria, Fritz Stein, Marcial Edwards – *r*: 134 min, col – *p*: Prochitel 1973

**Abastecimiento**
*d*: Raul Ruiz – *sc*: Raul Ruiz – *c*: Sergio Milhovilovic – *r*: 15 min, b/w – *p*: Chile Films 1973

**Dialogues d'exilés**
*d*: Raul Ruiz – *sc*: Raul Ruiz – *c*: Gilberto Orzello Azevedo – *l.p.*: Françoise Arnoul, Carla Cristi, Daniel Gélin, Sergio Hernandez, Percy Matas, Luis Poirot, Waldo Rojas, Carlos Solanos – *r*: 100 min, col – *p*: Percy Matas, Raul Ruiz 1974

**Le Corps dispersé et le monde à l'envers**
*d*: Raul Ruiz – *sc*: Raul Ruiz – *c*: Sami Kafati – *r*: 90 min, b/w – *p*: ZDF 1975

**Sotelo**
*d*: Raul Ruiz – *sc*: Raul Ruiz – *c*: Denis Lenoir – *r*: 15 min, col, 16 mm – *p*: United Nations 1976

**La Vocation suspendue**
*d*: Raul Ruiz – *sc*: Raul Ruiz, from the novel by Pierre Klossowski – *c*: Sacha Vierny – *l.p.*: Didier Flamand, Pascal Bonitzer, François Simon, Daniel Gélin, Edith Scob – *r*: 90 min, col, b/w, 16 mm – *p*: INA 1977

**Colloque de chiens**
*d*: Raul Ruiz – *sc*: Nicole Muchnik, Raul Ruiz – *c*: Denis Lenoir, Manuel Otero – *l.p.*: Eva Simonet, Silke Humel, Franck Lesne, Hugo Santiago, Raul Ruiz – *r*: 18 min, col – *p*: Filmoblic/OCC 1977

**L'Hypothèse du tableau volé**
*d*: Raul Ruiz – *sc*: Raul Ruiz, Pierre Klossowski, from the novel by Pierre Klossowski – *c*: Sacha Vierny – *l.p.*: Jean Rougeul, Anne Debois, Chantal Palay, Alix Comte, Jean Narboni, Christian Broutin – *r*: 65 min, b/w – *p*: INA 1979

**Petit Manuel d'histoire de France**
*d*: Raul Ruiz – *sc*: Raul Ruiz, from television archives of **Les Enigmes de l'histoire, La Caméra explore le temps, Les grandes Batailles du passé** and **Présence du passé** – *r*: 2 x 60 min, col, b/w – *p*: INA 1979

**Le Débat (Fantômes de la vidéo)**
*d*: Raul Ruiz – *sc*: Raul Ruiz – *r*: 90 min, col, video – *p*: INA 1980

**Le Jeu de l'oie**
*d*: Raul Ruiz – *sc*: Raul Ruiz – *l.p.*: Pascal Bonitzer, Jean-Loup
Rivière – *r*: 30 min, b/w – *p*: Antenne 2 1980

**Le Borgne**
*d*: Raul Ruiz – *sc*: Raul Ruiz – *c*: Jacques Bouquin – *l.p.*: François
Ede, Frank Ogier, Pascal Bonitzer, Manuelle Lipski, Jean-Christophe
Bouvet – *r*: 75 min (4 episodes), col, 16 mm – *p*: Les Films du
Dimanche 1980

**Les Divisions de la nature**
*d*: Raul Ruiz – *sc*: Raul Ruiz – *c*: Henri Alekan – *r*: 29 min, col, 16
mm – *p*: INA/Antenne 2 1981

**Le Toit de la baleine**
*d*: Raul Ruiz – *sc*: Raul Ruiz – *c*: Henri Alekan – *l.p.*: Willeke Van
Ammelrooy. Jean Badin, Fernando Bordeu, Hubert Curiel, Amber de
Grauw, Luis Mora, Emie Navarro – *r*: 90 min, b/w – *p*: Springtime
film bv 1981

**Des grands Événements et des gens ordinaires**
*d*: Raul Ruiz – *sc*: Raul Ruiz, François Ede – *c*: Jacques Bouquin,
Dominique Forgue – *r*: 60 min, col, 16 mm – *p*: INA 1983

**Le Territoire**
*d*: Raul Ruiz – *sc*: Raul Ruiz, Gilbert Adair – *c*: Henri Alekan – *l.p.*:
Isabelle Weingarten, Rebecca Pauly, Geoffrey Carey, Jeffry Kune,
Paul Getty Jr., Ethan Stone – *r*: 100 min, col – *p*: VO Films/Pierre
Cottrell/Paolo Branco 1983

**Les trois Couronnes du matelot**
*d*: Raul Ruiz – *sc*: Raul Ruiz – *c*: Sacha Vierny – *l.p.*: Jean-Bernard
Guillard, Philippe Deplanche, Jean Badin, Nadège Clair, Lisa Lyon,
Claude Derepp – *r*: 117 min, b/w, col – *p*: INA/Antenne 2 1983

**La Ville des pirates**
*d*: Raul Ruiz – *sc*: Raul Ruiz – *c*: Acacio de Almeida – *l.p.*: Hugues
Quester, Anne Alvaro, Melvil Poupaud, André Engel – *r*: 111 min,
col – *p*: Les films du Passage/Metro Filmes 1984

**La Présence réelle**
*d*: Raul Ruiz – *sc*: Raul Ruiz – *c*: Jacques Bouquin – *r*: 60 min, col, 16
mm – *p*: INA/FR3/Festival d'Avignon 1984

**L'Eveillé du Pont de l'Alma**
*d*: Raul Ruiz – *sc*: Raul Ruiz – *c*: François Ede – *l.p.*: Michel
Lonsdale, Jean-Bernard Guillard, Olimpia Carlisi, Jean Badin, Melvil
Poupaud – *r*: 85 min, col and b/w – *p*: Paolo Bianco/Les Films du
Passage 1985

**Régime sans pain**
*d*: Raul Ruiz – *sc*: Raul Ruiz – *c*: Acacio Almeida – *l.p.*: Anne Alvaro, Olivier Angèle, Gérard Maimone – *r*: 75 min, col – *p*: La Maison de la Culture de Grenoble 1986

**Les Destins de Manoel/Manoel dans l'île des merveilles**
*d*: Raul Ruiz – *sc*: Raul Ruiz – *c*: Acacio Almeida – *l.p.*: Ruben de Freitas, Marco Paulo de Freitas, Aurélie Chazel – *r*: 25 min, col – *p*: Les Films du Passage/Rita Filmes/INA 1986

**Mammame**
*d*: Raul Ruiz – *sc*: Jean-Claude Gallota – *c*: Acacio Almeida – *l.p.*: The Emile Dubois dance group – *r*: 65 min, col – *p*: Arcanal/ Cinémathèque de danse/La Maison de la Culture de Grenoble/ Théâtre de la ville de Paris 1986

**Mémoire des apparences**
*d*: Raul Ruiz – *sc*: Raul Ruiz, from the play by Calderon – *c*: Jacques Bouquin – *l.p.*: Sylvain Thirolle, Roch Leibovici, Bénédict Sire, Jean-Bernard Guillard – *r*: 90 min, b/w – *p*: INA/Maison de la culture du Havre 1986

**L'Ile au trésor**
*d*: Raul Ruiz – *sc*: Raul Ruiz, from the novel by Stevenson – *c*: Acacio de Almeida – *l.p.*: Vic Tayback, Jean-Pierre Léaud, Martin Landau, Anna Karina, Lou Castel, Jean-François Stevenin – *p*: Argos Film 1986

**La Chouette aveugle**
*d*: Raul Ruiz – *sc*: Raul Ruiz – *c*: Patrice Cologne – *l.p.*: Jean-Marie Boglin, Jean-François Capalus, Jean-Bernard Guillard – *r*: 90 min, col, 16 mm – *p*: Maison de la Culture du Havre/La Sept 1987

**Le Professeur Taranne**
*d*: Raul Ruiz – *sc*: Raul Ruiz, from the play by Adamov – *c*: Denis Lenoir – *l.p.*: Jacqueline Bollen, Marie-Luce Bonfanti, Ionna Gkizas, Brigitte Kaquet, Brigitte Simon – *r*: 65 min, b/w – *p*: Centre de l'Audiovisuel Bruxelles/Maison de la Culture du Havre 1987


**Coline SERREAU.**
Born in Paris in 1947. Daughter of theatre director Jean-Marie Serreau. Studied music, dance and acrobatics. At first actress for stage and television between 1970 and 1976. Appeared in the following films: **Un peu beaucoup, passionnément** (Enrico, 1970), **On s'est trompé d'Histoire d'amour** (Bertucelli, 1974), **Sept Morts sur ordonnance**, (Rouffio, 1975). Also scripted **On s'est trompé d'Histoire d'amour.**

**Mais qu'est-ce qu'elles veulent?**
*d*: Coline Serreau – *sc*: Coline Serreau – *c*: Jean-François Robin – *l.p.*: documentary interviews with various women – *r*: 90 min, col, 16 mm – *p*: INA/Copra Films 1978 (made in 1975)

**Pourquoi pas?**
*d*: Coline Serreau – *sc*: Coline Serreau – *c*: Jean-François Robin – *l.p.*:
Sami Frey, Mario Gonzalez, Christine Murillo, Nicole Jamet, Michel
Aumont – *r*: 93 min, col – *p*: Dimage/SND 1977

**Qu'est qu'on attend pour être heureux**
*d*: Coline Serreau – *sc*: Coline Serreau – *c*: Jean-Noël Ferragut – *l.p.*:
Romain Bouteille, Evelyne Buyle, Henri Garcin, André Gille, Pierre
Vernier, Marthe Souverbie – *r*: 92 min, col – *p*: Elephant Production/
UGC/Top 1 1982

**Trois Hommes et un couffin**
*d*: Coline Serreau – *sc*: Coline Serreau – *c*: Jean-Yves Escoffier – *l.p.*:
Roland Giraid, Michel Boujenah, André Dussolier, Philippine Leroy
Beaulieu, Dominique Lavanant – *r*: 106 min, col – *p*: Flach Films/
Soprofilm/TFI Films 1985

**Romuald et Juliette**
*d*: Coline Serreau – *sc*: Coline Serreau – *c*: Jean-Noël Ferragut – *l.p.*:
Daniel Auteuil, Firmine Richard, Pierre Vernier, Maxime Leroux – *r*:
108 min, col – *p*: Cinéa/FR3 Films 1989


**Bertrand TAVERNIER**
Born in Lyons in 1941. Educated in Paris. At first journalist and
creator of Nickelodéon film club. Assistant to Melville for **Léon
Morin Prêtre**. Attaché de presse for Georges de Beauregard.
Contributor to *Positif*, *Cahiers du cinéma*, *Combat*, *Les Lettres
françaises*. Author of several works on American cinema.

**Le Jeu de la chance** (one episode of **La Chance et l'amour**)
*d*: Bertrand Tavernier – *sc*: Bertrand Tavernier, Nicolas Vogel – *c*:
Alain Levent – *l.p.*: Michel Auclair, Bernard Blier – *r*: 20 min, b/w –
*p*: Georges de Beauregard 1964

**Le Baiser de Judas** (one episode of **Les Baisers**)
*d*: Bertrand Tavernier – *sc*: Bertrand Tavernier, Claude Nahon – *c*:
Raoul Coutard – *l.p.*: Laetitia Roman, Judy del Carril, Bernard
Rousselet, William Sabatier – *r*: 22 min, b/w – *p*: Georges de
Beauregard/Rome-Paris Films 1965

**L'Horloger de Saint-Paul**
*d*: Bertrand Tavernier – *sc*: Jean Aurenche, Pierre Bost, from the
novel by Georges Simenon, *L'Horloger d'Everton* – *c*: Pierre-
William Glenn – *l.p.*: Philippe Noiret, Jean Rochefort, Sylvain
Rougerie, Jacques Denis, Clothilde Joano – *r*: 105 min, col – *p*:
Lira Films 1974

**Que la Fête commence**
*d*: Bertrand Tavernier – *sc*: Jean Aurenche, Bertrand Tavernier – *c*:
Pierre-William Glenn – *l.p.*: Philippe Noiret, Jean Rochefort, Jean-

Pierre Marielle, Christine Pascal, Marina Vlady – *r*: 120 min, col – *p*: Michèle de Broca/Productions de la Guéville 1975

**Le Juge et l'assassin**
*d*: Bertrand Tavernier – *sc*: Bertrand Tavernier – *c*: Pierre-William Glenn – *l.p.*: Philippe Noiret, Michel Galabru, Isabelle Huppert, Jean-Claude Brialy – *r*: 110 min, col – *p*: Raymond Davos/Lira Films 1976

**Des Enfants gâtés**
*d*: Bertrand Tavernier – *sc*: Bertrand Tavernier, Christine Pascal – *c*: Alain Levent – *l.p.*: Michel Piccoli, Christine Pascal, Michel Aumont, Gérard Jugnot – *r*: 110 min, col – *p*: Films 66/Little Bear/Sara Films/Gaumont 1977

**La Mort en direct**
*d*: Bertrand Tavernier – *sc*: Bertrand Tavernier, from the novel by David Compton – *c*: Pierre-William Glenn – *l.p.*: Romy Schneider, Harvey Keitel, Harry Dean Stanton, Thérèse Liotard, Max Von Sydow, William Russell – *r*: 129 min, col – *p*: Seita Films/Little Bear/A2/Sara Films/Gaumont/SFP 1980

**Une Semaine de vacances**
*d*: Bertrand Tavernier – *sc*: Bertrand Tavernier, Colo Tavernier – *c*: Pierre-William Glenn – *l.p.*: Nathalie Baye, Gérard Lanvin, Michel Galabru, Flore Fitzgerald, Philippe Léotard – *r*: 102 min, col – *p*: Sara Films/Little Bear/A2 1980

**Coup de torchon**
*d*: Bertrand Tavernier – *sc*: Jean Aurenche, from the novel *Pop 1280* by Jim Thompson – *c*: Pierre-William Glenn – *l.p.*: Philippe Noiret, Isabelle Huppert, Jean-Pierre Marielle, Stéphane Audran, Eddy Mitchell, Guy Marchand – *r*: 128 min, col – *p*: Les Films de la Tour/A2/Little Bear 1981

**Mississipi Blues**
*d*: Bertrand Tavernier – *sc*: Bertrand Tavernier – *c*: Pierre-William Glenn – *r*: 107 min, col – *p*: Little Bear/Odessa Films/Films A2 1984

**Un Dimanche à la campagne**
*d*: Bertrand Tavernier – *sc*: Bertrand Tavernier, Colo Tavernier, from the novel by Pierre Bost – *c*: Bruno de Keyser – *l.p.*: Louis Ducreux, Sabine Azéma, Michel Aumont, Monique Chaumette – *r*: 94 min, col – *p*: Sara Films/Films A2 1984

**Autour de minuit (Round Midnight)**
*d*: Bertrand Tavernier – *sc*: Bertrand Tavernier – *c*: Bruno de Keyser – *l.p.*: Dexter Gordon, François Cluzet, Gabrielle Hakers, Sandra Reaves-Phillips – *r*: 130 min, col – *p*: Irwin Winkler/Warner Bros 1986

**La Passion Béatrice**
*d*: Bertrand Tavernier – *sc*: Colo Tavernier O'Hagan – *c*: Bruno de Keyser – *l.p.*: Bernard-Pierre Donnadieu, Julie Delpy, Nils Tavernier,

Monique Chaumette – *r*: 131 min, col – *p*: Clea Productions/AMLF/
TFI Films/Little Bear 1987

**La Vie et rien d'autre**
*d*: Bertrand Tavernier – *sc*: Jean Cosmos, Bertrand Tavernier – *c*:
Bruno de Keyser – *l.p.*: Philippe Noirct, Sabine Azéma, Pascale
Vignal – *r*: 134 min, col – *p*: Hachette Première/Gpe Europe/AB
Films/Little Bear/Films A2 1989

**André TECHINÉ**
Born 1943 in Valence d'Agen. 1964-7 critic for *Cahiers du cinéma*
and assistant to Marc'O and Jacques Rivette

**Paulina s'en va**
*d*: André Techiné – *sc*: André Techiné – *c*: Jean Genret and Pierre-
William Glenn – *l.p.*: Bulle Ogier, Marie-France Pisier, Laura Betti,
Michèle Moretti, Yves Beneyton, André Julien, Denis Berry – *r*: 90
min, col – *p*: Télé Hachette Dovidis 1969

**Souvenirs d'en France**
*d*: André Techiné – *sc*: André Techiné, Marilyn Goldin – *c*: Bruno
Nuytten – *l.p.*: Jeanne Moreau, Michel Auclair, Marie-France Pisier,
Claude Mann, Orane Demazis, Aram Stéphan, Hélène Surgère, Julien
Guiomar, Michèle Moretti, Pierre Baillot – *r*: 95 min, col – *p*:
Stephan Films/Buffalo Films/Renn Productions/Belstar Productions/
Simar Films 1975

**Barocco**
*d*: André Techiné – *sc*: André Techiné, Marilyn Goldin – *c*: Bruno
Nuytten – *l.p.*: Isabelle Adjani, Gérard Depardieu, Marie-France
Pisier, Jean-Claude Brialy, Julien Guiomar, Hélène Surgère, Jean-
François Stevenin – *r*: 105 min, col – *p*: André Génovès, Alain Sarde
1976

**Les Soeurs Brontë**
*d*: André Techiné – *sc*: André Techiné, Pascal Bonitzer, Jean Gruault
– *c*: Bruno Nuytten – *l.p.*: Isabelle Adjani, Marie-France Pisier,
Isabelle Huppert, Pascal Greggory, Patrick Magee, Hélène Surgère,
Roland Berton, Alice Sapritch, Roland Barthes – *r*: 115 min, col – *p*:
Action Films/Gaumont/FR3 1979

**Hôtel des Amériques**
*d*: André Techiné – *sc*: Gilles Taurand, André Techiné – *c*: Bruno
Nuytten – *l.p.*: Catherine Deneuve, Patrick Dewaere, Etienne Chicot,
Josiane Balasko, Sabine Haudepin – *r*: 93 min, col – *p*: Alain Sarde
(Sara Films)/RMC/Antenne 2 1981

**La Matiouette**
*d*: André Techiné – *sc*: André Techiné, Jacques Nolot – *c*: Pascal
Marti – *l.p.*: Jacques Nolot, Patrick Fierry – *r*: 47 min, b/w, 16 mm –
*p*: INA 1983

**L'Atelier**
*d*: André Techiné – *sc*: André Techiné and extracts of texts by Ingmar Bergman, Pascal Bruckner, Dostoievsky – *c*: Renato Berta – *l.p.*: Sophie Paul, Laurent le Doyen, Marianne Chemelky, Pierre-Loup Rajot, Olivier Rabourdin, Véronique Costamagna-Poat, Christine Citti, Christophe Bernard, Claire Rigollier, Sophie Lefou de la Colonge, Marie Carré, Nathalie Schmidt, Francis Trappat, Christine Vézinet, Nicholas Baby – *r*: 40 min, b/w, 16 mm – *p*: Nanterre Amandiers/INA 1984

**Rendez-vous**
*d*: André Techiné – *sc*: André Techiné, Olivier Assayas – *c*: Renato Berta – *l.p.*: Juliette Binoche, Lambert Wilson, Wadeck Stanczak, Jean-Louis Trintignant, Dominique Lavanant, Anne Wiazemsky, Jean-Louis Vitrac, Jacques Nolot – *r*: 87 min, col – *p*: Alain Terzian (T. Films) 1985

**Le Lieu du crime**
*d*: André Techiné – *sc*: André Techiné, Olivier Assayas, Pascal Bonitzer – *c*: Pascal Marti – *l.p.*: Catherine Deneuve, Victor Laroux, Danielle Darrieux, Wadeck Stanczak, Nicolas Giraudi, Jacques Nolot – *r*: 90 min, col – *p*: Alain Terzian (T. Films) 1986

**Les Innocents**
*d*: André Techiné – *sc*: André Techiné, Pascal Bonitzer – *c*: Renato Berta – *l.p.*: Sandrine Bonnaire, Simon de la Brosse, Abdel Kechiche, Jean-Claude Brialy – *r*: 100 min, col – *p*: Philippe Carcassonne (Cinéa)/Alain Terzian (T. Films) 1987

**François TRUFFAUT**
Born in Paris in 1932. Died 1984.

**Une Visite**
*d*: François Truffaut – *sc*: François Truffaut – *c*: Jacques Rivette – *l.p.*: Florence Doniol-Valcroze, Jean-José Richer, Laura Mauri, Francis Cognany – b/w 1955

**Les Mistons**
*d*: François Truffaut – *sc*: François Truffaut – *c*: Jean Malige – *l.p.*: Gérard Blain, Bernadette Lafont – *r*: 26 min, b/w – *p*: Les Films du Carrosse 1957

**Une Histoire d'eau**
*d*: François Truffaut, Jean-Luc Godard – *sc*: Jean-Luc Godard – *c*: Michel Latouche – *l.p.*: Jean-Claude Brialy, Caroline Dim – *r*: 18 min, b/w – *p*: Pierre Braunberger/Films de la Pléiade 1958

**Les 400 coups**
*d*: François Truffaut – *sc*: François Truffaut – *c*: Henri Decaë – *l.p.*: Jean-Pierre Léaud, Patrick Auffay – *r*: 101 min, b/w – *p*: Les Films du Carrosse 1959

322

**Tirez sur le Pianiste**
*d*: François Truffaut – *sc*: François Truffaut, Marcel Moussy, from the novel *Down There*, by David Goodis – *c*: Raoul Coutard – *l.p.*: Charles Aznavour, Marie Dubois, Nicole Berger – *r*: 80 min, b/w – *p*: Les Films de la Pléiade 1969

**Jules et Jim**
*d*: François Truffaut – *sc*: François Truffaut, Jean Gruault, from the novel by Henri-Pierre Roché – *c*: Raoul Coutard – *l.p.*: Jeanne Moreau, Oskar Werner, Henri Serre, Marie Dubois, Sabine Haudepin – *r*: 105 min, b/w – *p*: Les Films du Carrosse 1961

**Antoine et Colette** (one episode of **L'Amour à vingt ans**)
*d*: François Truffaut – *sc*: François Truffaut – *c*: Raoul Coutard – *l.p.*: Jean-Pierre Léaud, Marie-France Pisier, Patrick Auffay – *p*: Ulysse Productions/Pierre Roustang 1962

**La Peau douce**
*d*: François Truffaut – *sc*: François Truffaut – *c*: Raoul Coutard – *l.p.*: Jean Desailly, Françoise Dorléac, Daniel Ceccaldi – *r*: 115 min, b/w – *p*: Les Films du Carrosse 1964

**Farenheit 451**
*d*: François Truffaut – *sc*: François Truffaut, from the novel by Ray Bradbury – *c*: Nicolas Roeg – *l.p.*: Julie Christie, Oskar Werner, Cyril Cusack – *r*: 112 min, col – *p*: Anglo Enterprise/Vineyard Films 1966

**La Mariée était en noir**
*d*: François Truffaut – *sc*: François Truffaut, Jean-Louis Richard, from the novel *The Bride wore Black*, by William Irish – *l.p.*: Jeanne Moreau, Claude Rich, Jean-Claude Brialy, Michel Bouquet, Michel Lonsdale, Charles Denner, Daniel Boulanger, Alexandra Stewart – *r*: 107 min, col – *p*: Les Films du Carrosse/Artistes Associés/Dino de Laurentis 1967

**Baisers volés**
*d*: François Truffaut – *sc*: François Truffaut, Claude de Givray – *c*: Denys Clerval – *l.p.*: Jean-Pierre Léaud, Delphine Seyrig, Claude Jade, Michel Lonsdale, Daniel Ceccaldi – *r*: 91 min, col – *p*: Les Films du Carrosse 1968

**La Sirène du Mississippi**
*d*: François Truffaut – *sc*: François Truffaut, from the novel by William Irish, *Waltz into Darkness* – *c*: Denys Clerval – *l.p.*: Jean-Paul Belmondo, Catherine Deneuve, Michel Bouquet – *r*: 123 min, col – *p*: Les Films du Carrosse 1969

**L'Enfant sauvage**
*d*: François Truffaut – *sc*: François Truffaut, Jean Gruault, based on the *Mémoire* by Jean Itard – *c*: Nestor Almendros – *l.p.*: Jean-Pierre Cargol, François Truffaut – *r*: 84 min, b/w – *p*: Les Films du Carrosse 1969

**Domicile conjugale**
*d*: François Truffaut – *sc*: François Truffaut, Claude de Givray – *c*: Nestor Almendros – *l.p.*: Jean-Pierre Léaud, Kika Markham, Stacey Tendeter, Daniel Ceccaldi – *r*: 97 min, col – *p*: Les Films du Carrosse 1970

**Les deux Anglaises et le continent**
*d*: François Truffaut – *sc*: François Truffaut – *c*: Nestor Almendros – *l.p.*: Jean-Pierre Léaud, Kika Markham, Stacey Tendeter – *r*: 108 min, col – *p*: Les Films du Carrosse 1971

**Une belle Fille comme moi**
*d*: François Truffaut – *sc*: Jean-Loup Dabadie, François Truffaut, from the novel *Such a Gorgeous Kid Like Me*, by Henri Farrell – *c*: Pierre-William Glenn – *l.p.*: Bernadette Lafont, Claude Brasseur, Charles Denner, Guy Marchand, André Dussolier, Philippe Léotard – *r*: 100 min, col – *p*: Les Films du Carrosse/Columbia 1972

**La Nuit américaine**
*d*: François Truffaut – *sc*: François Truffaut, Jean-Louis Richard, Suzanne Schiffman – *c*: Pierre-William Glenn – *l.p.*: Jacqueline Bisset, Valentine Cortese, Alexandra Stewart, Jean-Pierre Aumont, Jean-Pierre Léaud, François Truffaut, Nathalie Baye – *r*: 120 min, col – *p*: Les Films du Carrosse 1973

**L'Histoire d'Adèle H.**
*d*: François Truffaut – *sc*: François Truffaut, Jean Gruault, based on the diary of Adèle Hugo – *c*: Nestor Almendros – *l.p.*: Isabelle Adjani, Bruce Robinson, Sylvia Marriott – *r*: 95 min, col – *p*: Les Films du Carrosse 1975

**L'Argent de poche**
*d*: François Truffaut – *sc*: François Truffaut, Suzanne Schiffman – *c*: Pierre-William Glenn – *l.p.*: Geory Desmouceaux, Philippe Goldman, Claudio Deluca, Ewa Truffaut, Laura Truffaut, Jean-François Stevenin – *r*: 105 min, col – *p*: Les Films du Carrosse 1976

**L'Homme qui aimait les femmes**
*d*: François Truffaut – *sc*: François Truffaut, Michel Fermaud, Suzanne Schiffman – *c*: Nestor Almendros – *l.p.*: Charles Denner, Lesley Caron, Brigitte Fossey – *r*: 119 min, col – *p*: Les Films du Carrosse 1977

**La Chambre verte**
*d*: François Truffaut – *sc*: François Truffaut, Jean Gruault, based on *The Altar of the Dead*, *Friends of Friends* and *The Beast in the Jungle*, by Henry James – *c*: Nestor Almendros – *l.p.*: François Truffaut, Nathalie Baye, Jean Dasté – *r*: 94 min, col – *p*: Les Films du Carrosse 1978

**L'Amour en fuite**
*d*: François Truffaut – *sc*: François Truffaut – *c*: Nestor Almendros – *l.p.*: Jean-Pierre Léaud, Marie-France Pisier, Claude Jade – *r*: 94 min, col – *p*: Les Films du Carrosse 1979

**Le dernier Métro**
*d*: François Truffaut – *sc*: François Truffaut, Suzanne Schiffman – *c*: Nestor Almendros – *l.p.*: Catherine Deneuve, Gérard Depardieu, Jean Poiret – *r*: 128 min, col – *p*: Les Films du Carrosse 1980

**La Femme d'à côté**
*d*: François Truffaut – *sc*: François Truffaut, Suzanne Schiffman – *c*: William Lubtchansky – *l.p.*: Gérard Depardieu, Fanny Ardant, Henri Garcin – *r*: 106 min, col – *p*: Les Films du Carrosse/TFI 1981

**Vivement Dimanche**
*d*: François Truffaut – *sc*: François Truffaut, Suzanne Schiffman, Jean Aurel, based on the novel by Charles Williams, *The Long Saturday Night* – *c*: Nestor Almendros – *l.p.*: Fanny Ardant, Jean-Louis Trintignant, Jean-Pierre Kalfon – *r*: 111 min, b/w – *p*: Les Films du Carrosse/Films A2/Soprofilms 1983


**Agnès VARDA**
Born in Brussels in 1928. Father Greek and mother French. Brought up in Sète. Studied at the Ecole du Louvre and became photographer with the TNP. Commissioned to report from Germany, Portugal, China and Cuba. Married to Jacques Demy.

**La Pointe courte**
*d*: Agnès Varda – *sc*: Agnès Varda – *c*: Louis Stein, Paul Soulignac – *l.p.*: Philippe Noiret, Sylvia Montfort – *r*: 85 min, b/w – *p*: Films Tamaris 1955

**O Saisons, ô châteaux**
*d*: Agnès Varda – *sc*: Agnès Varda – *c*: Quinto Albicocco – *r*: 22 min, col – *p*: Films de la Pléiade/Ministère du tourisme 1958

**L'Opéra-Mouffe**
*d*: Agnès Varda – *sc*: Agnès Varda – *c*: Agnès Varda – *r*: 17 min, b/w, 16 mm – *p*: Agnès Varda 1958

**Du Côté de la Côte (d'Azur, d'Azur, d'Azur)**
*d*: Agnès Varda – *sc*: Agnès Varda – *c*: Quinto Albicocco – *r*: 32 min, col – *p*: Argos Films 1958

**Cléo de 5 à 7**
*d*: Agnès Varda – *sc*: Agnès Varda – *c*: Jean Rabier – *l.p.*: Corinne Marchand, Antoine Bousseiller, Dorothy Blank, Michel Legrand, Dominique Davray – *r*: 90 min, b/w – *p*: Rome-Paris Films 1962

**Salut les Cubains**
*d*: Agnès Varda – *sc*: Agnès Varda – *r*: 29 min, b/w – *p*: S.N. Pathé Cinéma 1964

**Le Bonheur**
*d*: Agnès Varda – *sc*: Agnès Varda – *c*: Jean Rabier – *l.p.*: Jean-Claude Drouot, Claire Drouot, Sandrine Drouot, Olivier Drouot, Marie-France Boyer – *r*: 80 min, col – *p*: Parc Film/Mag Bodard 1965

**Elsa la rose**
*d*: Agnès Varda – *sc*: Agnès Varda – *l.p.*: Elsa Triolet, Louis Aragon –
*r*: 23 min, b/w – *p*: ORTF 1966

**Les Créatures**
*d*: Agnès Varda – *sc*: Agnès Varda – *c*: Willy Kurant – *l.p.*: Michel
Piccoli, Catherine Deneuve, Eva Dahlbeck, Britta Petersen, Jacques
Charrier – *r*: 95 min, col – *p*: Parc Film/Madeleine Films 1966

**Loin du Vietnam** (one episode)
*d*: Agnès Varda, Jean-Luc Godard, William Klein, Joris Ivens, Claude
Lelouch, Alain Resnais – *sc*: by the same directors – *c*: Bernard
Ziterman, Théo Robiche – *l.p.*: contributions from Michel Ray, Roger
Pic, Marcelin Loridan, François Maspero, Chris Marker, Jacques
Sternberg, Jean Lacouture – *r*: 120 min, col and b/w – *p*: SLON 1967

**Uncle Yanco**
*d*: Agnès Varda – *sc*: Agnès Varda – *l.p.*: Yanco Varda – *r*: 20 min,
col – *p*: Ciné-Tamaris/Robert Greenfelder 1967

**Black Panthers**
*d*: Agnès Varda – *sc*: Agnès Varda – *c*: Agnès Varda, David Myes –
*l.p.*: Huey Newton and members of the Black Panthers – *r*: 25 min,
col, 16 mm – *p*: Ciné-Tamaris 1968

**Lion's Love**
*d*: Agnès Varda – *sc*: Agnès Varda – *c*: Stefan Larner – *l.p.*: Viva,
Jerome Ragni, James Rado, Shirley Clarke, Carlos Clarens, Eddie
Constantine, Agnès Varda – *r*: 110 min, col – *p*: Max L. Raab
Productions 1970

**Nausicaa**
*d*: Agnès Varda – *sc*: Agnès Varda – *r*: 90 min, b/w – *p*: ORTF 1970
(unscreened)

**Daguerréotypes**
*d*: Agnès Varda – *sc*: Agnès Varda – *c*: Nurith Aviv – *l.p.*: the
inhabitants and shopkeepers of the rue Daguerre in Paris – *r*: 80 min,
col – *p*: Agnès Varda/Ciné-Tamaris 1978 (made in 1975)

**Réponse de femmes**
*d*: Agnès Varda – *sc*: Agnès Varda – *r*: 8 min, col – *p*: Ciné-Tamaris
1975

**L'Une chante l'autre pas**
*d*: Agnès Varda – *sc*: Agnès Varda – *c*: Charlie van Damm, Nurith
Aviv – *l.p.*: Valérie Mairesse, Robert Dadiès, Thérèse Liotard, Gisèle
Halimi, Dominique Ducros, Ali Raffi, Jean-Pierre Pellegrin – *r*: 120
min, col – *p*: Ciné-Tamaris/SFP/INA 1977

**Plaisir d'amour en Iran**
*d*: Agnès Varda – *sc*: Agnès Varda – *r*: 6 min – *p*: Ciné-Tamaris 1977

**Mur murs**
*d*: Agnès Varda – *sc*: Agnès Varda – *c*: Bernard Auroux – *r*: 80 min, col – *p*: Ciné-Tamaris 1982

**Documenteur**
*d*: Agnès Varda – *sc*: Agnès Varda – *c*: Nurith Aviv – *l.p.*: Sabine Manion, Mathieu Demy, Lisa Blok, Tina Odom, Gary Feldman, Charles Southwood – *r*: 60 min, col – *p*: Ciné-Tamaris 1982

**Ulysse**
*d*: Agnès Varda – *sc*: Agnès Varda – *c*: Jean-Yves Escoffier – *l.p.*: commentary by Agnès Varda – *r*: 22 min, b/w – *p*: Garance 1982

**Une Minute pour une image**
*d*: Agnès Varda – *sc*: Agnès Varda – Varda's commentary on 170 photos – *r*: 2 x 170 min, col 1983

**Les Dites cariatides**
*d*: Agnès Varda – *sc*: Agnès Varda – commentary spoken by Varda, including poems by Baudelaire and Banville – *r*: 12 min, col – *p*: Ciné-Tamaris 1984

**7 P Cuis .. S de B**
*d*: Agnès Varda – *sc*: Agnès Varda – *l.p.*: Yolande Moreau, Saskia Cohen-Tangui – *r*: 26 min, col – *p*: Ciné-Tamaris 1984

**Sans Toit ni loi**
*d*: Agnès Varda – *sc*: Agnès Varda – *c*: Patrick Blossier – *l.p.*: Sandrine Bonnaire, Macha Méril, Stéphane Freiss – *r*: 105 min, col – *p*: Ciné-Tamaris/Films A2 1985

**T'as de beaux Escaliers, tu sais**
*d*: Agnès Varda – *sc*: Agnès Varda – *r*: 3 min, b/w – *p*: Ciné-Tamaris 1986

**Jane B. par Agnès V.**
*d*: Agnès Varda – *sc*: Agnès Varda – *c*: Nurith Aviv – *l.p.*: Jane Birkin, Philippe Léotard, Jean-Pierre Léaud, Farid Chopel, Alain Souchon, Laura Betti, Charlotte Gainsbourg, Mathieu Demy, Agnès Varda – *r*: 95 min, col – *p*: Ciné-Tamaris/La Sept 1987

**Kung-Fu Master**
*d*: Agnès Varda – *sc*: Agnès Varda, Jane Birkin – *c*: Pierre-Laurent Chenieux – *l.p.*: Jane Birkin, Mathieu Demy, Charlotte Gainsbourg, Eva Simonet, Lou Doillon, Judy Campbell – *r*: 80 min, col – *p*: Ciné-Tamaris/La Sept 1987

# Index of Film Titles

# Index

332

**334**

337